*f*P

HAMILTON'S REPUBLIC

Readings in the American
Democratic Nationalist Tradition

Edited and Introduced by

MICHAEL LIND

THE FREE PRESS
New York   London   Toronto   Sydney   Singapore

THE FREE PRESS
A Division of Simon & Schuster Inc.
1230 Avenue of the Americas
New York, NY 10020

THE FREE PRESS and colophon are trademarks of Simon & Schuster Inc.

Designed by Carla Bolte

Manufactured in the United States of America

10   9   8   7   6   5   4   3   2   1

Library of Congress Cataloging-in-Publication Data

Hamilton's republic : readings in the American democratic nationalist
    tradition / edited by Michael Lind.
        p.   cm.
    Includes index.
    ISBN 0-684-83160-0
    1. Hamilton, Alexander, 1757–1804—Contributions in political
science.   2. Political science—United States—History.
3. Nationalism—United States—History.   I. Lind, Michael, 1962–.
JC176.H27   1997
973.4'092—dc21   97-33438
                                                         CIP

CREDITS

Toomer, Jean, from Frederik L. Rusch (ed.), *A Jean Toomer Reader*, New York: Oxford University Press, 1993. Reprinted by permission of the Yale Collection of American Literature, Beinecke Rare Book and Manuscript Library, Yale University.

Zakaria, Fareed, from "The Ultimate Resume" (Review of Godfrey Hodgson, *The Colonel: The Life and Wars of Henry Stimson, 1867-1950*), *The National Interest*, Summer 1991. Reprinted by permission of *The National Interest*.

CONTENTS

PART THREE. A MORE PERFECT UNION

PART FOUR. THE COMMON DEFENSE

PART FIVE. THE GENERAL WELFARE

INTRODUCTION

At the end of the twentieth century in the United States, "nationalism" is a dirty word. The American left equates nationalism with authoritarian tyranny and the vicious repression of minorities. The mainstream right identifies nationalism with protectionism and a failure to understand the benefits of the global economy. For both left and right, the term nationalism evokes images of continental European ethnic cleansing or East Asian statism. Nationalism, it is thought, is un-American. Accused of being nationalists, American liberals and conservatives alike will usually reply angrily that they are really "internationalists" in some sense, which they will proceed to explain.

On closer examination, though, the distinction between good internationalism and bad nationalism in American public discourse breaks down. A substantial number of liberal and leftist thinkers, seeking to protect American workers from competition with poor workers abroad and foreign government–business combinations, argue in favor of economic nationalism, even if they repudiate nationalism in other areas. A similar inconsistency is found on the right. Mainstream American conservatives unite their cosmopolitan vision of a single, integrated world economy with a truculent unilateralism in foreign policy (symbolized by ridicule of the United Nations). And in recent years conservatives have posed as defenders of a single, common national culture and an egalitarian polity in danger of being "Balkanized" by multiculturalism and racial and gender preferences.

Both contemporary American liberalism and contemporary American conservatism, then, are hybrid doctrines, part internationalist and part nationalist. Liberal and conservative attitudes toward the federal government are similarly incoherent. Liberals idealize and trust the domestic welfare agencies of the federal government, while viewing its foreign policy, military, and police agencies with a suspicion that frequently becomes paranoid. Conservatives do the reverse. Conservatives revile the federal government's domestic policy agencies while singing the praises of the national security apparatus. Liberals vilify the CIA and the Pentagon and defend the Labor Department; conservatives vilify the IRS and HUD and defend the CIA and the Pentagon. (In recent years some extreme conservatives sympathetic to right-wing militias have joined the radical left in vilifying federal law enforcement agencies.)

The division between nationalism and internationalism, then, runs through both mainstream liberalism and mainstream conservatism, not between them. Under the rules of present-day American politics, it is acceptable to be half-nationalist, like the liberals in economic policy or the conservatives in foreign policy and cultural politics. If they agree on nothing else, half-nationalist liberals and half-nationalist conservatives agree that consistent nationalism in American politics would be frightening.

The liberal–conservative duopoly in American politics has been challenged in recent years by Jerry Brown, Ross Perot, and Patrick Buchanan. Although Brown, Perot, and Buchanan are associated with the political left, center, and right, all three individuals, and the movements that they have led, can be subsumed under the category of national populism. National populism unites the nationalism in economics, politics, and culture that are separated, in different ways, in conventional American liberal and conservative ideologies. At the same time, national populists have tended to indulge in conspiracy theories and overly simple policy gimmicks.

The exaggerations and antics of the national populists have made it easy for conventional liberals and conservatives to continue dismissing American nationalism in their rhetoric (even as they continue to incorporate particular nationalist themes into their ideologies). What has been missing in recent American politics is a liberal or democratic nationalism, a sober, enlightened nationalism that cannot be dismissed as demagogy or rejected as a threat to constitutional government, civil liberties, or capitalism.

In short, what is missing from the American political debate is a contemporary version of America's own two-century-old tradition of democratic nationalism: the Hamiltonian tradition.

The two great traditions in American politics are democratic nationalism and democratic localism. Each is identified with one or the other of two important Founding Fathers of the early republic. American democratic nationalism is often known as "Hamiltonianism," after the first United States Secretary of the Treasury, Alexander Hamilton, while democratic localism is frequently called "Jeffersonianism," after Thomas Jefferson, the third President of the United States and the principal author of the Declaration of Independence.

The democratic localist tradition of Jefferson and his disciples has envisioned the ideal United States as a highly decentralized confederation of internally homogeneous state and local communities, linked only by a minimal national government. The United States was to be a kind of Switzerland on a continental scale. Democratic nationalists of the school of Hamilton have envisioned the ideal United States as an equal to or successor to Great Britain—one of several great world powers, if not the dominant superpower—with a relatively centralized state capable of projecting force abroad, fostering (and regulating) an industrial capitalist economy, and extending the strong arm of the law to protect minorities in America's heterogeneous population from oppression by local majorities.

Throughout American history, Hamiltonians and Jeffersonians have taken opposing sides on several issues that go to the core of American identity:

The primary community. Democratic nationalists tend to view the American nation itself as the primary community; democratic localists, to see the United States as an aggregate of smaller, more homogeneous regional, racial, or religious communities.

The legitimacy of the federal government. Democratic nationalists have always stressed that the federal and state governments alike derive their powers directly and independently from the people, by means of the Constitution of 1787. Democratic localists often (though not always) have claimed that the Constitution established merely a revocable compact among the states. Even when they do not endorse the compact theory of the Constitution, Jeffersonians usually favor a broad interpretation of states' rights and a narrow construction of federal authority. Hamiltonians construe states' rights narrowly and federal authority broadly.

Power politics. From Hamilton and Washington through twentieth-century democratic nationalists like the two Roosevelts, policymakers and thinkers in the Hamiltonian tradition have believed that the United States must use the traditional means of power politics—fleets, armies, secret services, foreign aid—in order to defend its interests and secure its advantage in the dangerous and unstable arena of global politics. Jeffersonians, fearful that standing armies and secret services will be used to repress domestic dissent, have been drawn toward utopian schemes that promise escape from world politics (isolationism) or the transcendence of old-fashioned power politics by world federalism (collective security).

Government activism. Throughout American history, Hamiltonian democratic nationalists have favored intelligent activism by both the federal and the state governments to promote the public interest. At different times government activism has taken the form of sponsoring "internal improvements" or infrastructure projects like the construction of turnpikes, canals, railroads, the airline industry, and the Internet; raising tariffs to protect infant industries, and then pressing for reciprocal free trade with other countries when those industries had matured; and establishing national social insurance programs like Social Security, Medicare, and Medicaid to cushion workers against fluctuations in the economy. Each of those projects has been denounced by Jeffersonian proponents of states' rights, in different eras, as unconstitutional, tyrannical, and tending to promote "consolidation" or excessive centralization.

The historian Walter Russell Mead has warned that it is a mistake to equate Hamiltonian statism and realism with Gaullist or Germanic cognates. Despite their profound differences, Hamiltonians and Jeffersonians have shared the common heritage of Anglo-American democratic liberalism. American democratic nationalism and American democratic localism share a cluster of beliefs about the importance of civil rights, property rights, elected representatives, limited government, and written constitutions. The two schools have debated not whether liberal democracy is a good idea, but in what form the liberal-democratic idea can best be realized. Though Jefferson accused Hamilton's Federalists of seeking to restore aristocracy in America, the truth is that, considered as a group, Hamiltonians have been as committed to liberal democracy and social equality as Jeffersonians. If Hamilton was a social climber and a snob, Jefferson was an aristocratic planter who owned more than five hundred slaves and who bought and sold human beings to pay for his extravagant lifestyle. Insofar as most measures extending individual rights have been pushed through by the federal government, backed by national majorities, over the objection of oppressive local majorities, it can even be argued that Hamiltonian policies have done more for individual rights than Jeffersonian rhetoric. During the Revolutionary War, when several dozen of Jefferson's slaves were escaping to freedom behind British lines, Hamilton proposed emancipating and arming American slaves as a war measure—a proposal eventually adopted in a different war by that great Hamiltonian statesman Abraham Lincoln.

From this brief summary it should be apparent that, however powerful Jeffersonian rhetoric remains in American public discourse, it is the Hamiltonians who have won the major struggles to determine what kind of country the United States would be. Lincoln and Grant settled the question of whether the United States was a nation-state or a loose alliance among sovereign states. Lincoln and his successors in the Republican party of 1865–1932, by presiding over the industrialization of the United States, foreclosed the option that the United States would remain a rural society with an agrarian economy, as so many Jeffersonians had hoped. The New Deal of Franklin Delano Roosevelt and the Great Society of Lyndon Baines Johnson made a majority of American citizens direct beneficiaries of federal entitlement programs—to the horror of Jeffersonians, who beheld a virtuous population being corrupted by dependence on the state. Finally, and most important, the use of federal troops and federal judges to secure first the freedom of black Americans from slavery and then the vindication of their civil and political rights has led Americans of all categories to take it for granted that their basic rights as U.S. citizens should not be at the mercy of city councils or state legislatures.

The achievement of the Hamiltonian vision of American society was by no means inevitable. Indeed, the attempt to match the Hamiltonian and Jeffersonian persuasions with American political parties shows the striking inability of the Hamiltonian tradition to find an enduring political vehicle. Thomas Jefferson's Republican party evolved into the Democratic Republicans, which became the Democrats. From the time of Jefferson until the 1960s, the two core constituencies of the Democratic party were white Southern Protestants and their allies among urban European immigrants and their descendants—chiefly Irish Catholics—in the North. The "Boston–Austin" axis uniting John F. Kennedy and Lyndon Johnson on a ticket was remarkably similar to the alliance between Southerners like Thomas Jefferson and Irish allies in Northern cities. New York's Tammany Hall club was an important Republican/Democratic–Republican/Democratic institution from the 1790s to the 1960s.

Nothing like that continuity exists on the Hamiltonian side. The democratic nationalist impulse has been embodied in a series of parties and movements, each of which has tended to fall apart in only a generation or two: the Federalists; the National Republicans; the Whigs, the Republicans; the Progressives. The reason for the difference between Jeffersonian continuity and Hamiltonian combustibility can be found in the different political elites and cultures of the South and the North.

Until the mid-twentieth century, the Democratic party was, first and foremost, the Southern party, controlled by a homogeneous and determined Southern elite that monopolized not only political power but economic control and social authority in its region. That elite cohesion permitted Southerners to exert political influence far out of proportion to their numbers (and still does—as I write, the President, the Vice-President, the Speaker of the House, and the Senate Majority Leader of the United States are all from states of the former Confederacy).

By contrast, the Northern elite has always been weakened by a division between nationally minded Hamiltonians, on the one hand, and, on the other, members of a unique "moralist" subculture in New England and the states settled by New Englanders in the Great Lakes region, the Northern prairie and the Pacific Northwest. To put the matter simply and rather crudely, the Hamiltonian party has succeeded when Northern nationalists have collaborated with Southern and Western nationalists, and it has collapsed when Northern moralists offended potential allies in other regions with their zealotry on behalf of various causes, including the abolition of slavery and opposition to the War of 1812 and the Mexican and Vietnam wars.

That debilitating intra-Northern dynamic can be seen at work most clearly in the stunted career of Daniel Webster and the Whig party. In order to bring the Whigs to power in the White House and Congress, northern Whigs like Webster had to win the trust of Southern moderates by appeasing the Southern oligarchy on issues related to slavery. That strategy was denounced by the moralist wing of the northern Whigs, "Conscience Whigs" for whom Webster and his allies were cynical "Cotton Whigs" willing to abandon abolitionist principle for something as insignificant as averting civil war and preserving the union. Even during the Civil War, with most of the South no longer represented in the federal government, the more radical Northern abolitionists criticized Lincoln for being too conservative in his emancipation policy.

Disagreements over foreign policy between Northern nationalists and Northern moralists have been even more fatal to the Hamiltonian project. As the historian David Hackett Fischer has demonstrated, Southerners and Westerners, despite their hostility to strong government in general, have usually been ardent supporters of American war-fighting and preparedness, while the residents of greater New England have been consistent pacifists and isolationists. The opposition of New England Federalists to the War of 1812, which was popular in the South and West, discredited Hamilton's Federalist party in the eyes of Americans outside of New England. In exactly the same way the opposition of northern liberal Democrats to the Vietnam War and the Cold War convinced most American voters from 1968 to 1992 that the Democratic party—the more Hamiltonian of the two parties of the time—could not be trusted with the presidency in an era of geopolitical strife. (The tension between New England moralism and northern Hamiltonian realism was submerged during the Civil War, when both schools agreed on the goal of defeating the Confederacy, for different reasons.)

The formula for Hamiltonian success in national politics is simple, if unpalatable to the Massachusetts-to-Wisconsin moralists who provide the core constituency of today's liberal left. For Hamiltonians to gain power in Congress and the White House, pro-military Northerners must spurn the pacifism and zealotry of uncompromising Northern moralists and unite with moderate, nationally minded Southerners and Westerners. Whenever Northern nationalists have allied themselves with moralists in their own region instead of with nationalists in other regions, the result has been the political suicide of the Hamiltonian party and the triumph of a Southern/ Western Jeffersonian majority, checked only by an ineffectual Northern remnant made up of politicians who, like Adlai Stevenson, would rather be right than president.

Today we are in a period in which Jeffersonians based in the South and the West control the national government, as they did during the era from 1800 to 1860. Beginning with the capture of the Republican Party by the McCarthy–Goldwater movement, Southern and Western conservatives, most of them from Democratic backgrounds, have joined the GOP and transformed the party of Lincoln and Theodore Roosevelt into the party of Jefferson and Jackson. It does not follow, however, that today's Democrats are Hamiltonians. The shrunken Democratic party of today, with its geographic base in New England and the Great Lakes and Northern prairie regions, exhibits the characteristic attitudes of the centuries-old Northern moralist subculture derived from New England Puritanism—a revulsion against the use of force in foreign affairs, coupled with a highly idealistic, even zealous approach to politics, which makes compromise on matters like affirmative action or abortion appear to be betrayal. We have a Jeffersonian majority party in the Republicans and a Northern moralist minority party in the Democrats—but at the moment there is no Hamiltonian nationalist party uniting those in every region who favor strength abroad and activist government at home.

At the end of the twentieth century, some conservatives hope, and many liberals fear, that the long trend toward the centralization of political authority and the nationalization of the American body politic is on the verge of being reversed. It is worth recalling, however, that each surge of Hamiltonian democratic nationalism has been followed by a period of Jeffersonian reaction, in which the Hamiltonian innovations have been trimmed back but not eliminated. Washington and Adams, leaders of the state-building Federalist party, were succeeded by Thomas Jefferson's Republicans in 1800; Jefferson and his party, while denouncing Federalist principles, retained many Federalist institutions and measures. Following the expansion of federal power in the service of social reform during the Civil War and Reconstruction, the pendulum swung back toward the Jeffersonian side of the political spectrum; nevertheless, the country remained far more centralized than it had been, and slavery, if not segregation, had been eliminated forever. The neo-Jeffersonian Republicans of the 1920s did not restore the status quo ante from before World War I and the climax of Progressive reform, just as the

Eisenhower administration and the bipartisan conservative bloc in Congress in the 1950s limited itself to trimming, not repealing, the New Deal and the national security state bequeathed by FDR and Truman.

The conservative backlash that followed the Civil Rights Revolution and the Great Society era shows every sign of following the same pattern of consolidation and minor retrenchment rather than repeal. True, conservatives denounce affirmative action, but in the name of the original integrationist ideal behind the 1964 Civil Rights Act. And while conservatives have had some success in dismantling the federal safety net for the poor, not even Ronald Reagan at the height of his power attempted to abolish New Deal/Great Society programs popular with the middle class, like Social Security, Medicare, student loans, and Head Start. It is safe to predict that most of the innovations of the mid-twentieth-century New Deal/Cold War liberals, architects of the welfare state and the national-security state, will survive the current wave of Jeffersonian conservatism. Likewise, it is safe to predict that future crises—whether global, like the world wars and the Depression, or internal, like the Civil War—will further the unfinished democratic nationalist agenda, perhaps in ways that no one can now predict.

The Plan of This Book

The disappearance of Hamiltonian democratic nationalism as an option in American politics is likely to prove temporary. In the meantime, this book is the first attempt to collect the writings of the major thinkers in the Hamiltonian tradition of American democratic nationalism. The first section consists of the major writings of Alexander Hamilton himself. In the remainder of the book, the themes that informed Hamilton's thought and work are illustrated by excerpts from the speeches and writings of major figures in the Federalist–National Republican–Whig–Republican–Progressive–New Deal tradition. Following the order of priorities in the Preamble of the U.S. Constitution, these themes are "We the People" (national identity), "A More Perfect Union" (the democratic nationalist theory of the constitution), "The Common Defense" (national-interest foreign policy), and "The General Welfare" (activist federal government).

Although the integrationist/amalgamationist view or "melting pot" theory of American society is represented in the section entitled "We the People," I have chosen not to include a separate section on civil rights. Hamilton himself sought the abolition of slavery, and two of the greatest Hamiltonian presidents, Abraham Lincoln and Lyndon Johnson, presided over the destruction by federal power of slavery and segregation, respectively. As tempting as it would be to claim civil rights as a Hamiltonian legacy, it would be intellectually dishonest to do so—just as dishonest as the conventional treatment of American civil rights as footnotes to the rhetoric of Thomas Jefferson. The truth is that the extension of civil rights to different categories of Americans—poor whites, black men, white women, homosexuals—has been promoted at different times by different groups for different reasons. Antebellum Jacksonians promoted a *Herrenvolk* or master-race democracy, favoring political (though not economic) egalitarianism within the white population and strict subordination of black Americans; their Whig and American Party rivals opposed slavery while worrying about direct democracy and wondering whether Irish Catholics could be considered white. American abolitionism and support for women's suffrage grew not out of the Enlightenment theories of human rights embodied in the Declaration of Independence, as most Americans mistakenly believe, but rather out of the same Northern evangelical Protestantism that also inspired the temperance movement. Many turn-of-the-century Progressives favored extending the vote to native-born, middle-class white women—and at the same time favored purging poor Southern whites, immigrants, and blacks from voter lists. If Jeffersonian democratic localism, identified with Southern states'-rights conservatism for most of American history, has been consistently hostile to the extension of civil rights to previously disfranchised groups, Hamiltonian democratic nationalism has been only intermittently sympathetic to minority rights. For every Lincoln or Truman who cautiously extends civil rights as a national security measure, there has been a Clay or a Webster willing to sacrifice justice in order to preserve national unity.

I have also left out subjects about which Hamiltonians have disagreed among themselves. The separation of powers is one such topic. While American democratic nationalists in every era have favored a strong national government, Hamiltonians in different periods have preferred different branches of the federal government—the presidency, Congress, or even the federal judiciary. Usually they have sought to enhance the power of the branch that their party controlled or had a chance of controlling: the presidency during the Federalist Era, the Congress in the Jacksonian period, when the Whigs had little success in presidential elections. The same subordination of separation-of-powers theory to political expediency is found among the Jeffersonians, who have repeatedly promulgated expansive theories of presidential prerogative power when one of their persuasion—Jefferson, Jackson, Reagan—held the highest office in the land.

Another topic on which there has been no agreement among Hamiltonians is immigration. Hamilton favored the immigration of skilled artisans but worried that unchecked immigration would reduce the social homogeneity that he considered necessary in a successful republic. The Whigs, their successors in the nativist American party of the 1850s, and later the Progressives worried that European immigrants could not or would not assimilate to the norms of the majority. On the other hand, Lincoln, Seward, and other mid-century Republicans welcomed European immigrants as potential replacements for freed black Americans slaves, whom colonizationists like Lincoln hoped to resettle in other countries in Latin America or the Caribbean. In general Hamiltonians have been more hostile than favorable to large-scale immigration, which they have viewed as a threat to national cultural unity and, sometimes, to the wages of native-born workers. But there have been enough exceptions to justify the exclusion of immigration as a topic of this book.

American democratic nationalism is primarily a theory of the military, constitutional, and economic organization of the American nation-state; it is not a comprehensive theory of the good society. Many of the questions that agitate today's politics, such as those touching on sex and sex roles, cannot be answered by reference to the Hamiltonian tradition of state-building and economy-building—or, for that matter, by reference to the rival Jeffersonian tradition. What the Hamiltonian or Jeffersonian line on regulating pornography on the Internet or cloning should be is anyone's guess. That Abraham Lincoln has been invoked by both gay Republicans and Republican opponents of abortion shows how easily attempts to project contemporary viewpoints on historical figures can become ventriloquism in a cemetery.

Finally, I have decided not to include a section on the question of whether there is or can be a distinctive American art and literature. This is a perennial topic, usually debated with more heat than light. Some of the American artists who have been most vehement in their rejection of Old World influences turn out to have had their own foreign models, like Walt Whitman, who lifted his "American" free-verse style from that of a best-selling English writer of the 1840s, Martin Tupper, or Frank Lloyd Wright, whose "Prairie School" architecture owed less to the American prairie than to the British Arts and Crafts movement and traditional Japanese architecture. At the same time, there is surely some point to the protest that American artists and writers should do more than imitate foreign schools in art and literature, the way that the New York School of abstract painters recycled the stale ideas of the European avant-garde after 1945. The subject is fascinating, but it is too remote from the practical concerns of American democratic nationalist thinkers for its inclusion in this anthology to be justified.

A certain bias has inevitably been introduced simply by the selection of writings. Some of the greatest American Hamiltonian statesmen have written little or nothing of consequence. There is much truth in the old chestnut about government and politics: "Those who talk do not know, and those who know do not talk." Inevitably journalists like Herbert Croly and Walter Lippmann and theorists like Henry C. Carey and Samuel Huntington receive far more space than policymakers like Nicholas Biddle (President of the Second Bank of the United States), William Seward, John Hay, and Elihu Root, although much space is devoted to the writings of two exceptional geniuses who were both students and practitioners of statecraft, Hamilton himself and Theodore Roosevelt.

Because this anthology is organized by themes, I have preceded each excerpt with a descriptive title. In a few cases the original title has been used when it is sufficiently descriptive (e.g., Israel Zangwill's "The Melting Pot"). A more conventional approach to labeling excerpts would have baffled readers, because some sources (Washington's Farewell Address, for example) are excerpted in more than one section.

"Rich country, strong army"—this motto of Japan's Meiji Restoration might be that of Hamiltonians in the United States. Hamiltonian democratic nationalism is not the source of all that is good and just in American life; it is merely the source of most of what is sensible and sound in American foreign policy, constitutional law, and economic policy. Other traditions, perhaps even the Jeffersonian tradition, can contribute to making American society more free, more cultivated, more cosmopolitan, or more cohesive. Hamiltonian statesmen and thinkers will fulfill their duty in the future, as they have in the past, if they do nothing more than ensure that the United States is safe, well governed, and rich.

PART ONE

THE LEGACY OF
ALEXANDER HAMILTON

After the revolutions of 1989 brought down communism in Eastern Europe, many of the political and intellectual leaders of the emerging democracies turned for guidance to the United States. Americans of all political persuasions recommended the writings of such sages as Thomas Jefferson, James Madison, and Abraham Lincoln. Alexander Hamilton was seldom mentioned, even though his contributions to that compendium of political wisdom, The Federalist, far outweigh those of his co-authors Madison and John Jay. No one suggested that the theories and example of Hamilton might be far more relevant to the new democratic regimes struggling to consolidate their rule and build new governmental, financial, and military institutions on the remnants of Soviet colonialism.

That oversight is puzzling, if not tragic, because Hamilton was the most practical nation-builder among the Founding Fathers. Thanks largely to his vision and energy, the United States became what it is today: a relatively centralized nation-state with a military second to none in the world, a powerful presidency, a strong judiciary, and an industrial capitalist economy. John Marshall, the first Chief Justice of the United States, who did so much to fix Hamilton's expansive view of federal authority in law, thought that Hamilton and his mentor George Washington were the greatest of the Founders. One contemporary acquaintance, Judge Ambrose Spencer, who had clashed with Hamilton, nevertheless declared that he was "the greatest man this country ever produced. . . . He, more than any man, did the thinking of the time." The great French diplomat and statesman Talleyrand, who worked with Hamilton during the Revolution and the early years of the republic, put his "mind and character . . . on a par with [those of] the most distinguished statesmen of Europe, not even excepting Mr. Pitt and Mr. Fox."

Such praise was justified. In addition to serving as George Washington's valued aide-de-camp during most of the Revolutionary War and successfully reorganizing the Continental Army as one of his tasks, Hamilton helped to initiate the move toward a more centralized union that resulted in the Philadelphia convention of 1787 and the federal constitution. His view of the Constitution as the source of implied as well as enumerated powers became the dominant interpretation, thanks to his admirers and students John Marshall, Joseph Storey, and Daniel Webster, and his conception of expansive presidential war and foreign policy powers would prevail in the twentieth century. As secretary of the treasury (1789–95), Hamilton established the fiscal infrastructure of the new republic, including the Bank of the United States, precursor of the Federal Reserve. He not only articulated the theory of tariff-based industrial policy (an inspiration to later American, German, and Japanese modernizers) but organized the Society for the Promotion of Useful Manufactures (SUM), the first American research institute and industrial conglomerate, sited on 38 acres by the Passaic River falls in Paterson, New Jersey.

Today, however, those who remember the mastermind of the Washington administration (1789–97) tend to know only a caricature of Hamilton as a champion of the rich—the prototype of such Wall Street wizards as Andrew Mellon and Michael Milken. Now and then Hamilton's ideas are invoked by those seeking to justify policies of economic nationalism, but more often "Hamiltonianism" is used as shorthand for a blend of plutocracy and authoritarianism, the antithesis of the democratic idealism associated with Hamilton's lifelong political rival Thomas Jefferson. (Jefferson placed a bust of Hamilton on the right side of the entrance hall at Monticello, across from his own portrait on the left, explaining to visitors: "Opposed in death as in life.") Regardless of political orientation, American politicians today all claim to be Jeffersonians. Few, if any, will admit to being Hamiltonians. At the end of the twentieth century, it appears, the consensus holds that Noah Webster was right to name Hamilton "the evil genius of this country."

It is far easier to understand why Hamilton has been maligned than why he has been forgotten. His life was as dramatic as any in the annals of the early American republic. The only non-native among the Founding Fathers, he was born in the British West Indies, probably in 1755, the illegitimate son of an aristocratic Scot and a French Huguenot. Orphaned at thirteen, he supported himself as a clerk in the St. Croix office of a New York import-export firm, acquiring a skill at commerce that would further distinguish him from all the other Founders except Franklin. Hamilton so impressed his employers with his intelligence and industry that they, and other sponsors, sent him to the North American colonies to further his education. He enrolled in King's College (later Columbia University) in 1773, but academic pursuits were cut short by his involvement in the writing of anti-British pamphlets and the subsequent outbreak of war. Nevertheless, wide and thorough reading kept Hamilton abreast of intellectual developments in Britain and continental Europe. Perhaps one of the strongest influences on his thought was the work of the Scottish philosopher David Hume, whose skepticism about classical republicanism and yeoman virtues made him anathema to Jefferson and other American republican idealists.

During the Revolutionary War, as a member of what Washington called his "family," Hamilton made himself so indispensable that he almost missed his chance for martial glory. That finally came at the Battle of Yorktown, where the slight, still boyish-looking officer personally led his battalion in an assault on a British position. The bond forged with Washington, though subject to strains, would eventually bring Hamilton into the first president's administration. In the meantime, between the war's end and Washington's inauguration, Hamilton was never idle. He read and practiced law, started a family with Elizabeth Schuyler (a New York patrician's daughter whom he married in 1780), and became increasingly involved in New York and national politics. To the latter he brought his strong conviction that the weakly knit confederation established in 1782 could not work, a conviction that spurred his cogent defense of the proposed federal constitution in the essays that he and his collaborators, Madison and Jay, wrote between October 1787 and May 1788. At least two-thirds of the eighty-five essays eventually published as The Federalist came from Hamilton's pen.

As an immigrant, Hamilton lacked any ties to a particular region that might have qualified his devotion to the American nation in its entirety. Installed as Washington's Secretary of the Treasury, he took decisive steps to strengthen the efficiency and power of the federal government. To that end, and to make the new nation-state creditworthy, he arranged for the federal government to assume the debts accumulated by the states during and after the Revolution and devised a system of taxation to pay off the debt. A political pragmatist, he won support for his bitterly contested assertion of sovereignty by the federal government by agreeing to back Thomas Jefferson and other Southerners in their ambition to move the nation's capital to a site on the Potomac River. Though initially opposed to political parties because of their disruptive character, Hamilton helped to create and then took the helm of the Federalist Party to push his policies through the legislature. His rivals in what became the Republican Party, including Secretary of State Thomas Jefferson, fought just as hard to thwart Hamilton's agenda, which they denounced as pro-business, antidemocratic, and even monarchical. Hamilton's tendency to favor England over France during the wars of the French Revolution and to hold up England's powerful military, civil, and financial administrations as models only stoked his enemies' animosity. The efforts of the Republicans in Congress to drive their foe from office—including an attempt, abandoned before it got far, to capitalize on Hamilton's affair with a blackmailer named Maria Reynolds—finally succeeded in 1795, two years before the end of Washington's second term.

Still wielding power in private life—among other ways, through the *New York Post,* which he founded—Hamilton began to make enemies even among his fellow Federalists, opposing John Adams's reelection to the presidency in 1800 and supporting the Louisiana Purchase in 1803. Hamilton, who, like Napoleon, preferred to make war on allies, enraged another Federalist by speaking ill of his candidacy for the governorship of New York. The offended party, Aaron Burr, demanded satisfaction. Hamilton accepted, though in the resulting duel he took care to aim away from his challenger. Burr was not so gracious. Hamilton, who as a boy had hoped to become a physician, offered an immediate evaluation of his condition: "This is a mortal wound, Doctor." He died the next day—July 14, 1804.

His ideas could not be so easily extinguished. Like his rival Jefferson, Hamilton was a theorist as well as a statesman. His premature death prevented him from writing the "full investigation of the history and science of civil government and the various modifications of it upon the freedom and happiness of mankind," to which he had planned to devote his later years, according to an admirer, Chancellor Joseph Kent, an early Chief Justice of the Supreme Court of New York. Though he never wrote his treatise on government, Hamilton lived to see the republication of The Federalist and his polemical Pacificus letters defending presidential authority and national-interest realism in foreign affairs. Those and other occasional writings, together with the three great reports he made to Congress as Secretary of the Treasury—*The Report on the Public Credit* (1790), *The Report on the Bank of the United States* (1790), and *The Report on Manufactures* (1791)—constitute a substantial body of work explicating the principles of Hamiltonian democratic nationalism.

As Hamilton saw it, the United States was, and should always remain, a nation-state in which the states are clearly subordinated to a strong but not oppressive federal government. The national government must possess military forces capable not only of securing America's interests abroad but of suppressing domestic insurrection quickly and effectively—a lesson he learned in the Whiskey Rebellion, which President Washington, with Hamilton's aid, put down in 1794. The success of the federal government, in the view of Hamilton and his followers, depends upon an efficient and competent executive branch and a powerful federal judiciary, both insulated to a degree from the popularly elected legislature. "The test of good government," Hamilton wrote, "is its aptitude and tendency to produce a good administration." Holding that good administration requires first-rate officers with long tenure, Hamilton firmly rejected the Jeffersonian notion that a great and powerful state can be administered by amateur politicians and short-term, inexperienced appointees.

One of the duties of the federal government, according to the Hamiltonian philosophy, is the active promotion of a dynamic industrial capitalist economy—not by government ownership but by establishment of sound public finance, public investment in infrastructure, and promotion of new industrial sectors unlikely to be profitable in their early stages. "Capital is wayward and timid in lending itself to new undertakings, and the State ought to excite the confidence of capitalists, who are ever cautious and sagacious, by aiding them to overcome the obstacles that lie in the way of all experiments," Hamilton wrote in The Report on Manufactures.

Hamilton, who had studied Adam Smith's The Wealth of Nations, agreed with the Scottish economist on most points but criticized two of his ideas. He rejected Smith's notion that agriculture was preferable to manufacturing. And though Hamilton saw many benefits in trade and foreign investment, he believed that free trade was a mistaken policy in some circumstances. Hamilton had learned during the Revolutionary War how important it was for a country not to depend on others for "the manufactories of all the necessary weapons of war." He also advocated protection of infant American industries such as textiles, at least until they were capable of competing on an equal basis with foreign products. Finally, Hamilton thought it foolish for a country to open its commerce to countries that protected theirs. In short, Hamilton held that economic policymakers should be guided by results rather than by dogmas in promoting state interests such as national security and the diversification of the national economy.

With the collapse of the Federalist party a few years after Hamilton's death in 1804, his philosophy of a strong, centralized national government promoting industrial capitalism and defending America's concrete interests abroad with an effective professional military passed into partial eclipse in a couple of generations. Quite different conceptions—states' rights, minimal government, agrarianism, isolationism, a militia-based defense—inspired the Jeffersonian and Jacksonian Democrats who dominated antebellum American politics. "National Republicans," such as John Quincy Adams, and later Whigs, such as Daniel Webster and Henry Clay, kept the Hamiltonian legacy alive. The Whigs, fusing with antislavery Jacksonian Democrats in the 1850s, formed the new Republican party, which under Abraham Lincoln and his successors crushed the Confederacy, abolished slavery, and made America into a strong nation-state linked by a federally sponsored railroad infrastructure and industrialization behind high tariff walls.

The triumph of the Union in the Civil War was in many ways a vindication of Hamilton's vision of America's destiny, as was the rise of the United States as one of the world's great powers by the time of the Spanish–American War. "For many decades after the Civil War," Hamilton's biographer Forrest McDonald writes, "his niche in the pantheon of American demigods was beneath only Washington's, if indeed it was not at Washington's right hand." Even so, the industrial magnates of the Gilded Age, like Jay Gould, Edward H. Harriman, and J. P. Morgan, were not as a rule Hamiltonian in their philosophy. They tended to follow Herbert Spencer, the British philosopher of laissez-faire Social Darwinism. Moreover, many American business leaders were pacifists, believing that international capitalism, by increasing interdependence, would render war and economic rivalry between states obsolete.

The intellectual and political heirs of Hamilton operated largely outside the realm of business. The Harvard political scientist Samuel P. Huntington, in *The Soldier and the State* (1957), describes the rise and fall of a neo-Hamiltonian school between 1890 and 1920. It included such politicians as Theodore Roosevelt and Massachusetts Senator Henry Cabot Lodge as well as such intellectuals as Herbert Croly, Brooks Adams, and Alfred Thayer Mahan, the prophet of American navalism and great-power politics. This group of like-minded men often combined *Realpolitik* in foreign policy with support for progressive reform at home—in the interest more of national efficiency than of abstract social justice. They rejected the Gilded Age's celebration of the entrepreneur in favor of the patrician-military ideal of an elite that serves the public by serving the state. According to Huntington, "Brooks Adams even went so far as to suggest openly that America would do well to substitute the values of West Point for the values of Wall Street." (It should come as no surprise to learn that West Point was a scaled-down version of Hamilton's grandiose vision of a comprehensive military academy.)

At the beginning of this century, Hamilton's reputation reached its peak. In *The Promise of American Life* (1909), the founding editor of *The New Republic* and the most influential thinker of the Progressive movement, Herbert Croly, contrasted Hamilton's view that "the central government is to be used, not merely to maintain the Constitution, but to promote the national interest and to consolidate the national organization" with the Jeffersonian theory that "there should be as little government as possible." The latter view rested on what Croly considered a naïve belief in "the native goodness of human nature." To Croly and his Progressive allies, Jeffersonian doctrines, if they had ever been relevant, were obsolete in the new era of national and multinational corporations, mass organizations, technological warfare, and imperialism. Croly conceded that Hamilton's version of American nationalism had been inadequate because of its excessive distrust of popular democracy, but he held that the basic conception of an activist national government promoting the common good was as compatible with egalitarian as with aristocratic conceptions of a good social order.

Croly's *beau idéal* of an American statesman was Theodore Roosevelt, whom he praised for emancipating "American democracy from its Jeffersonian bondage." TR united progressive democratic nationalism in domestic policy with an assertive realism, based on military power, in foreign affairs—a realism manifest in his seizure of Panama and his mediation of the Russo-Japanese War in the interest of the Pacific balance of power (a feat for which he won the Nobel Peace Prize in 1904). Roosevelt, like his friend Henry Cabot Lodge, Chairman of the Senate Foreign Relations Committee, favored U.S. intervention in World War I but opposed Wilson's League of Nations Treaty because it committed the United States to a vague collective security arrangement rather than a traditional limited alliance. In his own biography of Hamilton, published in 1883, Lodge predicted that "so long as the people of the United States form one nation, the name of Alexander Hamilton will be held in high and lasting honor, and even in the wreck of governments that noble intellect would still command the homage of men."

Lodge spoke too soon. After World War I Hamilton's reputation, along with the Hamiltonian tradition of American democratic nationalism, went into sudden decline. The defeat, by the representatives of the conventional business elite, of the progressive wing of the Republican party led by TR made the Republicans hostile to overseas military intervention, high levels of military spending, and ideas of government activism in the economy, even on behalf of business. The liberal wing of the Democratic party inherited the legacy of Hamiltonian progressivism. But New Deal liberalism, as it evolved in the 1930s, was quite different from the nationalism of earlier Progressives like TR and Croly.

The claim is often made that the New Deal represented a fusion of the two great American traditions of government, which resulted in a new synthesis:

the pursuit of Jeffersonian ends by Hamiltonian means. The historian Merrill D. Peterson writes that during the New Deal, "national power and purpose grew without disturbing the axis of the democratic faith. For all practical purposes, the New Deal ended the historic Jefferson–Hamilton dialogue in American history." One might more plausibly argue that New Deal liberals abandoned the democratic and technocratic Hamiltonian nationalism of Herbert Croly in favor of the ideal of the lobby-based broker state.

Partly to shield themselves from accusations that the New Deal was the American version of fascism or communism, New Dealers stressed the *absence* of centralized state direction of the economy. The journalist John Chamberlain described Franklin Delano Roosevelt's "broker state" as a liberal-democratic alternative to the directive state of the Progressives (and totalitarians). Interest-group liberalism was seen as a pragmatic, democratic American version of corporatism or syndicalism. "We have equilibrated power," the theologian Reinhold Niebuhr wrote. "We have attained a certain equilibrium in economic society itself by setting organized power against organized power" in the form of unions, corporations, and professional associations.

New Deal liberals found a patron saint for interest-group liberalism not in Hamilton (who had been the hero of so many of the detested Republicans) but in Madison. Madison's Federalist Number 10, with its theory of factions in a democracy, had been forgotten until the historian Charles Beard drew attention to it shortly before World War I. New Deal liberals downplayed Madison's opposition to factions and enlisted Federalist 10 as a precedent for their ideology of harmony and equilibrium through pluralism. In the 1940s and 1950s Madison was elevated to the status of a patron saint of interest-group liberalism, while Hamilton, the principal author of The Federalist, was denounced by, among others, the historian Douglass Adair for allegedly having favored "an overruling, irresponsible, and unlimited government."

Franklin D. Roosevelt himself played an important role in expelling Hamilton from the American pantheon. FDR, a Tory Democrat from the landed gentry of the Hudson River, saw himself in the Tory democrat from Virginia. In his mind, Jefferson stood for popular government, not necessarily for weak or decentralized government, while Hamilton was a forerunner of Andrew Mellon and identified with the worst excesses of a callous plutocracy. Reviewing a book by Claude G. Bowers, *Jefferson and Hamilton: The Struggle for Democracy in America,* FDR suggested in 1925 that the common people needed a champion against the forces of plutocracy: "I have a breathless feeling, too, as I wonder if, a century and a quarter later, the same contending forces are not mobilizing." At the 1928 Democratic national convention, FDR, the keynote speaker, declared: "Hamiltons we have today. Is there a

Jefferson on the horizon?" Soon enough, Jefferson—or at least a sanitized Jefferson, whose racist views and small-government, states'-rights ideology were conveniently forgotten—came to stand at the head of a line leading, by way of Andrew Jackson, to President Franklin D. Roosevelt himself. The work of rewriting American history as a prelude to the New Deal was completed by the moderate-liberal consensus historians of the 1950s and 1960s. At least one dissenting historian, Samuel Eliot Morison, considered this dismissal of the Federalist-Whig-Republican tradition "unbalanced and unhealthy, tending to create a neoliberal stereotype." But Hamilton's stock remained low.

To the extent that the Hamiltonian tradition lived on after 1932, it was in foreign policy. The logic of the broker state did not apply to the centralized national security state that was assembled during World War II and consolidated into a permanent structure during the Korean War. Samuel P. Huntington notes "the curious way in which Theodore Roosevelt was the intellectual godfather of Democratic administrations after 1933" in foreign policy, and he sees a "clear line" from such neo-Hamiltonians as TR and Elihu Root to "Stimson to Marshall, Lovett, and McCloy."[1]

One might have expected the leaders of the civil rights movement of the 1950s and 1960s to have looked to Hamilton for inspiration. The civil rights struggle, after all, was largely carried out in the name of federal authority by federal judges, whose power and independence Hamilton strenuously defended (notably in Federalist Number 76). What is more, Hamilton was one of the more outspoken opponents of slavery and racism among the Founding Fathers. When he was aide-de-camp to Washington, Hamilton favored giving black slaves their freedom and citizenship and arming them as soldiers. "The contempt we have been taught to entertain for the blacks, makes us fancy many things that are founded neither in reason nor experience. . . . [T]he dictates of humanity and true policy equally interest me in favor of this unfortunate class of men." After the war, Hamilton—who had grown up in the slave society of the West Indies—helped organize the Society for Promoting the Manumission of Slaves. By contrast, Jefferson, who owned hundreds of slaves, opposed emancipation if it could not be accompanied by the immediate colonization of black Americans abroad, and his speculations about alleged black inferiority in his *Notes on the State of Virginia* (1784–85) made

---

1. The theory of Cold War American realism, however, owed little to Hamilton, TR, Lodge, or Mahan, and far more to European émigré intellectuals such as Nicholas Spykman, Hans Morgenthau, and Henry Kissinger (the one exception being the perennial critic of foreign-policy utopianism, Walter Lippmann, Croly's fellow *New Republic* editor).

him a founder of pseudoscientific racism in the United States. Nevertheless, the modern habit of attributing everything good in American life to the inspiration of Jefferson alone has resulted in the Virginia slaveowner's being given credit for convictions about black equality and freedom that he did not hold—and that Hamilton did.

The New Left (which was chiefly influenced by the Marxist radicalism of Jewish immigrants and émigrés from Central Europe) and the modern conservative movement (which finds its greatest strength among old-stock white Americans in the South and the West) both invoke "Jeffersonian" ideas and rhetoric, for different purposes. The pseudo-Jeffersonian Left stresses sexual and reproductive freedom, while the genuinely Jeffersonian Right stresses property rights. Left-Jeffersonians attack big business, while Right-Jeffersonians attack big government. For all their differences, there is a striking similarity in the paeans to the virtue of the people and the suspicion of authority and organization shared by the leaders of both the sexual revolution and the tax revolt—and a common dislike of Alexander Hamilton, the socially conservative proponent of big business *and* big government.

While liberals were redefining their tradition as one that stretched from Jefferson to Lincoln to FDR, leaving out Hamilton and Theodore Roosevelt, the conservatives of the 1950s were reading Hamilton out of the lineage of the contemporary American Right. The conservative writer Russell Kirk, who repeated the hoary Jeffersonian libel that Hamilton sought to ensure that the rich and the well-born "could keep their saddles and ride . . . like English squires," criticized Hamilton as an unwitting precursor of the New Deal welfare state. "A man on the Right," according to the historian Clinton Rossiter in 1955, "is not necessarily a conservative, and if Hamilton was a conservative, he was the only one of his kind." The McCarthy-Buckley-Goldwater conservative movement owed more to the old Southern Democrats than to the Federalist-Whig-Republican tradition. Its philosophical roots sank deep in Jeffersonian antistatism, states' rights, and free-market libertarianism, and its anti-elitism and anti-intellectualism originated in Southwestern populism. The defense of the Hamiltonian tradition fell to Northeastern moderate Republicans like Senator Jacob Javits of New York. In *Order of Battle* (1964), Javits sought to defend his conception of the Republican party against the ex-Democrat Goldwaterite conservatives of the South and West: "This is the spirit which has represented the dominant strain in Republican history. Hamilton-Clay-Lincoln–Theodore Roosevelt: they represent the line of evolution embodying this tradition."

The battle for the GOP, though, had been lost long before Javits by Theodore Roosevelt himself and the members of his short-lived Progressive party. By the time Ronald Reagan was elected in 1980, the Republican party had become a completely libertarian, antistatist party in economics, with serious disagreements in its ranks only over such social issues as abortion and school prayer. Though Kevin Phillips, a graduate of the Rockefeller-Nixon-Connally wing of the GOP, published a book, *Staying on Top: The Business Case for National Industry Strategy* (1984), advocating a conservative industrial policy that would target federal aid to "basic industries like steel or automobiles, or high-technology industry," he was in a minority. Another Republican dissident, the former Reagan trade negotiator Clyde Prestowitz, founded the Economic Strategy Institute (ESI) to contest orthodox laissez-faire theories and to advocate government–business partnership and a results-oriented trade policy.

Despite such efforts, the dominant group in the Republican party today consists of Southern and Western Jeffersonians in the Dixiecrat tradition, along with ex-Democrat intellectuals who, while retaining a strong cultural nationalism, have repudiated the New Deal and the Great Society in favor of laissez-faire economics and the libertarian ideal of minimal government. In 1990 George Will named Jefferson the "Person of the Millennium," writing that Jefferson "is what a free person looks like—confident, serene, rational, disciplined, temperate, tolerant, curious." Ronald Reagan, himself an apostate New Deal Democrat, recommended that we "pluck a flower from Thomas Jefferson's life and wear it in our soul forever."

Hamilton probably would have thought as little of the contemporary Republican right as it thinks of him. Reagan's brand of populist conservatism, contrasting the virtue of the people with the evils of the elite, would have found no favor with the meritocratic Hamilton. He despised politicians concerned with "what will *please* (and) not what will *benefit* the people." Though often maligned as a champion of plutocracy, Hamilton favored imposts on the luxuries of the rich as a means of "taxing their superior wealth," praised inheritance laws that would "soon melt down those great estates which, if they continued, might favor the power of the few," and denounced the poll tax in order "to guard the least wealthy part of the community from oppression." Though Hamilton was not alarmed by a moderate deficit, he would have been shocked by deficits produced, like Reagan's, by an unwillingness to levy taxes to match spending. In his *Second Report on the Public Credit* (1795) he noted that runaway debt is "the natural disease of all governments" and that it is difficult "to conceive anything more likely than this to lead to great and convulsive revolutions of empire." The first and greatest Secretary of the Treasury, who during the Whiskey Rebellion helped President Washington to mobilize the militia to collect taxes, would not have smiled upon the tax-revolt rhetoric of Howard Jarvis and Ronald Reagan.

Having seen the consequences of feeble government during the Revolutionary War and the years of the Articles of Confederation, Hamilton would have been appalled by Reagan's assertion that "government is not part of the solution; it is the problem." Indeed, during the French Revolution, Hamilton contemptuously dismissed the "pernicious system" that maintained "that but a small portion of power is requisite to Government . . . and that as human nature shall refine and ameliorate by the operation of a more enlightened plan, government itself will become useless, and Society will subsist and flourish free from its shackles."

"The American nation reached the peak of its greatness in the middle of the 20th century," the historian Forrest McDonald has lamented. "After that time it became increasingly Jeffersonian, governed by coercion and the party spirit, its people progressively more dependent and less self-reliant, its decline candy-coated with the rhetoric of liberty and equality and justice for all: and with that decline Hamilton's fame declined apace." Repudiated by ersatz Jeffersonians and Jacksonians on the Left and Right alike, Hamilton, by the mid-twentieth century, was even being cast as a villain in American fiction and poetry. In his book-length poem *Paterson* (1946–58), William Carlos Williams, one of America's leading midcentury modernist poets, chose the site of Hamilton's early industrial experiments as a symbol of the blighting of the American spirit in the era of centralized government and concentrated industry. The poem is interlarded with quotations from a crackpot pamphlet Williams had read attacking Hamilton and the Federal Reserve, entitled "Tom Edison on the Money Subject." Not long afterward, the poet Robert Bly wrote an anti–Vietnam War poem that included the following lines:

> This is Hamilton's triumph.
> This is the triumph of a centralized bank.
> B-52s come from Guam. Teachers
> die in flames. The hopes of Tolstoy fall asleep in the ant heap.
> Do not ask for mercy.

In the ultimate insult, Gore Vidal, writing from an eccentric populist perspective, cast Hamilton as a sinister foil to the man who murdered him in a duel in his bestselling historical novel *Burr* (1976). Never had Hamilton's reputation been lower.

In recent years Hamiltonianism has been reintroduced into American political debate by way of Japan. Whereas the neo-Hamiltonians of the late nineteenth century looked to Hamilton as a guide to power politics, the

Hamiltonians of today are more likely to view him as the patron saint of industrial policy and economic nationalism.

The architects of the postwar Japanese economic miracle in the Ministry of International Trade and Industry (MITI) and the Ministry of Finance (MOF) were inspired not only by the examples of nineteenth-century Germany and America but by the theories of the nineteenth-century German-American economic nationalist Friedrich List, who, when he lived for a time in Pennsylvania, absorbed Hamilton's ideas about the protection of infant industries. By the late 1970s the remarkable if temporary success of modern Japan in promoting its high-tech industry and banking sectors by combining protectionism and industrial policy with the targeting of open foreign markets—chiefly that of the United States—was presenting a challenge to orthodox American economists and politicians, who had been committed to unilateral free trade since the aftermath of World War II. Working within the neoclassical paradigm, architects of "the new trade theory" (which is little more than a recycling of the old Hamilton–List theory of industrial policy) began to question the view that free trade is always beneficial to a country.

By the 1980s and 1990s a growing number of American politicians and public policy thinkers were advocating the emulation, in the United States, of aspects of Japanese industrial policy. It would be a mistake, however, to describe all American proponents of protectionism as "Hamiltonians." Hamilton and List advocated protectionism only as a temporary measure, to be discarded once world-class national industries had emerged. The failure to do so, by the United States in the 1920s and Japan in the 1970s, not only punished consumers but warped international trade and finance. What is more, most of the industrial-policy advocates in recent decades have been left-liberal Democrats, such as Robert Reich, Robert Kuttner, Lester Thurow, and Laura Tyson, whose interest in different (and sometimes conflicting) versions of national industrial policy grew out of a desire to help American workers threatened by foreign competition. Given a choice, many of these liberals would prefer a "global New Deal" regulating the excesses of transnational capitalism to American economic nationalism in the service of American self-sufficiency and geopolitical preeminence. They are better described as neo-Keynesians rather than neo-Hamiltonians. And the brands of economic nationalism promoted by Ross Perot and Patrick Buchanan owed more to Jacksonian populism than to Hamilton's principles.

The genuine Hamiltonians of today, one can argue, are the politicians and national-security experts more concerned about the U.S. defense industrial base than about union jobs in Detroit. The United States has long had its own military-led industrial policy, in the form of Pentagon-funded research and development. Military procurement has been largely responsible for the post-World War II U.S. lead in industries characterized by high risk and high research costs requiring government support: computers, aircraft, and communications equipment. The chief Pentagon agency—the American MITI, as it were—was the Defense Advanced Research Projects Agency or DARPA (President Clinton dropped the word "Defense" from the agency's name). During the 1980s DARPA funded R&D in sectors including very-high-speed integrated circuits (VHSIC), fiber optics, advanced lasers, computer software, and composite materials, which promised to have commercial applications as well as military uses.

The leading Hamiltonians to emerge from the military-industrial complex have not fared well in politics or in the private sector. DARPA director Craig Fields, an advocate of industrial policy, was forced out of his job by the Bush administration in 1990. The view that prevailed in that administration was one attributed to Michael J. Boskin, Chairman of the Council of Economic Advisors: "It doesn't matter whether the United States makes computer chips or potato chips." Admiral Bobby Ray Inman, the former National Security Agency (NSA) Director who grew concerned about American technological dependence in the 1980s, left government for an unsuccessful stint as the head of a government-backed computer consortium, Microelectronics and Computer Technology Corporation (MCC), in Austin, Texas. It might be useful to recall, however, that Hamilton failed both in his political efforts to promote an industrial policy and in his private attempt to jump-start American industrialization with his Society for Useful Manufactures in Paterson, New Jersey—only to be posthumously vindicated by later generations that adopted certain aspects of his program for national development.

If the neo-Hamiltonians of the 1890s gave a one-sided emphasis to Hamilton's foreign policy realism, the Hamiltonians of today may be overstressing his approach to trade and industry. To Hamilton, foreign policy and economic policy alike were mere means to achieving the goals to which he devoted his life: the unity of the American nation and the competence of its agent, the national state. The circumstances of the 1990s are far different from those of the 1790s, and the United States is a far different country—thanks, in no small part, to Hamilton and his successors. And yet the questions of national unity and competent government are as important in our day as in his.

Today the greatest threat to national unity comes not from sectionalism but from multiculturalism—the idea that there is no single nation comprising Americans of all races, ancestries, and religions, but only an aggregate of biologically defined "cultures" existing under a minimal framework of law. Neither Hamilton nor those of his contemporaries who shared his opposition to slavery gave any sustained thought to the requirements of a multiracial but unicultural society. Still, Hamilton's impassioned vision of a "continentalist" American society can inspire us indirectly as we seek to integrate the American nation in the aftermath of both segregation and multiculturalism.

When it comes to the problem of effective democratic government, Hamilton's legacy is more relevant today than ever. For a generation the United States has suffered from political gridlock, symbolized by, but not limited to, an inability to make tax revenues match spending. What Jonathan Rauch has called "demosclerosis" is a lethal by-product of the interest-group liberalism of the New Deal, a system now in advanced decay. Rauch, along with other conservatives and libertarians, argues for a "Jeffersonian" solution involving the radical reduction of government at all levels and the dispersal of authority from the central government to the states. However, in the conditions of the twenty-first century, when the United States is likely to face geopolitical competition with rising technological powers, mercantilist economic rivalries, and the threat of mass immigration from poor countries, minimal government will almost certainly not be a realistic option. Because the quantity of national government will not be significantly reduced, the quality of national governance will have to be improved. That will mean repudiating the ideal of the directionless broker state—now three-quarters of a century old—and attempting to realize the Hamiltonian and Progressive ideal of a strong but not authoritarian executive branch that is led by a meritocratic elite and capable of resisting interest-group pressures without ceasing to be ultimately accountable to elected representatives.

Elsewhere in the world, the Hamiltonian approach to building democratic capitalism in ex-communist and Third World societies could not be more timely. In the immediate aftermath of the Cold War, Americans urged a "Jeffersonian" model of reconstruction on societies everywhere, thinking that immediate elections and rapid marketization of collectivist economies would solve all problems. The result, in Russia and much of Eastern Europe and Latin America, has been economic stagnation, massive corruption, and popular disillusionment with democracy. The leaders of new democracies can learn from Hamilton and his mentor Washington that it is not enough to hold elections and establish free markets. A struggling new democratic government must be able to defend its borders against foreign enemies, suppress insurrection and criminality, and guide industrial development in the nation's interest—if necessary, at the expense of free trade and investment.

Not only contemporary Americans, then, but people everywhere have much to learn from Hamilton and Hamiltonianism in the century ahead. In the words of Clinton Rossiter, Alexander Hamilton "was conservative and radical, traditionalist and revolutionary, Tory and Whig all thrown into one. He is a glorious source of inspiration and instruction to modern conservatives, but so is he to modern liberals."

ALEXANDER HAMILTON

The Federalist (1787–88)

Hamilton was the organizer and chief author of the Federalist Papers, the most celebrated defense and explanation of the constitution of the United States. In the Federalist Hamilton, along with his co-authors Madison and Jay, argue for the superiority of the constitution, establishing a strong federal nation-state, over the earlier Articles of Confederation, which had created merely a weak league of states.

The selections from the Federalist that follow deal with the military, political, and economic advantages of a stronger Union. Essays dealing with checks and balances, the separation of powers, and the federal judiciary have not been included, because Hamilton's views on those topics have not necessarily been shared by later American democratic nationalists like the nineteenth-century Whigs and Republicans.

The Fate of an Empire

From *Federalist* 1

After an unequivocal experience of the inefficiency of the subsisting federal government, you are called upon to deliberate a new Constitution for the United States of America. The subject speaks its own importance, comprehending in its consequences nothing less than the existence of the UNION, the safety and welfare of the parts of which it is composed, the fate of an empire in many respects the most interesting in the world. It has been frequently remarked that it seems to have been reserved to the people of this country, by their conduct and example, to decide the important question, whether societies of man are really capable or not of establishing good government from reflection and choice, or whether they are forever destined to depend for their political constitutions on accident and force. If there be any truth in the remark, the crisis at which we are arrived may with propriety be regarded as the era in which that decision is to be made; and a wrong election of the part we shall act may, in this view, deserve to be considered as the general misfortune of mankind.

This idea will add the inducements of philanthropy to those of patriotism, to heighten the solicitude which all considerate and good men must feel for the event. Happy will it be if our choice should be directed by a judicious estimate of our true interests, unperplexed and unbiased by considerations not connected with the public good. . . .

And yet . . . we already have sufficient indications that it will happen in this as in all former cases of great national decision. A torrent of angry and malignant passions will be let loose. To judge from the conduct of the opposite parties, we shall be led to conclude that they will mutually hope to evince the justness of their opinions, and to increase the number of their converts by the loudness of their declamations and by the bitterness of their invectives. An enlightened zeal for the energy and efficiency of government will be stigmatized as the offspring of a temper fond of despotic power and hostile to the principles of liberty. An over-scrupulous jealousy of danger to the rights of the people, which is more commonly the fault of the head than of the heart, will be represented as mere pretense and artifice, the stale bait for popularity at the expense of public good. It will be forgotten, on the one hand, that jealousy is the usual concomitant of violent love, and that the noble enthusiasm of liberty is too apt to be infected with a spirit of narrow and illiberal distrust. On the other hand, it will be equally forgotten that the vigor of government is essential to the security of liberty; that, in the contemplation of a sound and well-informed judgment, their interests can never be separated; and that a dangerous ambition more often lurks behind the specious mask of zeal for the rights of the people than under the forbidding appearance of zeal for the firmness and efficiency of government. History will teach us that the former has been found a much more certain road to the introduction of despotism than the latter, and that of those men who have overturned the liberties of republics, the greatest number have begun their career by paying an obsequious court to the people, commencing demagogues and ending tyrants.

Union or Civil War

From *Federalist* 6

A man must be far gone in Utopian speculations who can seriously doubt that if these States should either be wholly disunited, or only united in partial confederacies, the subdivisions into which they might be thrown would have frequent and violent contests with each other. To presume a want of motives for such contests as an argument against their existence would be to forget that men are ambitious, vindictive, and rapacious. To look for a continuation of harmony between a number of independent, unconnected sovereignties situated in the same neighborhood would be to disregard the uniform course of human events, and to set at defiance the accumulated experience of ages.

The causes of hostility among nations are innumerable. There are some which have a general and almost constant operation upon the collective bodies of society. Of this description are the love of power or the desire of preeminence and dominion—the jealousy of power, or the desire of equality and safety. There are others which have a more circumscribed though an equally operative influence within their spheres. Such are the rivalries and competitions of commerce between commercial nations. And there are others, not less numerous than either of the former, which take their origin entirely in private passions; in the attachments, enmities, interests, hopes, and fears of leading individuals in the communities of which they are members. Men of this class, whether the favorites of a king or of a people, have in too many instances abused the confidences they possessed; and assuming the pretext of some public motive, have not scrupled to sacrifice the national tranquility to personal advantage or personal gratification. . . .

There have been, if I may so express it, almost as many popular as royal wars. The cries of the nation and the importunities of their representatives have, upon various occasions, dragged their monarchs into war, or continued them in it, contrary to their inclination, and sometimes contrary to the real interests of the state. . . .

Have we not already seen enough of the fallacy and extravagance of those idle theories which have amused us with promises of an exemption from the imperfections, the weaknesses, and the evils incident to society in every shape? Is it not time to awake from the deceitful dream of a golden age and to adopt as a practical maxim for the direction of our political conduct that we, as well as the other inhabitants of the globe, are yet remote from the happy empire of perfect wisdom and perfect virtue?

[It] has from long observation of the progress of society become a sort of axiom in politics that vicinity, or nearness of situations, constitutes nations' natural enemies.

From *Federalist* 7

The probability of incompatible alliances between the different States, or confederacies, and different foreign nations, and the effects of this situation upon the peace of the whole, have been sufficiently unfolded in some preceding papers. From the view they have exhibited of this part of the subject, this conclusion is to be drawn, that America, if not connected at all, or only by the feeble tie of a simple league, offensive and defensive, would, by the operation of such jarring alliances, be gradually entangled in all the pernicious labyrinths of European politics and wars; and by the destructive contentions of the parts into which she was divided, would be likely to become a prey to the artifices and machinations of powers equally the enemies of them all. *Divide et impera* must be the motto of every nation that either hates or fears us. . . .

From *Federalist* 8

War between the States, in the first period of their separate existence, would be accompanied with much greater distresses than it commonly is in those countries where regular military establishments have long obtained. The disciplined armies always kept on foot on the continent of Europe, though they bear a malignant aspect to liberty and economy, have, notwithstanding, been productive of the signal advantage of rendering sudden conquests impracticable, and of preventing that rapid desolation which used to mark the progress of war prior to their introduction. . . .

In this country the scene would be altogether reversed. The jealousy of military establishments would postpone them as long as possible. The want of fortifications, leaving the frontiers of one State open to another, would facilitate inroads. The populous states would, with little difficulty, overrun their less populous neighbors. Conquests would be as easy to be made as difficult to be retained. War, therefore, would be desultory and predatory. Plunder and devastation ever march in the train of irregulars. The calamities of individuals would make the principal figure in the events which would characterize our military exploits. . . .

If we are wise enough to preserve the Union we may for ages enjoy an advantage similar to that of an insulated situation. Europe is at a great distance from us. Her colonies in our vicinity will be likely to continue too much disproportioned in strength to be able to give us any dangerous annoyance. Extensive military establishments cannot, in this position, be necessary to our security. But if we should be disunited, and the integral parts should either remain separated, or, which is most probable, should be thrown together into two or three confederacies, we should be, in a short course of time, in the predicament of the continental powers of Europe—our liberties would be a prey to the means of defending ourselves against the ambition and jealousy of each other.

The Economic Advantages of Union

From *Federalist* 11

The importance of the Union, in a commercial light, is one of those points about which there is at least room to entertain a difference of opinion, and which has, in fact, commanded the most general assent of men who have any acquaintance with the subject. This applies as well to our intercourse with foreign countries as with each other. . . .

If we continue united, we may counteract a policy . . . unfriendly to our prosperity in a variety of ways. By prohibitory regulations, extending at the same time throughout the States, we may oblige foreign countries to bid against each other for the privileges of our markets. . . .

A further resource for influencing the conduct of European nations towards us, in this respect, would arise from the establishment of a federal navy. There can be no doubt that the continuance of the Union under an efficient government would put it in our power, at a period not very distant, to create a navy which, if it could not vie with those of the great maritime powers, would at least be of respectable weight if thrown into the scale of either of two contending parties. . . . By a steady adherence to the Union, we may hope, erelong, to become the arbiter of Europe in America, and to be able to incline the balance of European competitions in this part of the world as our interest may dictate. . . .

I shall briefly observe that our situation invites and our interests prompt us to aim at an ascendant in the system of American affairs. The world may politically, as well as geographically, be divided into four parts, each having a distinct set of interests. Unhappily for the other three, Europe, by her arms and her negotiations, by force and by fraud, has in different degrees extended her dominion over them all. Africa, Asia, and America have successively felt her domination. The superiority she has long maintained has tempted her to plume herself as the mistress of the world, and to consider the rest of mankind as created for her benefit. Men admired as profound philosophers have in direct terms attributed to her inhabitants a physical superiority and have gravely asserted that all animals, and with them the human species, degenerate in America—that even dogs cease to bark after having breathed awhile in our atmosphere. Facts have too long supported these arrogant pretensions of the European. It belongs to us to vindicate the honor of the human race, and to teach that assuming brother moderation. Union will enable us to do it. Disunion will add another victim to his triumphs. Let Americans disdain to be the instruments of European greatness! Let the thirteen States, bound together in a strict and indissoluble Union, concur in erecting one great American system superior to the control of all transatlantic force or influence and able to dictate the terms of the connection between the old and the new world!

The Need for Direct and Plenary Federal Authority

From *Federalist* 15

The great and radical vice in the construction of the existing confederation is the principle of legislation for states or governments, in their corporate or collective capacities, and as contradistinguished from the individuals of whom they consist. Though this principle does not run through all the powers delegated to the Union, yet it pervades and governs those on which the efficacy of the rest depends. Except as to the rule of apportionment, the United States have an indefinite discretion to make requisitions for men and money; but they have no authority to raise either by regulations extending to the individual citizens of America. The consequence of this is that though in theory their resolutions concerning those objects are laws constitutionally binding on the members of the Union, yet in practice they are mere recommendations which the States observe or disregard at their option.

From *Federalist* 16

[The federal government] must carry its agency to the persons of the citizens. It must stand in need of no intermediate legislations, but must itself be empowered to employ the arm of the ordinary magistrate to execute its own resolutions. The majesty of the national authority must be manifested through the medium of the courts of justice. The government of the Union, like that of each State, must be able to address itself immediately to the hopes and fears of individuals; and to attract to its support those passions which have the strongest influence upon the human heart. It must, in short, possess all the means, and have a right to resort to all the methods, of executing the powers with which it is intrusted, that are possessed and exercised by the governments of the particular States.

From *Federalists* 23

The principal purposes to be answered by union are these—the common defence of the members; the preservation of the public peace, as well against internal convulsions as external attacks; the regulation of commerce with other nations and between the states; the superintendence of our intercourse, political and commercial, with foreign countries.

The authorities essential to the common defense are these: to raise armies; to build and equip fleets; to prescribe rules for the government of both; to direct their operations; to provide for their support. These powers ought to exist without limitation, because it is impossible to foresee or to define the extent and variety of national exigencies, and the correspondent extent and variety of the means which may be necessary to satisfy them. The circumstances that endanger the safety of nations are infinite, and for this reason no constitutional shackles can wisely be imposed on the power to which the care of it is committed. This power ought to be coextensive with all the possible combinations of such circumstances; and ought to be under the direction of the same councils which are appointed to preside over the common defense. . . .

Whether there ought to be a federal government intrusted with the care of the common defense is a question in the first instance open to discussion; but the moment it is decided in the affirmative, it will follow that government ought to be clothed with all the powers requisite to complete execution of its trust. And unless it can be shown that the circumstances which may affect the public safety are reducible within certain determinate limits; unless the contrary of this position can be fairly and rationally disputed, it must be admitted as a necessary consequence that there can be no limitation of that authority which is to provide for the defense and protection of the community in any matter essential to its efficacy—that is, in any matter essential to the formation, direction, or support of the national forces.

The Need for a Strong and Permanent Military

From *Federalist* 23

If . . . it should be resolved to extend the prohibition [against standing armies] to the *raising* of armies in time of peace, the United States would then exhibit the most extraordinary spectacle which the world has yet seen—that of a nation incapacitated by its Constitution to prepare for defense before it was actually invaded. As the ceremony of a formal denunciation of war has of late fallen into disuse, the presence of an enemy within our territories must be waited for as the legal warrant to the government to begin its levies of men for the protection of the State. We must receive the blow before we could even prepare to return it. All that kind of policy by which nations anticipate distant danger and meet the gathering storm must be abstained from, as contrary to the genuine maxims of a free government. We must expose our property and liberty to the mercy of foreign invaders and invite them by our weakness to seize the naked and defenseless prey, because we are afraid that rulers, created by our choice, dependent on our will, might endanger that liberty by an abuse of the means necessary to its preservation. . . .

Here I expect to be told that the militia of the country is its natural bulwark, and would be at all times equal to the national defense. This doctrine, in substance, had like to have lost us our independence. It cost millions to the United States that might have been saved. The facts which from our own experience forbid a reliance of this kind are too recent to permit us to be the dupes of such a suggestion. The steady operations of war against a regular and disciplined army can only be successfully conducted by a force of the same kind. Considerations of economy, not less than of stability and vigor, confirm this position. The American militia, in the course of the late war, have, by their valor on numerous occasions, erected eternal monuments to their fame; but the bravest of them feel and know that the liberty of their country could not have been established by their efforts alone, however great and valuable they were. War, like most other things, is a science to be acquired and perfected by diligence, by perseverance, by time, and by practice.

The Federal Power of Taxation

From *Federalist* 31

A government ought to contain in itself every power requisite to the full accomplishment of the objects committed to its care, and to the complete execution of the trusts for which it is responsible, free from every other control but a regard to the public good and to the sense of the people.

As the duties of superintending the national defense and of securing the public peace against foreign or domestic violence involve a provision for casualties and dangers to which no possible limits can be assigned, the power of making that provision ought to know no other bounds than the exigencies of the nation and the resources of the community.

As revenue is the essential engine by which the means of answering the national exigencies must be procured, the power of procuring that article in its full extent must necessarily be comprehended in that of providing for those exigencies.

As theory and practice conspire to prove that the power of procuring revenue is unavailing when exercised over the States in their collective capacities, the federal government must of necessity be invested with an unqualified power of taxation in the ordinary modes.

From *Federalist* 33

The residue of the argument against the provisions of the Constitution in respect to taxation is ingrafted upon the following clauses. The last clause of the eighth section of the first article authorizes the national legislature "to make all laws which shall be necessary and proper for carrying into execution the powers by that Constitution vested in the government of the United States, or in any department or officer thereof"; and the second clause of the sixth article declares that "the Constitution and the laws of the United States made in pursuance thereof and the treaties made by their authority shall be the supreme law of the land, anything in the constitution or laws of any state to the contrary notwithstanding. . . ."

But it may be again asked, Who is to judge of the necessity and propriety of the laws to be passed for executing the powers of the Union? I answer first that this question arises as well and as fully upon the simple grant of those powers as upon the declaratory clause; and I answer in the second place that the national government, like every other, must judge, in the first instance, of the proper exercise of its powers, and its constituents in the last. If the federal government should overpass the just bounds of its authority and make a tyrannical use of its powers, the people, whose creature it is, must appeal to the standard they have formed, and take such measures to redress the injury done to the Constitution as the exigency may suggest and prudence justify.

A Nation Without a National Government

From *Federalist* 85

A nation, without a national government, is, in my view, an awful spectacle. The establishment of a Constitution, in time of profound peace, by the voluntary consent of a whole people, is a prodigy, to the completion of which I look forward with trembling anxiety.

The Report on Manufactures (1791)

> Along with his reports on the national debt and the need for a national
> bank, Hamilton's report to Congress encouraging the federal promotion
> of American industry is one of the great public papers of American his-
> tory. In *The Report on Manufactures,* Hamilton laid out a view of state-
> sponsored industrialization and economic nationalism that inspired
> generations of economists and policymakers and influenced economic
> theory and statecraft in Bismarckian Germany, Meiji Japan, and many
> other countries in the nineteenth and twentieth centuries.

The expediency of encouraging manufactures in the United States, which was
not long since deemed very questionable, appears at this time to be pretty
generally admitted. The embarrassments which have obstructed the progress
of our external trade have led to serious reflections on the necessity of enlarg-
ing the sphere of our domestic commerce. The restrictive regulations, which,
in foreign markets, abridge the vent of the increasing surplus of our agricultural produce, serve to beget an earnest desire that a more extensive demand
for that surplus may be created at home; and the complete success which has
rewarded manufacturing enterprise in some valuable branches, conspiring
with the promising symptoms which attend some less mature essays in others,
justify a hope that the obstacles to the growth of this species of industry are
less formidable than they were apprehended to be, and that it is not difficult
to find, in its further extension, a full indemnification for any external disadvantages, which are or may be experienced, as well as an accession of resources, favorable to national independence and safety.

There are still, nevertheless, respectable patrons of opinions unfriendly to
the encouragement of manufactures. . . .

If the system of perfect liberty to industry and commerce were the prevailing system of nations, the arguments which dissuade a country in the predicament of the United States from the zealous pursuit of manufactures would
doubtless have great force. It will not be affirmed that they might not be permitted, with few exceptions, to serve as a rule of national conduct. In such a
state of things, each country would have the full benefit of its peculiar advantages to compensate for its deficiencies or disadvantages. If one nation were in
a condition to supply manufactured articles on better terms than another,
that other might find an abundant indemnification in a superior capacity to
furnish the produce of the soil. And a free exchange, mutually beneficial, of
the commodities which each was able to supply, on the best terms, might be
carried on between them, supporting, in full vigor, the industry of each. And

though the circumstances which have been mentioned, and others which will be unfolded hereafter, render it probable that nations, merely agricultural, would not enjoy the same degree of opulence in proportion to their numbers, as those which united manufactures with agriculture, yet the progressive improvement of the lands of the former might, in the end, atone for an inferior degree of opulence in the meantime; and in a case in which opposite considerations are pretty equally balanced, the option ought, perhaps, always be in favor of leaving industry to its own direction.

But the system which has been mentioned is far from characterizing the general policy of nations. The prevalent one has been regulated by an opposite spirit. The consequence of it is that the United States are, to a certain extent, in the situation of a country precluded from foreign commerce. They can, indeed, without difficulty, obtain from abroad the manufactured supplies of which they are in want; but they experience numerous and very injurious impediments to the emission and vent of their own commodities. Nor is this the case in reference to a single foreign nation only. The regulations of several countries with which we have the most extensive intercourse throw serious obstructions in the way of the principal staples of the United States.

In such a position of things, the United States cannot exchange with Europe on equal terms; and the want of reciprocity would render them the victim of a system which should induce them to confine their views to agriculture, and refrain from manufactures. A consistent and increasing necessity on their part for the commodities of Europe, and only a partial and occasional demand for their own, in return, could not but expose them to a state of impoverishment, compared with the opulence to which their political and natural advantages authorize them to aspire.

Remarks of this kind are not made in the spirit of complaint. It is for the nations whose regulations are alluded to, to judge for themselves whether, by aiming at too much, they do not lose more than they gain. It is for the United States to consider by what means they can render themselves least dependent on the combinations, right or wrong, of foreign policy. . . .

The remaining objections to a particular encouragement of manufactures in the United States now require to be examined.

One of these turns on the proposition that industry, if left to itself, will naturally find its way to the most useful and profitable employment. Whence it is inferred that manufactures, without the aid of government, will grow up as soon and as fast as the natural state of things and the interest of the community may require.

Against the solidity of this hypothesis, in the full latitude of the terms, very cogent reasons may be offered. These have relation to the strong influence of

habit and the spirit of imitation; the fear of want of success in untried enterprises; the intrinsic difficulties incident to first essays towards a competition
with those who have previously attained to perfection in the business to be attempted; the bounties, premiums, and other artificial encouragements with
which foreign nations second the exertions of their own citizens in the
branches in which they are to be rivalled.

Experience teaches that men are often so much governed by what they are
accustomed to see and practice that the simplest and most obvious improvements, in the most ordinary occupations, are adopted with hesitation, reluctance, and by slow gradations. The spontaneous transition to new pursuits, in
a community long habituated to different ones, may be expected to be attended with proportionately greater difficulty. When former occupations
ceased to yield a profit adequate to the subsistence of their followers, or when
there was an absolute deficiency of employment in them, owing to the super-
abundance of hands, changes would ensue: but these changes would be likely
to be more tardy than might consist with the interest either of individuals or
of the society. In many cases they would not happen, while a bare support
could be insured by an adherence to ancient courses, though a resort to a more
profitable employment might be practicable. To produce the desirable
changes as early as may be expedient may therefore require the incitement and
patronage of government.

The apprehension of failing in new attempts is, perhaps, a more serious
impediment. There are dispositions apt to be attracted by the mere novelty of
an undertaking; but these are not always the best calculated to give it success.
To this it is of importance that the confidence of cautious, sagacious capitalists, both citizens and foreigners, should be excited. And to inspire this description of persons with confidence it is essential that they should be made to
see in any project which is new—and for that reason alone, if for no other,
precarious—the prospect of such a degree of countenance and support from
government as may be capable of overcoming the obstacles inseparable from
first experiments.

The superiority antecedently enjoyed by nations who have preoccupied
and perfected a branch of industry constitutes a more formidable obstacle
than either of those which have been mentioned, to the introduction of the
same branch into a country in which it did not before exist. To maintain, between the recent establishments of one country, and the long-matured establishments of another country, a competition upon equal terms, both as to
quality and price, is, in most cases, impracticable. The disparity, in the one or
in the other or in both, must necessarily be so considerable as to forbid a successful rivalship without the extraordinary aid and protection of government.

But the greatest obstacle of all to the successful prosecution of a new branch of industry in a country in which it was before unknown consists, as far as the instances apply, in the bounties, premiums, and other aids which are granted in a variety of cases by the nations in which the establishments to be imitated are previously introduced. It is well known (and particular examples, in the course of this report, will be cited) that certain nations grant bounties on the exportation of particular commodities, to enable their own workmen to undersell and supplant all competitors in the countries to which those commodities are sent. Hence the undertakers of a new manufacture have to contend, not only with the natural disadvantages of a new undertaking, but with the gratuities and remunerations which other governments bestow. To be enabled to contend with success it is evident that the interference and aid of their own governments are indispensable.

Combinations by those engaged in a particular branch of business in one country to frustrate the first efforts to introduce it in another, by temporary sacrifices, recompensed, perhaps, by extraordinary indemnifications of the government of such country, are believed to have existed, and are not to be regarded as destitute of probability. The existence or assurance of aid from the government of the country in which the business is to be introduced may be essential to fortify adventurers against the dread of such combination; to defeat their efforts, if formed; and to prevent their being formed, by demonstrating that they must in the end prove fruitless.

Whatever room there may be for an expectation that the industry of a people, under the direction of private interest, will, upon equal terms, find out the most beneficial employment for itself, there is none for a reliance that it will struggle against the force of unequal terms, or will, of itself, surmount all the adventitious barriers to a succcessful competition which may have been erected, either by the advantages naturally acquired from practice and previous possession of the ground, or by those which may have sprung from positive regulations and an artificial policy. This general reflection might alone suffice as an answer to the objection under examination, exclusively of the weighty considerations which have been particularly urged. . . .

Not only the wealth but the independence and security of a country appear to be materially connected with the prosperity of manufactures. Every nation, with a view to those great objects, ought to endeavor to possess within itself all the essentials of national supply. These comprise the means of subsistence, habitation, clothing, and defense.

The possession of these is necessary to the perfection of the body politic; to the safety as well as to the welfare of the society. The want of either is the want of an important organ of political life and motion; and in the various crises which await a state, it must severely feel the effects of any such deficiency. The extreme embarrassments of the United States during the late war, from an incapacity of supplying themselves, are still matter of keen recollection; a future war might be expected again to exemplify the mischiefs and dangers of a situation to which that incapacity is still, in too great a degree, applicable, unless changed by timely and vigorous exertion. To effect this change, as fast as shall be prudent, merits all the attention and all the zeal of our public councils: 'tis the next great work to be accomplished.

The want of a navy, to protect our external commerce, as long as it shall continue, must render it a peculiarly precarious reliance for the supply of essential articles, and must serve to strengthen prodigiously the arguments in favor of manufactures. . . .

It is not uncommon to meet with an opinion that, though the promoting of manufactures may be the interest of a part of the Union, it is contrary to that of another part. The Northern and Southern regions are sometimes represented as having adverse interests in this respect. Those are called manufacturing, these agricultural states; and a species of opposition is imagined to subsist between the manufacturing and agricultural interests. . . .

Ideas of a contrariety of interests between the Northern and Southern regions of the Union are, in the main, as unfounded as they are mischievous. The diversity of circumstances, on which such contrariety is usually predicated, authorizes a directly contrary conclusion. Mutual wants constitute one of the strongest links of political connection; and the extent of these bears a natural proportion to the diversity in the means of mutual supply.

Suggestions of an opposite complexion are ever to be deplored, as unfriendly to the steady pursuit of one great common cause, and to the perfect harmony of all the parts. . . .

A question has been made concerning the constitutional right of the Government of the United States to apply this species of encouragement [to manufacturing industry], but there is certainly no good foundation for such a question. The National Legislature has express authority "to lay and collect taxes, duties, imposts, and excises, to pay the debts, and provide for the common defence and general welfare," with no other qualifications than that "all duties, imposts, and excises shall be uniform throughout the United States; and that no capitation or other direct tax shall be laid, unless in proportion to numbers ascertained by a census or enumeration, taken on the principles prescribed in the Constitution," and that "no tax or duty shall be laid on articles exported from any State."

These three qualifications excepted, the power to raise money is plenary and indefinite, and the objects to which it may be appropriated are no less comprehensive than the payment of the public debts, and the providing for the common defense and general welfare. The terms "general welfare" were doubtless intended to signify more than was expressed or imported in those which preceded; otherwise, numerous exigencies incident to the affairs of a nation would have been left without a provision. The phrase is as comprehensive as any that could have been used, because it was not fit that the constitutional authority of the Union to appropriate its revenues should have been restricted within narrower limits than the "general welfare," and because this necessarily embraces a vast variety of particulars, which are susceptible neither of specification nor of definition.

It is, therefore, of necessity left to the discretion of the National Legislature to pronounce upon the objects which concern the general welfare, and for which, under that description, an appropriation of money is requisite and proper. And there seems to be no room for a doubt that whatever concerns the general interests of learning, of agriculture, of manufactures, and of commerce, are within the sphere of the national councils, as far as regards an application of money. . . .

In countries where there is great private wealth, much may be effected by the voluntary contribution of patriotic individuals; but in a community situated like that of the United States, the public purse must supply the deficiency of private resource. In what can it be so useful, as in prompting and improving the efforts of industry?

The *Pacificus* Letters (1793)

In the winter of 1793 the revolutionary government of France beheaded Louis XVI and plunged into war with Great Britain, Holland, and Spain. President George Washington issued a proclamation of U.S. neutrality in the conflict. That infuriated Secretary of State Thomas Jefferson and his allies, who romanticized the French republicans and believed that the United States should maintain the alliance it had had with France under the monarchy. Many of the Jeffersonians went so far as to encourage "Citizen Genet," an envoy of the revolutionary French regime who sought to appeal directly to the American people and to launch attacks on British vessels from the United States.

Between June 29 and July 27, 1793, Hamilton, using the pseudonym "Pacificus," published seven essays to defend the constitutionality and prudence of the neutrality proclamation. Hamilton's intention was to shift public opinion in favor of the policies that he and Washington favored.

"For God's sake, my dear sir," Jefferson wrote to his fellow Virginian and political ally James Madison, "take up your pen, select the most striking heresies and cut him to pieces in the face of the public. There is nobody else who can & will enter the lists with him."

The Pacificus essays are chiefly of interest today for their unsentimental and realistic view of power politics and their ever timely warning against allowing attachments to particular foreign states to influence American foreign policy.

Morality and Foreign Policy

From *Pacificus* 3

Between individuals, occasion is not unfrequently given for the exercise of gratitude. Instances of conferring benefits from kind and benevolent dispositions or feelings toward the person benefited, without any other interest on the part of the person who renders the service, than the pleasure of doing a good action, occur every day among individuals. But among nations they perhaps never occur. It may be affirmed as a general principle that the predominant motive of good offices from one nation to another is the interest or advantage of the nation which performs them.

Indeed, the rule of morality in this respect is not precisely the same between nations as between individuals. The duty of making its welfare the guide of its actions is much stronger upon the former than upon the latter; in proportion to the greater magnitude and importance of national compared with individual happiness, and to the greater permanency of the effects of national than of individual conduct. Existing millions, and for the most part future generations, are concerned in the present measures of a government; while the consequences of the private actions of an individual ordinarily terminate with himself, or are circumscribed within a narrow compass.

Whence it follows that an individual may, on numerous occasions, meritoriously indulge the emotions of generosity or benevolence, not only without an eye to, but even at the expense of, his own interest. But a government can rarely, if at all, be justifiable in pursuing a similar course; and, if it does so, ought to confine itself within much stricter bounds.[2] Good offices which are

---

2. This conclusion derives confirmation from the reflection that under every form of government rulers are only trustees for the happiness and interest of their nation, and cannot, consistently with their trust, follow the suggestions of kindness or humanity toward others, to the prejudice of their constituents. [footnote in the original.]

indifferent to the interest of a nation performing them, or which are compensated by the existence or expectation of some reasonable equivalent, or which produce an essential good to the nation to which they are rendered, without real detriment to the affairs of the benefactors, prescribe perhaps the limits of national generosity or benevolence.

It is not here meant to recommend a policy absolutely selfish or interested in nations; but to show that a policy regulated by their own interest, as far as justice and good faith permit, is, and ought to be, their prevailing one; and that either to ascribe to them a different principle of action, or to deduce, from the supposition of it, arguments for a self-denying and self-sacrificing gratitude on the part of a nation which may have received from another good offices, is to misrepresent or misconceive what usually are, and ought to be, the springs of national conduct.

France's Motives in Helping the United States

From *Pacificus* 5

France, the rival, time immemorial, of Great Britain, had, in the course of the war which ended in 1763, suffered from the successful arms of the latter the severest losses and the most mortifying defeats. Britain from that moment had acquired an ascendant in the affairs of Europe, and in the commerce of the world, too decided and too humiliating to be endured without extreme impatience, and an eager desire of finding a favorable opportunity to destroy it, and to repair the breach which had been made in the national glory. The animosity of wounded pride conspired with calculations of interest to give a keen edge to that impatience, and to that desire.

The American revolution offered the occasion. It early attracted the notice of France, though with extreme circumspection. As far as countenance and aid may be presumed to have been given prior to the epoch of the acknowledgment of our independence, it will be no unkind derogation to assert that they were marked neither with liberality nor with vigor; that they wore the appearance rather of a desire to keep alive disturbances which might embarrass a rival, than of a serious design to assist a revolution, or a serious expectation that it could be affected.

The victories of Saratoga, the capture of an army, which went a great way toward deciding the issue of the contest, decided also the hesitations of France. They established in the government of that country a confidence of our ability to accomplish our purpose, and, as a consequence of it, produced the treaties of alliance and commerce.

It is impossible to see in all this any thing more than the conduct of a jealous competitor, embracing a most promising opportunity to repress the pride and diminish the power of a dangerous rival, by seconding a successful resistance to its authority, with the object of lopping off a valuable portion of its dominions. The dismemberment of this country from Great Britain was an obvious and a very important interest of France. It cannot be doubted that it was both the determining motive and an adequate compensation for the assistance afforded to us.

Men of sense, in this country, derived encouragement to the part which their zeal for liberty prompted them to take in our revolution, from the probability of the cooperation of France and Spain. It will be remembered that this argument was used in the publications of the day; but upon what was it bottomed? Upon the known competition between those nations and Great Britain, upon their evident interest to reduce her power and circumscribe her empire; not certainly from motives of regard to our interest, or of attachment to our cause. Whoever should have alleged the latter, as the grounds of the expectation held out, would have been then justly considered as a visionary or a deceiver. And whoever shall now ascribe to such motives the aid which we did receive would not deserve to be viewed in a better light.

Nations Are Not Grateful

From *Pacificus* 6

The assistance derived from France was afforded by a great and powerful nation, possessing numerous armies, a respectable fleet, and the means of rendering it a match for the force to be encountered. The position of Europe was favorable to the enterprise; a general disposition prevailing to see the power of Britain abridged. The cooperation of Spain was very much a matter of course, and the probability of other Powers becoming engaged on the same side not remote. Great Britain was alone, and likely to continue so; France had a great and persuasive interest in the separation of this country from her. In this situation, with much to hope and little to fear, she took part in our quarrel.

France is at this time singly engaged with the greatest part of Europe, including all the first-rate Powers except one; and in danger of being engaged with the rest. To use the emphatic language of a member of the national convention, she has but one enemy, and that is all Europe. Her internal affairs are, without doubt, in serious disorder; her navy comparatively inconsiderable. The United States are a young nation; their population, though rapidly increasing, still small; their resources, though growing, not great; without armies, without fleets; capable, from the nature of the country and the spirit of its inhabitants, of immense exertions for self-defense, but little capable of those external efforts which could materially serve the cause of France. So far from having any direct interest in going to war, they have the strongest motives of interest to avoid it. By embarking with France in the war, they would have incomparably more to apprehend than to hope.

This contrast of situations and inducements is alone a conclusive demonstration that the United States are not under an obligation, from gratitude, to join France in the war. The utter disparity between the circumstances of the services to be rendered, and of the service received, proves that the one cannot be an adequate basis of obligation for the other.

Foreign Influence

From *Pacificus* 6

[This] ought to teach us not to overrate foreign friendships, and to be upon our guard against foreign attachments. The former will generally be found hollow and delusive; the latter will have a natural tendency to lead us aside from our own true interest, and to make us the dupes of foreign influence. Both serve to introduce a principle of action which in its effects, if the expression may be allowed, is anti-national. Foreign influence is truly the Grecian horse to a republic. We cannot be too careful to exclude its entrance. Nor ought we to imagine that it can only make its approaches in the gross form of direct bribery. It is then most dangerous when it comes under the patronage of our passions, under the auspices of national prejudice and partiality.

I trust the morals of this country are yet too good to leave much to be apprehended on the score of bribery. Caresses, condescensions, flattery, in unison with our prepossessions, are infinitely more to be feared; and as far as there is opportunity for corruption, it is to be remembered that one foreign power can employ this resource as well as another, and that the effect must be much greater when it is combined with other means of influence than where it stands alone.

PART TWO

WE THE PEOPLE

Nationalism requires a nation. American democratic nationalism presupposes the existence of an American nation whose members are defined as part of a single community by characteristics other than the political characteristic of being citizens of the United States. A moment's reflection will show why the nation cannot be defined in political terms. The American nation, acting through its leaders, could not choose among different governments—the colonial governments under Great Britain, the loose confederation set up by the Articles of Confederation, and the federal nation-state established by the 1787 federal constitution—unless the nation had an identity that was not affected by mere alterations of governments or constitutions.

With that in mind, we can examine rival theories of American national identity. I have argued elsewhere[1] that it is possible to distinguish five major conceptions of American identity: nativism, cultural pluralism, multiculturalism, democratic universalism, and the melting-pot theory or transracial nationalism. Of those five conceptions, three—cultural pluralism, multiculturalism, and democratic universalism—may be dismissed at once by an American democratic nationalist.

Cultural pluralism, an early-twentieth-century philosophy associated with the leftist thinkers Randolph Bourne and Horace Kallen, held that the European immigrant groups in the United States should preserve their dis-

---

1. Michael Lind, *The Next American Nation: The New Nationalism and the Fourth American Revolution* (New York: Free Press, 1995).

tinctive languages and subcultures. The assimilation of European immigrants and the ongoing amalgamation of their descendants into a single white population (and perhaps, in time, into a mixed-race population) has rendered cultural pluralism irrelevant. Multiculturalism, the child of the marriage of generations-old black nationalism with the Marx-inspired radicalism of the 1960s, agrees with the older cultural pluralist tradition that the United States is a "nation of nations," a multinational democracy. In the multicultural conception, the constituent "nations" that share common American governmental institutions, but little else, are not the European "ethnic groups" of the cultural pluralists but the five official races or quasi-races that the federal government has recognized since the 1970s: whites, blacks (or African-Americans), Hispanics (or Latinos), Asian-Americans (or Asians and Pacific Islanders), and Native Americans. This fivefold schema, familiar as it has become, is absurd; as a matter of anthropology, it is preposterous to classify Americans and Ghanaian immigrants together in a single category, "African-Americans," and Latinos or Hispanics are a diverse group of people of different conventionally defined races whose members share nothing except Latin American or Caribbean ancestry (speaking Spanish as a first language is not even required). Even more absurdly, the Asian and Pacific Islander category adopted by the U.S. government in the 1970s puts Pakistanis, Chinese, and Malays together into one pseudo-racial caste.

Even if the federal government's official five-race classification were not insulting to common sense and politically divisive, the multicultural conception of the United States as a multinational democracy would not follow from the existence of historic racial categories in American society. The sloppy use of the word "culture" as a synonym for "race" obscures the fact that culture and race are different, sometimes even opposite, concepts. White Southerners and black Southerners have shared the same broadly defined culture for centuries, even as they were divided by the arbitrary rules of the American caste system.

Instead of seeking to obliterate all traces of the old caste system, multiculturalism reinforces them. The hierarchical multiculturalism of slavery and segregation is replaced by a compensatory multiculturalism, in which members of the four minority "races"—blacks, Hispanics, Asians, and Native Americans—are given affirmative-action preferences in hiring, schooling, and politics at the expense of members of the majority white caste (who are presumed to inherit guilt for white supremacist policies before their time). It is easy to see that the chief beneficiaries of multiculturalism are white racists, who can find new recruits among whites injured by racial preferences and whose belief that nonwhite Americans really, in some sense, belong to a different "nation" or "people" appears to be endorsed by multicultural theory.

Democratic nationalists are bound to reject the idea, shared by cultural pluralists and multiculturalists alike, that the United States is a multinational democracy instead of a nation-state. Democratic nationalists must reject, as well, the theory of democratic universalists that the United States is a post-national or nonnational state. According to democratic universalism, the United States is a nation of individuals united solely by their devotion to liberal-democratic ideals, as expressed by the Declaration of Independence and the Gettysburg Address. The problems with this idea are obvious. Hundreds of millions of people in Europe, Asia, Latin America, and Africa share American democratic ideals, without thereby becoming American citizens. What is more, the democratic universalist theory seems to suggest that if the American people ceased to believe in liberal-democratic ideals, they would cease to be "American." That is a mere play on words, which confuses "American" as a term of praise with "American" as a description of a member of one of many independent communities in the world. It would be unfortunate if a majority of Americans repudiated liberal democracy in favor of one or another illiberal political creed, but they would still be Americans. Changing your mind does not change your nationality.

If the United States is considered a nation-state, rather than a multinational state (cultural pluralism, multiculturalism) or a postnational idea-state (democratic universalism), the question remains of how the extrapolitical American nation is to be defined. Nativism has tended to define membership in the core American national community narrowly, in terms of race and religion; a "real" American is an Anglo-American Protestant, or a West European Christian, or a Caucasian of Christian or Jewish belief or background. The racial-religious definition of American identity, whether broad or narrow, holds that the American nation cannot be altered too much by immigration or cultural change without losing its very identity.

A quite different perspective is provided by the melting-pot theory. The melting-pot theory holds that, at any one time, there is only one predominant cultural nation in the United States; but unlike the nativist theory, the melting-pot model envisions the American national majority as changing gradually over time, from the merger of native-born Americans with successive groups of immigrants, with cultural syncretism usually being followed, in time, by intermarriage and fusion of previously separate groups into a single population. It should be noted that the melting-pot ideal is amalgamation (the formation of a new culture and population from several), not assimilation (the conformity of all new groups to the standards of the previously dominant majority). Nativists cherish purity; melting-pot advocates favor hybridization.

Like the nativist conception of the American nation, the melting-pot conception has been enlarged over time. The earliest "melting pot" was that which blended Anglo-Americans (and numbers of Dutch and Germans) into a single population by the eve of American independence. By the middle of the twentieth century, the melting pot had been enlarged to include European immigrants from a variety of nations—but not native-born Americans or immigrants of other races. The Civil Rights Revolution, which among its other accomplishments struck down laws against interracial marriage, provided an opportunity to promote the idea of a new mixed-race, melting-pot majority. Unfortunately the depth of white racist sentiment against racial intermarriage, combined with the desire of black radicals to preserve a separate black American nation-within-the-nation, discouraged integrationist liberals from pursuing such a line of reasoning, at least in public. A quarter-century after the Civil Rights Revolution, the idea of the transracial melting pot is once again gaining favor, partly as the result of a backlash against multiculturalism and affirmative action among dissident liberals as well as conservatives, and partly as the result of high rates of intermarriage between whites and members of the burgeoning Hispanic and Asian immigrant communities. Today a growing if still small number of "mixed-race" Americans are demanding that the government cease pigeonholing them in one or another of the five official races. It remains to be seen whether black Americans are absorbed into a unified mixed-race population. A melting pot limited to whites, Hispanics, and Asians might do no more than replace the white–black dichotomy of the seventeenth through the twentieth century with a "tan–black" dichotomy in the twenty-first and twenty-second centuries.

The melting-pot conception of American identity, then, sees the formation of a common American cultural community as a precursor to the formation of a common American gene pool. Insofar as this is an ethnocultural conception of nationality, it is worth pausing to consider the criticisms that have been made of ethnocultural nationalism, and the proposed alternatives.

The term "nationalism" seldom appears in American journalism or scholarship, unless it is prefaced by pejorative adjectives: "xenophobic," "reactionary," or "irrational." In part this results from the identification of nationalism with the imperialism of Nazi Germany, Fascist Italy, and Imperial Japan. A more important factor, though, was the division of American intellectual life during the Cold War between liberal globalism and Marxist international socialism. (Cold War conservatism, which wedded anticommunist internationalism to free-trade ideology, in effect was a version of Wilsonian liberal globalism, in its rhetoric if not in practice.)

For half a century, from Pearl Harbor to the toppling of the Berlin Wall, Wilsonian liberal globalism—distinct from Hamiltonian democratic nationalism and Jeffersonian democratic localism—has provided the public philosophy of the United States. The distinct identity of the American nation, and the distinct interests of the American nation-state, have been downplayed in the interest of American leadership of the antifascist and anticommunist alliances. Americans were told that World War II was fought on behalf of "the democracies" and "the United Nations." They were told that World War III, the Cold War, was not an American effort but a joint crusade by "the Free World." For two generations, mainstream scholars and opinion leaders have repeated the Wilsonian myth that the United States is the dominant province in a transnational federation of sorts, variously styled as the Free World or the West. The abstract political principles that united America and its principal allies were stressed, at the expense of the ethnic, cultural, and historical legacies that continued to distinguish Americans from Germans, French, British, or Japanese.

In the interests of transnational alliances, American national history was rewritten by Wilsonian globalists, who sought to portray the United States as a kind of political church militant, an aggregate of "peoples" or "nationalities" held together by ideology, a liberal mirror image of the multinational, ideological Soviet Union. Soviet ideology was matched by American ideology, point by point. If the Soviets had the writings of Marx and Lenin, the United States and, by implication, the entire Free World, would have its own sacred texts, in the form of The Federalist Papers and Toqueville's *Democracy in America.* Madison's Federalist Number 10, which had languished unread until Charles Beard drew attention to it, was enlisted, rather implausibly, as the proof text of American "pluralism" in combat with communist totalitarianism. By the 1980s young Cold War conservatives—the political descendants of the Wilsonian globalists of the 1950s—recited out-of-context passages from Tocqueville and Madison as though they were sayings of Mao—or, more to the point in America's heavily Protestant culture, verses from the Bible.

Beginning in the 1960s, Wilsonian democratic globalism was attacked from the left, by multiculturalism—a variant of Marxism, invented when Marxists despaired of the white working classes in North America and Europe and pinned their hopes for revolution on nonwhite minorities at home and nonwhite "Third World" nations abroad. An old American tradition, black nationalism, was revived, to become the model for various pseudo-ethnic separatist movements—Hispanic nationalism, radical feminism, queer nationalism. For the past generation, the conversation about American identity has been little more than a sterile debate between the liberal globalist advocates of America as a theory and the multicultural theorists of America as a collection of various racial, immigrant, or sexual subcultures masquerading as "nations."

The liberal nationalist revolutions of 1989 in Eastern Europe and 1991 in the Soviet Union stunned Wilsonian globalists and multiculturalists alike. Wilsonian globalists, convinced that abstract principles should count more than historic nationalities, were appalled that anticommunist demonstrators in Europe should chant "Germany!" or "Russia!" instead of "Constitution!" or "Civil Society!" The breakup of multinational federations into more homogeneous nation-states—a process that was peaceful in Czechoslovakia and violent in Yugoslavia—was interpreted as barbaric regression by liberal globalists, for whom progress means the continual absorption of smaller communities of ancestry and fate by large entities defined by abstract principle. Multiculturalists were no more pleased, because the new nation-states did not remake themselves as smaller versions of the multinational federations they had left, but insisted on laws governing language, citizenship, and immigration that would identify the state with a majority nation. In short, both Wilsonian liberals and neo-Marxist leftists found themselves disoriented in a world for which they were not prepared, although there was little that would have surprised a liberal nationalist of 1848 or 1919.

Marxists, multicultural and otherwise, have gone into catatonic shock, as have many liberal globalists of the old school. The more resilient liberal globalists, in the United States, Canada, and Europe, have sought to recycle liberal globalism as a form of nationalism. The claim is often made that there are two kinds of nationalism—a good kind, in which the nation is defined by voluntary adherence to liberal political principles, and a bad kind, in which nationality is defined by language, culture, descent, or religion. The bad kind of nationalism is usually called "ethnic nationalism" (a redundancy, as I shall argue below). The name of the good sort of nationalism has not been settled. The German philosopher Jurgen Habermas calls it "constitutional patriotism" *(Verfassungspatriotismus)*. The American writer Liah Greenfeld and the Canadian writer Michael Ignatieff call the good, enlightened version of nationalism "civic nationalism," a term more widely used in the English-speaking world.

The distinction between civic nationalism and ethnic nationalism is very appealing, insofar as it permits us to put German Nazis and Serb irredentists in a completely different category from American patriots and French republicans. Unfortunately, the distinction is bogus. "Civic nationalism" exists only in the minds of professors, editorialists, and politicians. In the real world, there are no "civic" nations, that is, nations in which ethnic identity has been superseded by political ideology. All genuine nations are "ethnic," that is, defined as communities by one or more extrapolitical traits—language, culture, religion, race. The countries that are held forth as examples of civic nations—the United States, France, Canada, Switzerland—are either nation-states with a dominant ethnocultural nationality whose language is that of the state (the United States, France) or multinational states in which the primary loyalties of most people are to descent-group or language-group, not to the federal unit (Canada, Switzerland).

The attempt to create a nonethnic, pan-territorial, purely political identity, transcending the ties of language, culture, and descent, has failed in Canada and Belgium, as it also failed in Lebanon, the Soviet Union, and Yugoslavia. The reason for the weakness of "civic nationalism" in comparison with "ethnic nationalism" is no mystery. States come and go; nations, though not quite immortal, last for generations, and in some cases centuries and millennia. In the twentieth century, some ethnic Czechs and ethnic Germans and ethnic Hungarians have lived under a bewildering variety of states and constitutions—Austria-Hungary, its successor states, the Third Reich, communist dictatorships, and now postcommunist democracies. Borders have expanded and contracted, governments have risen and fallen, armies have swept back and forth across the landscape, whole populations have been resettled, even massacred. Through all of this political instability, the self-definition of people as members of the Czech or German or Hungarian ethnic nation has remained relatively stable. One could be a Czech nationalist, throughout the twentieth century; one could not be an Austro-Hungarian patriot after 1919.

The attempt to define a purely political form of nationalism, then, is doomed to failure. Since nation, or nationality, in the modern sense, is simply a synonym for ethnic group, a nonethnic nationalism is a meaningless play on words. The nation-state is the ethnic-state.

How is nationality or ethnicity to be defined? Here we encounter real divisions, not false dichotomies like the civic/ethnic distinction. Nationality may be, and has been, defined according to a number of extrapolitical characteristics: language, customs, religion, descent, or race. At one end is the most inclusive characteristic—language—at the other, the most exclusive—race, or biological identity. Practically all modern liberal nationalists (though not their nineteenth-century and early-twentieth-century predecessors) would reject race and religion as criteria for membership in a nation (although the state of Israel, a relatively liberal democracy, is illiberal insofar as it limits first-class citizenship to Jews, defined by religion and descent). Practically all liberal nationalists would emphasize the need for all members of a nation to speak the same language or mutually intelligible dialects of the same language. The "gray area," then, between the inclusiveness of linguistic nationalism and the exclusiveness of racial or religious nationalism involves customs, or folkways, although this is of more theoretical than practical importance (Americans are not stripped of their citizenship for refusing to celebrate Thanksgiving).

As long as we are content to remain in the realm of theory, we might replace the false theoretical distinction between civic nationalism and ethnic nationalism with a more useful distinction, between liberal or minimalist ethnic nationalism (language, culture) and illiberal or maximal nationalism (religion, race). Once we turn to the real world, however, even that distinction stands in need of revision, for the simple reason that in almost every country in the world membership in the ethnic nation, as well as state citizenship, is determined by descent. In most countries the only way to acquire citizenship is to be born to citizen parents. In the minority of countries where citizenship comes with birth in the territory—as in the United States and other Western Hemisphere states—the theoretical implications are more interesting than the practical consequences, since the number of children born to resident aliens, legal or illegal, is tiny as a proportion of the whole. Almost all Americans become American by being born to parents who are American, by birth or naturalization.

The point is that the identification of a nation with a descent-group—deplorable though it may be in theory—is inescapable in practice, even in the most liberal of liberal democracies. In most countries descent is a more or less accurate surrogate for nationality. The United States, sometimes described as a "nation of immigrants," is and always has been a nation of native-born descendants of immigrants. At no point since the eighteenth century have the number of immigrants in the U.S. population amounted to more than a fifth of the whole. As for the children of immigrants, they cannot be called "immigrants," since immigration is an experience that cannot be inherited. At most the children of immigrants are members of enclave ethnicities, which in the absence of continual immigration from the "old country" tend to dissolve after a generation or two.

A word about "ethnicity" in the American context is in order here. Elsewhere in the world "ethnicity" and "nationality" tend to be used interchangeably. In the United States the word "ethnicity" is used, in a very confusing manner, for descent-groups which may or may not be assimilated to the mainstream American national culture. Under this bizarre American convention, a Magyar-speaking immigrant may be lumped together with a fourth-generation descendant of Hungarians who knows no Magyar as "Hungarian-Americans." If language and culture define American nationality, then the fourth-generation American of Hungarian descent shares more in common with natives and assimilated immigrants of other ancestries—Chinese, Irish, German, Mexican—than he does with the Magyar-speaking immigrant.

This is more than just a quibble. By calling the assimilated descendants of immigrants "immigrants" and confusing real and merely residual ethnicity, all too many American historians and publicists have painted a misleading portrait of the United States as a "nation of immigrants" or a "multinational" democracy. The purpose, in many cases, has been to discourage the idea that the United States is a conventional liberal nation-state, corresponding to a predominant American cultural nation, and to portray the United States as a liberal-globalist United Nations in miniature, or a potential postnational socialist workers' paradise.

In reality, the great divisions within American society have not been ethnocultural divisions between descendants of different immigrant subcultures, but racial and religious differences. Unlike immigrant ethnic enclave cultures, which have tended to evaporate after contributing to the American idiom or American cuisine, religion and race are lasting divisions between Americans who otherwise share a common national culture.

Race and ethnicity, although they are usually confused in American discourse, are completely different things. Race or caste is based on biological descent (for example, in the United States "black" is defined as having one or more sub-Saharan African ancestors); ethnicity is based on behavior (speaking Italian instead of English). Though it is difficult, one can change one's ethnicity by acquiring a new language and culture; one cannot change one's race, which is always defined in an objective, if arbitrary, way. The rules of the historic American caste system show the distinction between race and ethnicity clearly. An immigrant who was ethnically Italian and could speak no English was automatically assigned to the "white" caste, whereas an American with any West African ancestors, notwithstanding the "ethnic" characteristics he shared with a white American (English as a native language, Protestantism, folkways and food-ways) was automatically assigned to the "black" caste on the basis of the "one-drop" rule. The "ethnic" differences between native-born white and black Americans—language, religion, customs—have been minor for centuries, but the racial caste system has been rigid, cruel, and enduring nevertheless.

Religion, like race, should not be confused with ethnicity. Like race in America, religion in America tends to be much more permanent and stable than ethnicity. The pattern in the U.S. has been that immigrant churches become de-ethnicized or Americanized after only a few generations. Irish, German, and Polish Catholicism have given way to a common American

Catholicism. The postethnic American religion or denomination may continue to be divided, but it will be divided along theological or political lines (the North–South division among denominations like the Methodists and Baptists originated from political disputes over slavery). Thus differences among Polish, German, and Russian Jews have been replaced by divisions among Reform, Conservative, and Orthodox Jews in America. (The exception to this rule—the continued racial division of American Protestantism—simply proves the point that race is distinct from, and far more durable than, ethnicity.)

It can be argued that the nonethnic basis of both American racism and American religiosity have contributed to nation-building in America, if sometimes in sinister ways. American racism may have helped Europeans shed their immigrant ethnicities more rapidly, by defining them as members of a privileged, larger group—white Americans. Similarly, the evolution of supraethnic forms of American Protestantism, Catholicism, and Judaism (and, perhaps, in the future, American Islam) may have enabled the descendants of immigrants to jettison some aspects of their heritage (language, folkways) while retaining another aspect of their inherited identity (religious affiliation). From the eighteenth century to the mid-twentieth century, the informal but predominant conception of American nationality, over and beyond mere political citizenship, evolved from Anglo-Protestant to West European–Christian to white–Judeo-Christian. If high rates of intermarriage among whites, Latinos, and Asian Americans (if not black Americans) continue, and if American Muslims succeed in gaining the recognition that has been accorded to American Jews, the next stage in this process, in the twenty-first and twenty-second centuries, may be an informal redefinition of the national majority as mixed-race and theist.

The point is that the existence of a common, evolving, transracial, and ecumenical American ethnicity—a common language and set of folkways—is not disproved by the continued existence of racial and religious divisions in the United States. The American nation has always been divided by race and religion and will continue to be divided along religious lines even if race fades away as a concept; but those are divisions within a nation, not between nations.

The Wilsonian globalist claim that the United States is not an ethnocultural nation-state but something else, a "multinational democracy" or "postnational democracy" or "civic democracy," then, cannot withstand analysis. Even if it could, that conception would be incompatible with the American theory of popular (i.e. national) sovereignty. That theory assumes that there is an American nation (one, not several) of which American governments (federal and state) are mere agents. That American cultural nation, originating in the seventeenth and eighteenth centuries, was already distinct by 1776. The Revolution was fought, and the Articles of Confederation and, later, the federal constitution were adopted, by that preexisting nation. It is not just wrong but ludicrous to say that the American nation was "created" by the Declaration of Independence or the U.S. Constitution, just as it is ridiculous to say that Abraham Lincoln and his fellow Republicans "created" the modern American nation. The signers of the Declaration and the drafters and ratifiers of the Constitution, like the Unionists during the Civil War, were members of a community that already existed as one of the nations of the world; they did not conjure a people up out of thin air. Governments may be created "by reflection and choice" (to use Hamilton's words in the Federalist), but genuine nations are not the handiwork of any individual or elite. They are the result of centuries of gradual social evolution, which individuals and elites can influence but not control.

If today's Wilsonian opponents of nationalism, even in its liberal and democratic forms, are wrong about America, they are just as wrong about the world. The history of the twentieth century does not bear out the Wilsonian equations of the supranational with the civilized and the national with the archaic. The communists and fascists alike sought to obliterate smaller nation-states, even to exterminate national minorities, not in the interest of moderate linguistic-cultural nationalism but in order to create supranational, expandible empires—the international socialist commonwealth, the Aryan racial empire. Each of the three world conflicts resulted in the disintegration of one or more despotic multinational empires—the Romanov, the Hapsburg, the Nazi, the Japanese, the British, the French, the Soviet—into more ethnically homogeneous successor states, many though not all of them becoming stable and successful liberal democracies. In the anti-Soviet European revolutions of 1989, liberalism and nationalism were linked against an illiberal internationalism in a way that reminded the historically aware of the European revolutions of 1848, in which liberals and nationalists united against defenders of reactionary multinational empires. The speed with which a number of new nation-states in Central Europe applied for admission to the European Union and NATO on gaining their sovereignty demonstrates that national sovereignty need not be an obstacle to international cooperation in the form of alliances or trading blocs; indeed, formal sovereignty for nation-based republics may be a precondition for international cooperation that is both voluntary and legitimate.

Democratic or liberal nationalism, then, is no contradiction in terms. Nationalism and authoritarianism or totalitarianism are not synonyms. Indeed, the nation-state appears to be the natural vehicle for liberal democratic government, rather than the globe or the province. In practice, all of the supranational entities that have been effective states, rather than mere alliances or trade blocs, have been despotic regimes, from which national groups have seceded at the first opportunity; even the relatively liberal British empire was based on despotic rule over unwilling populations. Now that the danger from totalitarian empires is past (if only for the moment), a new danger has appeared, in the form of the diffusion of government authority from national governments to lesser actors: mafias, tribes, warlords, banditti. In much of the world today, the greatest threat to liberty and prosperity comes from the feebleness of central governments unable to enforce the law on their own national territories—an observation that will come as no surprise to Hamiltonians, though it undercuts Jeffersonian optimism about the lowest levels of government. The nation-state has survived the threat of empire; whether it can survive the threat of warlordism in much of the world remains to be seen.

Both Hamiltonians and Jeffersonians can adhere to the melting-pot theory of the American nation as a conventional ethnocultural nation in the process of formation (as indeed, both Hamiltonians and Jeffersonians can adhere to the rival nativist or racist theory of America as a white Christian or white Judeo-Christian nation). Jeffersonians, in addition, can subscribe to democratic universalism, cultural pluralism, and even multiculturalism, since their ideal of homogeneous local communities does not necessarily require a national community; indeed, the thought of modern advocates of multiculturalism like Lani Guinier is remarkably similar, in its emphasis on minority protections and privileges, to the theory of the "concurrent majority" set forth by the greatest constitutional thinker in the Jeffersonian tradition, the nineteenth-century South Carolina Senator John C. Calhoun. Hamiltonian democratic nationalists, by contrast, must be either nativists or melting-pot nationalists, if their conception of the United States as a nation-state is to be consistent.

Most of the great Hamiltonians, insofar as they shared the religious and racial prejudices of the Anglo-American Protestant elite to which they belonged, can be classified as nativists. Indeed, the anti-Catholic American Party or "Know-Nothing" Party of the 1850s (the nickname is an allusion to its secretive membership, not to their ignorance) contained many former Whigs who would later join the Republican Party of Abraham Lincoln and William Seward. At the beginning of the twentieth century, Henry Cabot Lodge and Theodore Roosevelt shared not only neo-Hamiltonian views but an ideal of the American nation as a pan-Nordic or pan-Germanic people. TR muted his views and publicly favored a more expansive conception of the melting pot, while Lodge helped lead the ultimately successful movement to restrict European immigration to the United States.

The most articulate advocates of melting-pot nationalism, throughout most of American history, have been members of minority groups, such as Frederick Douglass and Jean Toomer (both of mixed race, though conventionally classified as black) and Israel Zangwill, an English Jew whose 1909 play *The Melting-Pot* popularized the idea. Given the extent of white American skepticism about racial amalgamation (shared even by Abraham Lincoln, who tried to arrange for freed black slaves to leave the United States), the transracial melting-pot tradition has only a limited, if distinguished, intellectual pedigree. Melting-pot nationalism is included here as a topic because it offers the only definition of the American people that will be compatible with American democratic nationalism in the generations to come, given the shrinking of the white majority and the blurring, through intermarriage, of the dubious racial categories that have divided Americans from one another for so long.

RALPH WALDO EMERSON

Ralph Waldo Emerson (1803–82) is best known today for his Harvard Phi Beta Kappa Address of 1837, "The American Scholar," a declaration of intellectual independence from the Old World which, ironically, was clearly inspired by contemporary British and German romanticism. Emerson was the presiding genius of the New England Transcendentalists, a literary circle that included Margaret Fuller and Henry David Thoreau. Emerson hailed Whitman as the great poet that America had been waiting for (although Emerson later had his doubts). Like many unworldly literati, Emerson tended toward extremism in his politics, idealizing John Brown the way that later Northeastern intellectuals would idealize the Black Panthers or Che Guevara. His thought places him not in the Hamiltonian Federalist-Whig-Republican tradition but rather in the rival Northern tradition of secularized Puritan radicalism, which has always coexisted uneasily with Hamiltonian nationalism. His early statement of the melting-pot theory of American identity in his Journal (1845), however, is worth reprinting.

The Smelting-Pot

As in the old burning of the Temple at Corinth, by the melting and intermixture of silver and gold and other metals a new compound more precious than any, called Corinthian brass, was formed: so in this continent,—asylum of all nations,—the energy of Irish, Germans, Swedes, Poles, and Cossacks, and all the European tribes,—of the Africans, and the Polynesians,—will construct a new race, a new religion, a new state, a new literature, which will be as vigorous as the new Europe which came out of the smelting-pot of the Dark Ages.

HENRY HIGHLAND GARNET

Henry Highland Garnet (1815–81) was a leading black American abolitionist whose books include *An Address to the Slaves of the United States of America* (1843) and *The Past and the Present Condition and the Destiny of the Colored Race* (1848). In this excerpt from the latter book, Garnet predicts the eventual formation of a mixed-race majority in the United States and rejects the idea that the homeland of black Americans is Africa rather than North America.

A Mixed Race

This western world is destined to be filled with a mixed race. Statesmen, distinguished for their forecast, have gravely said that the blacks must either be removed, or such as I have stated will be the result. It is a stubborn fact that it is impossible to separate the pale man and the man of color, and therefore the result which to them is so fearful, is inevitable.

Some people of color say that they have no home, no country. I am not among that number. It is empty declamation. It is unwise. It is not logical— it is false. . . . America is my home, my country, and I have no other. I love whatever good there may be in her institutions. I hate her sins. I loathe her slavery, and I pray Heaven that ere long she may wash away her guilt in tears of repentance. I love the green-hills which my eyes first beheld in infancy. I love every inch of soil which my feet pressed in my youth, and I mourn because the accursed shade of slavery rests upon it. I love my country's flag, and I hope that soon it will be cleansed of its stains, and be hailed by all nations as the emblem of freedom and independence.

HERMAN MELVILLE

Herman Melville (1819–91), a novelist and poet best remembered today for *Moby-Dick* (1851) and the posthumously published *Billy Budd,* achieved success in his lifetime only for his novels of South Sea adventure, based on his own experience as a young man aboard whaling ships. From one of these, *Redburn: His First Voyage* (1849), the following famous description of American nationality is drawn.

The Blood of the Whole World

There is something in the contemplation of the mode in which America has been settled, that, in a noble breast, should forever extinguish the prejudices of national dislike. Settled by the people of all nations, all nations may claim her for their own. You cannot spill a drop of American blood without spilling the blood of the whole world. . . . We are not a narrow tribe of men . . . whose blood has been debased in the attempt to ennoble it, by maintaining an exclusive succession among ourselves. No; our blood is as the flood of the Amazon, made up of a thousand noble currents all pouring into one. We are not a nation, so much as a world. . . . On this Western Hemisphere all tribes and peoples are forming into one federal whole.

FREDERICK DOUGLASS

Frederick Douglass (1817–95) was the archetype of an American, as a self-made man (a runaway slave who became a world-famous intellectual and leader), a champion of civil rights for nonwhite Americans and women, and—not least—as an individual of mixed heritage (he was the son of a white father and an enslaved black mother). Escaping from a Maryland plantation in 1838, Frederick Augustus Washington Bailey borrowed a new name from a character in a novel by Sir Walter Scott and joined the abolitionist movement in Massachusetts. He lectured in Britain, where British supporters purchased his freedom from his former master. Returning to the United States, he edited a weekly, *The North Star* (later *Frederick Douglass' Paper*), established his independence from white abolitionists like William Lloyd Garrison, and played a minor role in John Brown's conspiracy. During the Civil War he aided the Union cause by recruiting black troops. He was rewarded by being made United States Marshal for the District of Columbia (1887) and U.S. Minister to Haiti (1889).

In the excerpt below, from "The Future of the Colored Race" (May 1886), Douglass argues that a racially amalgamated American majority would emerge in time. Unlike today's civil rights establishment, Douglass did not believe that the continuing existence of white racism made a strict race-neutral legal and political regime any less necessary. When the black nationalist Martin Delany proposed that jobs in the federal government be given to blacks on the basis of their proportion in the population (a proposal that was implemented in the 1960s under the misleading name "affirmative action"), Douglass pointedly asked whether Germans and Irish would receive quotas too. "A nation within a nation is an anomaly," he wrote. "There can be but one American nation under the American government, and we are Americans."[2]

---

2. Frederick Douglass, "The Nation's Problem," in Howard Brotz, *African-American Social and Political Thought, 1850–1920* (New Brunswick, NJ: TransAction Publishers, 1992), p. 320.

Racial Amalgamation in America

My strongest conviction as to the future of the Negro . . . is, that he will not be expatriated nor annihilated, nor will he forever remain a separate and distinct race from the people around him, but that he will be absorbed, assimilated, and will only appear finally, as the Phoenicians now appear on the shores of the Shannon, in the features of a blended race. I cannot give at length my reasons for this conclusion, and perhaps the reader may think that the wish is the father to the thought, and may in his wrath denounce my conclusion as utterly impossible. To such I would say, tarry a little, and look at the facts. Two hundred years ago there were two distinct and separate streams of human life running through this country. They stood at opposite extremes of ethnological classification: all black on the one side, all white on the other. Now, between these two extremes, an intermediate race has arisen, which is neither white nor black, neither Caucasian nor Ethiopian, and this intermediate race is constantly increasing. I know it is said that marital alliance between these races is unnatural, abhorrent and impossible; but exclamations of this kind only shake the air. They prove nothing against a stubborn fact like that which confronts us daily and which is open to the observation of all. If this blending of the two races were impossible we should not have at least one-fourth of our colored population composed of persons of mixed blood, ranging all the way from a dark-brown color to the point where there is no visible admixture. Besides, it is obvious to common sense that there is no need of the passage of laws, or the adoption of other devices, to prevent what is in itself impossible.

Of course this result will not be reached by any hurried or forced process. It will not arise out of any theory of the wisdom of such blending of the two races. If it comes at all, it will come without shock or noise or violence of any kind, and only in the fullness of time, and it will be so adjusted to surrounding conditions as hardly to be observed. I would not be understood as advocating intermarriage between the two races. I am not a propagandist, but a prophet. I do not say that what I say *should* come to pass, but what I think is likely to come to pass, and what is inevitable. While I would not be understood as advocating the desirability of such a result, I would not be understood as deprecating it. Races and varieties of the human family appear and disappear, but humanity remains and will remain forever. The American people will one day be truer to this idea than now, and will say with Scotia's inspired son:

A man's a man for a' that.

When that day shall come, they will not pervert and sin against the verity of language as they now do by calling a man of mixed blood, a Negro;

they will tell the truth. . . . The opposition to amalgamation, of which we hear so much on the part of colored people, is for the most part the merest affectation, and will never form an impassable barrier to the union of the two varieties.

THEODORE ROOSEVELT

After Alexander Hamilton, Theodore Roosevelt (1858–1919) is perhaps the key philosopher-statesman in the pantheon of American democratic nationalism. This intellectual scion of a patrician New York family graduated from Harvard in 1880 and, unlike most members of his class, plunged into public life. From New York State politics the Republican Roosevelt moved on to help reform the U.S. Civil Service and the New York police commission. In 1897 TR became Secretary of the Navy. During the Spanish–American War his leadership of the "Rough Riders" in combat made him the equivalent of a modern media celebrity. The Republican political bosses who thought that they had got rid of this boisterous reformer by making him McKinley's Vice President were shocked when, on McKinley's assassination in 1900, TR became the nation's youngest President at forty-two. As President, TR promoted a "Square Deal" (ancestor of his cousin FDR's New Deal), which included passage of the Pure Food and Drug Act, interstate commerce reform, and conservationist measures like increasing the number of national parks. His views and achievements in domestic and foreign policy will be discussed in greater detail in a later section of this book.

TR has always been a controversial figure. Many have shared H. G. Wells's view that TR was "a big noise," and the isolationist Left of later generations has condemned him as a crypto-fascist. In his day conservative Republicans considered TR to be a dangerous radical, and TR was well to the left of Woodrow Wilson when he ran for President as the head of the Progressive party in 1912. TR's macho style, which grew out of the fear of late-nineteenth-century Anglo-American patricians that their class was becoming soft, had enormous if not always acknowledged influence on the American Left—one need only think of Jack London or Ernest Hemingway. The feminized, pacifist American Left of the post-

1960s era is a reincarnation of the older, genteel Northern Protestant tradition against which TR, among others, was rebelling. For some time the Left has ceded machismo, along with populism, to the American Right.

Like other Progressives, TR was concerned about the erosion of national unity as a result of mass immigration and growing class differences in the new industrial economy. Though he shared many of the prejudices of the elite to which he belonged, TR offended conservatives in the South and elsewhere by inviting the black leader Booker T. Washington to dine in the White House. In the following excerpt from "True Americanism" (*Forum,* April 1894, reprinted in *American Ideals,* 1897), his vigorous defense of the melting-pot conception of a single American national identity against the separatism of regional, class, and ethnic subcultures remains relevant today, even if his language may seem undiplomatic to genteel readers accustomed to the proprieties of political correctness.

True Americanism

Patriotism was once defined as "the last refuge of a scoundrel"; and somebody has recently remarked that when Dr. Johnson gave this definition he was ignorant of the infinite possibilities contained in the word "reform." Of course both gibes were quite justifiable, insofar as they were aimed at people who use noble names to cloak base purposes. Equally of course the man shows little wisdom and a low sense of duty who fails to see that love of country is one of the elemental virtues, even though scoundrels play upon it for their own selfish ends; and, inasmuch as abuses continually grow up in civic life as in all other kinds of life, the statesman is indeed a weakling who hesitates to reform these abuses because the word *reform* is often on the lips of men who are silly or dishonest.

What is true of patriotism and reform is true also of Americanism. There are plenty of scoundrels always ready to try to belittle reform movements or to bolster up existing iniquities in the name of Americanism; but this does not alter the fact that the man who can do most in this country is and must be the man whose Americanism is most sincere and intense. Outrageous though it is to use a noble idea as the cloak for evil, it is still worse to assail the noble idea itself because it can thus be used. The men who do iniquity in the name of patriotism, of reform, of Americanism, are merely one small division of the class that has always existed and will always exist—the class of hypocrites and demagogues, the class that is always prompt to steal the watchwords of righteousness and use them in the interests of evildoing.

The stoutest and truest Americans are the very men who have the least sympathy with the people who invoke the spirit of Americanism to aid what is vicious in our government or to throw obstacles in the way of those who strive to reform it. It is contemptible to oppose a movement for good because that movement has already succeeded somewhere else, or to champion an existing abuse because our people have always been wedded to it. To appeal to national prejudice against a given reform movement is in every way unworthy and silly. It is as childish to denounce free trade because England has adopted it as to advocate it for the same reason. It is eminently proper, in dealing with the tariff, to consider the effect of tariff legislation in time past upon other nations as well as the effect upon our own; but in drawing conclusions it is in the last degree foolish to try to excite prejudice against one system because it is in vogue in some given country, or to try to excite prejudice in its favor because the economists of that country have found that it was suitable to their own peculiar needs. In attempting to solve our difficult problem of municipal government it is mere folly to refuse to profit by whatever is good in the examples of Manchester and Berlin because these cities are foreign, exactly as it is mere folly blindly to copy their examples without reference to our own totally different conditions. As for the absurdity of declaiming against civil service reform, for instance, as "Chinese," because written examinations have been used in China, it would be quite as wise to declaim against gunpowder because it was first utilized by the same people. In short, the man who, whether from mere dull fatuity or from an active interests in misgovernment, tries to appeal to American prejudice against things foreign, so as to induce Americans to oppose any measure for good, should be looked on by his fellow countrymen with the heartiest contempt. So much for the men who appeal to the spirit of Americanism to sustain us in wrongdoing. But we must never let our contempt for these men blind us to the nobility of the idea which they strive to degrade. . . .

There are two or three sides to the question of Americanism, and two or three senses in which the word Americanism can be used to express the antithesis of what is unwholesome and undesirable. In the first place we wish to be broadly American and national, as opposed to being local or sectional. We do not wish, in politics, in literature, or in art, to develop that unwholesome parochial spirit, that overexaltation of the little community at the expense of the great nation, which produces what has been described as the patriotism of the village, the patriotism of the belfry. Politically, the indulgence of this spirit was the chief cause of the calamities which befell the ancient republics of Greece, the medieval republics of Italy, and the petty states of Germany as it was in the last century. It is this spirit of provincial patriotism, this inability to take a view of broad adhesion to the whole nation that has been the chief among the causes that have produced such anarchy in the South American states, and which have resulted in presenting to us not one great Spanish-American federal nation stretching from the Rio Grande to Cape Horn, but a squabbling multitude of revolution-ridden states, not one of which stands even in the second rank as a power. However, politically this question of American nationality has been settled once for all. We are no longer in danger of repeating in our history the shameful and contemptible disasters that have befallen the Spanish possessions on this continent since they threw off the yoke of Spain. Indeed, there is, all through our life, very much less of this parochial spirit than there was formerly. Still there is an occasional outcropping here and there; and it is just as well that we should keep steadily in mind the futility of talking of a northern literature or a southern literature, an eastern or a western school of art or science. Joel Chandler Harris is emphatically a national writer; so is Mark Twain. They do not write merely for Georgia or Missouri or California any more than for Illinois or Connecticut; they write as Americans and for all people who can read English. St. Gaudens lives in New York; but his work is just as distinctive of Boston or Chicago. It is of very great consequence that we should have a full and ripe literary development in the United States, but it is not of the least consequence whether New York, or Boston, or Chicago, or San Francisco becomes the literary or artistic center of the United States.

There is a second side to this question of a broad Americanism, however. The patriotism of the village or the belfry is bad, but the lack of all patriotism is even worse. There are philosophers who assure us that, in the future, patriotism will be regarded not as a virtue at all, but merely as a mental stage in the journey toward a state of feeling when our patriotism will include the whole human race and all the world. This may be so; but the age of which these philosophers speak is still several eons distant. In fact, philosophers of this type are so very advanced that they are of no practical service to the present generation. It may be, that in ages so remote that we cannot now understand any of the feelings of those who will dwell in them, patriotism will no longer be regarded as a virtue, exactly as it may be that in those remote ages people will look down upon and disregard monogamic marriage; but as things now are and have been for two or three thousand years past, and are likely to be for two or three thousand years to come, the words *home* and *country* mean a great deal. Nor do they show any tendency to lose their significance. At present, treason, like adultery, ranks as one of the worst of all possible crimes.

One may fall very far short of treason and yet be an undesirable citizen in the community. The man who becomes Europeanized, who loses his power of doing good work on this side of the water, and who loses his love for his native land, is not a traitor; but he is a silly and undesirable citizen. He is as emphatically a noxious element in our body politic as is the man who comes here from abroad and remains a foreigner. Nothing will more quickly or more surely disqualify a man from doing good work in the world than the acquirement of that flaccid habit of mind which its possessors style cosmopolitanism.

It is not only necessary to Americanize the immigrants of foreign birth who settle among us, but it is even more necessary for those among us who are by birth and descent already Americans not to throw away our birthright, and, with incredible and contemptible folly, wander back to bow down before the alien gods whom our forefathers forsook. It is hard to believe that there is any necessity to warn Americans that, when they seek to model themselves on the lines of other civilizations, they make themselves the butts of all right-thinking men; and yet the necessity certainly exists to give this warning to many of our citizens who pride themselves on their standing in the world of arts and letters, or, perchance, on what they would style their social leadership in the community. It is always better to be an original than an imitation, even when the imitation is of something better than the original; but what shall we say of the fool who is content to be an imitation of something worse? Even if the weaklings who seek to be other than Americans were right in deeming other nations to be better than their own, the fact yet remains that to be a first-class American is fiftyfold better than to be a second-class imitation of a Frenchman or Englishman. As a matter of fact, however, those of our countrymen who do believe in American inferiority are always individuals who, however cultivated, have some organic weakness in their moral or mental makeup; and the great mass of our people, who are robustly patriotic, and who have sound, healthy minds, are justified in regarding these feeble renegades with a half-impatient and half-amused scorn.

We believe in waging relentless war on rank-growing evils of all kinds, and it makes no difference to us if they happen to be of purely native growth. We grasp at any good, no matter whence it comes. We do not accept the evil attendant upon another system of government as an adequate excuse for that attendant upon our own; the fact that the courtier is a scamp does not render the demagogue any less a scoundrel. But it remains true that, in spite of all our faults and shortcomings, no other land offers such glorious possibilities to the man able to take advantage of them, as does ours; it remains true that no one of our people can do any work really worth doing unless he does it primarily as an American. It is because certain classes of our people still retain their spirit of colonial dependence on, and exaggerated deference to, European opinion, that they fail to accomplish what they ought to. It is precisely along the lines where we have worked most independently that we have accomplished the greatest results; and it is in those professions where there has been no servility to, but merely a wise profiting by foreign experience, that we have produced our greatest men. Our soldiers and statesmen and orators; our explorers, our wilderness-winners, and commonwealth-builders; the men who have made our laws and seen that they were executed; and the other men whose energy and ingenuity have created our marvellous material prosperity—all these have been men who have drawn wisdom from the experience of every age and nation, but who have nevertheless thought, and worked, and conquered, and lived, and died, purely as Americans; and on the whole they have done better work than has been done in any other country during the short period of our national life.

On the other hand, it is in those professions where our people might have striven hardest to mold themselves in conventional European forms that they have succeeded the least; and this holds true to the present day, the failure being of course most conspicuous where the man takes up his abode in Europe, where he becomes a second-rate European, because he is overcivilized, oversensitive, overrefined, and has lost the hardihood and manly courage by which alone he can conquer in the keen struggle of our national life. Be it remembered, too, that this same being does not really become a European; he only ceases to be an American, and becomes nothing. He throws away a great prize for the sake of a lesser one, and does not even get the lesser one. The painter who goes to Paris, not merely to get two or three years' thorough training in his art, but with the deliberate purpose of taking up his abode there, and with the intention of following in the ruts worn deep by ten thousand earlier travellers, instead of striking off to rise or fall on a new line, thereby forfeits all chance of doing the best work. He must content himself with aiming at that kind of mediocrity which consists in doing fairly well what has already been done better; and he usually never even sees the grandeur and picturesqueness lying open before the eyes of every man who can read the book of America's past and the book of America's present. Thus it is with the undersized man of letters, who flees his country because he, with his delicate, effeminate sensitiveness, finds the conditions of life on this side of the water crude and raw; in other words, because he finds that he cannot play a man's part among men, and so goes where he will be sheltered from the winds that harden stouter souls. This émigré may write graceful and pretty verses, essays, novels; but he will never do work to compare with that of his brother, who is strong enough to stand on his own feet, and do his work as an American. Thus it is with the scientist who spends his youth in a German university, and can thenceforth work only in the fields already fifty times furrowed by the German ploughs. Thus it is with that most foolish of parents who sends his children to be educated abroad, not knowing—what every clear-sighted American from Washington and Jay down has known—that the American who is to make his way in America should be brought up among his fellow Americans. It is among the people who like to consider themselves, and, indeed, to a large extent are, the leaders of the so-called social world, especially in some of the northeastern cities, that this colonial habit of thought, this thoroughly provincial spirit of admiration for things foreign, and inability to stand on one's own feet, becomes most evident and most despicable. We believe in every kind of honest and lawful pleasure, so long as the getting is not made man's chief business; and we believe heartily in the good that can be done by men of leisure who work hard in their leisure, whether at politics or philanthropy, literature or art. But a leisure class whose leisure simply means idleness is a curse to the community, and insofar as its members distinguish themselves chiefly by aping the worst—not the best—traits of similar people across the water, they become both comic and noxious elements of the body politic.

The third sense in which the word *Americanism* may be employed is with reference to the Americanizing of the newcomers to our shores. We must Americanize them in every way, in speech, in political ideas and principles, and in their way of looking at the relations between church and state. We welcome the German or the Irishman who becomes an American. We have no use for the German or Irishman who remains such. We do not wish German-Americans and Irish-Americans who figure as such in our social and political life; we want only Americans, and, provided they are such, we do not care whether they are of native or of Irish or of German ancestry. We have no room in any healthy American community for a German-American vote or an Irish-American vote, and it is contemptible demagogy to put planks into any party platform with the purpose of catching such a vote. We have no room for any people who do not act and vote simply as Americans, and as nothing else. Moreover, we have as little use for people who carry religious prejudices into our politics as for those who carry prejudices of caste or nationality. We stand unalterably in favor of the public-school system in its entirety. We believe that English, and no other language, is that in which all the school exercises should be conducted. We are against any division of the school fund, and against any appropriation of public money for sectarian purposes. We are against any recognition whatever by the state in any shape or form of state-aided parochial schools. But we are equally opposed to any discrimination against or for a man because of his creed. We demand that all citizens, Protestant and Catholic, Jew and Gentile, shall have fair treatment in every way; that all alike shall their rights guaranteed them. The very reasons that make us unqualified in our opposition to state-aided sectarian schools make us equally bent that, in the management of our public schools, the adherents of each creed shall be given exact and equal justice, wholly without regard to their religious affiliations; that trustees, superintendents, teachers, scholars, all alike shall be treated without any reference whatsoever to the creed they profess. We maintain that it is an outrage, in voting for a man for any position, whether state or national, to take into account his religious faith, provided only he is a good American. . . .

The mighty tide of immigration to our shores has brought in its train much of good and much of evil; and whether the good or the evil shall predominate depends mainly on whether these newcomers do or do not throw themselves heartily into our national life, cease to be Europeans, and become Americans like the rest of us. . . . If they remain alien elements, unassimilated, and with interests separate from ours, they are mere obstructions to the current of our national life, and, moreover, can get no good from it themselves. In fact, though we ourselves also suffer from their perversity, it is they who really suffer most. It is an immense benefit to the European immigrant to change him into an American citizen. To bear the name of American is to bear the most honorable titles; and whoever does not so believe has no business to bear the name at all, and, if he comes from Europe, the sooner he goes back there the better. Besides, the man who does not become Americanized nevertheless fails to remain a European, and becomes nothing at all. The immigrant cannot possibly remain what he was, or continue to be a member of the old-world society. If he tries to retain his old language, in a few generations it becomes a barbarous jargon; if he tries to retain his old customs and ways of life, in a few generations he becomes an uncouth boor. He has cut himself off from the Old World, and cannot retain his connection with it; and if he wishes ever to amount to anything he must throw himself heart and soul, and without reservation, into the new life to which he has come. . . .

From his own standpoint, it is beyond all question the wise thing for the immigrant to become thoroughly Americanized. Moreover, from our standpoint, we have a right to demand it. We freely extend the hand of welcome and of good-fellowship to every man, no matter what his creed or birthplace, who comes here honestly intent on becoming a good United States citizen like the rest of us; but we have a right, and it is our duty, to demand that he shall indeed become so and shall not confuse the issues with which we are struggling by introducing among us old-world quarrels and prejudices. . . . He must revere only our flag; not only must it come first, but no other flag should even come second. He must learn to celebrate Washington's birthday rather than that of the queen or kaiser, and the Fourth of July instead of St. Patrick's Day. Our political and social questions must be settled on their own merits, and not complicated by quarrels between England and Ireland, or France and Germany, with which we have nothing to do: it is an outrage to fight an American political campaign with reference to questions of European politics. Above all, the immigrant must learn to talk and think and *be* United States.

The immigrant of today can learn much from the experience of the immigrants of the past, who came to America prior to the Revolutionary War. We were then already, what we are now, a people of mixed blood. . . .

But I wish to be distinctly understood on one point. Americanism is a question of spirit, conviction, and purpose, not of creed or birthplace. The politician who bids for the Irish or German vote, or the Irishman or German who votes as an Irishman or German, is despicable, for all citizens of this commonwealth should vote solely as Americans; but he is not a whit less despicable than the voter who votes against a good American, merely because that American happens to have been born in Ireland or Germany. Knownothingism, in any form, is as utterly un-American as foreignism. It is a base outrage to oppose a man because of his religion or birthplace, and all good citizens will hold any such effort in abhorrence. . . .

We Americans can only do our allotted task well if we face it steadily and bravely, seeing but not fearing the dangers. Above all we must stand shoulder to shoulder, not asking as to the ancestry or creed of our comrades, but only demanding that they be in very truth Americans, and that we all work together, heart, hand, and head, for the honor and the greatness of our common country.

HERBERT CROLY

Along with Theodore Roosevelt, Herbert Croly (1869–1930), the leading editor and writer of the Progressive movement, was chiefly responsible for renovating Hamiltonian nationalism as a force in twentieth-century American politics. Croly's father, David Goodman Croly (1829–89), was a journalist who emigrated to the United States from Ireland. A crude racist like many Irish-American Democrats in the North, the elder Croly coined the term "miscegenation" in an anti-Lincoln pamphlet of 1864, which purported to be the Republicans' announcement of a plan for promoting race-mixing by abolishing slavery: "All that is needed to make us the finest race on earth is to engraft upon our stock the negro element which providence has placed by our side on this continent. We must become a yellow-skinned, black-haired people, if we would attain the fullest results of civilization."[3] It comes as no surprise that Croly's son, like many other Progressives, was indifferent to the situation of black Americans. The elder Croly was also a champion of August Comte's Positivism, an ideology of utopian secular reform. Positivism doubtless influenced Herbert Croly's vision of a strong national government undertaking major projects of reform.

Herbert Croly was a sickly young man who entered and withdrew from Harvard several times; while there, he came under the influence of the philosopher Josiah Royce, who converted him to Christianity. After a stint at editing Architectural Record (a position he obtained through his late father's connections), Croly married a wealthy woman whose money enabled him to write *The Promise of American Life* over a four-year period. When *The Promise of American Life* was published in 1910,

---

3. Quoted in *Dictionary of American Biography* (New York: Charles Scribner's Sons, 1929), vol. 2, part 1, p. 560.

Massachusetts Senator Henry Cabot Lodge recommended it to his friend Theodore Roosevelt (then on safari in Africa after his retirement from the presidency). TR became an admirer and enlisted Croly's help in drafting his "New Nationalism" speech at Osawatomie (reprinted later in this book). Two other admirers, a wealthy couple named Willard and Dorothy Straight, gave Croly the money to found *The New Republic* in 1914 as a pro-TR Progressive journal opposed to Woodrow Wilson (who was then identified with the laissez-faire right). Within a few years *The New Republic,* whose editors included Walter Lippmann and Walter Weyl, had become supporters of the Wilson administration (Lippmann even joined the administration and helped shape the "Fourteen Points" program). Disillusioned by the Treaty of Versailles, Croly lost interest in politics and dabbled in mysticism, and his magazine drifted into marginality in the 1920s. (*The New Republic* became a journal of pro-communist fellow-travelers for most of the century; in recent decades, under the ownership of Martin Peretz, it has become a libertarian conservative journal that shares its publisher's intense focus on Israel.)

During the decade in which he was a significant and influential political thinker, Croly, at the height of his powers, helped to shape an alternative to the laissez-faire, antigovernment ideology that was dominant in his time (and is resurgent in ours). Like other Progressive thinkers, who tended to ignore blacks and favor the assimilation of European immigrants to a Northern–Midwestern Anglo-American norm, Croly devoted more thought to the relationship of nation and state than to the composition of the American nation itself. In the following passage from *The Promise of American Life* (1909), Herbert Croly makes the argument that, wherever possible, the citizenry of a democratic state ought to correspond more or less to a single ethnocultural or "historical" nation.

Democracy and the Historical Nation

[T]he constructive national democrat must necessarily differ from the old school of democratic "liberals." A nationalized democracy is not based on abstract individual rights, no matter whether the individual lives in Colorado, Paris, or Calcutta. Its consistency is chiefly a matter of actual historical association. . . . A people that lack the power of basing their political association on an accumulated national tradition and purpose is not capable of either nationality or democracy. . . .

ISRAEL ZANGWILL

Israel Zangwill (1864–1926), who is associated more closely than anyone else with the idea of the American melting pot, was not an American at all. This playwright and polemicist was an English subject and a secular Jew who devoted much of his life to Zionism. His 1909 play *The Melting-Pot* caused a sensation at a time when the dominant view of American nationality identified the American nation with the Anglo-Saxon or Anglo-Celtic "race." In the early twentieth century the melting-pot idea was attacked not only by the racist right but by leftist proponents of "cultural pluralism" like the Americans Randolph Bourne and Horace Kallen, who, like modern multiculturalists, preferred the idea of the United States as a mosaic of distinct ethnic nationalities, each of which would retain its own language and folkways.

In 1912, three years after he dedicated *The Melting-Pot* to Theodore Roosevelt, Zangwill wrote the former President to ask whether he still supported the concept. TR replied: "But, my dear Sir, the idea that I have forgotten the 'Melting-Pot,' and its dedication to me! Now as a matter of fact that particular play I shall always count among the very strong and real influences upon my thought and my life. It has been in my mind continually, and on my lips often during the last three years. It not merely dealt with 'the melting pot,' with the fusing of all foreign nationalities into an American nationality, but it also dealt with the great ideals which it is just as essential for the native born as for the foreign to realize and uphold if the new nationality is to represent a real addition to the sum total of human achievement."[4]

---

4. TR to Israel Zangwill, November 27, 1912, in Roosevelt Collection, Library of Congress.

The Melting-Pot

To Theodore Roosevelt:
In respectful recognition of his strenuous struggle against the forces that threaten to shipwreck the great republic which carries mankind and its fortunes, this play is, by his kind permission, cordially dedicated.

ACT ONE

Vera: So your music finds inspiration in America?

David: Yes—in the seething of the Crucible.

Vera: The Crucible? I don't understand!

David: Not understand! You, the Spirit of the Settlement! [*He rises and crosses to her and leans over the table, facing her.*] Not understand that America is God's Crucible, the great Melting-Pot where all the races of Europe are melting and re-forming! Here you stand, good folk, think I, when I see them at Ellis Island, here you stand [*Graphically illustrating it on the table*] in your fifty groups, with your fifty languages and histories, and your fifty blood hatreds and rivalries. But you won't be long like that, brothers, for these are the fires of God you've come to—these are the fires of God. A fig for your feuds and vendettas! Germans and Frenchmen, Irishmen and Englishmen, Jews and Russians—into the Crucible with you all! God is making the American.

Mendel: I should have thought the American was made already—eighty millions of him.

David: Eighty millions! [*He smiles toward* Vera *in good-humoured derision.*] Eighty millions! Over a continent! Why, that cockleshell of a Britain has forty millions! No, uncle, the real American has not yet arrived. He is only in the Crucible, I tell you—he will be the fusion of all races, perhaps the coming superman. . . .

ACT FOUR

Vera: [*They stand quietly hand in hand.*] Look! How beautiful the sunset is after the storm! [David *turns. The sunset, which has begun to grow beautiful just after* Vera's *entrance, has now reached its most magnificent moment; below there are narrow lines of saffron and pale gold, but above the whole sky is one glory of burning flame.*]

David: [*Prophetically exalted by the spectacle*] It is the fires of God round His Crucible. [*He drops her hand and points downward.*] There she lies, the great Melting-Pot—listen! Can't you hear the roaring and the bubbling! There gapes her mouth [*He points east*]—the harbour where a thousand mammoth feeders come from the ends of the world to pour in their human freight. Ah, what a stirring and a seething! Celt and Latin, Slav and Teuton, Greek and Syrian—black and yellow—

Vera: [*Softly, nestling to him*] Jew and Gentile—

David: Yes, East and West, and North and South, the palm and the pine, the pole and the equator, the crescent and the cross—how the great Alchemist melts and fuses them with his purging flame! Here shall they all unite to build the Republic of Man and the Kingdom of God. Ah, Vera, what is the glory of Rome and Jerusalem where all nations and races come to worship and look back, compared with the glory of America, where all races and nations come to labour and look forward! [*He raises his hands in benediction over the shining city.*] Peace, peace, to all ye unborn millions, fated to fill this giant continent—the God of our *children* give you Peace. [*An instant's solemn pause. The sunset is swiftly fading, and the vast panorama is suffused with a more restful twilight, to which the many-gleaming lights of the town add the tender poetry of the night. Far back, like a lonely, guiding star, twinkles over the darkening water the torch of the Statue of Liberty. From below comes up the softened sound of voices and instruments joining in "My Country, 'tis of Thee." The curtain falls slowly.*]

Zangwill on the Melting Pot

In a 1914 appendix to *The Melting-Pot,* Zangwill expanded on his ideas. Note that the British Zangwill, unlike some American proponents of the melting-pot idea, does not believe that the American nation is unique; other nations in the Western Hemisphere, and even Old World nations like the English, are melting-pot nations as well. Note also that Zangwill believes—indeed, fears—that immigration restrictions would accelerate the formation of a common nationality from groups of immigrants.

The process of amalgamation is not assimilation or simple surrender to the dominant type, as is popularly supposed, but an all-round give-and-take by which the final type may be enriched or impoverished. . . .

Once America slams her doors, the crucible will roar like a closed furnace. Heaven forbid, however, that the doors shall be slammed for centuries yet. . . .

Whether any country will ever again be based like those of the Old World upon a unity of race or religion is a matter of doubt. . . .

Though the peoples now in process of formation in the New World are being recruited by mainly economic forces, it may be predicted they will ultimately harden to homogeneity of race, if not even of belief. For internationalism in religion seems to be again receding in favour of national religion (if, indeed, these were ever more than superficially superseded), at any rate in favour of nationalism raised into religion.

If racial homogeneity has not yet been evolved completely even in England—and, of course, the tendency can never be more than asymptotic—it is because cheap and easy transport and communication, with freedom of economic movement, have been late developments and are still far from perfect. Hence, there has never been a thorough shake-up and admixture of elements, so that certain counties and corners have retained types and breeds peculiar to them. But with the ever-growing interconnection of all parts of the country, and with the multiplication of labour bureaux, these breeds and types will be—alas, for local colour!—increasingly absorbed in the general mass. For fusion and unification are part of the historic life-process. "Normans and Saxons and Danes" are we here in England, yes and Huguenots and Flemings and Gascons and Angevins and Jews and many other things.

In fact . . . there is hardly an ethnic element that has not entered into the Englishman. . . .

Thus every country has been and is a "Melting Pot." But America, exhibiting the normal fusing process magnified many thousand diameters and diversified beyond all historic experience, and fed not by successive waves of immigration but by a hodgepodge of simultaneous hordes, is, in Bacon's phrase, an "ostensive instance" of a universal phenomenon. America is *the* "Melting Pot."

Her people has already begun to take on such a complexion of its own, it is already so emphatically tending to a new race, crossed with every European type, that the British illusion of a cousinly Anglo-Saxon people with whom war is unthinkable is sheer wilful blindness. Even to-day, while the mixture is still largely mechanical not chemical, the Anglo-Saxon element is only preponderant; it is very far from being the sum total.[5]

---

5. In the play, Zangwill hints that "black and yellow" have a place in the American melting pot—though he segregates the two categories by a hyphen from "Celt and Latin, Slav and Teuton, Greek and Syrian." In his appendix, however, he shows that he shares the racist assumptions of his era about blacks: "This is not to deny that the prognathous face is an ugly and undesirable type of countenance or that it connotes a lower average of intellect and ethics, or that white and black are as yet too far apart for profitable fusion." Zangwill warns that "in view of all the unpleasantness, both immediate and contingent, that attends the blending of colours, only heroic souls on either side should dare the adventure of intermarriage. Blacks of this temper, however, would serve their race better by making Liberia a success or building up an American negro State . . . or at least asserting their rights as American citizens which without their labour could never have been opened up." In short, like most of his audience, Zangwill assumed that the melting pot in the United States (and other white-settler countries like Canada, Brazil, and Argentina) was for European groups only.

JEAN TOOMER

In the twentieth century, as in the nineteenth, the greatest champion of
the idea of the American people as a transracial melting-pot nation has
been a black American—although Jean Toomer (1894–1967) would
have resisted that and any other racial classification. Toomer, best known
today for his 1923 novel *Cane*, a lyrical narrative about black American
life, was the son of a father of white, black, and Native American descent
and the grandson of Pinckney Benton Stewart Pinchback, the mixed-race
governor of Louisiana during Reconstruction. Dissatisfied with critics
and publishers who were interested only in stereotypically "Negro" material, Toomer, who was influenced by the then fashionable Russian mystic
Georges I. Gurdjieff and later by Quakerism, came to see himself as a
prophet of a postracist Americanism and a new humanism. In the post-
1960s era of identity politics, in which integrationism has lost out among
black American leaders and intellectuals to black nationalism and multiculturalism, Toomer has been neglected.

The American Race

Letter to James Weldon Johnson, July 11, 1930

My view of this country sees it composed of people who primarily are
Americans, who secondarily are of various stocks or mixed stocks. The matter of descent, and of divisions presumably based on descents, has been
given, in my opinion, due emphasis, indeed over-emphasis. I aim to stress
the fact that we are all Americans. I do not see things in terms of Negro,
Anglo-Saxon, Jewish, and so on. As for me personally, I see myself an
American, simply an American.

71

As regards art I particularly hold this view. I see our art and literature as primarily American art and literature. I do not see it as Negro, Anglo-Saxon, and so on.

Accordingly, I must withdraw from all things which emphasize or tend to emphasize racial or cultural divisions. I must align myself with things which stress the experiences, forms, and spirit we have in common.

This does not mean that I am necessarily opposed to the various established racial or sociological groupings. Certainly it does not mean that I am opposed to the efforts and forces which are trying to make these groups creative. On the contrary, I affirm these efforts. I recognize, for example, that the Negro art movement has had some valuable results. It is, however, for those who have and who will benefit by it. It is not for me. My poems are not Negro poems, nor are they Anglo-Saxon or white or English poems. My prose, likewise. They are, first, mine. And, second, in so far as general race or stock is concerned, they spring from the result of racial blendings here in America which have produced a new race or stock. We may call this stock the American stock or race. . . .

A New Race in America

From "A New Race in America," 1931

There is a new race in America. I am a member of this new race. It is neither white nor black nor in-between. It is the American race, differing as much from white and black as white and black differ from each other. It is possible that there are Negro and Indian bloods in my descent along with English, Spanish, Welsh, Scotch, French, Dutch, and German. This is common in America; and it is from all these strains that the American race is being born. But the old divisions into white, black, brown, red, are outworn in this country. They have had their day. Now is the time of the birth of a new order, a new vision, a new ideal of man.

An American People

From "Not Typically American," March 13, 1935

The typically American thing is for a man, if he is white, to live all his life as a white man, and to have queer unreal views of the people of all other groups; if colored, to live all his life as a colored man, and to have queer unreal views of people of other groups; if Jewish to live all his life as a Jew, and to have queer unreal views of the people of other groups; if an Indian to live all his life as an Indian and to have queer unreal views of the people of all other groups. If of English descent to live among people of English descent, if Scotch or Irish or Welsh or German or French or Italian or Spanish or Greek or what not, to live amongst those of similar descent all his life. In the typical view, matters of genesis overshadow matters of Being. . . .

In short, the typically American thing is for people to group themselves (or to be grouped) and adhere to racial or religious or nationalistic separatisms. Though in ideal one country, united and indivisible, though our biological actuality approaches this ideal (we are undoubtedly forming an American race) we are, sociologically, a replica of Europe's mutually repellent nationalisms with the red man and something of Africa and the Orient thrown in for good measure. Our social psychology lags far behind our spiritual ideals on the one hand and our physical realities on the other. . . .

If the old world fatherlands of our new world citizens were to feed their respective children in this country with inflammatory nationalistic propaganda they could stir up in no time a world war within the borders of the United States. Technically of course it would be called a civil war. Whatever called, it would be explosive evidence of the fact that though we are citizens we are not yet a people—and we are not yet a people owing to two main causes: first, that there has not yet been time enough for such a consolidation; and, second, because the natural process of consolidation has been artificially checked by certain powers in this country who, for their own profit and with characteristic shortsight, have maneuvered to divide us and keep us divided. . . .

More than three hundred years were required in order to consolidate and blend a mixture of stocks into the present day English people. More than three hundred years will be required to consolidate and blend the mixtures existing here into an American people.

The American Race

From "The Americans," undated

There is a new race here. For the present we may call it the American race. That, to date, not many are aware of its existence, that they do not realize that they themselves belong to it—this does not mean it does not exist; it simply means it does not yet exist for them because they, under the suggestion of hypnotic labels and false beliefs, are blind to it. But these labels and beliefs will die. They too must and will die. And the sight of people will be freed from them, and the people will become less blind and they will use their sight and see.

This new race is neither white nor black nor red nor brown. These are old terms for old races, and they must be discarded. This is a new race; and though to some extent, to be sure, white and black and red and brown strains have entered into its formation, we should not view it as part white, part black, and so on. For when different elements come together in chemico-biological blendings, a new substance is produced, a new substance with new qualities in a new form. Water, though composed of two parts of hydrogen and one part of oxygen, is not hydrogen and oxygen; it is *water,* a new substance with a new form produced by the blending of hydrogen and oxygen. So the blending of different racial strains, taking place in the geographical setting of the American continent, has given rise to a new race which is uniquely itself. Save in the case of those who only recently have come here, it includes *everyone* in the country.

MICHAEL LIND

The American Cultural Nation

From *The Next American Nation*, 1995

If . . . we conceive of the United States as a liberal nation-state, then we must reject the idea that liberty in America requires what might be called separation of nation and state. There is no analogy between state neutrality, with respect to religion, and state neutrality, with respect to nationality. There is not, and should not be, an established religion in the United States; but there is, and should be, an established nationality—that is, a language, culture, and folkways, which are privileged above those of other nationalities that happen to reside in U.S. territory (German-speaking Amish, unassimilated Chinese and Poles and Nigerians). With respect to religion, the United States is neutral, not tolerant; with respect to nationality, the United States is tolerant, not neutral. From the perspective of minority nationalities, the United States is a tolerant liberal nation-state, not a neutral nonnation-state. Enclave nationalities, foreign residents, and unassimilated immigrants should be treated with respect, but they should not be given a veto over the loose but real identification of the American state with the American cultural nation.

Of all the elements of a national culture, language is by far the most important. To be a member of a cultural nation is not merely to speak the language—foreigners can learn that; it is to speak it idiomatically, without a significant accent, with the fluency of a native, to be alive to all the subtle nuances in intonation and vocabulary, to recognize the allusions that make any nation's language a repository of its past. It is possible for foreigners to become not merely citizens of the state, but members of the majority cultural nation; but such acculturation is very difficult, particularly for adult immigrants, requiring years of immersion in the national language and the complex of conceptions and sentiments to which the vernacular language grants access. . . .

There is more to the national culture than the national language, though the language is both the primary index of nationality and its major means of transmission. In addition, there are folkways—not abstract moral codes, but particular ways of acting, ways of dressing, conventions of masculinity and femininity, ways of celebrating major events like births, marriages, and funerals, particular kinds of sports and recreations, conceptions of the proper boundaries between the secular and religious spheres. And there is also a body of material—ranging from historical events that everyone is expected to know about to widely shared but ephemeral knowledge of sports and cinema and music—that might be called common knowledge. Common language, common folkways, common knowledge—these, rather than race or religion or political philosophy, are what identify a member of the American cultural nation.

The national culture is not fixed, like the canon of an established religion; on the other hand, it is not as ephemeral as the most superficial manifestations of popular culture. It is neither carved in stone nor writ in water; rather it is embedded like boulders in a glacier that moves over time, altering the landscape as it flows, but so slowly that at any given moment it seems to be frozen and still. A national culture is like the national language that tends to be its most important element. Contemporary Polish is different in many ways from eighteenth-century Polish, but the one has recognizably evolved from the other. Because the national culture changes relatively slowly, it is possible to describe it in some detail, even though, like a dictionary, any lexicon of shared traditions is doomed to leave out many new usages and include much that is already obsolete. . . .

The term melting pot, trite though it has become, really does express the nature of the American national culture much more accurately than do metaphors like mosaic or salad bowl or quilt or orchestra. The common culture of the American nation is a unique blend of elements contributed by Algonquian Indians and Midwestern Quakers and black Americans and Mexican mestizos and New England patricians. The national culture is not a white culture; black Americans have shaped it far more than the most numerous white immigrant group, German-Americans. Nor is it middle-class; black-derived musical forms like jazz, soul, gospel, and R&B, as well as country and western music, have been frowned upon by the respectable middle classes of every generation. It most certainly is not European culture transplanted overseas without alteration; the national culture of English-speaking North America is just as distinctly a product of the Western Hemisphere as is the hybrid European-African-Indian culture of Portuguese-speaking Brazil. . . .

A mere list of ingredients—English, African, Algonquian, Chinese, German, Mexican, Italian—makes American culture sound much more open to novelty than it really is. Precisely because it is so often selective, cultural borrowing does not necessarily represent openness to genuine novelty on the part of a nation. Indeed, members of a nation often borrow only those aspects of foreign cultures that can be easily fitted into the preexisting pattern of their own. . . .

The American national vernacular culture—American English, and a living tradition that has its own slowly changing grammar as well as its own rapidly fluctuating idiom—is what defines the majority nationality in the United States, a uniquely American nationality that largely overlaps with, but is distinct from, the class of United States citizens, a nationality that today includes people whose ancestors lived on every populated continent. If ethnicity can be defined by language and culture, there is a multiracial and multireligious but unicultural American ethnic nation. We might speak, without contradiction, of the Ethnic American. . . .

The liberal nationalist definition of American identity extends it to anyone whose primary, or adopted, culture is America's "mulatto" mainstream. This is an extremely inclusive conception. It is therefore hard to understand why so many American liberals, influenced by democratic universalism, would want to define American nationality solely in terms of political citizenship or subjective opinion. After all, if American identity is bestowed by the government, then the government can take it away. If American identity is bestowed by public opinion, then public disrespect can dis-bestow it. If to be American is to be a U.S. citizen, then black Americans only became Americans with the enactment of the Fourteenth Amendment. If to be American is to be considered American by the American majority, then one's very identity depends on the prejudices of other people. What is so liberal about these notions? According to the linguistic-cultural test of nationality, from the very earliest years of the colonial period, English-speaking, North American–born black Americans were members of the American cultural nation, even when most were slaves and not citizens, even when most white Americans considered black Americans, wrongly, to be another people. . . .

The dramatic figures about the approaching time when nonwhites are a majority in the United States look much less significant, when one realizes that the American *cultural majority* is much larger than the *white racial majority*. This transracial American ethnic group is continually growing, even if the proportion of its members of exclusively European descent is slowly diminishing. The gradual diminution in the relative numbers of Americans of British and European descent need not mean a diminution of the *real*

American majority, whose members include black Mississippians, Californians of Asian descent, and Texans of Mexican ancestry, and growing numbers of mixed-race people whose very existence renders our racial categories obsolete.

PART THREE

A MORE PERFECT UNION

All Americans in the Hamiltonian tradition of democratic nationalism, whatever their other differences may have been, have agreed on one priority: the unification of the American nation in a single nation-state. The nightmare of nationalists from Washington and Hamilton to Webster and Lincoln was the division of the American people among rival, petty republics, like those among which the culturally similar Latin Americans have been divided since they achieved independence from Spain.

The arguments that democratic nationalists in America have made for Union have been primarily practical arguments, based on the benefits of a common defense and a common internal market. In addition, there have been sentimental arguments for national unity, of the kind made famous by Daniel Webster and Abraham Lincoln. In the selections that follow, those practical and sentimental arguments for the establishment and preservation of a single comprehensive American nation-state are emphasized, at the expense of technical legal arguments from the federal constitution. While this principle of selection results in the neglect of great nationalist legal thinkers like Marshall, Kent, Choate, and Storey, it gets the priorities right. History has shown that Americans who are not persuaded by either the pragmatic or the emotional arguments for national unity are not likely to be reasoned into submission by legal subtleties.

It is worth pausing, however, to outline the constitutional theory of American democratic nationalism. From the earliest days of the republic, two distinct and incompatible theories of the American nation-state have been debated by generations of American politicians and scholars. The states'-rights or compact theory, associated with Southern conservatives in the Jeffersonian tradition, holds that the United States, even under the Federal Constitution that went into effect in 1789, should be considered a loose confederation of "sovereign" states. The rival nationalist or popular sovereignty theory of the mostly Northern Hamiltonians has denied "sovereignty" in the premodern sense to either the state governments or the federal government. The People (a term that is used in American discourse where "Nation" would be used in other countries) are the sovereign, delegating different portions of their power to different levels of government. Adherents of the popular sovereignty theory, it should be noted, do not deny that the states have powers under the Constitution that should not be usurped by the federal government; they do deny, however, that the individual states or their populations have any recourse to self-help measures like nullification of laws or secession. What the people/nation as a whole created, only the people/nation as a whole can alter.

The Civil War put an end to any thought of secession by states against the will of the national majority (though perhaps not forever—one cannot know what the centuries ahead may hold). This section ends, as the debate over union effectively ended, with selections from the addresses and writings of leading nationalist leaders and thinkers of the Civil War era, including Abraham Lincoln and Francis Lieber.

PREAMBLE TO THE UNITED STATES CONSTITUTION (1789)

The first object mentioned in the Preamble to the Constitution is the formation of a "more perfect union" by the sovereign "People" of the United States—not the several "peoples" of the several states.

We the People of the United States, in order to form a more perfect union, establish justice, insure domestic tranquility, provide for the common defence, promote the general welfare, and secure the blessings of liberty to ourselves and our posterity, do ordain and establish this Constitution for the United States of America.

SAMUEL H. BEER

In the following excerpt from *To Make a Nation: The Rediscovery of American Federalism* (1993), Samuel H. Beer, Eaton Professor of the Science of Government, Emeritus, at Harvard, summarizes the popular sovereignty theory held by Alexander Hamilton and his successors.

The Nationalist Theory of Federalism

Intrinsic to [the national idea as a] way of looking at democratic nationalism in America is a theory of federalism. This theory is about the division of authority between the federal and the state governments and about the purposes which this distribution of power is expected to serve. It is a theory in the sense that it is a coherent body of thought describing and justifying the federal system in the light of certain fundamental principles. These are the principles of democracy and nationality on which the Constitution as a whole is based. . . . [T]his curious arrangement of a constitutionally protected vertical division of power is an intentional and functional institution—not an historical accident or the upshot of mere compromise—of the self-governing American people as they seek over time to make and remake themselves as a nation.

The significance of this theory as a choice among possible regimes is brought out by the contrast with compact theory. From the viewpoint of compact theory, federalism and nationalism, the states and the nation, are opposed. This is opposition in a quite fundamental sense: not merely a conflict between state government and federal government but between state and nation as political communities. For, if the center of political life is in each of the separate states of the nation, it cannot be in the nation as a whole. Or, to put the matter even more bluntly, in so far as the compact model is a correct description, the true nation in America is not the United States but the separate states of which it is composed. We are not one people but several.

Radically different conclusions follow from the opposing view of the location of our nationality, the source of our democracy, and the function of the federal–state division of authority. In contrast with compact theory, national theory takes a far more generous view of the powers and responsibilities of the federal government. Throughout our history, it has informed and supported the broad against the narrow construction of the constitutional power of the federal government. National theory, however, is not merely a doctrine of centralization. As its advocates at the time of the founding continually emphasized, the national point of view not only tolerates but indeed requires a federal arrangement.

In this conception the American republic is one nation served by two levels of government, the object of both being to protect and enhance the well-being of the nation. The states are not rival communities carved out of the greater jurisdiction which, although they are incapable of real material or moral independence, seek to act on an exclusive and inward-looking concern for their distinct interests. Like the federal government, state governments also express the national will. The nation can use both levels or either level of government to make itself more of a nation: that is, to make the United States a freer, wealthier, more powerful, and indeed more virtuous human community. . . .

Like the other Founders, Hamilton sought to establish a regime of republican liberty, that is, a system of government which would protect the individual rights of person and property and which would be founded upon the consent of the governed. He was by no means satisfied with the legal framework produced by the Philadelphia Convention. Fearing the states, he would have preferred a much stronger central authority, and, distrusting the common people, he would have set a greater distance between them and the exercise of power. He was less concerned, however, with the legal framework than with the use that would be made of it. He saw in the Constitution not only a regime of liberty, but also and especially the promise of nationhood.

He understood, moreover, that this promise of nationhood would have to be fulfilled if the regime of liberty itself was to endure. The scale of the country almost daunted him. At the Philadelphia Convention, as its chief diarist reported, Hamilton "confessed he was much discouraged by the amazing extent of Country in expecting the desired blessings from any general sovereignty that could be substituted." This fear echoed a common opinion of the time. The great Montesquieu had warned that popular government was not suitable for a large and diverse country. If attempted, he predicted, its counsels would be distracted by "a thousand private views" and its extent would provide cover for ambitious men seeking despotic power.

One reply to Montesquieu turned this argument on its head by declaring that such pluralism would be a source of stability. In his famous Federalist 10 James Madison argued that the more extensive republic, precisely because of its diversity, would protect popular government by making oppressive combinations far less likely. As elaborated by Madison, Hamilton, and other champions of the new regime, their hopes for a more extensive republic rested on more than its promise of a mechanical balance of groups. Hamilton summarized these views in the farewell address that he drafted for Washington in 1796. Its theme was the importance of union if the regime of liberty was to survive. This union would not consist merely in a strong central government or a common framework of constitutional law. It would be rather a condition of the American people, uniting them by sympathy as well as interest in what Washington termed "an indissoluble community of interest as *one nation.*"

JAMES WILSON

It is perhaps no coincidence that the two most uncompromising nationalists among the American Founders were two immigrants—Alexander Hamilton, born and raised in the West Indies, and the Scots immigrant James Wilson (1742–87). Immigrants not only lack parochial regional, class, or ethnic loyalties that might eclipse their perception of the common good, but they sometimes compensate for their status as outsiders by zeal for the community that has adopted them. Among the examples that come to mind are Napoleon (a Corsican), Stalin (a Georgian), and T.S. Eliot, the American expatriate who became the most exquisitely English of twentieth-century Englishmen.

Educated at the University of Edinburgh, Wilson emigrated to the American colonies in 1765 and became Latin tutor at the College of Philadelphia. In 1767 he was admitted to the Pennsylvania bar. This prosperous lawyer, essayist, and scholar wrote pro-independence pamphlets and served in the Continental Congress and later in the Constitutional Convention. Wilson dominated the Pennsylvania ratifying convention. Washington appointed him to the Supreme Court in 1789. Wilson's last years were troubled by financial problems and by the deaths of his first wife and an infant son. He died, feeling depressed and persecuted, without achieving his dream of writing the American equivalent of Blackstone's commentaries on law. Nevertheless, his views on popular sovereignty and the federal constitution influenced a greater Supreme Court justice, John Marshall, and through him became part of the American public philosophy.

Wilson's contributions to American constitutional thought have long been overshadowed by those of his more familiar contemporaries like Hamilton, Jefferson, and Madison. This neglect has resulted in a real loss to American self-understanding, inasmuch as Wilson's speech before the

Ratifying Convention of Pennsylvania (October 6, 1787), reproduced here, sets forth the democratic nationalist theory of the United States Constitution more concisely and eloquently than even the celebrated Federalist papers of Hamilton, Madison, and Jay. It is easy to understand why Lord Bryce, in *The American Commonwealth* (1888), declared that Wilson had been "one of the deepest thinkers and most exact reasoners" among the American Founders and "in the front rank of the political thinkers of his age."

Popular Sovereignty and the Constitution

The system proposed, by the late convention, for the government of the United States, is now before you. Of that convention I had the honor to be a member. As I am the only member of that body who have the honor to be also a member of this, it may be expected that I should prepare the way for the deliberations of this assembly, by unfolding the difficulties which the late convention were obliged to encounter; by pointing out the end which they proposed to accomplish; and by tracing the general principles which they have adopted for the accomplishment of that end.

To form a good system of government for a single city or state, however limited as to territory, or inconsiderable as to numbers, has been thought to require the strongest efforts of human genius. With what conscious diffidence, then, must the members of the convention have revolved in their minds the immense undertaking which was before them. Their views could not be confined to a small or a single community, but were expanded to a great number of states, several of which contain an extent of territory, and resources of population, equal to those of some of the most respectable kingdoms on the other side of the Atlantic. Nor were even these the only objects to be comprehended within their deliberations. Numerous states yet unformed, myriads of the human race, who will inhabit regions hitherto uncultivated, were to be affected by the result of their proceedings. It was necessary, therefore, to form their calculations on a scale commensurate to a large portion of the globe.

For my own part, I have often been lost in astonishment at the vastness of the prospect before us. To open the navigation of a single river was lately thought, in Europe, an enterprise adequate to imperial glory. But could the commercial scenes of the Scheldt be compared with those that, under a good government, will be exhibited on the Hudson, the Delaware, the Potomac, and the numerous other rivers that water and are intended to enrich the dominions of the United States?

The difficulty of the business was equal to its magnitude. No small share of wisdom and address is requisite to combine and reconcile the jarring interests that prevail, or seem to prevail, in a single community. The United States contain already thirteen governments mutually independent. Those governments present to the Atlantic a front of fifteen hundred miles in extent. Their soil, their climates, their productions, their dimensions, their numbers are different. In many instances a difference and even an opposition subsists among their interests; and a difference and even an opposition is imagined to subsist in many more. An apparent interest produces the same attachment as a real one, and is often pursued with no less perseverance and vigor. When all these circumstances are seen and attentively considered, will any member of this honorable body be surprised that such a diversity of things produced a proportioned diversity of sentiment? Will he be surprised that such a diversity of sentiment rendered a spirit of mutual forbearance and conciliation indispensably necessary to the success of the great work? And will he be surprised that mutual concessions and sacrifices were the consequences of mutual forbearance and conciliation? When the springs of opposition were so numerous and strong, and poured forth their waters in courses so varying, need we be surprised that the stream formed by their conjunction was impelled in a direction somewhat different from that which each of them would have taken separately?

I have reason to think that a difficulty arose in the minds of some members of the convention from another consideration—their ideas of the temper and disposition of the people for whom the constitution is proposed. The citizens of the United States, however different in other respects, are well known to agree in one strongly marked feature of their character—a warm and keen sense of freedom and independence. This sense has been heightened by the glorious result of their late struggle against all the efforts of one of the most powerful nations of Europe. It was apprehended, I believe, by some, that a people so high spirited would ill brook the restraints of an efficient government. I confess that this consideration did not influence my conduct. I knew my constituents to be high spirited, but I knew them also to possess sound sense. I knew that, in the event, they would be best pleased with that system of government which would best promote their freedom and happiness. . . .

A very important difficulty arose from comparing the extent of the country to be governed with the kind of government which it would be proper to establish in it. It has been an opinion, countenanced by high authority, "that the natural property of small states is to be governed as a republic; of middling ones, to be subject to a monarch; and of large empires, to be swayed by a despotic prince; and that the consequence is that, in order to preserve the principals of the established government, the state must be supported in the extent it has acquired; and that the state will alter in proportion as it extends or contracts its limits."[1] This opinion seems to be supported, rather than contradicted, by the history of the governments in the Old World. Here then the difficulty appeared in full view. On one hand, the United States contain an immense extent of territory, and, according to the foregoing opinion, a despotic government is best adapted to that extent. On the other hand, it was well known that, however the citizens of the United States might, with pleasure, submit to the legitimate restraints of a republican constitution, they would reject, with indignation, the fetters of despotism. What then was to be done? The idea of a confederate republic presented itself. This kind of constitution has been thought to have "all the internal advantages of a republican, together with the external force of a monarchical government."[2] Its description is, "a convention by which several states agree to become members of a larger one which they intend to establish. It is a kind of assemblage of societies that constitute a new one, capable of increasing by means of farther association."[3] The expanding quality of such a government is peculiarly fitted for the United States, the greatest part of whose territory is yet uncultivated.

But while this form of government enabled us to surmount the difficulty last mentioned, it conducted us to another of which I am now to take notice. It left us almost without precedent or guide, and consequently without the benefit of that instruction which, in many cases, may be derived from the constitution and history and experience of other nations. Several associations have frequently been called by the name of confederate states which have not, in propriety of language, deserved it. The Swiss cantons are connected only by alliances. The United Netherlands are indeed an assemblage of societies, but this assemblage constitutes no *new one,* and therefore it does not correspond with the full definition of a confederate republic. The Germanic body is composed of such disproportioned and discordant materials, and its structure is so intricate and complex, that little useful knowledge can be drawn from it. Ancient history discloses, and barely discloses to our view, some confederate republics—the Achaean league, the Lycian confederacy, and the Amphyctyonic council. But the facts recorded concerning their constitutions are so few and general, and their histories are so unmarked and defective, that no satisfactory information can be collected from them concerning many particular circumstances, from an accurate discernment and comparison of which alone, legiti-

---

1. Wilson is quoting Montesquieu, *Spirit of the Laws,* b.8.c.20.

2. *Ibid.,* b.9.c.1.

3. *Ibid.*

mate and practical inferences can be made from one constitution to another. Besides, the situation and dimensions of those confederacies, and the state of society, manners and habits in them, were so different from those of the United States that the most correct descriptions could have supplied but a very small fund of applicable remark. Thus in forming this system we were deprived of many advantages which the history and experience of other ages and other countries would, in other cases, have afforded us.

Permit me to add, in this place, that the science even of government itself seems yet to be almost in its state of infancy. Governments, in general, have been the result of force, of fraud, and of accident. After a period of six thousand years has elapsed since the Creation, the United States exhibit to the world the first instance, as far as we can learn, of a nation unattacked by external force, unconvulsed by domestic insurrections, assembling voluntarily, deliberating fully, and deciding calmly, concerning that system of government under which they would wish that they and their posterity should live. The ancients, so enlightened on other subjects, were very uninformed with regard to this. They seem scarcely to have had any idea of any other kinds of governments than the three simple forms designated by the epithets monarchical, aristocratical, and democratical. I know that much and pleasing ingenuity has been exerted, in modern times, in drawing entertaining parallels between some of the ancient constitutions and some of the mixed governments that have since existed in Europe. But I much suspect that, on strict examination, the instances of resemblance will be found to be few and weak, to be suggested by the improvements which in subsequent ages have been made in government, and not to be drawn immediately from the ancient constitutions themselves, as they were intended and understood by those who framed them. . . .

One thing is very certain, that the doctrine of representation in government was altogether unknown to the ancients. Now the knowledge and practice of this doctrine is, in my opinion, essential to every system that can possess the qualities of freedom, wisdom and energy.

It is worthy of remark, and the remark may, perhaps, excite some surprise, that representation of the people is not, even at this day, the sole principle of any government in Europe. Great Britain boasts, and she may well boast, of the improvement she has made in politics by the admission of representation, for the improvement is important as far as it goes; but it by no means goes far enough. Is the executive power of Great Britain founded on representation? This is not pretended. Before the revolution, many of the kings claimed to reign by divine right, and others by hereditary right; and even at the revolution, nothing farther was effected or attempted than the recognition of certain parts of an original contract supposed at some remote period to have been made between the king and the people. A contract seems to exclude, rather than to imply, delegated power. The judges of Great Britain are appointed by the crown. The judicial authority, therefore, does not depend upon representation, even in its most remote degree. Does representation prevail in the legislative department of the British government? Even here it does not predominate, though it may serve as a check. The legislature consists of three branches, the king, the lords, and the commons. Of these, only the latter are supposed by the constitution to represent the authority of the people. This short analysis clearly shows to what a narrow corner of the British constitution the principle of representation is confined. I believe it does not extend farther, if so far, in any other government in Europe. For the American States were reserved the glory and the happiness of diffusing this vital principle through all the constituent parts of government. Representation is the chain of communication between the people and those to whom they have committed the exercise of the powers of government. This chain may consist of one or more links, but in all cases it should be sufficiently strong and discernible.

To be left without guide or precedent was not the only difficulty in which the convention were involved by proposing to their constituents a plan of a confederated republic. They found themselves embarrassed with another of peculiar delicacy and importance; I mean that of drawing a proper line between the national government and the governments of the several states. It was easy to discover a proper and satisfactory principle on the subject. Whatever object of government is confined in its operation and effects within the bounds of a particular state should be considered as belonging to the government of that state; whatever object of government extends its operation or effects beyond the bounds of a particular state should be considered as belonging to the government of the United States. But though this principle be sound and satisfactory, its application to particular cases would be accompanied with much difficulty, because in its application room must be allowed for great discretionary latitude of construction of the principle. In order to lessen or remove the difficulty arising from discretionary construction on this subject, an enumeration of particular instances in which the application of the principle ought to take place has been attempted with much industry and care. It is only in mathematical science that a line can be described with mathematical precision. But I flatter myself that, upon the strictest investigation, the enumeration will be found to be safe and unexceptionable, and accurate, too, in as great a degree as accuracy can be expected in a subject of this nature. Particulars under this head will be more properly explained when we descend to the minute view of the enumeration which is made in the proposed constitution.

After all, it will be necessary that, on a subject so peculiarly delicate as this, much prudence, much candor, much moderation and much liberality should be exercised and displayed both by the federal government and by the governments of the several states. It is to be hoped that those virtues in government will be exercised and displayed when we consider that the powers of the federal government and those of the state governments are drawn from sources equally pure. If a difference can be discovered between them, it is in favor of the federal government, because that government is founded on a representation of the whole union, whereas the government of any particular state is founded only on the representation of a part, inconsiderable when compared with the whole. Is it not more reasonable to suppose that the counsels of the whole will embrace the interest of every part, than that the counsels of any part will embrace the interests of the whole?

I intend not, sir, by this description of the difficulties with which the convention were surrounded, to magnify their skill or their merit in surmounting them, or to insinuate that any predicament in which the convention stood should prevent the closest and most cautious scrutiny into the performance which they have exhibited to their constituents and to the world. My intention is of far other and higher aim—to evince by the conflicts and difficulties which must arise from the many and powerful causes which I have enumerated that it is hopeless and impracticable to form a constitution which will, in every part, be acceptable to every citizen, or even to every government, in the United States; and that all which can be expected is to form such a constitution as, upon the whole, is the best that can possibly be obtained. Man and perfection!—a state and perfection!—an assemblage of states and perfection! Can we reasonably expect, however ardently we wish, to behold the glorious union?

I can well recollect, though I believe I cannot convey to others, the impression which, on many occasions, was made by the difficulties which surrounded and pressed the convention. The great undertaking, at some times, seemed to be at a stand; at other times, its motions seemed to be retrograde. At the conclusion, however, of our work, many of the members expressed their astonishment at the success with which it terminated.

Having enumerated some of the difficulties which the convention were obliged to encounter in the course of their proceedings, I shall next point out the end which they proposed to accomplish. Our wants, our talents, our affections, our passions, all tell us that we were made for a state of society. But a state of society could not be supported long or happily without some civil restraint. It is true that, in a state of nature, any one individual may act uncontrolled by others; but it is equally true that, in such a state, every other individual may act uncontrolled by him. Amidst this universal independence, the dissensions and animosities between interfering members of the society would be numerous and ungovernable. The consequence would be that each member, in such a natural state, would enjoy less liberty, and suffer more interruption, than he would in a regulated society. Hence the universal introduction of governments of some kind or other into the social state. The liberty of every member is increased by this introduction, for each gains more by the limitation of the freedom of every other member than he loses by the limitation of his own. The result is that civil government is necessary to the perfection and happiness of man. In forming this government, and carrying it into execution, it is essential that the interest and authority of the whole community should be binding on every part of it.

The foregoing principles and conclusions are generally admitted to be just and sound with regard to the nature and formation of single governments, and the duty of submission to them. In some cases they will apply, with much propriety and force, to states already formed. The advantages and necessity of civil government among individuals in society are not greater or stronger than, in some situations and circumstances, are the advantages and necessity of a federal government among states. A natural and a very important question now presents itself. Is such the situation—are such the circumstances of the United States? A proper answer to this question will unfold some very interesting truths.

The United States may adopt any one of four different systems. They may become consolidated into one government in which the separate existence of the states shall be entirely absorbed. They may reject any plan of union or association, and act as separate and unconnected states. They may form two or more confederacies. They may unite in one federal republic. Which of these systems ought to have been proposed by the convention?

To support with vigor a single government over the whole extent of the United States would demand a system of the most unqualified and the most unremitted despotism. Such a number of separate states, contiguous in situation, unconnected and disunited in government, would be, at one time, the prey of foreign force, foreign influence, and foreign intrigue; at another, the victim of mutual rage, rancor, and revenge. Neither of these systems found advocates in the late convention; I presume they will not find advocates in this.

Would it be proper to divide the United States into two or more confederacies? It will not be unadvisable to take a more minute survey of this subject. Some aspects under which it may be viewed are far from being, at first sight, uninviting. Two or more confederacies would be each more compact and more manageable than a single one extending over the same territory. By dividing the United States into two or more confederacies, the great collision of interests, apparently or really different and contrary, in the whole extent of their dominion, would be broken, and in a great measure disappear in the several parts. But these advantages, which are discovered from certain points of view, are greatly overbalanced by inconveniences that will appear on a more accurate examination. Animosities, and perhaps wars, would arise from assigning the extent, the limits, and the rights of the different confederacies. The expenses of governing would be multiplied by the number of federal governments. The danger resulting from foreign influence and mutual dissensions would not, perhaps, be less great and alarming in the instance of different confederacies than in the instance of different though more numerous unassociated states. These observations, and many others that might be made on the subject, will be sufficient to evince that a division of the United States into a number of separate confederacies would probably be an unsatisfactory and an unsuccessful experiment.

The remaining system which the American States may adopt is a union of them under one confederate republic. It will not be necessary to employ much time or many arguments to show that this is the most eligible system that can be proposed. By adopting this system, the vigor and decision of a widespreading monarchy may be joined to the freedom and beneficence of a contracted republic. The extent of territory, the diversity of climate and soil, the number and greatness and connection of lakes and rivers with which the United States are intersected and almost surrounded, all indicate an enlarged government to be fit and advantageous for them. The principles and dispositions of their citizens indicate that in this government liberty shall reign triumphant. Such indeed have been the general opinions and wishes entertained since the era of our independence. If those opinions and wishes are as well founded as they have been general, the late convention were justified in proposing to their constituents one confederate republic as the best system of a national government for the United States. . . .

We have remarked that civil government is necessary to the perfection of society; we now remark that civil liberty is necessary to the perfection of civil government. Civil liberty is natural liberty itself, divested only of that part which, placed in the government, produces more good and happiness to the community than if it had remained in the individual. Hence it follows that civil liberty, while it resigns a part of natural liberty, retains the free and generous exercise of all the human faculties, so far as it is compatible with the public welfare.

In considering and developing the nature and end of the system before us, it is necessary to mention another kind of liberty, which has not yet, as far as

I know, received a name. I shall distinguish it by the appellation of *federal liberty*. When a single government is instituted, the individuals of which it is composed surrender to it a part of their natural independence which they before enjoyed as men. When a confederate republic is instituted, the communities of which it is composed surrender to it a part of their political independence which they before enjoyed as states. The principles which directed, in the former case, what part of the natural liberty of the man ought to be given up, and what part ought to be retained, will give similar directions in the latter case. The states should resign to the national government that part, and that part only, of their political liberty, which, placed in that government, will produce more good to the whole than if it had remained in the several states. While they resign this part of their political liberty, they retain the free and generous exercise of all their other faculties as states, so far as it is compatible with the welfare of the general and superintending confederacy.

Since states as well as citizens are represented in the constitution before us, and form the objects on which that constitution is proposed to operate, it was necessary to notice and define federal as well as civil liberty. . . .

We now see the great end which [the convention] proposed to accomplish. It was to frame, for the consideration of their constituents, one federal and national constitution—a constitution that would produce the advantages of good, and prevent the inconveniences of bad government—a constitution whose beneficence and energy would pervade the whole union, and bind and embrace the interests of every part—a constitution that would ensure peace, freedom, and happiness to the states and people of America.

We are now naturally led to examine the means by which they proposed to accomplish this end. This opens more particularly to our view the important discussion before us. But previously to our entering upon it, it will not be improper to state some general and leading principles of government which will receive particular applications in the course of our investigations.

There necessarily exists in every government a power from which there is no appeal; and which, for that reason, may be termed supreme, absolute, and uncontrollable. Where does this power reside? To this question writers on different governments will give different answers. Sir William Blackstone will tell you that in Britain the power is lodged in the British parliament; that the parliament may alter the form of the government; and that its power is absolute and without control. The idea of a constitution limiting and superintending the operations of legislative authority seems not to have been accurately understood in Britain. There are, at least, no traces of practice conformable to such a principle. The British constitution is just what the British parliament pleases. When the parliament transferred legislative authority to

Henry the Eighth, the act transferring it could not, in the strict acceptation of the term, be called unconstitutional.

To control the power and conduct of the legislature by an overruling constitution was an improvement in the science and practice of government reserved to the American States.

Perhaps some politician who has not considered with sufficient accuracy our political systems would answer that, in our governments, the supreme power was vested in the constitutions. This opinion approaches a step nearer to the truth, but does not reach it. The truth is that, in our governments, the supreme, absolute, and uncontrollable power remains in the people. As our constitutions are superior to our legislatures, so the people are superior to our constitutions. Indeed the superiority, in this last instance, is much greater; for the people possess, over our constitutions, control in act, as well as in right.

The consequence is that the people may change the constitutions whenever and however they please. This is a right of which no positive institution can ever deprive them.

These important truths, sir, are far from being merely speculative; we, at this moment, speak and deliberate under their immediate and benign influence. To the operation of these truths, we are to ascribe the scene, hitherto unparalleled, which America now exhibits to the world—a gentle, a peaceful, a voluntary, and a deliberate transition from one constitution of government to another. In other parts of the world, the idea of revolutions in government is, by a mournful and indissoluble association, connected with the idea of wars and all the calamities attendant on wars. But happy experience teaches us to view such revolutions in a very different light—to consider them only as progressive steps in improving the knowledge of government and increasing the happiness of society and mankind.

Oft have I viewed with silent pleasure and admiration the force and prevalence, through the United States, of this principle—that the supreme power resides in the people; and that they never part with it. It may be called the *panacea* in politics. There can be no disorder in the community but may here receive a radical cure. If the error be in the legislature, it may be corrected by the constitution; if in the constitution, it may be corrected by the people. There is a remedy, therefore, for every distemper in the government, if the people are not wanting to themselves. For a people wanting to themselves, there is no remedy; from their power, as we have seen, there is no appeal; to their error, there is no superior principle of correction.

There are three simple species of government—monarchy, where the supreme power is in a single person—aristocracy, where the supreme power is in a select assembly, the members of which either fill up, by election, the vacancies in their own body, or succeed to their places in it by inheritance, property, or in respect of some personal right or qualification—a republic or democracy, where the people at large retain the supreme power, and act either collectively or by representation.

Each of these species of government has its advantages and disadvantages.

The advantages of monarchy are strength, dispatch, secrecy, unity of counsel. Its disadvantages are tyranny, expense, ignorance of the situation and wants of the people, insecurity, unnecessary wars, evils attending elections or successions.

The advantages of aristocracy are wisdom arising from experience and education. Its disadvantages are dissensions among themselves, oppression to the lower orders.

The advantages of democracy are liberty, equal, cautious and salutary laws, public spirit, frugality, peace, opportunities of exciting and producing abilities of the best citizens. Its disadvantages are dissensions, the delay and disclosure of public counsels, the imbecility of public measures retarded by the necessity of a numerous consent.

A government may be composed of two or more of the simple forms abovementioned. Such is the British government. It would be an improper government for the United States, because it is inadequate to such an extent of territory, and because it is suited to an establishment of different orders of men. . . .

What is the nature and kind of that government which has been proposed for the United States by the late convention? In its principle, it is purely democratical; but that principle is applied in different forms, in order to obtain the advantages, and exclude the inconveniences of the simple modes of government.

If we take an extended and accurate view of it, we shall find the streams of power running in different directions, in different dimensions, and at different heights, watering, adorning, and fertilizing the fields and meadows, through which their courses are led; but if we trace them we shall discover that they all originally flow from one abundant fountain. In this constitution, all authority is derived from THE PEOPLE.

JOHN JAY

John Jay (1745–1829) is remembered today as one of the authors of The Federalist, along with Alexander Hamilton, the principal author, and James Madison. Jay, a lawyer from an elite New York family, had a varied career as a member of the Continental Congress, a diplomat in Spain and France during and after the American War of Independence, and, until Thomas Jefferson arrived to take over, as acting secretary of state for the new government created by the federal constitution. Washington appointed Jay to be the first Chief Justice of the United States; while serving in that capacity (the federal judiciary did not yet have much to do), Jay was sent to Britain to resolve issues that the conclusion of the war had left outstanding. "Jay's Treaty" of 1794 was denounced by those who thought that too many concessions to the British had been made. Hamilton, who had guided Jay from afar during the negotiations, was actually stoned by a mob when he tried to speak in public in the treaty's favor. Jay resigned from the Supreme Court to become the Federalist Governor of New York, 1794–1800. His last twenty-eight years were spent in comfortable retirement.

In this excerpt from *The Federalist*, no. 2 (1787), Jay invokes two of the themes common to nationalists around the world: the relation of members of the nation to one another, and of the nation to its territorial homeland.

The American Nation and Its Homeland

It has until lately been a received and uncontradicted opinion that the prosperity of the people of America depended on their continuing firmly united, and the wishes, prayers, and efforts of our best and wisest citizens have been constantly directed to that object. But politicians now appear who insist that this opinion is erroneous, and that instead of looking for safety and happiness in union, we ought to seek it in a division of the States into distinct confederacies or sovereignties. . . .

It has often given me pleasure to observe that independent America was not composed of detached and distant territories, but that one connected, fertile, well-spreading country was the portion of our western sons of liberty. Providence has in a particular manner blessed it with a variety of soils and productions and watered it with innumerable streams for the delight and accommodation of its inhabitants. A succession of navigable waters forms a kind of chain round its borders, as if to knit it together; while the most noble rivers in the world, running at convenient distances, present them with highways for the easy communication of friendly aids and the mutual transportation and exchange of their various commodities.

With equal pleasure I have as often taken notice that Providence has been pleased to give this one connected country to one united people—a people descended from the same ancestors, speaking the same language, professing the same religion, attached to the same principles of government, very similar in their manners and customs, and who, by their joint counsels, arms, and efforts, fighting side by side throughout a long and bloody war, have nobly established their general liberty and independence.

This country and this people seem to have been made for each other, and it appears as if it was the design of Providence that an inheritance so proper and convenient for a band of brethren, united to each other by the strongest ties, should never be split into a number of unsocial, jealous, and alien sovereignties.

GEORGE WASHINGTON

George Washington (1732–99) achieved mythic status in his own life-time, receiving poetic encomia from English poets as different as William Blake and Byron, who contrasted Washington favorably with the despotic Napoleon (Byron also made the American frontiersman Daniel Boone a symbol of liberty). His contemporaries were impressed by the fact that the general who led a successful revolution did not establish a personal dictatorship, like Cromwell or Napoleon or any number of "lib-erators" in the nineteenth and twentieth centuries. An austere and remote figure, Washington has always inspired admiration rather than the idol-ization that Lincoln earned with his eloquence and folksiness and that Jefferson won with the seductive brilliance of his radical rhetoric.

During his first presidency, Washington attempted to be a nonparti-san figure, but he could do nothing to arrest the division of the political elite into the Federalists, led by his protégé and Treasury Secretary, Alexander Hamilton, and the Republicans grouped around his Secretary of State, Thomas Jefferson. Much to the horror of Jefferson, who con-cluded that the great man had become senile, Washington's political views were aligned completely with those of Hamilton. Like John Marshall (who wrote an admiring multivolume biography of the first President), Washington was a Southern planter with nationalist princi-ples. Unlike Jefferson, who wrote of liberty while owning hundreds of slaves, Washington provided for the manumission of his own slaves upon his death.

The regional divisions that would lead to the Civil War were already evident during Washington's two administrations in the split between the mostly Northern Federalists and the predominantly Southern Republicans. In his Farewell Address to the American people (1796), drafted with the help of Hamilton, Washington warned against "every attempt to alienate any portion of our country from the rest."

The Unity of Government

Interwoven as is the love of liberty with every ligament of your hearts, no recommendation of mine is necessary to fortify or confirm the attachment.

The unity of government which constitutes you one people is also now dear to you. It is justly so, for it is a main pillar in the edifice of your real independence, the support of your tranquillity at home, your peace abroad; of your safety; of your prosperity; of that very liberty which you so highly prize. But as it is easy to foresee that from different causes, and from different quarters, much pains will be taken, many artifices employed, to weaken in your minds the conviction of this truth; as this is the point in your political fortress against which the batteries of internal and external enemies will be most constantly and actively (though covertly and insidiously) directed, it is of infinite moment that you should properly estimate the immense value of your national Union, to your collective and individual happiness; that you should cherish a cordial, habitual, and immoveable attachment to it; accustoming yourselves to think and speak of it as the palladium of your political safety and prosperity; watching for its preservation with jealous anxiety; discountenancing whatever may suggest even a suspicion that it can in any event be abandoned; and indignantly frowning upon the first dawning of every attempt to alienate any portion of our country from the rest, or to enfeeble the sacred ties which now link together its various parts.

For this you have every inducement of sympathy and interest. Citizens by birth or choice of a common country, that country has a right to concentrate your affections. The name of AMERICAN, which belongs to you, in your national capacity, must always exalt the just pride of patriotism, more than any appellation derived from local discriminations. With slight shades of difference, you have the same religion, manners, habits and political principles. You have in a common cause fought and triumphed together; the independence and liberty you possess are the work of joint councils and joint efforts, of common dangers, sufferings, and successes.

But these considerations, however powerfully they address themselves to your sensibility, are greatly outweighed by those which apply more immediately to your interest. Here every portion of our country finds the most commanding motives for carefully guarding and preserving the union of the whole.

The North, in an unrestrained intercourse with the South, protected by the equal laws of a common government, finds in the productions of the latter great additional resources of maritime and commercial enterprise, and precious materials of manufacturing industry. The South, in the same intercourse, benefiting by the agency of the North, sees its agriculture grow and its commerce expand; turning partly into its own channels the seamen of the North, it finds its particular navigation invigorated—and while it contributes, in different ways, to nourish and increase the general mass of the national navigation, it looks forward to the protection of a maritime strength to which itself is unequally adapted. The East, in a like intercourse with the West, already finds, and in the progressive improvement of interior communication by land and water, will more and more find, a valuable vent for the commodities which it brings from abroad, or manufactures at home. The West derives from the East supplies requisite to its growth and comfort—and what is perhaps of still greater consequence, it must of necessity owe the secure enjoyment of indispensable outlets for its own productions to the weight, influence, and the future maritime strength of the Atlantic side of the Union, directed by an indissoluble community of interest as one Nation. Any other tenure by which the West can hold this essential advantage, whether derived from its own separate strength, or from an apostate and unnatural connection with any foreign power, must be intrinsically precarious.

While, then, every part of our country thus feels an immediate and particular interest in Union, all the parts combined cannot fail to find, in the united mass of means and efforts, greater strength, greater resource, proportionately greater security from external danger, a less frequent interruption of their peace by foreign nations, and, what is of inestimable value! they must derive from union an exemption from those broils and wars between themselves which so frequently afflict neighboring countries not tied together by the same government; which their own rivalships alone would be sufficient to produce, but which opposite foreign alliances, attachments and intrigues would stimulate and embitter. Hence likewise, they will avoid the necessity of those over-grown establishments which under any form of government are inauspicious to liberty, and which are to be regarded as particularly hostile to republican liberty; in this sense it is, that your Union ought to be considered as a main prop of your Liberty, and that the love of the one ought to endear to you the preservation of the other.

These considerations speak a persuasive language to every reflecting and virtuous mind, and exhibit the continuance of the Union as a primary object of patriotic desire. Is there a doubt whether a common government can embrace so large a sphere? Let experience solve it. To listen to mere speculation in such a case were criminal. We are authorized to hope that a proper organization of the whole, with the auxiliary agency of governments for the respective subdivisions, will afford a happy issue to the experiment. 'Tis well worth a fair and full experiment. With such powerful and obvious motives to Union, affecting all parts of our country, while experience shall not have demonstrated its impracticability, there will always be reason to distrust the patriotism of those who, in any quarter, may endeavor to weaken its bands.

In contemplating the causes which may disturb our Union, it occurs as a matter of serious concern that any ground should have been furnished for characterizing parties by geographical discriminations, Northern and Southern, Atlantic and Western; whence designing men may endeavor to excite a belief that there is a real difference of local interests and views. One of the expedients of party to acquire influence, within particular districts, is to misrepresent the opinions and aims of other districts. You cannot shield yourselves too much against the jealousies and heart-burnings which spring from these misrepresentations; they tend to render alien to each other those who ought to be bound together by fraternal affection. . . .

To the efficacy and permanency of your Union, a government for the whole is indispensable. No alliances, however strict, between the parties can be adequate substitute; they must inevitably experience the infractions and interruptions which all alliances in all times have experienced. Sensible of this momentous truth, you have improved upon your first essay by the adoption of a constitution of government better calculated than your former for an intimate Union, and for the efficacious management of your common concerns. This government, the offspring of our own choice, uninfluenced and unawed, adopted upon full investigation and mature deliberation, completely free in its principles, in the distribution of its powers, uniting security with energy, and containing within itself a provision for its own amendment, has just claim to your confidence and your support. Respect for its authority, compliance with its laws, acquiescence in its measures, are duties enjoined by the fundamental maxims of true liberty. The basis of our political systems is the right of the people to make and to alter their constitutions of government; but the constitution which at any time exists, till changed by an explicit and authentic act of the whole people, is sacredly obligatory upon all. The very idea of the power, and the right of the people to establish government, presupposes the duty of every individual to obey the established government.

All obstructions to the execution of the laws, all combinations and associations, under whatever plausible character, with the real design to direct, control, counteract, or awe the regular deliberation and action of the constituted authorities, are destructive of this fundamental principle, and of fatal tendency. They serve to organize faction, to give it an artificial and extraordinary force—to put in the place of the delegated will of the nation, the will of a party, often a small but artful and enterprising minority of the community; and, according to the alternate triumphs of different parties, to make the public administration the mirror of the ill-concerted and incongruous projects of faction, rather than the organ of consistent and wholesome plans, digested by common councils, and modified by mutual interests.

However combinations or associations of the above description may, now and then, answer popular ends, they are likely in the course of time and things to become potent engines by which cunning, ambitious and unprincipled men will be enabled to subvert the power of the people, and to usurp for themselves the reins of government; destroying afterwards the very engines which have lifted them to unjust dominion.

Towards the preservation of your government, and the permanency of your present happy state, it is requisite not only that you steadily discountenance irregular oppositions to its acknowledged authority, but also that you resist with care the spirit of innovation upon its principles, however specious the pretexts. One method of assault may be to effect, in the forms of the Constitution, alterations which will impair the energy of the system, and thus to undermine what cannot be directly overthrown. In all the changes to which you may be invited, remember that time and habit are at least as necessary to fix the true character of governments, as of other human institutions—that experience is the surest standard by which to test the real tendency of the existing constitution of a country—that facility in changes upon the credit of mere hypothesis and opinion exposes to perpetual change, from the endless variety of hypothesis and opinion; and remember, especially, that for the efficient management of your common interests, in a country as extensive as ours, a government of as much vigor as is consistent with the perfect security of liberty is indispensable. Liberty itself will find in such a government, with powers properly distributed and adjusted, its surest guardian. It is, indeed, little else than a name, where the government is too feeble to withstand the enterprises of faction, to confine each member of the society within the limits prescribed by the laws, and to maintain all in the secure and tranquil enjoyment of the rights of persons and property.

JOHN MARSHALL

Appointed Chief Justice of the United States by President John Adams in 1801, John Marshall (1755–1835) served until his death during the second term of President Andrew Jackson. He used his influence and his example to promote the strong, independent judiciary that Hamilton had praised in the Federalist as one of the advantages of the federal constitution. The power of the Supreme Court to strike down laws passed by Congress as unconstitutional was established in *Marbury* v. *Madison* (1803). In addition, he vindicated the power of the federal courts over state courts (*Cohens* v. *Virginia,* 1821), gave an expansive reading of the interstate commerce clause (*Gibbons* v. *Ogden,* 1824). In *McCulloch* v. *Maryland* (1819), Marshall provided a broad interpretation of the implied powers of the federal government.

Marshall, a Virginia planter who served in Congress and as a diplomat before his appointment to the Supreme Court, was a distant relative of Thomas Jefferson. Marshall, though, like Washington, was a Southerner with Northern nationalist principles. Jefferson hated him, particularly after Marshall thwarted Jefferson's attempt to convict his Vice President, Aaron Burr, of treason. (Ironically, Marshall's insistence that justice be done in the Burr case may have saved the murderer of Alexander Hamilton from being hanged at the instigation of Hamilton's arch-enemy, Jefferson.) Jefferson referred to Marshall's Supreme Court as a "subtle corps of sappers and miners," which was "constantly working underground to undermine our confederated fabric." When Marshall's five-volume biography of George Washington was published (1804–7), President Jefferson ordered federal postmasters not to take orders for it, ruining the prospects for its sale. Marshall was despised with equal warmth by President Andrew Jackson, who said of Marshall's opinion in *Worcester* v. *Georgia* that Jackson's Cherokee removal policy was unconstitutional: "John Marshall has made his decision, now let him enforce it."

Marshall's opinion in *McCulloch* v. *Maryland* (4 Wheaton 403, 1819) which follows sets forth the nationalist theory of the federal constitution simply and elegantly.

Popular Sovereignty and the Constitution

The Convention which framed the Constitution was, indeed, elected by the State legislatures. But the instrument, when it came from their hands, was a mere proposal, without obligation or pretensions to it. It was reported to the then existing Congress of the United States, with a request that it might "be submitted to a Convention of Delegates, chosen in each State by the people thereof, under the recommendation of its legislatures, for their assent and ratification." This mode of proceeding was adopted; and by the Convention, by Congress, and by the State Legislatures, the instrument was submitted to the people. They acted upon it in the only manner in which they can act safely, effectively, and wisely, on such a subject, by assembling in Convention. It is true, they assembled in their several States—and where else should they have assembled? No political dreamer was ever wild enough to think of breaking down the lines which separate the States, and of compounding the American people into one common mass of consequence; when they act, they act in their States. But the measures they adopt do not, on that account, cease to be the measures of the people themselves, or become the measures of the State governments.

From these conventions the Constitution derives its whole authority. The government proceeds directly from the people; is "ordained and established" in the name of the people; and is declared to be ordained "in order to form a more perfect union, establish justice, ensure domestic tranquillity, and secure the blessings of liberty to themselves and to their posterity." The assent of the States, in their sovereign capacity, is implied in calling the Convention, and thus submitting that instrument to the people. But the people were at perfect liberty to accept or reject it; and their act was final. It required not the affirmance, and could not be negatived, by the State governments. The constitution as thus adopted was of complete obligation, and bound the State sovereignties.

It has been said that the people had already surrendered all their powers to the State sovereignties, and had nothing more to give. But, surely, the question whether they may resume and modify the powers granted to government does not remain to be settled in this country. Much more might the legitimacy of the general government be doubted had it been created by the States. The powers delegated to the State sovereignties are to be exercised by themselves and not by a distinct and independent sovereignty created by themselves. For the formation of a league, such as was the confederation, the State sovereignties were certainly competent. But when, "in order to form a more perfect union," it was deemed necessary to change this alliance into an effective government, possessing great and sovereign powers, and acting directly on the people, the necessity of referring it to the people, and of deriving its powers directly from them, was felt and acknowledged by all.

DANIEL WEBSTER

Daniel Webster (1782–1852) shared with Henry Clay the distinction of being the greatest exponent of democratic nationalism in the United States between the era of John Marshall and John Quincy Adams and that of Abraham Lincoln. Webster, a New Hampshire native, served as a Senator from Massachusetts from 1827 to 1841. He and Clay formed the Whig Party, which opposed President Andrew Jackson's ultimately successful effort to destroy the Second Bank of the United States (the successor to the Bank of the United States fostered by Hamilton). In addition to distinguished service in the Senate, Webster served as Secretary of State for Presidents Harrison, Tyler, and Fillmore and was an unsuccessful presidential candidate of the Whig Party.

During his lifetime he was one of the most famous orators in the English-speaking world, no minor accomplishment in an era when oratory modeled on Greek and Roman precedents was one of the principal literary genres. Among his most famous speeches are his arguments before the Supreme Court in *Dartmouth College* v. *Woodward* (1818) and *Gibbons* v. *Ogden* (1824); the Plymouth Oration (1820); the First Bunker Hill Address (1825); and the Commemorative Discourse on Adams and Jefferson (1826). He expounded the democratic nationalist view of the United States in his most famous speeches in the U.S. Senate: the Second Reply to Hayne (1830), the Reply to Calhoun (1833), and the Constitution and the Union Speech (1850).

The Second Reply to Hayne, excerpted here from "Second Speech on Foot's Resolution" (U.S. Senate, January 26, 1830), was a landmark in the development of American democratic nationalism. Earlier generations of American nationalists, like Hamilton and Wilson, tended to rest their case for American national unity on pragmatic grounds—a strategy that reflected not only the temper of eighteenth-century rationalism but the relative youth of the country and the absence of collective memories. By Webster's time, however, the republic already had a pantheon of heroes and a memory of glorious victories in bygone struggles, celebrated by orators like Webster himself. Webster's conception of "national conservatism" (his term) was influenced by the conservatism of Edmund Burke, with its emphasis on tradition and on the sentimental bonds of community. Gone is the Augustan and Federalist preference for abstraction and antithesis, replaced by a fluid style, now conversational, now histrionic. Tradition and hero-worship were enlisted in the service of the doctrine of national unity and popular sovereignty that the Whigs inherited from the Federalists and would pass on to the Republicans. In Webster, American patriotism ceases to be instrumental and becomes sentimental.

The occasion for the Second Reply to Hayne was a debate in the Senate about the power of the federal government to support a favorite Hamiltonian enterprise, internal improvements, or infrastructure development—in this case, a canal in Ohio. Senator Robert Hayne of South Carolina had put forth the traditional Southern states'-rights arguments against this federal project, not suspecting that he had ensured that he would be remembered by posterity only as Webster's foil. Webster's speech was the most widely read Congressional speech of its era and inspired a once-famous 1851 painting by G. P. A. Healy. The impression it made upon a young Whig named Abraham Lincoln can be observed in the Gettysburg Address, which echoes one of Webster's famous formulations in the Second Reply to Hayne: "the people's Constitution, the people's government, made for the people, made by the people, and answerable to the people."

The Second Reply to Hayne

Mr. President—When the mariner has been tossed for many days in thick weather, and on an unknown sea, he naturally avails himself of the first pause in the storm, the earliest glance of the sun, to take his latitude, and ascertain how far the elements have driven him from his true course. Let us imitate this prudence and, before we float farther on the waves of this debate, refer to the point from which we departed, that we may at least be able to conjecture where we now are. I ask for the reading of the resolution before the Senate. . . .

This leads, Sir, to the real and wide difference in political opinion between the honorable gentleman and myself. On my part, I look upon all these objects [of federal policy] as connected with the common good, fairly embraced in its object and its terms; he, on the contrary, deems them all, if good at all, only local good. This is our difference. The interrogatory which he proceeded to put at once explains this difference. "What interest," asks he, "has South Carolina in a canal in Ohio?" Sir, this very question is full of significance. It develops the gentleman's whole political system; and its answer expounds mine. Here we differ. I look upon a road over the Alleghenies, a canal round the falls of the Ohio, or a canal or railway from the Atlantic to the Western waters, as being an object large and extensive enough to be fairly said to be for the common benefit. The gentleman thinks otherwise, and this is the key to his construction of the powers of the government. He may well ask what interest has South Carolina in a canal in Ohio. On his system, it is true, she has no interest. On that system, Ohio and Carolina are different governments, and different countries; connected here, it is true, by some slight and ill-defined bond of union, but in all main respects separate and diverse. On that system, Carolina has no more interest in a canal in Ohio than in Mexico. The gentleman, therefore, only follows out his own principles; he does no more than arrive at the natural conclusions of his own doctrines; he only announces the true results of that creed which he has adopted himself, and would persuade others to adopt, when he thus declares that South Carolina has no interest in a public work in Ohio.

Sir, we narrow-minded people of New England do not reason thus. Our *notion* of things is entirely different. We look upon the states, not as separated, but as united. We love to dwell on that union, and on the mutual happiness which it has so much promoted, and the common renown which it has so greatly contributed to acquire. In our contemplation, Carolina and Ohio are parts of the same country; states, united under the same general government, having interests, common, associated, intermingled. In whatever is within the proper sphere of the constitutional power of this government, we look upon the states as one. We do not impose geographical limits to our patriotic feeling or regard; we do not follow rivers and mountains, and lines of latitude, to find boundaries beyond which public improvements do not benefit us. We who come here, as representatives of these narrow-minded and selfish men of New England, consider ourselves as bound to regard with an equal eye the good of the whole, in whatever is within our powers of legislation. Sir, if a railroad or canal, beginning in South Carolina and ending in South Carolina, appeared to me of national importance and national magnitude, believing, as I do, that the power of government extends to works of that description, if I were to stand up here and ask, What interest has Massachusetts in a railroad in South Carolina? I should not be willing to face my constituents. These same narrow-minded men would tell me that they had sent me to act for the whole country, and that one who possessed too little comprehension, either of intellect or feeling, one who was not large enough, both in mind and in heart, to embrace the whole, was not fit to be entrusted with the interest of any part. . . .

This leads us to inquire into the origin of this government and the source of its power. Whose agent is it? Is it the creature of the state legislatures, or the creature of the people? If the government of the United States be the agent of the state governments, then they may control it, provided they can agree in the manner of controlling it; if it be the agent of the people, then the people alone can control it, restrain it, modify or reform it. It is observable enough, that the doctrine for which the honorable gentleman contends leads him to the necessity of maintaining, not only that this general government is the creature of the states, but that it is the creature of each of the states severally, so that each may assert the power for itself of determining whether it acts within the limits of its authority. It is the servant of four-and-twenty masters, of different wills and different purposes, and yet bound to obey all. This absurdity (for it seems no less) arises from a misconception as to the origin of this government and its true character. It is, Sir, the people's constitution, the people's government, made for the people, made by the people, and answerable to the people. The people of the United States have declared that this Constitution shall be the supreme law. We must either admit this proposition or dispute their authority. The states are, unquestionably, sovereign as far as their sovereignty is not affected by this supreme law. But the state legislatures, as political bodies, however sovereign, are yet not sovereign over the people. So far as the people have given power to the general government, so far the grant is unquestionably good, and the government holds of the people, and not of the state governments. We are all agents of the same supreme power, the people. The general government and the state governments derive their authority from the same source. . . .

If anything be found in the national constitution, either by original provision or subsequent interpretation, which ought not to be in it, the people know how to get rid of it. If any construction, unacceptable to them, be established, so as to become practically a part of the constitution, they will amend it, at their own sovereign pleasure. But while the people choose to maintain it as it is, while they are satisfied with it, and refuse to change it, who has given, or who can give, to the state legislatures a right to alter it, either by interference, construction, or otherwise? Gentlemen do not seem to recollect that the people have any power to do anything for themselves. They imagine there is no safety for them any longer than they are under the close guardianship of the state legislatures. Sir, the people have not trusted their safety, in regard to the general constitution, to these hands. They have required other security, and taken other bonds. They have chosen to trust themselves, first, to the plain words of the instrument, and to such construction as the government themselves, in doubtful cases, should put on their own powers, under their oaths of office, and subject to their responsibility to them; just as the people of a state trust their own state governments with a similar power. Secondly, they have reposed their trust in the efficacy of frequent elections, and in their own power to remove their own servants and agents whenever they see cause. Thirdly, they have reposed trust in the judicial power, which, in order that it might be trustworthy, they have made as respectable, as disinterested, and as independent as was practicable. Fourthly, they have seen fit to rely, in case of necessity, or high expediency, on their known and admitted power to alter or amend the constitution, peaceably and quietly, whenever experience shall point out defects or imperfections. And, finally, the people of the United States have at no time, in no way, directly or indirectly, authorized any state legislature to construe or interpret *their* high instrument of government; much less, to interfere, by their own power, to arrest its course and operation.

If, Sir, the people in these respects had done otherwise than they have done, their constitution could neither have been preserved, nor would it have been worth preserving. And if its plain provisions shall now be disregarded, and these new doctrines interpolated in it, it will become as feeble and helpless a being as its enemies, whether early or more recent, could possibly desire. It will exist in every state, but as a poor dependent on state permission. It must borrow leave to be; and will be, no longer than state pleasure, or state discretion, sees fit to grant the indulgence, and to prolong its poor existence.

But, Sir, although there are fears, there are hopes also. The people have preserved this, their own chosen constitution, for forty years, and have seen their happiness, prosperity, and renown grow with its growth, and strengthen with its strength. They are now, generally, strongly attached to it. Overthrown by direct assault, it cannot be; evaded, undermined, NULLIFIED, it will not be, if we, and those who shall succeed us here, as agents and representatives of the people, shall conscientiously and vigilantly discharge the two great branches of our public trust, faithfully to preserve, and wisely to administer it.

Mr. President, I have thus stated the reasons of my dissent to the doctrines which have been advanced and maintained. I am conscious of having detained you and the Senate much too long. I was drawn into the debate with no previous deliberation, such as is suited to the discussion of so grave and important a subject. But it is a subject of which my heart is full, and I have not been willing to suppress the utterance of its spontaneous sentiments. I cannot, even now, persuade myself to relinquish it, without expressing once more my deep conviction that, since it respects nothing less than the Union of the states, it is of most vital and essential importance to the public happiness. I profess, Sir, in my career hitherto, to have kept steadily in view the prosperity and honor of the whole country, and the preservation of our federal Union. It is to that Union we owe our safety at home, and our consideration and dignity abroad. It is to that Union that we are chiefly indebted for whatever makes us most proud of our country. That Union we reached only by the discipline of our virtues in the severe school of adversity. It had its origin in the necessities of disordered finance, prostrate commerce, and ruined credit. Under its benign influence, these great interests immediately awoke, as from the dead, and sprang forth with newness of life. Every year of its duration has teemed with fresh proofs of its utility and its blessings; and although our territory has stretched out wider and wider, and our population spread farther and farther, they have not outrun its protection or its benefits. It has been to us all a copious fountain of national, social, and personal happiness.

I have not allowed myself, Sir, to look beyond the Union, to see what might lie hidden in the dark recess behind. I have not coolly weighed the chances of preserving liberty when the bonds that unite us together shall be broken asunder. I have not accustomed myself to hang over the precipice of disunion, to see whether, with my short sight, I can fathom the depth of the abyss below; nor could I regard him as a safe counselor in the affairs of this government, whose thoughts should be mainly bent on considering, not how the Union may be best preserved, but how tolerable might be the condition of the people when it should be broken up and destroyed. While the Union lasts, we have high, exciting, gratifying prospects spread out before us, for us and our children. Beyond that I seek not to penetrate the veil. God grant that in my day, at least, that curtain may not rise! God grant that on my vision never may be opened what lies behind! When my eyes shall be turned to behold for the last time the sun in heaven, may I not see him shining on the broken and dishonored fragments of a once glorious Union; on states dissevered, discordant, belligerent; on a land rent with civil feuds, or drenched, it may be, in fraternal blood! Let their last feeble and lingering glance rather behold the gorgeous ensign of the republic, now known and honored throughout the earth, still full high advanced, its arms and trophies streaming in their original lustre, not a stripe erased or polluted, nor a single star obscured, bearing for its motto no such miserable interrogatory as "What is all this worth?" nor those other words of delusion and folly, "Liberty first and Union afterwards" but everywhere, spread all over in characters of living light, blazing on all its ample folds, as they float over the sea and over the land, and in every wind under the whole heavens, that other sentiment, dear to every true American heart, — Liberty *and* Union, now and for ever, one and inseparable!

EDWARD EVERETT

Edward Everett (1794–1865) was one of the most celebrated and influential American literary figures of the nineteenth century. In his long career he was a Unitarian pastor in Boston, professor of Greek at Harvard, editor of the *North American Review,* Governor of Massachusetts (1835–38), U.S. Minister to England (1840–45), and president of his alma mater, Harvard University (1846–49). He succeeded his friend and fellow Whig Daniel Webster as Secretary of State upon Webster's death in 1852. In 1853 he became a U.S. Senator from Massachusetts, and in 1860 he agreed to be nominated for Vice President on the ticket of the Constitutional Union party, whose presidential nominee was John Bell (the Constitutional Union party, in the tradition of Whigs like Clay and Webster, was more willing to compromise with the South in order to preserve the Union than was the Republican party, which drew on other ex-Whigs like Lincoln).

The reputation of the great Whig orator Edward Everett, like that of Daniel Webster, has shared in the eclipse of oratory as a genre. In his lifetime Everett was renowned both as a poet and as an orator; his speeches, like "The Circumstances Favorable to the Progress of Literature in America" (1824), were collected in *Orations and Speeches* (1859). If Everett is remembered at all today, it is as the speaker who delivered the main address at Gettysburg, following Lincoln's brief and immortal remarks. Some have sought to elevate Lincoln by denigrating Everett and his speech. Lincoln needs no such assistance. Everett's 1863 address at Gettysburg was a model of its kind, setting forth, with the amplification the genre required, the same democratic nationalist view of the Civil War that Lincoln encapsulated in his brief remarks on the same occasion. Everett's observations on "the bonds that unite us as one people" refute the claim of modern democratic universalists that midcentury American

Unionists like Lincoln and Everett conceived of the United States as an armed doctrine, rather than as a conventional nation-state corresponding to an ethnocultural nation residing in a particular homeland.

The Bonds That Unite Us

The bonds that unite us as one people—a substantial community of origin, language, belief, and law (the four great ties that hold the societies of men together); common national and political interests; a common history; a common pride in a glorious ancestry; a common interest in this great heritage of blessings; the very geographical features of the country; the mighty rivers that cross the lines of climate and thus facilitate the interchange of natural and industrial products, while the wonder-working arm of the engineer has leveled the mountain-walls which separate the East and West . . . these bonds of union are of perennial force and energy, while the causes of alienation are imaginary, factitious and transient.

FRANCIS LIEBER

Francis Lieber (1800–1872) belonged to a small but distinguished group of nineteenth-century German-American National Liberals, including the political economist Friedrich List, the U.S. general and Senator Carl Schurz, and (much later) the anthropologist Franz Boas, who infused German liberal nationalist ideas into American political and economic thought. Lieber was born in Germany and fought in the Napoleonic Wars. As a student, he was arrested as a subversive follower of the German liberal nationalist Friedrich Ludwig Jahn. After fighting and becoming disillusioned in the Greek war of independence in 1822, Lieber was arrested in Germany for his liberal activities again in 1824. He made his way to Britain, then in 1827 arrived in Boston, where he gained attention by creating the *Encyclopaedia Americana*. In 1835, he was appointed to the chair of history and political economy at South Carolina College (now the University of South Carolina). In that uncongenial environment he wrote *Manual of Political Ethics* (1838–39), *Legal and Political Hermeneutics* (1839) and *On Civil Liberty and Self-Government* (2 volumes, 1853). Lieber sought to develop an American democratic nationalist political philosophy to counteract the sophisticated states'-rights conservatism of South Carolina's brilliant conservative Senator John C. Calhoun, while at the same time avoiding the excesses of French Jacobinism and the kind of naïve radicalism he had encountered in revolutionary Greece. Lieber's combination of enthusiasm for national unity with praise, reminiscent of Edmund Burke's, for moderate "Anglican" or Anglo-American liberty (as opposed to "Gallican" or French radicalism) won him the praise of Hamiltonian Whigs including Henry Clay, Rufus Choate, and Chancellor Joseph Kent. Lieber also translated Toqueville (who was a friend and correspondent) and, during the Civil War, drew up a codification of the laws of war that was adopted by the U.S. military and by numerous other nations, including Bismarck's united Germany. In 1857 Lieber received an appointment at Columbia. He taught law at Columbia from 1865 until his death in 1872.

During the Civil War Lieber was an ardent partisan of the Union, advising President Lincoln and writing pro-Union pamphlets. He was not an armchair warrior; in his youth, he had nearly died as a result of wounds he received in the fighting that led up to Waterloo. Of his three sons, two fought for the Union, with one (appropriately named Hamilton) losing an arm in his country's cause. Another son, Oscar, who loved the South of his childhood, fought and died on the Southern side.

In "Nationalism: A Fragment of Political Science" (1868), Lieber tried to sum up decades of thinking about the relationship among nationalism, constitutional civil liberty, and democracy. Despite its awkward and pedantic style, this small essay is important for its attempt to view the formation and growing centralization of the American union as one example of a process occurring in Germany, Italy, and other regions where nations were throwing off outmoded imperial or confederal structures for modern—and modernizing—nation-states.

Nationalism

The National Polity is the normal type of Modern Government; Civil Liberty resting on Institutional Self-Government is the highest political calling of this period; Absolutism, whether Monarchical or Democratic, intelligent and brilliant or coarse, its pervading danger; and increasing International Neighborliness with growing Agreement of National Forms and Concepts, its fairest Gauge of the Spreading Progress of our Kind.

NORMAL TYPES OF GOVERNMENT. NATIONALIZATION

As the city-state was the normal type of free communities in antiquity, and as the feudal system must be considered as one of the normal types of government in the forbidding middle ages, so is the national polity the normal type of our own epoch—not indeed centralism.

The highest national polity yet developed is the representative national government, equally distant from the market-republic of old and the despotism of Asia and Europe, or absorbing centralism. Centralism may be intensely national, even bigottedly so; it may be intelligent, and formulated with precision; but centralism remains an inferior species of government, and decentralization becomes necessary as self-government or liberty are longed for and present themselves clearer to the mind of a people waxing in manliness and independence. Centralism may be national, but National Polity and Centralism are not equivalent terms. . . .

WHAT IS A NATION IN THE MODERN SENSE OF THE WORD?

The word Nation, in the fullest adaptation of the term, means, in modern times, a numerous and homogeneous population (having long emerged from the hunter's and nomadic state), permanently inhabiting and cultivating a coherent territory, with a well-defined geographic outline, and a name of its own—the inhabitants speaking their own language, having their own literature and common institutions, which distinguish them clearly from other and similar groups of people; being citizens or subjects of a unitary government, however subdivided it may be, and feeling an organic unity with one another, as well as being conscious of a common destiny. Organic intellectual, and political, internal unity, with proportionate strength, and a distinct and obvious demarcation from similar groups, are notable elements of the idea of a modern nation in its fullest sense. A nation is a nation only when there is but one nationality; and the attempt at establishing a nationality within a nationality is more inconsistent and mischievious even than the establishment of "an empire within an empire."

No groupings of human beings, short of nations, are adequate to the high demands of modern civilization. Without a national character, states cannot obtain that longevity and continuity of political society which is necessary for our progress. Even our patriotism has become pre-eminently national. Modern patriotism is not satisfied with the narrow bounds of a city, as of old, or the limits of a province, though it be the fairest. Nothing but a Country, that is the dwelling-place of a Nation, suffices for the *patria* of modern men. . . .

In the organic unity lies the difference between the terms *Nation* and *People*. People generally means the aggregate of the inhabitants of a territory. . . .

Extensive and organized political power over large populations does not suffice to make a nation. . . . Nor does common extraction and demarcating institutions, not even a peculiar religion, necessarily constitute a nation in the modern sense. . . . Nor does a common language alone constitute a nation. . . .

However striking a characteristic of a nation may be found in a separate language, and however important a separate name for a country or a nation may be, neither is absolutely necessary. We are an illustration. We have not our separate language; and more than two distinctly separate nations may speak the English tongue, before the Cis-Caucasian race passes into the twentieth century. Long before the American Independence was actually declared the consciousness of our forming a national identity was ripening. The Continental Congress used the words Country and America in its official acts—in resolutions and appointments—before that day of mark, the Fourth of July. The very name Continental Congress, continental army and money shows that the idea of a national unity was present to the minds of all—at home as well as abroad. Unfortunately no name had formed itself for our portion of the globe. No one can say in what bed our history would have coursed, had there been a distinct name for our country, and had Philadelphia become the national capital.[4] As it was, general names came to be used. Chatham and his contemporaries always used the name America; Washington was appointed to the command in order to defend and protect "American liberty," before the Declaration of Independence; but whether there was a distinct name or not, all felt that we were a nation. . . .

The nationality of our people and their government used to be strenuously denied by the adherents of what was called the States-Rights doctrine; probably it is still; not however because we have not our own language, nor, unfortunately, a distinct name for our country (not quite unlike the deficiency of the English language itself in not possessing a word for *Patrie* or *Vaterland*), but because they preferred provincialism to nationalism and clung to the effete form of government of a confederacy of petty sovereignties. They denied even that Congress was a government. . . .

POLITICAL CHARACTERISTICS OF OUR AGE

The three main characteristics of the political development which mark the modern epoch are:

The national polity;

The general endeavor to define more clearly, and to extend more widely, human rights and civil liberty (not unconnected as this movement is with the pervading critical spirit of the age, and the wedlock of Knowledge and Labor which marks the nineteenth century);

And the decree which has gone forth that many leading nations shall flourish at one and the same time, plainly distinguished from one another; yet striving together, with one public opinion, under the protection of one law of nations, and in the bonds of one common moving civilization.

---

4. Lieber was not the first to fret about the lack of a distinct name for the American nation; in the 1840s, a New York historical society had proposed that the U.S.A. be renamed "Alleghenia," after the mountain chain that, by linking North and South, symbolized national unity.

The universal monarchy. . . ; a single leading nation; confederacies of petty sovereigns; a civilization confined to one spot or portion of the globe—all these are obsolete ideas, wholly insufficient for the demands of advanced civilization, and attempts at their renewal have led and must lead to ruinous results, the end of all anachronisms recklessly pursued.

ABRAHAM LINCOLN

Unlike many of the figures in the Hamiltonian tradition of American democratic nationalism, Abraham Lincoln (1809–65) needs no introduction to contemporary readers. Indeed, Lincoln's assassination resulted in a cult which has lasted to the present day. Like most cults, the Lincoln cult robs its subject of his historically specific identity and turns him into an abstract symbol of ideas and values which he did not necessarily share.

For most Americans today, Lincoln as the Great Emancipator symbolizes civil rights, even though Lincoln subordinated the emancipation of the slaves to the restoration of the Union—and even though he favored the removal of black Americans, once freed, to colonies in the Caribbean or Central America. In addition to Lincoln the Great Emancipator, there is Lincoln the Mystical Unionist. This image is closer to the truth, but in the absence of an explanation of Lincoln's vision of American society his Unionism can seem to be obsessive, even sinister—as it does in the work of Edmund Wilson and Gore Vidal.

The real Lincoln was neither an unworldly proponent of a color-blind society nor a ruthless and half-mad Bismarckian statist; he was a conventional Whig-Republican, in the tradition of Clay, Webster, and ultimately Hamilton. Among his contemporaries, Lincoln was distinguished by his political skills and his intelligence, but he was original neither as a thinker nor as a policymaker (such originality is not part of the job description of great politicians). His task as President, as he saw it, was to save the Union and to help his fellow Republicans in the Cabinet and Congress enact the Hamiltonian economic agenda that had been thwarted for decades by states'-rights Southern Democrats. In both tasks, he succeeded.

Lincoln himself contributed to later misunderstandings by his rhetorical appropriation of the words and image of Thomas Jefferson in his antislavery and pro-Union speeches. There was not a single element of the Jeffersonian program—states' rights, agrarianism, strict construction of the federal constitution—that Lincoln, as a Whig and then as a Republican politician, did not reject with passion. Nevertheless, he realized that if the Republican party was to be more successful than the failed Whigs, it had to recruit Democratic voters in the West and the border South who idolized Thomas Jefferson and Andrew Jackson. Lincoln's solution was to turn Jeffersonian rhetoric against Jefferson's own Southern Democratic political heirs, by a kind of intellectual ju-jitsu. Lincoln's Jefferson was little more than the author of the Declaration of Independence, which itself was reduced to the phrase "all men are created equal." Although the nineteenth-century abolitionist movement arose from the moral fervor of Northern Protestants and had no significant roots at all in Jefferson's or Locke's secular natural-rights doctrines, Lincoln pretended that the antislavery movement was a natural development of Jefferson's Enlightenment belief in human equality. What is more, like a mathematician demonstrating a topological inversion, Lincoln turned the Declaration of Independence, a manifesto of secession, into a symbol of Unionism, arguing that the preservation of the Union was necessary to achieve the goal of the Declaration: equality. This was sophistry of the highest order. Thus did Lincoln, one of the most cunning debaters in American history, enlist Jeffersonian rhetoric for Hamiltonian ends. In a somewhat similar manner an equally clever politician, Franklin D. Roosevelt, would later claim to be in a supposed Jefferson–Lincoln tradition while presiding over an expansion of federal authority and American military power beyond Hamilton's wildest dreams. Indeed, it is common for politicians seeking to win votes from the rival party to claim the legacy of the rival party's heroes; Ronald Reagan and Newt Gingrich have frequently invoked the memories of FDR and John F. Kennedy to lend legitimacy to policies both Democratic Presidents would have abhorred.

Lincoln as a great but conventional Hamiltonian nationalist may be a less inspiring figure than the alternate "Lincolns," but the others are phantoms of the patriotic imagination. The genuine patron saint of civil rights in America is not Abraham Lincoln but Frederick Douglass, the prophet of American racial amalgamation and equality for women. Lincoln should be remembered as the Great Nationalist, the greatest of all of the American statesmen in the Hamiltonian tradition of democratic nationalism. Lincoln more than any other single individual saved the United States from disintegration and set it on the road to becoming the dominant industrial and military power of the twentieth century. Those were accomplishments enough for a human being, if not for a demigod.

Before saving the Union, Lincoln had frequently argued for it. His case for the Union combined the practical arguments made by Hamilton and Washington, the legal arguments of nationalist jurists like Marshall, and—perhaps most important—the sentimental, if not mystical, vision of the Union derived from Daniel Webster.

The Myth of State Sovereignty

From the President's Message to Congress in Special Session, July 4, 1861

Our States have neither more nor less power than that reserved to them in the Union by the Constitution—no one of them ever having been a State out of the Union. The original ones passed into the Union even before they cast off their British colonial dependence; and the new ones each came into the Union directly from a condition of dependence, excepting Texas. And even Texas, in its temporary independence, was never designated a State. The new ones only took the designation of States on coming into the union, while that name was first adopted for the old ones in and by the Declaration of Independence. Therein the "United Colonies" were declared to be "free and independent States;" but, even then, the object plainly was not to declare their independence of one another, or of the Union, but directly the contrary, as their mutual pledge, and their mutual action, before, at the time, and afterwards, abundantly show. The express plighting of faith by each and all of the original thirteen in the Articles of Confederation, two years later, that the Union shall be perpetual, is most conclusive. Having never been States, either in substance or in name, outside of the Union, whence this magical omnipotence of "State rights," asserting a claim of power to lawfully destroy the Union itself? Much is said about the "sovereignty" of the States; but the word, even, is not in the national Constitution; nor, as is believed, in any of the State constitutions. What is "sovereignty," in the political sense of the term? Would it be far wrong to define it "a political community, without a political superior"? Tested by this, no one of our States, except Texas, ever was a sovereignty. And even Texas gave up the character on coming into the Union; by which act she acknowledged the Constitution of the United States and the laws and treaties of the United States made in pursuance of the Constitution to be, for her, the supreme law of the land. The States have their status in the Union, and they have no other legal status. If they break from this, they can only do so against law and by revolution. The Union, and not themselves separately, procured their independence and their liberty. By conquest, or purchase, the Union gave each of them whatever of independence and liberty it has. The Union is older than any of the States; and, in fact, it created them as States. Originally some dependent colonies made the Union, and, in turn, the Union threw off their old dependence for them, and made them States, such as they are. Not one of them ever had a State constitution independent of the Union. Of course, it is not forgotten that all of the new States framed their constitutions before they entered the Union; nevertheless, dependent upon, and preparatory to, coming into the Union.

Unquestionably the States have the powers and rights reserved to them in and by the national Constitution; but among these, surely, are not included all conceivable powers, however mischievous or destructive; but, at most, such only as were known in the world, at the time, as governmental powers; and certainly a power to destroy the Government itself had never been known as a governmental—as a merely administrative power. This relative matter of national power and State rights, as a principle, is no other than the principle of generality and locality. Whatever concerns the whole should be confided to the whole—to the General Government; while whatever concerns only the State should be left exclusively to the State. This is all there is of original principle about it. Whether the National Constitution in defining boundaries between the two has applied the principle with exact accuracy, is not to be questioned. We are all bound by that defining, without question.

The Natural Frontiers of the American Nation-State

From the President's Annual Message to Congress, December 1, 1862

A nation may be said to consist of its territory, its people, and its laws. The territory is the only part of it which is of certain durability. "One generation passeth away and another generation cometh; but the earth abideth forever." It is of the first importance to duly consider, and estimate, this ever-enduring part. That portion of the earth's surface which is owned and inhabited by the people of the United States, is well adapted to be the home of one national family; and it is not well adapted for two, or more. Its vast extent, and its variety of climate and productions, are of advantage, in this age, for one people, whatever they might have been in former ages. Steam, telegraphs, and intelligence have brought these to an advantageous combination for one united people. . . .

There is no line, straight or crooked, suitable for a national boundary, upon which to divide. Trace through, from east to west, upon the line between the free and slave country, and we shall find a little more than one-third of its length are rivers, easy to be crossed, and populated, or soon to be populated, thickly upon both sides; while nearly all its remaining length are merely surveyor's lines, over which people may walk back and forth without any consciousness of their presence. No part of this line can be made any more difficult to pass, by writing it down on paper, or parchment, as a national boundary. . . .

But there is another difficulty. The great interior region, bounded east by the Alleghenies, north by the British dominions, west by the Rocky Mountains, and south by the line along which the culture of corn and cotton meet, and which includes part of Virginia, part of Tennessee, all of Kentucky, Ohio, Indiana, Michigan, Wisconsin, Illinois, Missouri, Kansas, Iowa, Minnesota, and the Territories of Dakota, Nebraska, and part of Colorado, already has above ten millions of people, and will have fifty millions within fifty years, if not prevented by any political folly or mistake. It contains more than one third of the country owned by the United States—certainly more than one million of square miles. Once half as populous as Massachusetts already is, it would have more than seventy-five millions of people. A glance at the map shows that, territorially speaking, it is the great body of the republic. The other parts are but marginal borders to it, the magnificent region sloping west from the Rocky Mountains to the Pacific, being the deepest and also the richest in undeveloped resources. In the production of provisions, grains, grasses, and all which proceed from them, this great interior region is naturally one of the most important in the world. Ascertain from the statistics the small proportion of the region which has, as yet, been brought into cultivation, and also the large and rapidly increasing amount of its products, and we shall be overwhelmed with the magnitude of the prospect presented. And yet this region has no sea-coast, touches no ocean anywhere. As part of one nation, its people now find, and may forever find, their way to Europe by New York, to South America and Africa by New Orleans, and to Asia by San Francisco. But separate our common country into two nations, as designated by the present rebellion, and every man of this great interior region is thereby cut off from some one or more of these outlets, not, perhaps, by a physical barrier, but by embarrassing and onerous trade regulations.

And this is true, wherever a dividing, or boundary line, may be fixed. Place it between the now free and slave country, or place it south of Kentucky, or north of Ohio, and still the truth remains, that none south of it, can trade to any port or place north of it, and none north of it, can trade to any port or place south of it, except upon terms dictated by a government foreign to them. These outlets, east, west, and south, are indispensable to the well-being of the people inhabiting, and to inhabit, this vast interior region. Which of the three may be the best, is no proper question. All, are better than either, and all, of right, belong to that people, and their successors forever. True to themselves, they will not ask where a line of separation shall be, but will vow, rather, that there shall be no such line. Nor are the marginal regions less interested in these communications to, and through them, to the great outside world. They, too, and each of them, must have access to this Egypt of the West, without paying toll at the crossing of any national boundary.

The Gettysburg Address

Address Delivered at the Dedication of the Cemetery at Gettysburg, November 19, 1863

In this, the most famous speech by an American political leader, the theory of American democratic nationalism worked out by Lincoln's predecessors, including Hamilton and Webster, is presented in a form as pure and memorable as a catechism. Attempts by later generations to read their own preoccupations into the Gettysburg Address should not be allowed to obscure what it is—the crystallization of the traditional Whig-Republican conception of the American nation-state.[5]

Four score and seven years ago our fathers brought forth on this continent, a new nation, conceived in Liberty, and dedicated to the proposition that all men are created equal.

Now we are engaged in a great civil war, testing whether that nation, or any nation so conceived and so dedicated, can long endure. We are met on a great battle-field of that war. We have come to dedicate a portion of that field, as a final resting place for those who here gave their lives that that nation might live. It is altogether fitting and proper that we should do this.

---

5. An example of this misconception is found in Garry Wills's *Lincoln at Gettysburg: The Words That Remade America* (1992), in which Wills claims that Lincoln used the speech to "effect an intellectual revolution." Curiously, nobody present at the occasion, including Lincoln's secretary and future biographer John Hay, noticed the "intellectual revolution."

But, in a larger sense, we can not dedicate—we can not consecrate—we can not hallow—this ground. The brave men, living and dead, who struggled here, have consecrated it, far above our poor power to add or detract. The world will little note, nor long remember what we say here, but it can never forget what they did here. It is for us the living, rather, to be dedicated here to the unfinished work which they who fought here have thus far so nobly advanced. It is rather for us to be here dedicated to the great task remaining before us—that from these honored dead we take increased devotion to that cause for which they gave the last full measure of devotion—that we here highly resolve that these dead shall not have died in vain—that this nation, under God, shall have a new birth of freedom—and that government of the people, by the people, for the people, shall not perish from the earth.

PART FOUR

THE COMMON DEFENSE

The phrase "the national interest" sums up the complex of ideas animating the foreign policies preferred by Alexander Hamilton and his successors in the nineteenth and twentieth centuries. A myth has grown up that Hamiltonianism is the tradition of the American business elite. It is more accurate to say that it is the tradition of the American officer corps. The two greatest American philosopher-statesmen of this school—Alexander Hamilton and Theodore Roosevelt—were not only military officers but military intellectuals, careful students of the history of war and power politics who were obsessed with marshaling the resources of the American nation in the service of American national security. Hamilton the immigrant orphan and TR the patrician shared a contempt for the business class, viewing financial and industrial elites at best as co-opted agents of national policy. The *Primat der Aussenpolitik,* or primacy of foreign policy, in their political thought links American Hamiltonians with certain Continental and East Asian counterparts, even as it alienates them from fellow Americans who think little of world politics and envision domestic politics chiefly as the stage for individual self-fulfillment, or as an arena for moral debates over slavery, prohibition, or sexual mores. Like European realists, American Hamiltonians have stressed the inevitability of conflict among states and nations and the necessity of a powerful military as the *ultima ratio regnum.* Neighboring countries, Hamilton believed, are "natural enemies"; the "true interest" of a state may be obscured by popular passions or foreign corruption; Americans, "as well as the other inhabitants of the globe, are yet remote from the happy empire of perfect wisdom and perfect virtue"—in expressing these sentiments, which his admirers and successors would endorse, Hamilton sounded no different from European theorists of *raison d'état* and the balance of power.

Unlike some European theorists, however, Americans in the Hamiltonian realist tradition have never seen military might or expansion as goals in themselves. What is more, American strategists (in common with their British and Dutch precursors) have placed great emphasis on commerce and international law. Hamiltonian democratic nationalists have differed from Jeffersonian democratic localists and Wilsonian democratic globalists in viewing commerce and law not as panaceas that will eliminate the need for national power in an era of "interdependence" but as public goods made possible by the possession of a preponderance of power by the United States, acting alone or in concert with other "civilized nations" (as Theodore Roosevelt and Henry Cabot Lodge would have put it). Still, most Americans in the Hamiltonian foreign policy tradition would not dismiss trade and law with contempt, after the manner of the more militaristic of European practitioners of *Machtpolitik*.

The Jeffersonian vision of the American republic completely inverts the priorities of the Hamiltonians. Whereas Hamilton and his successors have tried to create an American republic capable of holding its own if not achieving hegemonic leadership in the unstable realm of world politics, Jefferson and his disciples have tended to reason their way from abstract principles to the ideal constitution of society and then, as an afterthought, pondered the sort of world order in which such a utopia could exist—if, that is, they thought of foreign policy at all. From the eighteenth to the twentieth century, Jeffersonians conceived of the United States as a kind of early-modern Switzerland on a continental scale—a decentralized agrarian republic, with a racially and culturally homogeneous population in which class differences were minimal chiefly because the majority of Americans would be family farmers. This ideal republic would be free of the repressive institutions of the premodern European state, like a monarchy and an established church, and free as well of the expensive and coercive institutions of modern European and Asian states, like central government bureaucracies, standing armies, general staffs, secret police, and espionage agencies. Most decisions would be made at the state and local levels, by citizen-legislators, and security against crime and invasion would be provided by citizen militias. By keeping government limited and by blurring the distinction between the political elite and the citizenry with devices like frequent elections and citizen-armies, Jeffersonians hoped to prevent the emergence of a despotic, uncontrollable state—an ambition that even the most ardent Hamiltonians must concede to be legitimate, given the atrocities perpetrated by modern tyrannies.

In its classical form, Jeffersonian democratic localism assumes that the United States will not face domestic upheavals or foreign threats that cannot be dealt with by the constabulary or the militia. To admit the need for defending the nation against foreign enemies by means of a massive, permanent military establishment, financed by federal taxes that are collected by a central bureaucracy, is to surrender to Hamiltonian nationalists on the central point of the debate. To this objection Jeffersonians have provided two answers. The first—the proposition that the geographic isolation of the continental United States from Old World conflicts makes an American national security apparatus unnecessary—was never credible, inasmuch as the oceans did not prevent Britain from warring on American soil during the Napoleonic Wars or prevent German submarines during World War I from threatening the American coastline. (In the age of ballistic missiles, the point is moot.) A second answer is provided by a policy of neutrality—if the United States shuns alliances with other powers and acts as a neutral in world politics, then it will avoid antagonizing possible enemies. In the Jeffersonian view, whether American isolation is the providential product of geography or follows from a conscious policy of geopolitical neutrality, or both, the result will be the same: the absence of a need for a massive military and diplomatic establishment and intelligence agencies that absorb taxes and threaten individual liberty.

The disagreement between the two great American traditions can be summed up thus: Hamiltonians are more afraid of the world than of their own government, while Jeffersonians are more afraid of their own government than of the world.

From the early years of the United States, national-interest realists have had to struggle to present their strategic programs in terms palatable to the majority of American citizens, whose political culture is permeated by a Jeffersonian hostility to military establishments and to policies reminiscent of allegedly devious and unprincipled "Old World" diplomacy and imperialism. Whenever possible, American statesmen have clothed realist policies in idealist rhetoric. For example, FDR camouflaged his geopolitical conceptions during World War II, speaking in public about "the United Nations" and "the Four Freedoms," while musing off the record about a postwar concert of four great powers, with their own spheres of influence—the United States, the Soviet Union, Britain, and Nationalist China. In somewhat the same manner, Frederick the Great, that arch-Machiavellian, wrote and published a treatise denouncing Machiavelli. Theodore Roosevelt was probably the last President who could speak more or less honestly about what he was doing in foreign affairs. His successors have treated the American people as naïve idealists, sometimes effectively (as during the Gulf War, when President George Bush declared that Iraq's dictator Saddam Hussein was "worse than Hitler") and sometimes disastrously (as during the Vietnam War, when a succession of presidents failed to explain adequately to an increasingly skeptical public the geopolitical reasons for U.S. intervention in Southeast Asia—reasons that were actually quite plausible, in a realist perspective).

To the anthologist, this divergence between the reality of American foreign policy and the rhetoric employed to obtain public support for it presents a dilemma. American elected leaders tend to defend their policies in terms of noble-sounding pabulum (FDR's "Four Freedoms," which no one can ever quite remember), while elite appointees and lifelong public servants tend not to engage in public debate or tend to echo their political masters. The best analyses of American strategy from a realist perspective are usually penned by journalists or academics, who need not fear the censure of the public or the press or, for that matter, the displeasure of foreign governments. This fact, and not their actual influence on the making of U.S. foreign policy, is responsible for the prominence given in the section that follows to journalists like Herbert Croly, Walter Lippmann, James Chace, and Fareed Zakaria. Paul H. Nitze and Samuel P. Huntington are among the rare figures who have both served in government at high levels and written intelligently about foreign policy, though Nitze has been primarily a public servant and Huntington is best known as a scholar. In an ideal world, policymakers would be acquainted with useful scholarship, and scholars could bring experience of government service to their formulation of theories about world politics. To hope for such a union, or at least association, of practice and theory is to push Hamiltonian realism as close to utopianism as it can go.

GEORGE WASHINGTON

President George Washington's 1796 Farewell Address, drafted by Hamilton, contains one of the earliest expositions of American national-interest realism. No single strategy could serve the United States in all its successive permutations. The strategy of neutrality and isolation that President George Washington favored in the late 1790s was prudent when the United States was a weak republic threatened by the turmoil of the Napoleonic wars; a similar strategy of neutrality and isolation would have been a disastrous mistake in the twentieth century, when only American military power was capable of preventing German or Soviet hegemony in Eurasia and perhaps the world. Isolationists in the twentieth century have invoked the Farewell Address as authority for the proposition that the United States should stay out of wars in Europe (and, by extension, in Asia). Such an interpretation ignores the fact that Washington was advocating only a short-term strategy to ensure that the United States did not risk destruction at the hands of Britain by entering the wars of the French Revolution as an ally of France. Washington himself foresees that the United States, if it avoids dismemberment in war and disintegration in civil war, "at no great distant period" will be a "great nation." At that point Americans will be able "to choose peace or war, as our interest, guided by justice, shall counsel."

Our Interest

Observe good faith and justice towards all nations; cultivate peace and harmony with all; religion and morality enjoin this conduct; and can it be that good policy does not equally enjoin it? It will be worthy of a free, enlightened,

and, at no great distant period, a great nation, to give to mankind the mag-
nanimous, and too novel, example of a people always guided by an exalted
justice and benevolence. Who can doubt that in the course of time and things,
the fruits of such a plan would richly repay any temporary advantages which
might be lost by a steady adherence to it? Can it be that Providence has not
connected the permanent felicity of a nation with its virtue? The experiment,
at least, is recommended by every sentiment which ennobles human nature.
Alas! It is rendered impossible by its vices!

In the execution of such a plan, nothing is more essential than that permanent, inveterate antipathies against particular nations, and passionate attachments for others, should be excluded; and that, in place of them, just and
amicable feelings towards all should be cultivated. The nation which indulges
towards another an habitual hatred, or an habitual fondness, is in some degree
a slave; it is a slave to its animosity or to its affection, either of which is sufficient to lead it astray from its duty and its interest. Antipathy in one nation
against another disposes each more readily to offer insult and injury, to lay hold
of slight causes of umbrage, and to be haughty and intractible when accidental
or trifling occasions of dispute occur. Hence frequent collisions, obstinate, en-
venomed, and bloody contests. The nation prompted by ill-will and resentment sometimes impels to war the government, contrary to the best
calculations of policy. The government sometimes participates in the national
propensity, and adopts through passion what reason would reject; at other
times it makes the animosity of the nation subservient to projects of hostility,
instigated by pride, ambition, and other sinister and pernicious motives; —the
peace often, sometimes, perhaps, the liberty of nations, has been the victim.

So, likewise, a passionate attachment of one nation for another produces a
variety of evils. Sympathy for the favorite nation, facilitating the infusion of
an imaginary common interest, in cases where no real common interest exists,
and infusing into one the enmities of the other, betrays the former into a participation in the quarrels and wars of the latter, without adequate inducement
or justification. It leads also to concessions to the favorite nation of privileges
denied to others, which is apt doubly to injure the nation making the concessions, by unnecessarily parting with what ought to have been retained, and by
exciting jealousy, ill-will, and a disposition to retaliate, in the parties from
whom equal privileges are withheld; and it gives to ambitious, corrupted, or
deluded citizens, who devote themselves to the favorite nation, facility to be-
tray or sacrifice the interests of their own country, without odium, sometimes
even with popularity; gilding with the appearances of a virtuous sense of
obligation, a commendable deference for public opinion, or a laudable zeal

for public good, the base or foolish compliances of ambition, corruption, or infatuation.

As the avenues to foreign influence in innumerable ways, such attachments are particularly alarming to the truly enlightened and independent patriot. How many opportunities do they afford to tamper with domestic factions, — to practice the arts of seduction, —to mislead public opinion, —to influence or awe the public councils? Such an attachment of a small or weak, towards a great or powerful, nation, dooms the former to be the satellite of the latter.

Against the insidious wiles of foreign influence (I conjure you to believe me, fellow citizens) the jealousy of a free people ought to be constantly awake, since history and experience prove that foreign influence is one of the most baneful foes of a republican government. But that jealousy, to be useful, must be impartial, else it becomes the instrument of the very influence to be avoided, instead of a defence against it. Excessive partiality for one foreign nation, and excessive dislike of another, cause those whom they actuate to see danger only on one side, and serve to veil and even second the arts of influence on the other. Real patriots, who may resist the intrigues of the favorite, are liable to become suspected and odious, while its tools and dupes usurp the applause and confidence of the people, to surrender their interests.

The great rule of conduct for us, in regard to foreign nations, is in extending our commercial relations to have with them as little *political* connection as possible. So far as we have already formed engagements, let them be fulfilled with perfect good faith. —Here let us stop.

Europe has a set of primary interests, which to us have none, or a very remote relation. Hence she must be engaged in frequent controversies, the causes of which are essentially foreign to our concerns. Hence, therefore, it must be unwise in us to implicate ourselves by artificial ties in the ordinary vicissitudes of her politics, or the ordinary combinations and collisions of her friendships or enmities.

Our detached and distant situation invites and enables us to pursue a different course. If we remain one people, under an efficient government, the period is not far off when we may defy material injury from external annoyance; when we may take such an attitude as will cause the neutrality, we may at any time resolve upon, to be scrupulously respected; when belligerent nations, under the impossibility of making acquisitions upon us, will not lightly hazard the giving us provocation; when we may choose peace or war, as our interest, guided by justice, shall counsel.

SAMUEL P. HUNTINGTON

The Federalist party—the first in the series of American Hamiltonian parties that includes the Whigs and nineteenth-century Republicans—is unique among American parties in that foreign policy played a great, perhaps central, role in its formation and demise. Many of the Federalists like Washington and his principal aide Hamilton were former Continental Army line officers who wanted a stronger, more centralized Union in order to check threats in North America from European great powers like Britain and France. During the Wars of the French Revolution, foreign policy issues eclipsed others in the debates between Hamiltonian Federalists, who believed that the American national interest would best be served if Britain checked France, and Jeffersonian Republicans, who allowed their enthusiasm for the French Revolution to blind them to the dangers that a continental Europe consolidated under French control might pose to the Western Hemisphere.

Two crises undermined the Federalist party and helped to turn control of the United States over to Jeffersonians based in the South and West for half a century, beginning with Jefferson's election in 1800. The first crisis was a power struggle within the Federalist party between Alexander Hamilton and President John Adams. In 1798, as part of its war with Britain, France declared it would seize neutral vessels containing British products—a category that included most American merchant ships. In response to this "quasi-war" with France, Hamilton proposed that the United States outfit a navy and raise an army, which, in the event of all-out war with France, could invade and sieze Florida and Louisiana (then controlled by France's satellite, Spain). Anticipating the later Monroe Doctrine (which was also based on U.S.–British cooperation in the Western Hemisphere), Hamilton even suggested an alliance between the United States and Britain to liberate South America from Spain, thus depriving France of Latin American resources. George Washington came out of retirement to serve as the commander of the projected army, but only on condition that his favorite adviser, Hamilton, be given the key position of inspector general and the rank of major general. In practice, this made Hamilton the acting head of the army, precisely the outcome that President Adams had sought to avoid by enlisting Washington. Adams, a weak and resentful individual who knew that Hamilton was considered the guiding force in his own party, reversed course in 1799 by appeasing France. (Not until the late 1960s, when the opportunistic Robert Kennedy, hoping to replace Lyndon Johnson as President and leader of the Democratic party, metamorphosed from an anticommunist hawk into an antiwar dove, would strategy be sacrificed to personal ambition and resentment in so blatant a manner.)

The Federalist party, crippled by Adams's jealousy of Hamilton, ultimately expired as a result of Federalist opposition to the War of 1812. On purely geopolitical grounds the Federalists were right both to oppose the U.S. entry into the Napoleonic Wars on the side of France, which would have been a greater threat to U.S. security, had it triumphed, than Britain. However, the New England Federalists were not content to criticize the logic of the war; there was talk of New England's secession from the Union by a number of prominent New England Federalists, who met at the infamous Hartford Convention in 1814. This identified the Federalist party in the mind of most Americans as a party of New England traitors, and the party quickly collapsed. That debacle foreshadowed the pattern in later American history, when isolationist New Englanders, opposing a major war, paid the price by seeing their party rejected by a majority of Americans after the war. Just as Federalist opposition to the War of 1812 discredited the Federalist party, so Whig opposition to the Mexican War was one of the factors that led to that party's disappearance, and the opposition of the dominant New England and Northern Democrats to the Vietnam War and the Cold War after 1968 contributed to the collapse of the Democratic party into minority status. In other words, the inbred antimilitary sentiments of New Englanders and New England descendants in the Northern tier of states have undermined a succession of Hamiltonian parties based in those regions. It is probably no coincidence that the leaders in the Hamiltonian tradition who have been most at ease with the use of force on behalf of the national interest have come from regions outside of the North, like Hamilton himself, a native of the Caribbean island of St. Kitts; George Washington, a Virginian; Henry Clay, a Kentuckian; and Abraham

Lincoln, a native of Kentucky. (Even the New Yorker Theodore Roosevelt and his predecessor, the Midwesterner William McKinley, were attacked as warmongers from within their native North.)

During the brief years of its ascendancy from 1789 to 1800, before the machinations of John Adams and the antiwar ethos of New England marginalized it, the Federalist party under Hamilton's leadership promoted a far-sighted program for national military preparedness. In his classic history of civil-military relations in the United States, *The Soldier and the State* (1957), excerpted here, Samuel P. Huntington describes the different approaches of Hamilton and Jefferson to national security.

The Federalists

The failure of military professionalism to make institutional headway in the United States was . . . intimately connected with the failure of Federalism. The Federalists were almost classically conservative; their basic values closely resembled those of the military ethic. Responsible for the preservation of American security during the difficult first years, they had the conservative's interest in military affairs. "Hamilton's hobby was the Army," wrote John Adams, and the second president himself averred that national defense "has always been near to my heart." They stressed the need for military force and the primacy of national defense among the functions of government. The Federalists did not condemn nor eschew power politics; they played the game with some enjoyment and considerable finesse. Washington's Farewell Address advice that the nation should be strong enough and sensible enough so that it could "choose peace or war as our interest guided by justice shall counsel" even reflected the professional military concept of war as the rational instrument of state policy.

If Federalist conservatism had maintained its vitality as an intellectual current and political force into the nineteenth century, it would have been a fertile source of military professionalism. Instead, the Federalists disappeared before the science of war and the military profession became functionally feasible in America. . . .

Like other liberals, Jefferson had little interest in or use for regular military forces, and he had no recognition of the emerging character of professional military officership. Jefferson had no use for objective civilian control, condemning the distinction "between the civil and military, which it is for the happiness of both to obliterate." Unlike most subsequent liberals, however, he did have a definite plan for national defense. Jefferson did not scout the continuing threats to the United States nor the persistent possibility of war. His military policy had its roots in the same unstable state of international relations as did Hamilton's. But in substance it was vastly different, representing an effort to develop a liberal alternative to the Hamiltonian program which would embody the extreme of transmutation based on the "military sovereignty of the people." Far from wishing to disarm the United States, Jefferson desired to turn the nation into an armed camp. "None but an armed nation can dispense with a standing army; to keep ours armed and disciplined is, therefore, at all times important . . ." The militia should be universal in scope—"every citizen is a soldier" is a Jeffersonian motto—and well-organized, classified, disciplined, and equipped. In the end, Jefferson's military policy was no more successful than Hamilton's. To universalize the military obligation was in effect to abolish it. Instead of substituting a liberal force for a regular force, Congress preferred to limit the regular force to an inconsequential size. Extirpation triumphed over transmutation. . . .

The most notable and lasting manifestation of the Jeffersonian impact upon American militarism was in the military academy at West Point. Hamilton's recommendations of 1799 had proposed the creation of five schools: a Fundamental School in which students received instruction for two years in "all the sciences necessary to a perfect knowledge of the different branches of the military art"; and four advanced engineering and artillery, cavalry, infantry, and naval schools, to one of which students would go for specialized study after completing the fundamental courses. This would have been a true professional academy teaching the essence of military science as a whole as well as elements of its more specialized branches. In contrast, the institution which Jefferson established at West Point in 1802 was only one-fifth of the military university urged by Hamilton. It was created almost incidental to the creation of the Corps of Engineers. Its principal object was to produce engineers for military and civil employment. . . .

Thus, before the Civil War West Point was deficient in the two components of a preliminary professional military education. It did not give its students a broad grounding in the liberal arts; neither did it furnish them with the first essentials of military science.

Between the end of the Napoleonic Wars in 1815 and the end of the nineteenth century, the United States devoted itself to continental expansion. Revolts of American settlers in Spanish Florida and Mexican Texas led to the acquisition of those territories. Texas, kept out of the Union by the North for a decade because it proposed to enter as a slave state, was an independent—and bankrupt—republic from 1836 to 1845. The admission of Texas led to war with Mexico, which had never relinquished its claim. The defeat of Mexico by the United States in the Mexican War (1846–48) led to the annexation of California and the Southwest, for which the United States indemnified the Mexican government. The Whigs, the Hamiltonian party of the era, opposed further territorial expansion for fear that it would expand the region of slavery and add allies for the Southern planter oligarchy in national politics. Lincoln denounced President Polk's conduct of the war with Mexico with his famous "spot of blood" speech, in which he accused Polk of instigating the war unjustly. Lincoln and other Whig opponents of the war were wrong on the facts, and had Lincoln died in the 1850s he would be remembered, if at all, as the author of a rather unscrupulous example of partisan propaganda.

The extraordinary expansion in area of the United States took place in a period when the regular military was starved of funds and viewed with suspicion by Jeffersonian Democrats. The weakness of the federal armed forces may have contributed to the calculation of the Southern elite that the South could make good its secession from the Union in 1860–61. Had Hamilton succeeded in establishing a strong, permanent federal military establishment, Southern secession might have been nipped in the bud by a show of overwhelming force like that with which Washington and Hamilton had greeted the abortive Whiskey Rebellion of 1794.

The success of the federal armies during the Civil War seems to have led to a reversal of the way that some former Whigs in the Republican party viewed expansion. William Henry Seward, who served as Secretary of State under Lincoln, Johnson, and Grant, believed that the United States should annex not only a number of Caribbean and Pacific islands, but Canada and Mexico as well. He even speculated that Mexico City, because of its location, would be the ideal capital of the expanded United States of America. Seward had to settle for purchasing Alaska from Russia for seven million dollars (the Russians preferred that the United States take over Alaska to keep the territory out of the hands of their rival, the British Empire). Seward and those who shared his dreams of American imperial expansion were thwarted by anti-expansionists in the Senate, led by Massachusetts Senator Charles Sumner. The opposition to expansion reflected the deeply ingrained hostility of New England's moralistic subculture to foreign war and entanglement (New Englanders led the opposition to the Spanish-American and Philippine wars). Anti-expansionism also reflected the fear on the part of many white American leaders that expansion would lead to U.S. citizenship for Caribbean blacks, Latin American mestizos and Indians, and Pacific islanders. Had the United States been less racist in the nineteenth century, it might have been larger in the twentieth.

Although Seward's generation of great-power expansionists was thwarted in its ambitions, it cleared the way for the generation of Theodore Roosevelt. In the following excerpt from *The Soldier and the State* (1957), Samuel P. Huntington describes a small but influential elite at the turn of the century whom he labels "Neo-Hamiltonians."

The Neo-Hamiltonians

From roughly 1890 (the publication of *The Influence of Sea Power upon History, 1660–1783*) to 1920 (the rejection of Leonard Wood by the Republican National Convention), a group of statesmen and publicists and a school of thought existed in America which might be labeled Neo-Hamiltonian. The outstanding individuals in this group were Theodore Roosevelt, Henry Cabot Lodge, Elihu Root, Albert J. Beveridge, A. T. Mahan, Herbert Croly, Leonard Wood, Henry Adams, and Brooks Adams. The common bond among these diverse personalities was an outlook on politics which transcended the usual American categories. The Neo-Hamiltonians did not fall into the liberal tradition of Jefferson, Jackson, [Herbert] Spencer, and Wilson. Yet neither were they completely conservative, in the sense in which Calhoun was conservative. On economic issues, they bridged the gap from the reforming tendencies of Croly and the *New Republic* group to the staunch standpatism of Elihu Root. More significantly, the Neo-Hamiltonians also combined elements of military and civilian thinking. They were in fact the first important American social group whose political philosophy more or less consciously borrowed and incorporated elements of the professional military ethic. . . .

The civilian expressions of the Neo-Hamiltonian ethic—the writings and speeches of Theodore Roosevelt, the philosophizing of the Adamses, the policies of Elihu Root, the editorials of the pro-war *New Republic*—reveal a peculiar amalgam of liberal–conservative values. Neo-Hamiltonianism differed from liberalism and resembled the professional military viewpoint in its appreciation of the role of power in human affairs. Like the military and unlike the liberals, the Neo-Hamiltonians saw international politics as basically a struggle among independent nations with interests which not infrequently brought them into conflict with each other. Contrary to the optimistic doctrines of business pacifism, they held to the military view that war was far from obsolete. Also, like the military and unlike the liberals, the Neo-Hamiltonians argued that national policy must primarily reflect not abstract ideals but a realistic understanding of the national interest. This was the first responsibility of the statesmen [sic]. So long as nations exist, force is the ultimate arbiter. Consequently, nations must maintain adequate armaments to back up their national policies, the nature of national policy determining the size and nature of the forces required. The Neo-Hamiltonians shared with the military an essentially Clausewitzian view of the relations of policy and force. They supported the military in their efforts to build up the nation's defenses. They were more willing than most Americans to accept the military profession. Herbert Croly's *New Republic* in 1915 could pour a withering scorn at the liberal illusions of Bryan and Carnegie that a citizen army, springing to arms overnight, was sufficient for the nation's defense. Along with the military, the Neo-Hamiltonians rejected plutocracy and were bitter in their contempt for the prevailing commercialism, materialism, and the values inherent in an economically oriented way of life. They shared with the military a stress on loyalty, duty, responsibility, and subordination of the self to the requirements of the nation. Brooks Adams even went so far as to suggest openly that America would do well to substitute the values of West Point for the values of Wall Street.

EMORY UPTON

Emory Upton (1839–81) was a brilliant military intellectual as well as a great American soldier. A graduate of West Point, Upton rose rapidly in the Federal armies during the Civil War. In the 1870s Upton and two deputies toured Europe and Asia. The recommendations in the report that grew out of their study were ignored by Congress; Upton later published the report at his own expense. Assigned to command the Presidio of San Francisco, Upton, for reasons that remain obscure, committed suicide at the age of forty-one.

The following excerpt is from "The Military Policy of the United States," a manuscript completed in 1880 but not published until 1904, after Upton's death, with an introduction by then Secretary of War Elihu Root, who had rediscovered it. In the essay Upton, like other Hamiltonians, argues that the Jeffersonian traditions of reliance on citizen militias and inadequate funding for defense end up costing the United States both treasure and blood. Of greatest interest is his attempt to refute the deeply rooted American belief that a strong military and a liberal republic are incompatible.

Delusions About Defense

Shortly after the disastrous battle of Camden, Washington wrote to the President of Congress "what we need is a good army, not a large one." Unfortunately for the country, the object sought by this assertion, so thoroughly in harmony with our cherished institutions, has only been partially attained in time of peace.

In view of the growth of our neighbors, the vast extent of our territory, and the rapid increase of our floating population, the time must speedily arrive when all intelligent and law-abiding people will accept, and adhere to, the opinion of John Adams that "the National defense is one of the cardinal duties of a statesman."

Our military policy, or, as many would affirm, our want of it, has now been tested during more than a century. It has been tried in foreign, domestic, and Indian wars, and while military men, from painful experience, are united as to its defects and dangers, our final success in each conflict has so blinded the popular mind, as to induce the belief that as a nation we are invincible. . . .

Whether we may be willing to admit it or not, in the conduct of war, we have rejected the practice of the European nations and with little variation have thus far pursued the policy of China . . . .

Up to this time in our history our military policy has been largely shaped by the Anglo-Saxon prejudice against "standing armies as a dangerous menace to liberty." . . .

The same prejudice has led our people to another false conclusion. If standing armies are dangerous to liberty, then it ought to follow that officers of the army should be inimical to republican institutions. But here again, if the lessons of history be read and accepted, it will be admitted that of all forms of government the republican, or democratic, is most favorable to the soldier. There is not a well-read officer in our service who does not know that monarchy sets a limit to military ambition, while in republics military fame is frequently rewarded with the highest civic honors.

The history of Rome, Greece, and Carthage affords abundant support for this statement, while, on the other hand, that of England shows that of all her great heroes Cromwell alone, in the days of the Commonwealth, stepped from the head of the army to the head of the state. After the restoration, Marlborough and Wellington received titles and estates, but those were bestowed by the Crown instead of the people.

In France, Turenne and Condé added the luster of their achievements to the glory of the King, but the wars of the Revolution filled Europe with the fame of republican generals, Napoleon at their head. When through popular favor he became First Consul and finally rose to supreme power he gave rank and titles to his generals, but the fame of his marshals was merged in the glory of the Emperor. He knew how to exalt and how to abase; he could tolerate no rival; a line in the Moniteur could at any time make or destroy the reputation of a marshal.

In our day Bismarck planned the political unity of Germany, while Von Moltke alone made it possible by destroying in two campaigns the military power of Austria and France.

Had Germany been a republic both would have risen to the chief magistracy of the state, but under a monarchy they had to content themselves with fame, titles and estates, and the patronizing favor of a kind-hearted Emperor.

The French, on the contrary, after establishing a republic, elevated to the presidency the marshal who surrendered the Imperial army at Sedan.

Our own people, no less than the Romans, are fond of rewarding our military heroes. The Revolution made Washington President for two terms; the war of 1812 elevated Jackson and Harrison to the same office, the first for two terms, the latter for one; the Mexican war raised Taylor and Pierce to the Presidency, each for one term; the rebellion has already made Grant President for two terms, Hayes for one term, while the present Chief Magistrate, Garfield, owes his high office as much to his fame as a soldier as to his reputation as a statesman.

Long wars do not reward the highest commanders only. After the Revolution Knox, Dearborn, and Armstrong rose to the office of Secretary of War; Hamilton was Secretary of the Treasury; while Monroe, first Secretary of State, was finally elected President for two terms. During the Rebellion [i.e., the Civil War—Ed.] nearly 150 regular officers rose to the grade of brigadier and major general who, but for the four years' struggle, would have been unknown outside of the military profession.

Since the war, distinguished officers of volunteers have filled nearly every office in the gift of the people. They have been elected chief magistrates of their States, and today on both floors of Congress they are conspicuous alike for their numbers and influence. . . .

Foreign governments, surrounded by powerful neighbors, act on the theory that military commanders can be educated, no less than captains and lieutenants. The same theory is true of statesmen. A general does not so much regard the causes of war; his duty is to be familiar with military history and to know the details and principles upon which successful war is conducted.

The statesman, on the contrary, should study peace and the causes which tend to preserve or destroy it. History will teach him that peace ends in war and war again ends in peace. If the causes which terminate peace and produce war cannot be removed, and if the legislator does not recognize and know how to create a powerful army, he ceases to be a statesman. . . .

Again, our remoteness from powerful nations has led to another delusion—that we shall forever be free from foreign invasion. Within the present year (1880) a Senator of the United States, standing on the parapet of Fort Monroe and witnessing the firing of worthless smoothbore artillery, assured the author that we would not have another war in a century. No statesman would have made such a prediction. He would have recalled the Revolution, the War of 1812, and the Mexican War. He would have pointed to the British possessions on the north, to Mexico on the west, and Spain on the south; he would not have forgotten the affair of the *Virginius* and the frequent complications on the Rio Grande as proof that at any moment we may be plunged into another foreign war. He would, furthermore, have condemned the useless ordnance before him, and would have declared that wisdom and economy demand that we should be ready for any war whenever and wherever it may occur. . . .

The author is well aware that in suggesting this system he will be accused of favoring centralization and strong government. This is a charge which he would neither covet nor deny. No soldier in battle ever witnessed the flight of an undisciplined army without wishing for a strong government, but a government no stronger than was designed by the fathers of the Republic.

Founded in the affections of the people, the Constitution in time of danger gives Congress absolute power to raise and support armies and to lay its hands upon every man and every dollar within the territory of the nation.

Recognizing, moreover, that the individual life is to be sacrificed to the life of a state, the same Constitution permits the suspension of the writ of habeas corpus, giving to Congress and to the President power not only over life and property, but over the liberty of every citizen of the Republic. It is a popular delusion that armies make wars; the fact is wars inevitably make armies. No matter what the form of government, war, at the discretion of the rulers, means absolute despotism, the danger from which increases as the war is prolonged. Armies in time of peace have seldom if ever overthrown their governments, but in time of anarchy and war the people have often sought to dictate, and purchase peace at the expense of their liberty. If we would escape this danger we should make war with a strong arm. No foreign invader should ever be allowed a foothold on our soil. Recognizing, too, that under popular institutions the majority of the people create the government and that the majority will never revolt, it should be our policy to suppress every riot and stamp out every insurrection before it swells to rebellion. This means a strong government, but shall we find greater safety in one that is weaker? . . .

If in time of rebellion our own Government grew more despotic as it grew stronger, it is not to be inferred that there is any necessary connections between despotism and military strength.

Twenty thousand regular troops at Bull Run would have routed the insurgents, settled the question of military resistance, and relieved us from the pain and suspense of four years of war.

China, the most despotic of Governments, has no military strength; numbering 400,000,000 people, she has been twice conquered by a few despised

Tartars, and only a few years ago 20,000 English and French dictated peace at the walls of the capital. In Persia the Shah can lop off the heads of his subjects or wall them up alive at his pleasure, and yet it has been said that a single foreign battalion could overthrow his throne, while a brigade would starve in his dominions. . . .

Our forefathers hated Great Britain because she repeatedly subverted the government of the colonies. A large portion of their descendants, confusing states rights with state sovereignty, look upon the General Government as equally hostile to the States. When this feeling is abandoned; when it is understood that the life of the State is bound up in the life of the nation; when it is appreciated that republicanism, State and national, guaranteed by the Constitution, is the natural bulwark against the two forms of despotism—absolute monarchy on the one side and absolute democracy on the other—then, and not till then, will the views of the author be accepted.

ALFRED THAYER MAHAN

Another eminent Neo-Hamiltonian at the turn of the twentieth century was Alfred Thayer Mahan (1840–1914). Mahan was born at West Point, the son of a professor of engineering. After graduating from the U.S. Naval Academy in 1859, Mahan served in the U.S. Navy during and after the Civil War. In 1885 he became a lecturer in tactics and naval history at the new War College in Newport. His lectures, published as *The Influence of Sea Power Upon History, 1660–1783* (1890), made him an international celebrity in an era of great-power naval competition. A section from these lectures appears below. Kaiser Wilhelm declared that he was "devouring" Mahan's works, and Mahan dined with the Queen and the Prime Minister during a visit to Britain. As one might expect, Mahan's fame created a lot of animosity among his fellow naval officers. He retired from the navy in 1896, only to emerge to advise the government during the war with Spain. Many of Mahan's recommendations—including the acquisition of colonies that could serve as coaling stations for steam-powered warships—were adopted during and after the Spanish–American War, which ended with the acquisition by the United States of an extensive Caribbean and Pacific maritime empire, including the Philippines, which were subdued only after one of the most brutal and perhaps least justifiable wars that the United States has fought. (It should be noted that, had the United States not acquired the Philippines, the islands would almost certainly have come under British, German, or Japanese domination.)

Sea Power

If time be, as is everywhere admitted, a supreme factor in war, it behooves countries whose genius is essentially not military, whose people, like all free people, object to pay for large military establishments, to see to it that they are at least strong enough to gain the time necessary to turn the spirit and capacity of their subjects into the new activities which war calls for. If the existing force by land or sea is strong enough to hold out, even though at a disadvantage, the country may rely upon its natural resources and strength coming into play for whatever they are worth—its numbers, its wealth, its capacities of every kind. If, on the other hand, what force it has can be overthrown and crushed quickly, the most magnificent possibilities of natural power will not save it from humiliating conditions, nor, if its foe be wise, from guarantees which will postpone revenge to a distant future. The story is constantly repeated on the smaller fields of war: "If so-and-so can hold out a little longer, this can be saved or that can be done"; as in sickness it is often said: "If the patient can only hold out so long, the strength of his constitution may pull him through."

England to some extent is now such a country. Holland was such a country; she would not pay, and if she escaped, it was but by the skin of her teeth. . . .

That our own country is open to such a reproach is patent to all the world. The United States has not that shield of defensive power behind which time can be gained to develop its reserve of strength. As for a seafaring population adequate to her possible needs, where is it? Such a resource, proportionate to her coast-line and population, is to be found only in a national merchant shipping and its related industries, which at present scarcely exist. . . .

To turn now from the particular lessons drawn from the history of the past to the general question of the influence of government upon the sea career of its people, it is seen that that influence can work in two distinct but closely related ways.

First, in peace: The government by its policy can favor the natural growth of a people's industries and its tendencies to seek adventure and gain by way of the sea; or it can try to develop such industries and such sea-going bent, when they do not naturally exist; or, on the other hand, the government may by mistaken action, check and fetter the progress which the people left to themselves would make. In any one of these ways the influence of the government will be felt, making or marring the sea power of the country in the matter of peaceful commerce; upon which alone, it cannot be too often insisted, a thoroughly strong navy can be based.

Secondly, for war: The influence of the government will be felt in its most legitimate manner in maintaining an armed navy, of a size commensurate with the growth of its shipping and the importance of the interests connected with it. More important even than the size of the navy is the question of its intentions, favoring a healthful spirit and activity, and providing for rapid development in time of war by an adequate reserve of men and of ships and by measures for drawing out that general reserve power which has before been pointed to, when considering the character and pursuits of the people. Undoubtedly under this second head of war-like preparation must come the maintenance of suitable naval stations, in those distant parts of the world to which the armed shipping must follow the peaceful vessels of commerce. The protection of such stations must depend either upon direct military force, as do Gibraltar and Malta, or upon a surrounding friendly population, such as the American colonists once were to England, and, it may be presumed, the Australian colonists now are. Such friendly surroundings and backing, joined to a reasonable military provision, are the best of defenses, and when combined with decided preponderance at sea, make a scattered and extensive empire, like that of England, secure; for, while it is true that an unexpected attack may cause disaster in some one quarter, the actual superiority of naval power prevents such disaster from being general or irremediable. History has sufficiently proved this. England's naval bases have been in all parts of the world; and her fleets have at once protected them, kept open the communications between them, and relied upon them for shelter. . . .

As the practical object of this inquiry is to draw from the lessons of history inferences applicable to one's own country and service, it is proper now to ask how far the conditions of the United States involve serious danger, and call for action on the part of the government, in order to build again her sea power. It will not be too much to say that the action of the government since the Civil War, and up to this day, has been effectively directed solely to what has been called the first link in the chain which makes sea power. Internal development, great production, with the accompanying aim and boast of self-sufficingness, such has been the object, such to some extent the result. In this the government has faithfully reflected the bent of the controlling elements of the citizenry, though it is not always easy to feel that such controlling elements are truly representative, even in a free country. However that may be, there is no doubt that, besides having no colonies, the intermediate link of a peaceful shipping, and the interests involved in it, are now lacking. In short, the United States has only one link of the three.

The question is eminently one in which the influence of the government should make itself felt, to build up for the nation a navy which, if not capable of reaching distant countries, shall at least be able to keep clear the chief approaches to its own.

HERBERT CROLY

In *The Promise of American Life* (1909), from which a section appears here, Herbert Croly devoted most of his attention to arguing for a more expansive conception of the national government in domestic affairs. As the excerpts that follow show, however, the leading intellectual of the Progressive movement believed that an assertive foreign policy based on the national interest was the natural corollary of "democratic Hamiltonianism" at home.

During World War I Croly, having pinned his hopes on Woodrow Wilson rather than TR, was swept up by Wilson's utopianism and then bitterly disappointed by the "victors' justice" of the Treaty of Versailles. Unlike more realistic Progressives such as TR and Lodge, Croly and the *New Republic* circle had hoped that World War I would be followed by a new order based on international cooperation and social justice, not a continuation of old-fashioned spheres of influence and alliances. Describing Croly's reaction to the triumph of power politics over principle, John Judis writes: "For three days, Croly remained in seclusion, pacing the floor, but on the fourth, he directed the editorial meeting at which the magazine's editors decided unanimously to come out fighting against Wilson and the treaty."[1]

Nationalism and Militarism

One of the most difficult and (be it admitted) one of the most dubious problems raised by any attempt to establish a constructive relationship between

---

1. John Judis, *Grand Illusion: Critics and Champions of the American Century* (New York: Farrar, Straus & Giroux, 1992), p. 24.

these two principles [of nationality and democracy] hangs on the fact that hitherto national development has not apparently made for international peace. The nations of Europe are to all appearances as belligerent as were the former European dynastic states. Europe has become a vast camp, and its governments are spending probably a larger proportion of the resources of their countries for military and naval purposes than did those of the eighteenth century. How can these warlike preparations, in which all the European nations share, and the warlike spirit which they have occasionally displayed, be reconciled with the existence of any constructive relationship between the national and the democratic idea?

The question can best be answered by briefly reviewing the claims already advanced on behalf of the national principle. I have asserted from the start that the national principle was wholly different in origin and somewhat different in meaning from the principle of democracy. What has been claimed for nationality is, not that it can be identified with democracy, but that as a political principle it remained unsatisfied without an infusion of democracy. But the extent to which this infusion can go and the forms which it takes are determined by a logic and a necessity very different from that of an absolute democratic theory. National politics have from the start aimed primarily at efficiency—that is, at the successful use of the force resident in the state to accomplish the purposes desired by the Sovereign authority. . . . A national polity . . . always remains an organization based upon force. In internal affairs it depends at bottom for its success not merely upon public opinion, but, if necessary, upon the strong arm. It is a matter of government and coercion as well as a matter of influence and persuasion. So in its external relations its standing and success have depended, and still depend, upon the efficient use of force, just in so far as force is demanded by its own situation and the attitudes of its neighbors and rivals. The democrats who disparage efficient national organization are at bottom merely seeking to exorcise the power of physical force in human affairs by the use of pious incantations and heavenly words. That they will never do. . . .

War may be and has been a useful and justifiable engine of national policy. It is justifiable, moreover, not merely in such a case as our Civil War, in which a people fought for their own national integrity. It was, I believe, justifiable in the case of the two wars which preceded the formation of the modern German Empire. These wars may, indeed, be considered as decisive instances. Prussia did not drift into them, as we drifted into the Civil War. They were deliberately provoked by Bismarck at a favorable moment, because they were necessary to the unification of the German people under Prussian leadership; and I do not hesitate to say that he can be justified in the assumption of this enormous responsibility. The German national organization means increased security, happiness, and opportunity of development for the whole German people; and inasmuch as the selfish interests of Austria and France blocked the path, Bismarck had his sufficient warrant for a deliberately planned attack. . . . The unification of Germany and Italy has not only helped to liberate the energies of both the German and the Italian people, but it has made the political divisions of Europe conform much more nearly to the lines within which the people of Europe can loyally and fruitfully associate one with another. In fact, the whole national movement, if it has increased the preparations for war, has diminished the probable causes thereof; and it is only by diminishing the number of causes whereby a nation had more to gain from victory than it has to lose by defeat that war among the civilized powers can be gradually extinguished. . . .

A genuinely national policy must, of course, be based upon a correct understanding of the national interest in relation to those of its neighbors and associates. That American policy did obtain such a foundation during the early years of American history is to be traced to the sound political judgment of Washington and Hamilton. Jefferson and the Republicans did their best for a while to persuade the American democracy to follow the dangerous course of the French democracy, and to base its international policy not upon the firm ground of national interest, but on the treacherous sands of international democratic propagandism. After a period of hesitation, the American people, with their usual good sense in the face of a practical emergency, rallied to the principles subsequently contained in Washington's Farewell Address, and the Jeffersonian Republicans, when they came into control of the Federal government, took over this conception of American national policy together with the rest of the Federalist outlook. But like the rest of the Federalist organization and ideas, the national foreign policy was emasculated by the expression it received at the hands of the Republicans. The conduct of American foreign affairs during the first fifteen years of the century are an illustration of the ills which may befall a democracy during a critical international period, when its foreign policy is managed by a party of anti-national patriots. . . .

Hitherto, the American preference and desire for peace has constituted the chief justification for its isolation. At some future time, the same purpose, just in so far as it is sincere and rational, may demand intervention. The American responsibility in this respect is similar to that of any peace-preferring European Power. If it wants peace, it must be spiritually and physically prepared to fight for it. Peace will prevail in international relations, just as order prevails within a nation, because of the righteous use of superior force—because the power which makes for pacific organization is stronger than the power which makes for a warlike organization. It looks as if at some future time the power of the United States might well be sufficient, when thrown into the balance, to tip the scale in favor of a comparatively pacific settlement of international complications. Under such conditions a policy of neutrality would be a policy of irresponsibility and unwisdom.

THEODORE ROOSEVELT

Theodore Roosevelt attempted to put neo-Hamiltonian precepts into practice during his presidency (1901–1909). His achievements in foreign policy were dwarfed by those successors like FDR and Truman who led the United States during global conflicts. Still, by mediating a European dispute in Morocco as well as the end of the Russo-Japanese war (an accomplishment that earned him the Nobel Peace Prize in 1905), TR performed an important service in showing not just the world but the American public that the United States had emerged as a great power with interests worldwide.

In foreign policy, as in domestic policy, Theodore Roosevelt was the major link between the old Hamiltonianism of nineteenth-century Whigs and Republicans like Clay, Webster, and Lincoln, and the "democratic Hamiltonians" of the twentieth century: the Progressives, New Deal liberals, and Cold War liberals. Despite TR's modernity, his acceptance and indeed enjoyment of power, both national and personal, make him seem somewhat alien to elite Americans at the end of the twentieth century, who are used to seeing national self-assertion clothed in pious abstractions, and who have been trained to consider unapologetic patriotism a vulgar attribute of the uneducated working class. The faint of heart should exercise caution, in reading the following extracts from TR on foreign policy.

The Strenuous Life

From *The Strenuous Life*, 1900

I preach to you, then, my countrymen, that our country calls not for the life of ease but for the life of strenuous endeavor. The twentieth century looms before us big with the fate of many nations. If we stand idly by, if we seek merely swollen, slothful ease and ignoble peace, if we shrink from the hard contests where men must win at hazard of their lives and at the risk of all they hold dear, then the bolder and stronger peoples will pass us by, and will win for themselves the domination of the world. Let us therefore boldly face the life of strife, resolute to do our duty well and manfully; resolute to uphold righteousness by deed and by word; resolute to be both honest and brave, to serve high ideals, yet to use practical methods. Above all, let us shrink from no strife, moral or physical, within or without the nation, provided we are certain that the strife is justified, for it is only through strife, through hard and dangerous endeavor, that we shall ultimately win the goal of true national greatness.

The Big Stick

From "Speech at the Minnesota State Fair," September 2, 1901

Right here let me make as vigorous a plea as I know how in favor of saying nothing that we do not mean, and of acting without hesitation up to whatever we say. A good many of you are probably acquainted with the old proverb: "Speak softly and carry a big stick—you will go far." If a man continually blusters, if he lacks civility, a big stick will not save him from trouble; and neither will speaking softly avail, if back of the softness there does not lie strength, power. In private life there are few beings more obnoxious than the man who is always loudly boasting; and if the boaster is not prepared to back up his words his position becomes absolutely contemptible. So it is with the nation. It is both foolish and undignified to indulge in undue self-glorification, and, above all, in loose-tongued denunciation of other peoples. Whenever on any point we come in contact with a foreign power, I hope that we shall always strive to speak courteously and respectfully of that foreign power. Let us make it evident that we intend to do justice. Then let us make it equally evident that we will not tolerate injustice being done to us in return. Let us further make it evident that we use no words which we are not prepared to back up with deeds, and that while our speech is always moderate, we are ready and willing to make it good. Such an attitude will be the surest possible guarantee of that self-respecting peace, the attainment of which is and must ever be the prime aim of a self-governing people.

The Peace of Righteousness

From *America and the World War,* 1915

In 1864 there were in the North some hundreds of thousands of men who praised peace as the supreme good, as a good more important than all other goods, and who denounced war as the worst of all evils. These men one and all assailed and denounced Abraham Lincoln, and all voted against him for president. Moreover, at that time there were many individuals in England and France who said it was the duty of those two nations to mediate between the North and the South, so as to stop the terrible loss of life and destruction of property which attended our Civil War; and they asserted that any Americans who in such event refused to accept their mediation and to stop the war would thereby show themselves the enemies of peace. Nevertheless, Abraham Lincoln and the men back of him by their attitude prevented all such effort at mediation, declaring that they would regard it as an unfriendly act to the United States. Looking back from a distance of fifty years, we can now see clearly that Abraham Lincoln and his supporters were right. Such mediation would have been a hostile act, not only to the United States but to humanity. The men who clamored for unrighteous peace fifty years ago this fall were the enemies of mankind.

These facts should be pondered by the well-meaning men who always clamor for peace without regard to whether peace brings justice or injustice. Very many of the men and women who are at times misled into demanding peace, as if it were itself an end instead of being a means of righteousness, are men of good intelligence and sound heart who only need seriously to consider the facts, and who can then be trusted to think aright and act aright. There is, however, an element of a certain numerical importance among our people, including the members of the ultrapacifist group, who by their teachings do some real, although limited, mischief. They are a feeble folk, these ultrapacifists, morally and physically; but in a country where voice and vote are alike free, they may, if their teachings are not disregarded, create a condition of things where the crop they have sowed in folly and weakness will be reaped with blood and bitter tears by the brave men and high-hearted women of the nation.

The folly preached by some of these individuals is somewhat startling, and if it were translated from words into deeds it would constitute a crime against the nation. One professed teacher of morality made the plea in so many words that we ought to follow the example of China and deprive ourselves of all power to repel foreign attack. Surely this writer must have possessed the exceedingly small amount of information necessary in order to know that nearly half of China was under foreign dominion and that while he was writing the Germans and Japanese were battling on Chinese territory and domineering as conquerors over the Chinese in that territory. Think of the abject soul of a man capable of holding up to the admiration of free-born American citizens such a condition of serfage under alien rule!

Nor is the folly confined only to the male sex. A number of women teachers in Chicago are credited with having proposed, in view of the war, hereafter to prohibit in the teaching of history any reference to war and battles. Intellectually, of course, such persons show themselves unfit to be retained as teachers a single day, and indeed unfit to be pupils in any school more advanced than a kindergarten. But it is not their intellectual, it is also their moral shortcomings which are striking. The suppression of the truth is, of course, as grave an offense against morals as is the suggestion of the false or even the lie direct; and these teachers actually propose to teach untruths to their pupils.

True teachers of history must tell the facts of history; and if they do not tell the facts both about the wars that were righteous and the wars that were unrighteous, and about the causes that led to these wars and to success or defeat in them, they show themselves morally unfit to train the minds of boys and girls. If in addition to telling the facts they draw the lessons that should be drawn from the facts, they will give their pupils a horror of all wars that are entered into wantonly or with levity or in a spirit of mere brutal aggression or save under dire necessity. But they will also teach that among the noblest deeds of mankind are those that have been done in great wars for liberty, in wars of self-defense, in wars for the relief of oppressed peoples, in wars for putting an end to wrongdoing in the dark places of the globe.

Any teachers, in school or college, who occupied the position that these foolish, foolish teachers have sought to take, would be forever estopped from so much as mentioning Washington and Lincoln; because their lives are forever associated with great wars for righteousness. These teachers would be forever estopped from so much as mentioning the shining names of Marathon and Salamis. They would seek to blind their pupils' eyes to the glory held in the deeds and deaths of Joan of Arc, of Andreas Hofer, of Alfred the Great, of Arnold von Winkelried, of Kosciusko and Rakoczy. They would be obliged to warn their pupils against ever reading Schiller's "William Tell" or the poetry of Koerner. Such men are deaf to the lament running: "Oh, why, Patrick Sarsfield, did we let your ships sail/Across the dark waters from green Innisfail?"

To them Holmes's ballad of Bunker Hill and Whittier's "Laus Deo," MacMaster's "Ode to the Old Continentals" and O'Hara's "Bivouac of the Dead" are meaningless. Their cold and timid hearts are not stirred by the surge of the tremendous "Battle Hymn of the Republic." On them lessons of careers like those of Timoleon and John Hampden are lost; in their eyes the lofty self-abnegation of Robert Lee and Stonewall Jackson was folly; their dull senses do not thrill to the deathless deaths of the men who died at Thermopylae and at the Alamo—the fight of those grim Texans of which it was truthfully said that Thermopylae had its messengers of death but the Alamo had none.

It has actually been proposed by some of these shivering apostles of the gospel of national abjectness that, in view of the destruction that has fallen on certain peaceful powers of Europe, we should abandon all efforts at self-defense, should stop building battle-ships, and cease to take any measures to defend ourselves if attacked. It is difficult to seriously consider such a proposition. It is precisely and exactly as if the inhabitants of a village in whose neighborhood highway robberies had occurred should propose to meet the crisis by depriving the local policeman of his revolver and club.

There are, however, many high-minded people who do not agree with these extremists, but who nevertheless need to be enlightened as to the actual facts. These good people, who are busy people and not able to devote much time to thoughts about international affairs, are often confused by men whose business is to know better. For example, a few weeks ago these good people were stirred to a moment's belief that something had been accomplished by the enactment of Washington of a score or two of all-inclusive arbitration treaties; being not unnaturally misled by the fact that those responsible for the passage of the treaties indulged in some not wholly harmless bleating as to the good effects they would produce. As a matter of fact, they *probably* will not produce the smallest effect of any kind or sort. Yet it is *possible* they may have a mischievous effect, inasmuch as under certain circumstances to fulfill them would cause frightful disaster to the United States, while to break them, even although under compulsion and because it was absolutely necessary, would be fruitful of keen humiliation to every right-thinking man who is jealous of our international good name.

If, for example, whatever the outcome of the present war, a great tri-umphant military despotism declared that it would not recognize the Monroe Doctrine or seized Magdalena Bay, or one of the Dutch West Indies, or the Island of St. Thomas, and fortified it; or if—as would be quite possible—it announced that we had no right to fortify the Isthmus of Panama, and itself landed on adjacent territory to erect similar fortifications; then, under these absurd treaties, we would be obliged, if we happened to have made one of them with one of the countries involved, to go into an interminable discussion of the subject before a joint commission, while the hostile nation proceeded to make its position impregnable. It seems incredible that the United States government could have made such treaties; but it has just done so, with the warm approval of the professional pacifists.

These treaties were entered into when the administration had before its eyes at that very moment the examples of Belgium and Luxembourg, which showed beyond possibility of doubt, especially when taken in connection with other similar incidents that have occurred during the last couple of decades, that there are various great military empires in the Old World who will pay not one moment's heed to the most solemn and binding treaty, if it is to their interest to break it. If any one of these empires, as a result of the present contest, obtains something approaching to a position of complete predominance in the Old World, it is absolutely certain that it would pay no heed whatever to these treaties, if it desired to better its position in the New World by taking possession of the Dutch or Danish West Indies or of the territory of some weak American state on the mainland of the continent. In such event we would be obliged either instantly ourselves to repudiate the scandalous treaties by which the government at Washington has just sought to tie our hands—and thereby expose ourselves in our turn to the charge of bad faith—or else we should have to abdicate our position as a great power and submit to abject humiliation. . . .

We must insist on righteousness first and foremost. We must strive for peace always; but we must never hesitate to put righteousness above peace. In order to do this, we must put force back of righteousness, for, as the world now is, national righteousness without force back of it speedily becomes a matter of derision. To the doctrine that might makes right, it is utterly useless to oppose the doctrine of right unbacked by might.

It is not even true that what the pacifists desire is right. The leaders of the pacifists of this country who for five months now have been crying "Peace, peace" have been too timid even to say that they want the peace to be a righteous one. We needlessly dignify such outcries when we speak of them as well-meaning. The weaklings who raise their shrill piping for a peace that shall consecrate successful wrong occupy a position quite as immoral as and infinitely more contemptible than the position of the wrongdoers themselves. The ruthless strength of the great absolutist leaders—Elizabeth of England, Catherine of Russia, Peter the Great, Frederick the Great, Napoleon, Bismarck—is certainly infinitely better for their own nations and is probably better for mankind at large than the loquacious impotence, ultimately trouble-breeding, which has recently marked our own international policy. A policy of blood and iron is sometimes very wicked; but it rarely does as much harm, and never excites as much derision, as a policy of milk and water—and it comes dangerously near flattery to call the foreign policy of the United States under President Wilson and Mr. Bryan merely one of milk and water. Strength at least commands respect; whereas the prattling feebleness that dares not rebuke any concrete wrong, and whose proposals for right are marked by sheer fatuity, is fit only to excite weeping among angels and among men the bitter laughter of scorn. . . .

What befell Antwerp and Brussels will surely some day befall New York or San Francisco, and may happen to many an inland city also, if we do not shake off our supine folly, if we trust for safety to peace treaties unbacked by force. At the beginning of last month, by the appointment of the president, peace services were held in the churches of this land. As far as these services consisted of sermons and prayers of good and wise people who wished peace only it if represented righteousness, who did not desire that peace should come unless it came to consecrate justice and not wrongdoing, good and not evil, the movement represented good. Insofar, however, as the movement was understood to be one for immediate peace without any regard to righteousness or justice, without any regard for righting the wrongs of those who have been crushed by unmerited disaster, then the movement represented mischief, precisely as fifty years ago, in 1864, in our own country a similar movement for peace, to be obtained by acknowledgment of disunion and by the perpetuation of slavery, would have represented mischief. In the present case, however, the mischief was confined purely to those taking part in the movement in an unworthy spirit; for (like the peace parades and newspaper peace petitions) it was a merely subjective phenomenon; it had not the slightest effect of any kind, sort, or description upon any of the combatants abroad and could not possibly have any effect upon them. It is well for our own sakes that we should pray sincerely and humbly for the peace of righteousness; but we must guard ourselves from any illusion as to the news of our having thus prayed producing the least effect upon those engaged in the war.

There is just one way in which to meet the upholders of the doctrine that might makes right. To do so we must prove that right will make might, by backing right with might.

In his second inaugural address Andrew Jackson laid down the rule by which every national American administration ought to guide itself, saying: "The foreign policy adopted by our government is to do justice to all, and to submit to wrong by none."

The statement of the dauntless old fighter of New Orleans is as true now as when he wrote it. We must stand absolutely for righteousness. But to do so is utterly without avail unless we possess the strength and the loftiness of spirit which will back righteousness with deeds and not mere words. We must clear the rubbish from off our souls and admit that everything that has been done in passing peace treaties, arbitration treaties, neutrality treaties, Hague treaties, and the like, with no sanction of force behind them, amounts to literally and absolutely zero, to literally and absolutely nothing, in a time of serious crisis. We must recognize that to enter into foolish treaties that cannot be kept is as wicked as to break treaties which can and ought to be kept. We must labor for an international agreement among the great civilized nations which shall put the full force of all of them back of any one of them, and of any well-behaved weak nation, which is wronged by any other power. Until we have completed this purpose, we must keep ourselves ready, high of heart and undaunted of soul, to back our rights with our strength.

HENRY CABOT LODGE

The major rivals of Hamiltonian national-interest realism in the twentieth century have been Jeffersonian isolationism and Wilsonian globalism, the philosophy behind collective security. Collective security, the Wilsonian answer to the dilemmas of preserving a decentralized republic in a world of centralized power-states, is not as much a contradiction of Jeffersonian isolationism as one might suppose. Isolationists seek to stay out of global power politics; collective-security enthusiasts hope to replace power politics with world law under the aegis of the League of Nations or the United Nations. Either option would spare the United States the necessity of acting as a conventional great power with a strong central government and a military-industrial complex, and permit the American republic to remain, or become again, a decentralized democracy under minimal government. During his campaign for ratification of the League of Nations treaty, Wilson claimed that only by participating in a global collective-security pact could the United States be spared the necessity of maintaining a large and intrusive national security apparatus. A Wilsonian world order would provide the conditions in which the Jeffersonian utopia could be realized.

One of the most brilliant and effective critics of Wilsonian idealism was Massachusetts Senator Henry Cabot Lodge (1850–1924). A great-grandson of a leading Federalist, George Cabot, Lodge was taught at Harvard by the historian and philosopher Henry Adams (himself the descendant of two presidents, John Adams and John Quincy Adams). Obtaining a law degree from Harvard, Lodge soon abandoned the practice of law and resumed his education, receiving the first Ph.D. in political science from Harvard. He assisted Henry Adams in editing the *North American Review,* and wrote biographies of great Americans in the Federalist–Whig–Republican nationalist tradition: *Alexander Hamilton*

161

(1882), *Daniel Webster* (1882), and *George Washington* (1888). Following his heroes into politics, Lodge was elected to the Massachusetts House, then in 1886 won a seat in the U.S. Congress. His first cause was championship of the "Force Bill," a precursor of Lyndon Johnson's Voting Rights Act, which sought to provide federal supervision of elections to enable black Southerners to vote. He also collaborated with his friend Theodore Roosevelt on civil service reform. From 1893 until his death, he was a U.S. Senator from Massachusetts. He brought his expertise in international history and politics to bear as chairman of the Foreign Affairs Committee.

During and after World War II, Lodge was caricatured by Democratic propagandists as a narrow-minded provincial who abused his chairmanship of the Senate Foreign Relations Committee to block the passage of President Woodrow Wilson's League of Nations Treaty. Lodge's perfidy was held responsible not only for Wilson's collapse from a stroke while engaging in a frantic cross-country whistle-stop train campaign to mobilize public support for U.S. membership in the League, but even for the outbreak of World War II, which, it was said, would not have occurred had the League of Nations stopped Hitler and Japan. That was nonsense, of course. The British and the French, members of the League, did nothing when Nazi Germany, Fascist Italy, and Imperial Japan began their campaigns of aggressive expansion. If the democratic powers that were directly threatened by the Axis powers hesitated to act, it is doubtful that the United States, with its isolationist traditions and a majority determined to avoid intervention in another European war, would have supported preemptive wars in Europe and Asia. As it happened, Japan had to sink the U.S. Pacific fleet and Hitler had to declare war gratuitously on the United States before FDR finally was able to mobilize public support for all-out American intervention in World War II.

Lodge would have supported the League of Nations treaty if Wilson had acquiesced to his insistence that it be passed with reservations permitting the United States to decide whether to intervene in a particular war authorized by the League. Wilson's refusal to accept that commonsense revision doomed the treaty. During World War II, designers of the United Nations learned from Wilson's mistake by conditioning the participation of member states on observance of their own constitutional processes.

That reservation, and the built-in great-power concert that is the Security Council, with its five permanent members, made the United Nations closer than the League of Nations to Lodge's idea of an international organization. Still, it cannot be said that the success of the United Nations after 1945 proves that the League might have worked, because the United Nations has not been a success. The Security Council was deadlocked throughout the Cold War by U.S.–Soviet hostility. The majority of Third World countries in the General Assembly devoted themselves for decades to denouncing the United States, Israel, and the industrialized nations in general. For a few years after the Cold War, the Security Council acted as an echo chamber for the United States, but increasing Chinese hostility to the United States may renew the deadlock in that body.

Lodge's doubts about the effectiveness of a truly international body, then, have been vindicated. Lodge was no isolationist; he was an internationalist, but one whose internationalism was based on a realistic sense of power politics. Like Theodore Roosevelt, Lodge rejected the idea of collective security enforced by a world organization in favor of the notion of an alliance of "civilized nations" (the United States and Britain, and possibly France) that would have been powerful enough to deter states like Germany that sought to overturn the international order to America's disadvantage.

In the first excerpt that follows, Lodge expressed what he admitted was a utopian hope for an international organization. In his later criticism of President Wilson's ideas about collective security, Lodge admitted that he had grown much more skeptical about the prospects for a genuine league of nations.

Force and Peace

From Henry Cabot Lodge, "Force and Peace," Chancellor's Address at Union College, June 9, 1915

We can put it all into a sentence. What we see [in the war in Europe] is unchained physical force multiplied beyond computation by all the inventions and discoveries of an unresting science, as potent in destruction as it is in beneficence.

How is such a use of physical force, unlimited in its power, terrible in its consequences, to be avoided? How is peace to be established and maintained hereafter among the nations of the earth? One thing is certain, it cannot be done by words. Nothing will be accomplished by people who are sheltered under neutrality gathering outside the edges of the fight and from comfortable safety summoning the combatants to throw down their arms and make peace because war is filled with horrors and women are the mothers of men. The nations and the men now fighting, as they believe, for their lives and freedom and national existence know all this better than anyone else, and would heed such babble, if they heard it, no more than the twittering of the birds. In our Civil War, when we were fighting for our national life, England and France and other outsiders were not slow in telling us that the Union could not be saved, that the useless carnage ought to cease, that peace must be made at once. Except as an irritating impertinence we regarded such advice as of no more consequence than the squeaking of mice behind the wainscot when fire has seized upon the house. Neither present peace, nor established peace in the future for which we hope, is helped by fervent conversation among ourselves about the beauties of peace and the horrors of war, interspersed with virtuous exhortations to others, who are passing through the valley of the shadow, to give up all they are fighting for and accept the instructions of bystanders who are daring and sacrificing nothing and who have nothing directly at stake. Peace will not come in this way by vain shoutings nor by mere loudness in shrieking uncontested truths to a weary world. No men or women possessed of ordinary sense or human sympathies need arguments to convince them that peace among nations is a great good, to be sought for with all their strength, but the establishment and maintenance of peace cannot be accomplished by language proclaiming the virtues of peace and demonstrating the horrors of war. The many excellent people who may be described as habitual if not professional advocates of peace appear to be satisfied with making and listening to speeches about it. They seem to think great advances are made if we put our official names to a series of perfectly empty and foolish agreements which it is charitable to describe as harmless follies, for they weaken and discredit every real treaty which seeks to promote international good-will and settle international differences. They are so vain and worthless that, when the hour of stress came, no one would think it worthwhile even to tear them up. Treaty agreements looking to the peaceful settlement of international disputes, and which can be carried out, are valuable to the extent to which they go, but treaty agreements which go beyond the point of practical enforcement, which are not meant to be enforced, and which have neither a sense of obligation nor force to sustain that obligation behind them, are simply injurious. If we are to secure our own peace and do our part toward the maintenance of world peace, we must put rhetoric, whether in speech or on paper, aside. We must refuse to be satisfied with illusions. We must refuse to deceive ourselves and others. We must pass by mere words and vague shows, and come clear-eyed to the facts and the realities. The dominant fact today, I repeat, is the physical force now unchained in this great war. Some people seem to think that if you can abolish force and the instruments of force you can put an end to the possibilities of war. . . .

No one has suggested, not even the most ardent advocates of peace, that the police of our cities should be abolished on the theory that an organization of armed men whose duty it is to maintain order, even if they are compelled often to wound and sometimes to kill for that purpose, are by their mere existence an incitement to crime and violence. If order, peace, and civilization in a town, city, or state rest, as they do rest in the last analysis, upon force, upon what does the peace of a nation depend? It must depend, and it can only depend, upon the ability of the nation to maintain and defend its own peace at home and abroad. . . .

The people who urge the disarmament of one nation in an armed world confuse armament and preparation with the actual power upon which peace depends. They take the manifestation for the cause. Armament is merely the instrument by which the force of the community is manifested and made effective, just as the policeman is the manifestation of the force of the municipal community upon which local order rests. The fact that armies and navies are used in war does not make them the cause of war, any more than maintaining a fire in a grate to prevent the dwellers in the house from suffering from cold warrants the abolition of fire because where fire gets beyond control it is a destructive agent. Alexander the Great was bent on conquest, and he created the best army in the world at that time, not to preserve the peace of Macedonia, but for the purpose of conquering other nations, to which purpose he applied his instrument. The wars which followed were not due to the Macedonian phalanx, but to Alexander. The good or the evil of national armament depends, not on its existence or its size, but upon the purpose for which it is created and maintained. Great military and naval forces created for purposes of conquest are used in the war which the desire of conquest causes. They do not in themselves cause war. Armies and navies organized to maintain peace serve the ends of peace because there is no such incentive to war as a rich, undefended, and helpless country, which by its condition invites aggression. The grave objections to overwhelming and exhausting armaments are economic. A general reduction of armaments is not only desirable, but something to be sought for with the utmost earnestness. But for one nation to disarm and leave itself defenseless in an armed world is a direct incentive and invitation to war. . . . The first step, then, toward the maintenance of peace is for each nation to maintain its peace with the rest of the world by its own honorable and right conduct and by such organization and preparation as will enable it to defend its peace. . . .

We should never forget that if democracy is not both able and ready to defend itself, it will go down in subjection before military autocracy because the latter is then the more efficient. We must bear constantly in mind that from the conflict which now convulses the world there may possibly come events which would force us to fight with all our strength to preserve our freedom, our democracy, and our national life. . . . [T]here is no escape from the proposition that the peace of the world can be maintained only as the peace and order of a single community are maintained, as the peace of a single nation is maintained, by the force which united nations are willing to put behind the peace and order of the world. Nations must unite as men unite in order to preserve peace and order. The great nations must be so united as to be able to say to any single country, you must not go to war, and they can only say that effectively when the country desiring war knows that the force which the united nations place behind peace is irresistible. . . .

It may be easily said that this idea, which is not a new one, is impracticable, but it is better than the idea that war can be stopped by language, by speechmaking, by vain agreements which no one would carry out when the stress came, by denunciations of war and laudations of peace, in which all men agree; for these methods are not only impracticable, but impossible and barren of all hope of real result. It may seem Utopian at this moment to suggest a union of civilized nations in order to put a controlling force behind the maintenance of peace and international order, but it is through the aspiration for perfection, through the search for Utopias, that the real advances have been made.

Collective Security

From Henry Cabot Lodge, "The President's Plan for a World Peace,"
speech delivered in the Senate, February 7, 1917

It is not necessary, of course, to say anything as to the many general and just observations made by the President in regard to the horrors and miseries of war, or the dangers and complications with which the present conflict threatens the United States, or as to his or our duty as servants of humanity. Of course, we all agree most heartily with the proposition that peace—just and righteous peace—is infinitely better than war; that virtue is better than vice; that, in Browning's words:—

> It's better being good than bad;
> It's safer being meek than fierce;
> It's better being sane than mad.

In all these declarations we must be cordially and thoroughly of one mind. All that I desire to do is to speak briefly of the substantive propositions contained in the President's address and, by analysis, discover, if I can, precisely what policies and courses of action he is undertaking to commit the country. . . .

As I understand it, the President is aiming at two objects, both in the highest degree admirable—to bring to an end the war now raging in Europe, and to make provision for the future and permanent peace of the world. It is to the promotion of the second purpose that he proposes action on the part of the United States, saying that we should frankly formulate the conditions upon which this Government would feel justified in asking our people to approve its firm and solemn adherence to a league for peace. He then proceeds to state the two purposes in this way:

> The present war must first be ended; but we owe it to candor and to a just regard for the opinion of mankind to say that, so far as our participation in guarantees of future peace is concerned, it makes a great deal of difference in what way and upon what terms it is ended. The treaties and agreements which bring it to an end must embody terms which will create a peace that is worth guaranteeing and preserving, a peace that will win the approval of mankind, not merely a peace that will serve the several interests and immediate aims of the nations engaged. We shall have no voice in determining what those terms shall be, but we shall, I feel sure, have a voice in determining whether they shall be made lasting or not by the guarantees of a universal covenant; and our judgment upon what is fundamental and essential as a condition precedent to permanency should be spoken now, not afterwards, when it may be too late.

It will be observed that in this paragraph of his address the President says explicitly that the first condition precedent to any action for a league for peace must be the ending of the present war. He then declares that the treaties and agreements which bring the war to an end must create a peace which is worth guaranteeing and preserving. He says further that we shall have no voice in determining what those terms shall be, but that they can never be lasting or permanent unless they meet with our approval. It seems to me that this is equivalent to saying that we are to have no voice in what the terms of the peace which ends the present war shall be, but that at the same time the terms must be what we approve or we shall not be able to enter into any future league to preserve the peace of the world. In other words, our action is to be conditioned upon the terms of a peace which we are to have no voice in determining. If the belligerents when they come to make peace do not make all the terms satisfactory to us, they cannot look to us to aid them in making that peace lasting and permanent. The President then goes on to lay down the general principles upon which the terms of the peace, in which we are to have no voice, shall be based if the peace thus obtained is to be a peace worth having.

In the first place, it must be a peace without victory. It is not quite clear just what this means, unless it is intended to be a declaration in the interest of one group of belligerents who, having abandoned the original hope of complete victory, wish to make peace in the most advantageous way now open to them. This interpretation must be at once dismissed, for it is not to be supposed for a moment that this can be the President's object, because we all know how devoted he is to neutrality—how it has been his belief from the beginning that it was the duty of the American people to be neutral even in their thoughts— and he is, of course, well aware that it is as easy to be unneutral in forcing a peace favorable to one side as it is to help one side against the other while war is raging. Peace without victory can only mean, therefore, that neither side is to gain anything by the terms of peace through victory in the field, because if there are no victories on either side there can be neither gains nor losses in the final settlement except through the voluntary self-sacrifice and generosity of the combatants; in other words, all the lives have been given in this war and all the money spent in vain and Europe is to emerge from this conflict in exactly the same situation as when she entered it. It seems to me incredible that people who have made such awful sacrifices as have been made by the belligerents should be content to forgo the prospect of victory, in the hope of bringing the war to an end, with everything left just as it was. In such a result they might well think that all their efforts and losses, all their miseries and sorrows and sacrifices were a criminal and hideous futility. Both sides have been inspired by the hope of victory; both sides are still so inspired. Some of the belligerents, at least, believe as I believe that the one object of the war is to win a victory which will assure a permanent peace and would regard a reproduction of the old conditions, with all their menacing possibilities, as something far worse than war. They are determined that the dark peril which has overshadowed our own lives and threatened the independence and very existence of their own countries shall not be permitted to darken the future and be a curse to their children and their children's children. For this they are fighting and dying. Perhaps they ought not to think in this way; perhaps they ought to feel as the President does. But we must deal with things as they are; we must "uncover realities," and there is no doubt of the reality of the desire among many of the great nations of Europe to close this war with a victory which will give them a peace worth having, and not a mere breathing-space filled with the up-building of crushing armaments and then another and a worse war. Such, I think, is their point of view; but as a practical question for us, dealing with a condition on which we are to build a future league for peace to which we are to be a party, how are we going to provide that it shall be a peace without victory? How are we to arrange that there shall be no victories?

The President says that a peace won by victory would leave a bitter memory upon which peace terms could not rest permanently, but only as upon quicksand. There has been pretty constant fighting in this unhappy world ever since the time when history began its records, and in speaking of lasting peace in terms of history we can only speak comparatively. I think, however, that I am not mistaken in saying that since the fall of the Roman Empire the longest period of general peace which Europe and the Western World have enjoyed was during the forty years following the battle of Waterloo. During that time there were, of course, a few small and unimportant wars, but there was no great general conflict among great nations anywhere, and yet the peace of 1815 was a peace imposed upon France by the victorious allies if ever such a thing happened in the history of mankind. There was an attempt to settle that Napoleonic war by a treaty "without victory" and between equals. The treaty was signed at Amiens on March 27, 1802. This "peace without victory" lasted exactly thirteen months and nineteen days, and then war came again and continued for twelve years, and was ended by a peace through victory of the most absolute kind, and that peace lasted between England and France for a hundred years and has never been broken. Our war with Spain ended with a peace based on the complete victory of the United States by land and sea. There is no reason to suppose that because it was a peace obtained by victory that it is not a lasting peace. I might cite other examples, but one affirmative instance is enough to shatter a universal negative. As the Frenchman said, "No generalization is ever completely true, not even this one." It is a little hasty, therefore, to say that no peace can endure which is the fruit of victory. The peace which lasts is the peace which rests on justice and righteousness, and if it is a just and righteous peace it makes no difference whether it is based on the compromises and concessions of treaties or upon victories in the field. But I return to and repeat the main question before I leave this point. If peace without victory is to be a condition precedent of lasting peace to be maintained by the covenant in which we are to take part, how are we practically to compel or secure the existence of such a condition?

The next condition precedent stated by the President, without which we can have no peace that "can last or ought to last," is the universal acceptance of the idea that governments derive all their just powers from the consent of the governed and that any peace which does not recognize and accept this principle will inevitably be upset. Must the fact that any given government rests on the consent of the governed be determined by a popular vote or by the general acceptance by the people of the existing form of government? Who is to decide whether the principle is recognized under the different governments of the world with whom we are to form the League for Peace "supported by the organized major force of mankind"? If the recognition of this principle is to be essential to the lasting peace which we are to support—and every American, of course, believes in and admires the principle—what is to be done about Korea, or Hindustan, or Alsace-Lorraine, or the Trentino, or the Slav Provinces of Austria, or the Danish Duchies? Does the government of Armenia by Turkey, with its organized massacres, rest on the consent of the governed, and if it does not are we to take steps to remedy it, or is Turkey to be excluded from the league, or is the league to coerce Turkey to an observance of our principles? As a preliminary of the peace which we are to help enforce must we insist that it cannot exist if there are any people under any government who have been handed from sovereignty to sovereignty as if they were property? I am not contesting the justice of the principle—far from it—but we may well ask how we are going to compel the adoption of that principle by other goverments, and this is no idle question, but a real and practical one which cannot be evaded. If we enter upon this most desirable reform of other nations, there may be people sufficiently malevolent to ask whether we secured Louisiana by a vote of the people of that Territory, or California and other acquisitions from Mexico, or the Philippines, or Puerto Rico, or even Alaska, where there were Russian inhabitants who were handed over for a price, very much like property or as serfs. . . .

I have tried very briefly to set forth the conditions precedent which the President says are essential to a lasting peace. I have endeavored in a very general and independent way to "uncover the realities" and to be rid of all "soft concealments." Now, having clearly in our minds these conditions precedent, vital to the establishment of a lasting peace which we are to help bring about, I desire to consider the part which we are to take in maintaining it. . . .

If . . . voluntary arbitration and voluntary agreements, by convention or otherwise, without any sanction, have reached their limits, what is the next step? There is only one possible advance, and that is to put a sanction behind the decision of an international tribunal or behind an agreement of the nations; in other words, to create a power to enforce the decree of the international courts or the provisions of the international agreements. There is no other solution. I have given a great deal of thought to the question and I admit that at first it seemed to me that it might be possible to put force behind the world's peace. The peace and order of towns and cities, of states and nations, are all maintained by force. The force may not be displayed—usually there is no necessity for doing so—but order exists in our towns, in our cities, in our

States, and in our Nation, and the decrees of our courts are enforced solely because of the existence of overwhelming force behind them. It is known for example that behind the decrees of the courts of the United States there is an irresistible force. If the peace of the world is to be maintained as the peace of a city or the internal peace of a nation is maintained, it must be maintained in the same way—by force. To make an agreement among the nations for the maintenance of peace, and leave it to each nation to decide whether its force should be used in a given case to prevent war between two or more other nations of the world, does not advance us at all; we are still under the voluntary system. . . .

The President sees this clearly. He proposes that we should adhere to a league for peace and then says:

> It will be absolutely necessary that a force be created as a guarantor of the permanency of the settlement so much greater than the force of any nation now engaged or any alliance hitherto formed or projected that no nation, no probable combination of nations, could face or withstand it. If the peace presently to be made is to endure, it must be a peace made secure by the organized major force of mankind.

Nothing could be plainer or more direct than that statement, and if we are to advance from the voluntary stage, it must be, as the President says, by a league for peace behind which is the organized major force of mankind. I fully agree with the President that if we are to have a league such as he describes and are to enforce peace, it must be done in just the way he has stated. As a general proposition nothing could be more attractive for those who desire the peace of the world. I confess that when I first began to consider it some two years ago it presented great attractions to me, but the more I have thought about it the more serious the difficulties in the way of its accomplishment seem to be. . . . The first difficulty comes when the league is confronted by the refusal of a nation involved in dispute with another nation to abide by the decision of the league when that decision has been rendered by an international tribunal, or in any other way. Submission to such a decision can only be compelled as submission to a decision of the court is compelled—by force; in this case the organized major force of mankind. . . . The authorities of the league would, of necessity, have the power to call on every member of the league to send out its quota to the forces of the league and the nations forming the league would find themselves, of necessity, involved in war.

The first question that would occur to any one of us is what the numbers of the league force will be. I will not venture a guess myself, but I will quote the opinion of Professor Albert Bushnell Hart, the distinguished historian, a close student and high authority on all American policies and a most friendly critic of the President's address. In a very interesting article in the "New York Times" of January 28, 1917, Professor Hart says:

> He [the President] does incline toward the general plan which is pushed by the League to Enforce Peace. For, he says: "It will be absolutely necessary that a force be created as a guarantor of the permanency of the settlement so much greater than the force of any nation now engaged, or any alliance hitherto formed or projected, that no nation, no probable combination, could face or withstand it."
>
> If that means anything definite, it means an international police force of not less than 5,000,000 men, in which the share of the United States would be at least 500,000.

There is the estimate of a dispassionate and competent observer. Will it not be worth while to pause a moment before we commit ourselves to an army of 500,000 men, to be held ready for war at the pleasure of other nations in whose councils we shall have but one vote if we are true to the President's policy of the equality of nations? . . .

If we are to adhere to the principle of the equality of nations laid down by the President, each nation, great and small, having equality of rights, would have an equal voice in the decision of the league, and a majority would set the forces of the league in motion. It might happen that the majority would be composed of the smaller and weaker nations, who, if they are to have equality of rights, would thus be enabled to precipitate the greater nations into war, into a war, perhaps, with one of the greatest nations of the league. In the present state of human nature and public opinion is it probable that any nation will bind itself to go to war at the command of other nations and furnish its army and navy to be disposed of as the majority of the representatives of other nations may see fit? It seems to me that this is hardly possible, and yet in what other way can we come to the practical side of this question? In what other way are you to enforce the decisions of the league? . . .

I hear already the clamor of those who have been shrieking for peace at any price and denouncing all armaments, rising around us with the passionate demand that we shall immediately join a league for peace, about the details of which they neither know nor care, but which will compel the establishment of large naval and military forces and which may plunge us into war in any quarter of the globe at any moment at the bidding of other nations. Such is the magic of a word to those who are content with vocal sounds and ask only that the word they love be shouted with sufficient loudness. But they, too, if they persist, will meet the day when words are vain, and when they must face relentless, unforgiving realities.

The Interwar Period and World War II

The period from 1919 to 1941 was one in which both Wilsonian global-ists and Hamiltonian realists were frustrated by a resurgence of isola-tionism in the United States. The Wilsonians did not get their League, and the Hamiltonians did not get their navy or their alliances. The isolationists in-cluded not only Jeffersonians but many Progressives who believed that the United States should concentrate on improving itself. Pacifists and anti-im-perialist members of the U.S. Congress from New England and the Midwestern and Pacific Coast states settled by New Englanders, like Idaho's Senator Borah, held hearings in which they blamed American participation in World War I on the connivings of international bankers and "munitions mak-ers." (One of Borah's admirers, Idaho Senator Frank Church, would lead an equally irrational and destructive isolationist attack on American national se-curity institutions and policies in the 1970s.) In the 1920s the United States played an important role in the economy of Europe and the world, but this was brought to an end by the Great Depression that began in 1929. In the 1930s the fact that the United States was far weaker militarily than its eco-nomic strength would warrant encouraged the leaders of Nazi Germany and Japan in the mistaken belief that they could discount American hostility to their designs.

There was little that the United States could have done to prevent another war in Europe. It is sometimes said that the United States, along with Britain and France, should have threatened war with Nazi Germany in the mid-1930s. That might have deterred Hitler and might even have led to his being overthrown by the German military. It would have been more likely to lead to a war between the Western democracies and Germany, from which the only winner might have been the Soviet Union. We know from recently disclosed Soviet archival evidence that Stalin was hoping that a war of Britain and France against Germany would drain both sides and permit the Soviet Union to move into Europe to pick up the pieces. As it turned out, the Soviet Union, after starting World War II as Hitler's ally, ultimately bore the brunt of the losses in the war to destroy Nazi Germany, while the United States suffered least of all the major powers.

However limited America's options in Europe were during the 1930s, American policy in East Asia undoubtedly invited trouble. Having acquired the Philippines and Hawaii, the United States did not assign adequate armed forces to protect them from Japanese attack. Had the United States been able to negotiate from a position of strength, Japan might have been deterred from its campaign of conquest in China and Southeast Asia. Foolishly, the United States in the 1920s had pressured the British to end their alliance with Japan, which dated back to the early twentieth century. A decade later, the Japanese, seeking a great-power ally, chose Nazi Germany, which seemed at the time to be the rising power. The result was the Pacific War, which might have been avoided by a wiser American strategy backed up by adequate force. Forgetting TR's maxim, the United States during the interwar period spoke loudly and carried a twig.

WALTER LIPPMANN

Walter Lippmann (1889–1974) consistently played a supporting role in American foreign policy throughout his long career, from his role in drafting Woodrow Wilson's Fourteen Points during his youth to his reluctant opposition to the Vietnam War as an influential columnist in his final years. Born into an affluent German Jewish family in New York City, Lippmann obtained a philosophy degree from Harvard. He joined Herbert Croly as a founding editor of *The New Republic* and later edited the *New York World* newspaper before becoming a full-time syndicated columnist in 1931. He wrote a number of books, which benefited from the perspective he gained from his position at the intersection of the worlds of journalism, scholarship, and politics: *A Preface to Politics* (1913), *Drift and Mastery* (1914), *Public Opinion* (1922), *The Cold War* (1947), and *The Public Philosophy* (1955).

During World War I Lippmann helped President Wilson's adviser Colonel Edward House prepare for the Versailles Peace Conference. Lippmann's disillusioning experiences during World War I convinced him of the gap between the realities of power politics and public statements and perceptions (his book *Public Opinion* was inspired by his meditations on wartime propaganda). This selection is from *U.S. Foreign Policy: Shield of the Republic* (1943), in which Lippmann wrote about the origins of World War II and the possibilities for postwar peace from a realist perspective. The book remains a classic of American realist thought; if it is flawed, it is because Lippmann tends to concentrate too singlemindedly on abstract power relations and ignores the influences on foreign policy of constitutions, ideologies, and values. This bias later led Lippmann to misinterpret the Soviet Union and communist China as traditional great powers rather than dynamic, revolutionary regimes.

The Need to Balance Power and Commitments

[Americans] have forgotten the compelling and, once seen, the self-evident common principle of all genuine foreign policy—the principle that alone can force decisions, can settle controversy, and can induce agreement. This is the principle that in foreign relations, as in all other relations, a policy has been formed only when commitments and power have been brought into balance. This is the forgotten principle which must be recovered and restored to the first place in American thought if the nation is to achieve the foreign policy which it so desperately wants.

Without the controlling principle that the nation must maintain its objectives and its power in equilibrium, its purposes within its means and its means equal to its purposes, its commitments related to its resources and its resources adequate to its commitments, it is impossible to think at all about foreign affairs. Yet the history of our acts and of our declarations . . . will show that rarely, and never consistently, have American statesmen and the American people been guided by this elementary principle of practical life.

No one would seriously suppose that he had a fiscal policy if he did not consider together expenditure and revenue, outgo and income, liabilities and assets. But in foreign relations we have habitually in our minds divorced the discussion of our war aims, our peace aims, our ideals, our interests, our commitments, from the discussion of our armaments, our strategic position, our potential allies and our probable enemies. No policy could emerge from such a discussion. For what settles practical controversy is the knowledge that ends and means have to be balanced: an agreement has eventually to be reached when men admit that they must pay for what they want and that they must want only what they are willing to pay for. If they do not have to come to such an agreement, they will never except by accident agree. For they will lack a yardstick by which to measure their ideals and their interests, or their ways and means of protecting and promoting them. . . .

Before we examine the history of our insolvent foreign relations, we must be sure that we know what we mean by a foreign commitment and by the power to balance it.

> I mean by a *foreign commitment* an obligation, outside the continental limits of the United States, which may in the last analysis have to be met by waging war.

> I mean by *power* the force which is necessary to prevent such a war or to win it if it cannot be prevented. In the term necessary power I include the military force which can be mobilized effectively within the domestic ter-

ritory of the United States and also the reinforcements which can be obtained from dependable allies.

[A] foreign policy consists in bringing into balance, with a comfortable surplus of power in reserve, the nation's commitments and the nation's power. The constant preoccupation of the true statesman is to achieve and maintain this balance. Having determined the foreign commitments which are vitally necessary to his people, he will never rest until he has mustered the force to cover them. In assaying ideals, interests, and ambitions which are to be asserted abroad, his measure of their validity will be the force he can muster at home combined with the support he can find abroad among other nations which have similar ideals, interests, and ambition.

For nations, as for families, the level may vary at which a solvent balance is struck. If its expenditures are safely within its assured means, a family is solvent when it is poor, or is well-to-do, or is rich. The same principle holds true of nations. The statesman of a strong country may balance its commitments at a high level or at a low. . . . If he does not, he will follow a course that leads to disaster. . . .

The elementary means by which all foreign policy must be conducted are the armed forces of the nation, the arrangement of its strategic position, and the choice of its alliances. In the American ideology of our times these things have come to be regarded as militaristic, imperialistic, reactionary, and archaic; the proper concern of right-minded men was held to be peace, disarmament, and a choice between non-intervention and collective security.

We not only ignored the development of the means to achieve our ends: we chose as the ends of our efforts a set of ideals which were incompatible with all the means of achieving any ideals. The ideal of peace diverted our attention from the idea of national security. The ideal of disarmament caused us to be inadequately armed. The apparently opposed ideals of non-intervention on the one hand, and of collective security on the other, had at bottom the same practical result in that they inhibited us from forming our necessary alliances. Thus . . . we have had to wage war three times without being prepared to fight; and we have twice made peace without knowing what we wanted. . . .

1. "PEACE"

So we must examine our national prejudices, and we may begin by asking ourselves whether peace, as so many say, is the supreme end of foreign policy. Merely to ask the question would have seemed shocking a short while ago. At the moment, it is obvious that the survival of the nation in its independence and its security is a greater end than peace. . . .

If the logic of peace as the supreme national ideal leads to absurdity, then it must be a grave error to think and to say that peace is the supreme end. For national ideals should not express amiable but considered sentiments. They should express the serious purposes of the nation, and the vice of the pacifist ideal is that it conceals the true end of foreign policy. The true end is to provide for the security of the nation in peace *and* in war. This means that, as far as human foresight and prudence can make it so, the vital interests of the nation must be so legitimate that the people will think them worth defending at the risk of war—and that they must be safeguarded so that they can be defended successfully in case of war. A nation has security when it does not have to sacrifice its legitimate interests to avoid war and is able, if challenged, to maintain them by war.

This has always been the view of statesmen who understood their responsibilities. It is, I submit, what Washington meant when he said in the Farewell Address that "*we may choose peace or war, as our interest, guided by justice, shall counsel.*" Washington did not say that the nation should or could renounce war, and seek only peace. For he knew that the national "interest, guided by justice" might bring the Republic into conflict with other nations. Since he knew that the conflict might be irreconcilable by negotiation and compromise, his primary concern was to make sure that the national interest was wisely and adequately supported by armaments, suitable frontiers, and appropriate alliances.

The untoward result of the pacifist ideal is to cause the nation to neglect its defenses and to ignore its enemies. For national policy, we must never forget, controls at the most only national action: thus the pacifist nation can disarm itself but it does not disarm its enemies. This quandary is not resolved by saying that if all nations could be persuaded by argument or example to adopt the pacifist ideal, there would be no more wars and no further need to be prepared for war. This is the error of acting today on the assumption that you have already achieved what you dimly hope you may be able to achieve tomorrow. For until all the nation's rivals and potential enemies are irrevocably committed to the pacifist ideal, it is a form of criminal negligence to act as if they were already committed to it. . . .

We may call this the vicious circle of pacifism. In the name of peace the nation is made weak and unwilling to defend its vital interests. Confronted with the menace of superior force, it then surrenders its vital interests. The pacifist statesmen justify their surrenders on the ground, first, that peace is always preferable to war, and second, that because the nation wants peace so much, it is not prepared to wage war. Finally, with its back to the wall, the pacifist nation has to fight nevertheless. But then it fights against a strategically superior enemy; it fights with its own armaments insufficient and with its alliances shattered. This was the way in which the pacifist ideal led the peace-loving nations to the very edge of the catastrophe from which they are now saving themselves only at prodigious cost. The generation which most sincerely and elaborately declared that peace is the supreme end of foreign policy got not peace, but a most devastating war.

2. "DISARMAMENT"

In the interval between the two great wars the United States sought to promote peace by denouncing war, even by "outlawing" it, and by disarming itself, Great Britain, and France. The movement to limit armaments was, no doubt, inspired in considerable measure by sheer war-weariness and by the desire to save money. But the disinterested and idealistic theory of disarmament was that if everyone had less capacity to wage war, there would be a smaller likelihood of war. . . .

The story of the disarmament movement is the sorry tale of nations which lost sight of their own vital interests, and very nearly emasculated themselves fatally as a result. For more than a hundred years the marriage, in Jefferson's metaphor, of British and American sea power had supported the Monroe Doctrine. The American people did not know it, and, lacking the elementary principles of a foreign policy, they did not wish to hear about it. Though Britain and America had been allies in 1917–1918, yet in the twenty years which elapsed before they became allies again they acted as if they were potential enemies. This assumption controlled the disarmament movement— that extraordinary movement by which the partners of one great war disarmed one another in the short period which remained before they were to be partners again in an even greater war.

3. "NO ENTANGLING ALLIANCES"

The hard core of resistance to the formation of foreign policy has been the popular objection to alliances. For over a century Americans have believed that the undesirability of alliances was so self-evident as to be beyond the pale of discussion. Now an objection which men will not examine and debate is a prejudice. This prejudice rests, so most of us were brought up to believe, upon the teachings of the Founding Fathers of the Republic.

Yet as a matter of fact the Founding Fathers did not hold the prejudice against alliances which latter-day Americans have ascribed to them. The record of their words and acts shows that whenever they thought it would serve the national interest to have the support of allies, they were only too pleased to have allies. . . .

How then did we come to think that alliances were contrary to the example of the Founding Fathers, and therefore alien to the purest American tradition? . . . [A] few passages, torn from their context and then misread, were treated as the Holy Writ of American tradition.

These phrases come from Washington's Farewell Address (September 17, 1796) and from Jefferson's First Inaugural (March 4, 1801). The passage from Washington states that "Europe has a set of primary interests which to us have none or a very remote relation," and therefore "it must be unwise for us to implicate ourselves by artificial ties in the ordinary vicissitudes of her politics or the ordinary combinations and collisions of her friendships or enmities." . . .

Not wishing to be drawn into the European War on the side of France against England, he then went on to argue that the alliance made with France in 1778, which played such a decisive part in the War of Independence, should not be regarded as a *permanent* alliance to support France in all her wars. . . . What he objected to was the extending the French alliance to include the obligation to help France in Europe: "I repeat, therfore, let those engagements [with France] be observed in their genuine sense. But in my opinion it is *unnecessary and would be unwise to extend them.*" These are not the words of a man with a dogmatic prejudice against all alliances as such: these are the words of a man cautiously measuring the necessity and wisdom of extending an alliance.

Evidently, Washington, who had helped to send Franklin and others to the European capitals to obtain their support in an American war, was not the man to propose dogmatically that America would never need allies and must never form alliances. . . .

The celebrated injunction to seek "honest friendship with all nations, entangling alliances with none" comes from Jefferson's First Inaugural. It is no less clear that Jefferson, like Washington, had no dogmatic prejudice against alliances as such. For, where an American interest, as he conceived it, was at stake, he sought as a matter of course for the appropriate ally. . . .

Thus we are entitled to say that the objection of latter-day Americans to alliances is not based on the authority of the Founders of the Republic. It rests on an obscuration of the words, the acts, and the explicit beliefs of Washington, Jefferson, Madison and Monroe. . . .

4. "COLLECTIVE SECURITY"

When the prejudice against alliances encountered the desire to abolish war, the result was the Wilsonian conception of collective security. . . .

Wilson . . . not only shared the traditional prejudices against alliances but was deeply influenced also by the idea that the nations could be brought together by consent, as the thirteen American colonies had been brought together first in a confederation and then in a federal union. This analogy has long been cherished by Americans as affording the hope that it might become a model for the rest of the world.

Yet it is, I submit, a profoundly misleading analogy. For the thirteen colonies had been planted and had matured under one sovereign power, that of the English crown. . . .

They were not forming an altogether unprecedented union, they were perpetuating and perfecting a union which had always existed since the plantation of the British colonies. The fact that none of the Spanish or French colonies joined the union is fairly conclusive evidence that even in North America—three thousand miles from Europe—political unions do not become more comprehensive by voluntary consent. . . .

President Wilson's conception of collective security did not take into account this historic pattern. He held that there should be a union of fifty juridically equal but otherwise unequal states, and not the evolution of a union from a nucleus of firmly allied strong states. Refusing to regard alliances as the effective means by which collective security could be made to operate, Wilson forbade the founders of the League of Nations to perfect their alliance which had been tested in the fires of war. . . .

The American opponents of the League saw truly that if the League was actually going to enforce peace, then it must imply the equivalent of an Anglo-American alliance. If the League did not imply that, then the generalized commitments of the Covenant were too broad and too unpredictable to be intelligible. . . .

The dilemma was presented because Wilson was trying to establish collective security without forming an alliance. He wanted the omelet. He rejected the idea of cooking the eggs. . . .

The fundamental subject of foreign policy is how a nation stands in relation to the principal military powers. For only the great powers can wage great wars. Only a great power can resist a great power. Only a great power can defeat a great power. And therefore the relationship of his nation with the other great powers is the paramount—not by any means the sole, but the paramount—concern of the maker of foreign policy. Unless this relationship is such that the combination against him is not stronger than the combination to which he belongs, his foreign policy is not solvent: his commitments exceed his means, and he is leading his people into grave trouble.

Therefore, no great power can be indifferent to any of the other great powers. It must take a position in regard to all of them. No great power can stand alone against all the others. For none can be great enough for that. If its object is to win a war it has chosen to wage, or not to lose a war imposed upon it, a great power must have allies among the great powers. And if its object is, as ours must be, to preserve the peace, then it must form a combination of indisputably preponderant power with other great states which also desire peace.

Thus the statesman, who means to maintain peace, can no more ignore the order of power than an engineer can ignore the mechanics of physical force. He should not, to be sure, frivolously play "power politics." But he must with cold calculation organize and regulate the politics of power. If he does not do that, and do it correctly, the result must be a cycle of disastrous wars followed by peace settlements which breed more wars. . . .

The common error of the foreign policy of all the great powers [opposed to Nazi Germany and Imperial Japan] is that they did not take the precaution to become members of an indisputably powerful combination. The aggressor combination was not powerful enough to win: it was powerful enough only to plunge the world into war. The combination of the defenders was not formed until they were on the edge of catastrophe.

Thus we must conclude that in the order of power—in the relationship among the states which are great powers because they can raise great forces and can arm them—the object of each state must be to form a combination which isolates its enemy. From 1935 to 1940 it was Hitler's object to isolate Great Britain. He did not succeed and therefore he must lose the war. Since 1941 it has been the object of the United Nations to separate Germany and Japan and then defeat each of them separately. Every state, whether it is bent on aggression or on pacification, can achieve its purpose only if it avoids being isolated by a combination of the other great states.

To be isolated is for any state the worst of all predicaments. To be the member of a combination which can be depended upon to act together and, when challenged, to fight together, is to have achieved the highest degree of security which is attainable in a world in which there are many sovereign national states.

The world we live in is a world of many sovereign national states, and for the purposes of practical action this condition is given and is unalterable. A Roman Peace, in which one state absorbs and governs all the others, is so completely impossible in our time that we need not stop to argue whether it would be inferno or utopia. If there is to be peace in our time, it will have to be peace among sovereign national states, and the makers of foreign policy can be concerned with no other kind of peace.

Since the first concern of the makers of foreign policy in a sovereign national state must be to achieve the greatest possible security, their object must be to avoid isolation by becoming members of an adequate combination. If they are entirely successful, the adequate alliance to which they belong will either be unchallenged, and they will have peace without fighting for it, or it will be invincible and they will have peace after a victorious war. To be one against the many is the danger, to be among the many against the one is security.

It follows that when the alliance is inadequate because there is an opposing alliance of approximately equal strength, the stage is set for a world war. For then the balance of power is so nearly even that no state is secure. It cannot know whether it would win or would lose the war which it knows is probable. Therefore, it is confronted with the need to calculate the risks of striking first and seizing the advantage of the initiative, or of waiting to be attacked in the hope, usually vain, that it will become too strong to be attacked.

Europe from 1900 to 1914 was in this condition of unstable balance. There was no certain preponderance of force with the Triple Entente or with the Central Powers. The question was put to the test of battle, and it was not until the weight of America was drawn in from the outside that a decision was reached and the war could come to an end. From the rise of Hitler to Munich Europe was again in this condition. No one knew, not Hitler, not Stalin, nor Chamberlain or Daladier, the relative strength of the Axis and of the opposing combination. Only when Hitler succeeded at Munich in separating the Franco-British allies from Russia, had he so altered the balance of power in his favor that a war for the conquest of Europe was from his point of view a good risk.

If, then, the object is not only to provide for security against being defeated in war but also to organize a peace which prevents war, the alliance to be adequate must be so dependable and so overwhelmingly powerful that there is no way of challenging it. The combination must be so strong that war against it is not a calculated risk, in which much might be won at a great price, but is instead an obvious impossibility because there would be no chance whatever of winning it.

To form such an overwhelming combination and maintain it is not easy. That is why peace has never yet been made universal, and why, when it has been achieved, it has not lasted. The combinations have tended to dissolve under the pressure of special interests within their member states. Old powers decline and new powers emerge. And never yet have statesmen been equal to the task of passing from one order of power to another without gigantic and prolonged wars. The cycle of these wars continues until by the survival of the strongest in the struggle for existence the new order of power is formed by a preponderant combination. . . .

We are committed to defend at the risk of war the lands and the waters around them extending from Alaska to the Philippines and Australia, from

Greenland to Brazil to Patagonia. The area of these commitments is very nearly half the surface of the globe, and within this area we insist that no other great power may enlarge its existing dominion, that no new great power may establish itself.

The area of American defensive commitment is not quite 40 per cent of the land surface of the earth. But it contains a little less than 25 per cent of the population of the earth. The Old World contains 75 per cent of mankind living on 60 per cent of the land of this globe. Thus it is evident that the potential military strength of the Old World is enormously greater than that of the New World. . . .

These calculations may at first glance seem to some irrelevant because it must seem so unlikely that we should ever have to face the combined power of the Old World. Those who think this are already granting what I am attempting to demonstrate, namely that the New World cannot afford to be isolated against the combined forces of the Old World, and that it must, therefore, find in the Old World dependable friends. They should also remember that as a matter of historic fact this country's vital interests have been threatened by the combined powers of the Old World. This threat existed at the conclusion of the great wars a century ago. The threat was averted by the statesmanship of Monroe, Madison, and Jefferson, who seized upon Canning's offer to withdraw Great Britain "from their scale"—that is the European combination—and to shift it "into that of our two continents." Thus experience teaches us that the combination of the Old World against our commitments in the New World is not inconceivable, and wisdom requires that we should never ignore it.

The fact of our military inferiority as an isolated state becomes more portentous when we realize how vulnerable is our strategic position. We have to defend two thirds of the surface of the globe from our continental base in North America. We are an island. South America is an island. The Philippines are islands. Australia is an island. Greenland is an island. All these islands lie in an immense oceanic lake of which the other great powers control the shores. Thus, if we are isolated and have no allies among the great powers, we have to defend most of the lake without any strategic support upon the mainland from which an attack would be launched. . . .

If this estimate of our real position seems at first to be incredible, let us remember that it seems incredible only because we have talked about our isolation but have never been so foolish or so unlucky as to be in fact isolated. We were extricated in 1823 from the threat of true isolation by the statesmanship of Canning and Monroe. Their construction lasted until 1917 when we averted the threat of true isolation by Wilson's intervention. In 1940 we were so near to true isolation that for a whole appallingly dangerous year the issue hung precariously upon the valor and skill of the people of Britain, and upon the historic campaign which President Roosevelt waged to arouse this country in time to its awful peril.

The security which Monroe had been able to achieve by diplomacy, Wilson and Roosevelt were unable to accomplish without engaging in war. But in all three instances the United States was faced with the problem of averting the threat of military isolation. The fact that Monroe averted it by diplomacy, and, indeed, by secret diplomacy, and that Wilson and Roosevelt averted it by joining an alliance which was already in the field, has prevented many Americans from perceiving the realities of our position. They do not believe that the consequences of isolation would be so fatal as they would in fact be because, thus far in our history, we have always in the nick of time found adequate allies.

But our luck might not hold. Our improvisations at the eleventh hour might the next time be too little and too late. Thus we must safeguard the future by founding our foreign policy on the undeniable necessity of forming dependable alliances in the Old World. . . .

At the end of the eighteenth century and the beginning of the nineteenth century most of the nations of the New World won their sovereign independence from the parent nations in the Old World. But the separation, though it is absolute in the realm of self-government, has never existed in the realm of strategic security. The original geographic and historical connections across the Atlantic have persisted. The Atlantic Ocean is not the frontier between Europe and the Americas. It is the inland sea of a community of nations allied with one another by geography, history, and vital necessity.

The members of this community may not all love one another, and they have many conflicting interests. But that is true of any community except perhaps the community of the saints. The test of whether a community exists is not whether we have learned to love our neighbors but whether, when put to the test, we find that we do act as neighbors. By that test all the centuries of experience since the discovery of the Americas has shown that there is peace and order on this side of the Atlantic only when there is peace and order among our neighbors on the other side of the Atlantic. Whenever they have been involved in great wars, the New World has been involved. When they have had peace from great war, as they did have from Waterloo to the first invasion of Belgium, there have been no great international wars that concerned the Americas.

Not what men say, not what they think they feel, but what in fact when they have to act they actually do—that is the test of community. By that test there is a great community on this earth from which no member can be excluded and none can resign. This community has its geographical center in the great basin of the Atlantic.

The Cold War

The United States and its allies waged World War II on the assumption—which in hindsight looks like a great strategic error—that Germany and Japan had to be not only defeated and reformed but eliminated forever as significant military powers. During the war FDR speculated about a postwar great-power concert consisting of the United States, Britain, the Soviet Union, and Chiang Kai-shek's Nationalist China. A more realistic view was Lippmann's hope for a "nuclear alliance" or great-power concert consisting of the United States, Britain, and the Soviet Union. The power vacuums created by the defeat of Germany and Japan, in addition to the postwar bankruptcy of the British Empire, and the victory in China of Mao's communists, which made the world's most populous nation an ally of the Soviet Union for more than a decade, presented American statesmen with a situation far worse than they had expected. Without countervailing economic and military aid from the United States, it seemed likely that America's West European and Asian allies would feel compelled to appease the Soviet bloc and might even be threatened by Soviet-sponsored subversion or Soviet conquest.

The Truman administration responded with a series of bold diplomatic and military measures to check Soviet influence and neutralize Soviet intimidation. (Following the familiar pattern, these measures were opposed by Northern isolationists—Taft Republicans and northern Democrats who favored Progressive Party candidate Henry Wallace's strategy of appeasing the Soviet Union.) The Marshall Plan committed the United States to a massive and unprecedented program of postwar reconstruction in devastated Europe. Aid was offered not only to Western Europe but to Eastern Europe and the Soviet Union; Stalin rejected American help and proceeded to consolidate a totalitarian empire in half of Europe that lasted until the anticommunist revolutions of 1989 swept the puppets of the U.S.S.R. from power in Eastern Europe. Winston Churchill called the Marshall Plan "the most unsordid act in history."

The slow but steady recovery of the Soviet Union from the war, combined with the Soviet acquisition of atomic weapons, gave Stalin the confidence to probe American resolve in Europe and the Middle East and to encourage communist revolutionaries in East Asia like Mao, Korea's Kim II Sung, and Vietnam's Ho Chi Minh. In a report to President Truman entitled NSC-68, drafted by Dean Acheson and Paul Nitze among others, the case was made for a rapid and sustained buildup of America's armed forces, which had been scaled down immediately after the conclusion of World War II. The recommendations contained in NSC-68 were not implemented until the North Korean communist dictator Kim II Sung, with the advance knowledge and support of Stalin and Mao, invaded noncommunist South Korea and started the Korean War. In retrospect NSC-68 came to be considered a blueprint for America's policy of containment of the Soviet empire—a policy that ultimately succeeded in 1986, despite the military debacle in the Vietnam War and the misguided appeasement of the Soviet Union by the United States during the heyday of Northern left-liberal isolationism in Congress between 1968 and the Soviet invasion of Afghanistan in 1979. Ironically, the most important allies of the United States in the Second Cold War of 1979–86, in addition to communist China, were the very nations that the United States had sought during World War II to eliminate as significant factors in world politics—Germany (or rather its Western three-fourths) and Japan.

GEORGE C. MARSHALL

George C. Marshall (1880–1959) had a distinguished career as both a military officer and a diplomat. A graduate of the Virginia Military Institute and the Infantry and Cavalry School and Staff College at Fort Leavenworth, Kansas, Marshall achieved recognition as a staff officer in World War I and became an aide to Army Chief of Staff General John J. Pershing. During World War II, Marshall, by then a general, served as Army chief of staff and was the senior member of the Allied Combined Chiefs of Staff. He was the chief architect of the Allied strategy that led to the defeat first of Nazi Germany and then of Imperial Japan After the war, Marshall became an envoy to China for the Truman administration, and he was appointed secretary of state in 1947. In June 1947, during a commencement address at Harvard, Marshall proposed the $112 billion dollar European Recovery Program that became known as the Marshall Plan (for which Marshall was awarded the Nobel Peace Prize in 1953). Marshall served as secretary of defense during the first part of the Korean War, from 1950–1951. Marshall, with his combination of military expertise, political acumen, reserve, and integrity, reminded many of George Washington.

The Marshall Plan

I need not tell you gentlemen that the world situation is very serious. That must be apparent to all intelligent people. I think one difficulty is that the problem is one of such enormous complexity that the very mass of facts presented to the public by press and radio make it exceedingly difficult for the man in the street to reach a clear appraisement of the situation. Furthermore, the people of this country are distant from the troubled areas of the earth and it is hard for them to comprehend the plight and consequent reactions of the long-suffering peoples, and the effect of those reactions on their governments in connection with our efforts to promote peace in the world.

In considering the requirements for the rehabilitation of Europe, the physical loss of life, the visible destruction of cities, factories, mines, and railroads was correctly estimated, but it has become obvious during recent months that this visible destruction was probably less serious than the dislocation of the entire fabric of European economy. For the past 10 years conditions have been highly abnormal. The feverish preparation for war and the more feverish maintenance of the war effort engulfed all aspects of national economies. Machinery has fallen into disrepair or is entirely obsolete. Under the arbitrary and destructive Nazi rule, virtually every possible enterprise was geared into the German war machine. Long-standing commercial ties, private institutions, banks, insurance companies, and shipping companies disappeared, through loss of capital, absorption through nationalization, or by simple destruction. In many countries, confidence in the local currency has been severely shaken. The breakdown of the business structure of Europe during the war was complete. Recovery has been seriously retarded by the fact that two years after the close of hostilities a peace settlement with Germany and Austria has not been agreed upon. But even given a more prompt solution of these difficult problems, the rehabilitation of the economic structure of Europe quite evidently will require a much longer time and greater effort than had been foreseen. . . .

The truth of the matter is that Europe's requirements for the next three or four years of foreign food and other essential products—principally from America—are so much greater than her present ability to pay that she must have substantial additional help or face economic, social, and political deterioration of a very grave character.

The remedy lies in breaking the vicious circle and restoring the confidence of the European people in the economic future of their own countries and of Europe as a whole. The manufacturer and the farmer throughout wide areas must be able and willing to exchange their products for currencies the continuing value of which is not open to question.

Aside from the demoralizing effect on the world at large and the possibilities of disturbances arising as a result of the desperation of the people concerned, the consequences to the economy of the United States should be apparent to all. It is logical that the United States should do whatever it is able to do to assist in the return of normal economic health in the world, without which there can be no political stability and no assured peace. Our policy is directed not against any country or doctrine but against hunger, poverty, desperation, and chaos. Its purpose should be the revival of a working economy in the world so as to permit the emergence of political and social conditions in which free institutions can exist. Such assistance, I am convinced, must not be on a piecemeal basis as various crises develop. Any assistance that this Government may render in the future should provide a cure rather than a mere palliative. Any government that is willing to assist in the task of recovery will find full cooperation, I am sure, on the part of the United States Government. Any government which maneuvers to block the recovery of other countries cannot expect help from us. Furthermore, governments, political parties, or groups which seek to perpetuate human misery in order to profit therefrom politically or otherwise will encounter the opposition of the United States.

It is already evident that, before the United States Government can proceed much further in its efforts to alleviate the situation and help start the European world on its way to recovery, there must be some agreement among the countries of Europe as to the requirements of the situation and the part those countries themselves will take in order to give proper effect to whatever action might be undertaken by this Government. It would be neither fitting nor efficacious for this Goverment to undertake to draw up unilaterally a program designed to place Europe on its feet economically. This is the business of the Europeans. The initiative, I think, must come from Europe. The role of this country should consist of friendly aid in the drafting of a European aid program and of later support of such a program so far as it may be practical for us to do so. The program should be a joint one, agreed to by a number [of], if not all, European nations.

An essential part of any successful action on the part of the United States is an understanding on the part of the people of America of the character of the problem and the remedies to be applied. Political passion and prejudice should have no part. With foresight, and a willingness on the part of our people to face up to the vast responsibility which history has clearly placed upon our country, the difficulties I have outlined can and will be overcome.

NATIONAL SECURITY COUNCIL

NSC-68

From A *Report to the National Security Council by the Executive Secretary on United States Objectives and Programs for National Security,* April 14, 1950

A continuation of present trends would result in a serious decline in the strength of the free world relative to the Soviet Union and its satellites. This unfavorable trend arises from the inadequacy of current programs and plans rather than from any error in our objectives and aims. These trends lead in the direction of isolation, not by deliberate decision but by lack of the necessary basis for a vigorous initiative in the conflict with the Soviet Union.

Our position as the center of power in the free world places a heavy responsibility upon the United States for leadership. We must organize and enlist the energies and resources of the free world in a positive program for peace which will frustrate the Kremlin design for world domination by creating a situation in the free world to which the Kremlin will be compelled to adjust. Without such a cooperative effort, led by the United States, we will have to make gradual withdrawals under pressure until we discover one day that we have sacrificed positions of vital interest.

It is imperative that this trend be reversed by a much more rapid and concerted build-up of the actual strength of both the United States and the other nations of the free world. The analysis shows that this will be costly and will involve significant domestic financial and economic adjustments.

The execution of such a build-up, however, requires that the United States have an affirmative program beyond the solely defensive one of countering the threat posed by the Soviet Union. This program must light the path to peace and order among nations in a system based on freedom and justice, as contemplated in the Charter of the United Nations. Further, it must envisage the political and economic measures with which and the military shield behind which the free world can work to frustrate the Kremlin design by the strategy of the cold war; for every consideration of devotion to our fundamental values and to our national security demands that we achieve our objectives by the strategy of the cold war, building up our military strength in order that it may not have to be used. The only sure victory lies in the frustration of the Kremlin design by the steady development of the moral and material strength of the free world and its projection into the Soviet world in such a way as to bring about an internal change in the Soviet system. Such a positive program—harmonious with our fundamental national purpose and our objectives—is necessary if we are to regain and retain the initiative and to win and hold the necessary popular support and cooperation in the United States and the rest of the free world.

This program should contain a plan for negotiation with the Soviet Union, developed and agreed with our allies and which is consonant with our objectives. The United States and its allies, particularly the United Kingdom and France, should always be ready to negotiate with the Soviet Union on terms consistent with our objectives. The present world situation, however, is one which militates against successful negotiations with the Kremlin—for the terms of agreements on important pending issues would reflect present realities and would therefore be unacceptable, if not disastrous, to the United States and the rest of the free world. After a decision and a start on building up the strength of the free world has been made, it might then be desirable for the United States to take an initiative in seeking negotiations in the hope that it might facilitate the process of accommodation by the Kremlin to the new situation. Failing that, the unwillingness of the Kremlin to accept equitable terms or its bad faith in observing them would assist in consolidating popular opinion in the free world in support of the measures necessary to sustain the build-up.

In summary, we must, by means of a rapid and sustained build-up of the political, economic, and military strength of the free world, and by means of an affirmative program intended to wrest the initiative from the Soviet Union, confront it with convincing evidence of the determination and ability of the free world to frustrate the Kremlin design of a world dominated by its will. Such evidence is the only means short of war which eventually may force the Kremlin to abandon its present course of action and to negotiate acceptable agreements on issues of major importance.

The whole success of the proposed program hangs ultimately on recognition by this Government, the American people, and all free peoples, that the cold war is in fact a real war in which the survival of the free world is at stake.

Essential prerequisites to success are consultations with Congressional leaders designed to make the program the object of non-partisan legislative support, and a presentation to the public of a full explanation of the facts and implications of the present international situation. The prosecution of the program will require of us all the ingenuity, sacrifice, and unity demanded by the vital importance of the issue and the tenacity to persevere until our national objectives have been attained.

DEAN ACHESON

Dean Acheson (1893–1971), like most of the principal figures in the Hamiltonian tradition, came from an elite Northeastern Anglo-American background; his father was the Episcopal bishop of Connecticut. Educated at Yale (where he was Cole Porter's roommate), Acheson received his law degree from Harvard and spent the 1920s and 1930s as a corporate lawyer in New York, with the exception of a brief stint as an Under Secretary of the Treasury in 1933. In 1941 he became an Assistant Secretary of State, and then Under Secretary of State from 1945 to 1947. From 1947 to 1953 he served as Secretary of State under President Truman. In that capacity Acheson became one of the principal architects of America's successful Cold War grand strategy. During the Vietnam War he emerged from retirement to join the group of "Wise Men" of the foreign policy establishment who advised President Johnson to liquidate the costly and inconclusive proxy war with China and the Soviet Union in Indochina.

In the following excerpt from his memoirs (*Present at the Creation: My Years in the State Department,* 1969), he describes how the Wilsonian illusions and grandiose ambitions of American policymakers like Cordell Hull, FDR's Secretary of State, had to be discarded in favor of realism and improvisation. Among the delusions of Acheson's *bête noire* Hull, it should be noted, was the common misconception that free trade would lead to world peace. "Toward 1916 I embraced the philosophy I carried out throughout my twelve years as Secretary of State," the former Tennessee Senator recalled in his 1948 memoirs. "From then on, to me unhampered trade dovetailed with peace; high tariffs, trade barriers, and unfair economic competition with war."

The Struggle Through Illusion to Policy

Many times in the course of this book I have remarked upon our misconceptions of the state of the world around us, both in anticipating postwar conditions and in recognizing what they actually were when we came face to face with them. This was true not only of the extent of physical destruction, damage, and loss caused by the war, but even more of social, economic, and political dislocations undermining the very continuance of great states and empires. Only slowly did it dawn upon us that the whole world structure and order that we had inherited from the nineteenth century was gone and that the struggle to replace it would be directed from two bitterly opposed and ideologically irreconcilable power centers.

The first and perhaps most glaring example of our unawareness has appeared in the account of our slow realization of the extent of postwar relief and rehabilitation needs. At first we saw them almost as capable of being met by semiprivate charity, as in Belgium during the earlier phase of the European Civil War; gradually our conception enlarged to the international program of UNRRA, and then, three years after the end of the war, to the massive effort of the Marshall Plan and the associated foreign aid plans.

Again, as we looked further into political and economic problems, and particularly as we began to meet them, our preliminary idea appeared more and more irrelevant to the developing facts and the attitudes, purposes, and capabilities of other actors on the scene. Mr. Hull's establishment had drawn its blueprints from Wilsonian liberalism and a utopian dream. They were founded on a refurbished and strengthened League of Nations, which assumed continued cooperation of the wartime alliance in banishing war and the use of force. Economic arrangements—even the new ideas of Maynard Keynes—were to be brought into conformity with the classical economic goals of removing obstructions from the free movement of goods, people, and funds as means of expanding trade and development. And economic development was to take on an evangelistic character in support of social justice and democratic institutions.

Furthermore, within months, even weeks, of the surrender of Germany and Japan, unilateral disarmament was under way in the Western nations. In some cases military defeat, in others approaching bankruptcy and the end of lend-lease, in the United States the conviction that militarism had gone forever and a new day had dawned led to wholesale demobilization of armed forces. . . .

It was in that period [1945–48] that we awakened fully to the facts of the surrounding world and to the scope and kind of action required by the interests of the United States; the second period, that of President Truman's second administration, became the time for full action upon these conclusions and for meeting the whole gamut of reactions—favorable, hostile, and merely recalcitrant, foreign and domestic—that they produced. In the first period, the main lines of policy were set and begun; in the second, they were put into full effect amid the smoke and confusion of battle.

These lines of policy, which have guided the actions of our country for nearly two decades, were not sonorous abstractions—much less what President Lincoln called "pernicious abstractions"—written down in a sort of official book of proverbs. Nor were they rules or doctrines. Rather they were precedents and grew by the method of the Common Law into a *corpus diplomaticum* to aid the judgment of those who must make decisions. Its central aim and purpose was to safeguard the highest interest of our nation, which was to maintain as spacious an environment as possible in which free states might exist and flourish. Its method was common action with like-minded states to secure and enrich the environment and to protect one another from predators through mutual aid and joint effort.

The *corpus* differed from Mr. Hull's preconceptions by relegating to the future the attempt at universality in a sharply divided world. Like our own Constitution, the *corpus* in its order of priorities rated ahead of promotion of the general welfare the insurance of domestic tranquillity and provision for the common defense. It placed the strategic approach to practicable objectives, concretely and realistically conceived, ahead of generalizations, even those wearing the garb of idealism. It developed institutions and means to aid in achieving these more limited and, it was hoped, transitory ends.

In later years, the conceptions of this *corpus diplomaticum* have been criticized because its very success in meeting the urgent problems and dangers it was designed to meet in Europe and Korea has led our allies to relax their efforts, partly in the hope that they are no longer necessary and partly in the lurking belief that they were never quite so necessary as represented. Hardly had American leadership in collective political and military measures brought an end to Soviet aggressive activism initiated by the blockade of Berlin and the attack on South Korea when the successful measures were doubted by advocates of detente with the Soviet Union and disengagement abroad. Again illusions obscured reality, although the Soviet Union in Hungary in 1956 and in Czechoslovakia in 1968 showed with the most blatant brutality the nature of its fears, its intentions, and its capabilities. It is a mistake to interpret too literally and sweepingly the poet's admonition that things are not what they seem. Sometimes they are, and it is often essential to survival to know when they are and when they are not.

Another source of instability in foreign affairs is the popular conception that, as in women's fashions and automobile design, novelty and change are essential to validity and value. A combination of illusion and fashion leads to a demand for yearly models in diplomatic design. The pursuit of unity and strength in the face of Soviet aggressive hostility can almost overnight give way to popular demand for a detente style, then for an Asian motif recognizing Asia's hundreds of millions, that motif soon to be displaced by a new primacy accorded to the southern hemisphere. The simple truth is that perseverance in good policies is the only avenue to success, and that even perseverance in poor ones often gives the appearance of being so, as General de Gaulle has so continuously demonstrated.

The great exponent of perseverance, William the Silent, Prince of Orange, never wavered in the face of every hardship and disaster from striving for the unity and independence of the Netherlands. The immortal sentence in which he epitomized his life cannot be repeated too often: "It is not necessary to hope in order to act, or to succeed in order to persevere."

PAUL H. NITZE

Paul Nitze (b. 1907) is one of the most distinguished practitioners and students of statecraft in American history. During World War II he served in various capacities, including that of vice chairman of the Strategic Bombing Survey, for which he was awarded the Medal of Merit by President Truman. As director of the State Department's Policy Planning Staff in 1950, he helped to design the policy of containment of the Soviet Union. He later served Secretary of the Navy in the 1960s and as a chief U.S. arms negotiator with the Soviet Union in both the 1970s and the 1980s. For half a century he played a leading role in American foreign policy as a leading public servant rather than as an elected politician.

Nitze was one of the principal authors of NSC-68 (1950), one of the key documents in the development of America's Cold War grand strategy. In the following excerpt from a speech delivered to the faculty and students of the Naval War College in 1953, Nitze defends the strategy of containment against possible alternatives.

The Seven Pillars of Unwisdom

From *Paul H. Nitze on Foreign Policy,* 1989

The approach which I propose to take may appear to be somewhat theoretical and analytic. In certain circumstances such an approach may clarify rather than confuse.

But to dive into the heart of the subject, I should like to start by discussing three interrelated concepts.

The first of these is the preservation of the republic, the second is the reduction of Soviet power and influence, and the third is the avoidance of war.

These three concepts, stated in various ways, appear explicitly or implicitly in almost every statement of our national aims. The way in which they are phrased is important; perhaps more important is the way in which these concepts are conceived of as being interrelated.

It has seemed to us in the Policy Planning Staff that the first of these concepts, the preservation of the republic, is different in kind from the other two. The concept of the reduction of Soviet power and influence is a contingent concept which depends from an external fact, the fact that today the principal threat to our republic comes from the power and influence of the Soviets. The third concept, the avoidance of war, is also contingent in that there clearly are circumstances under which we could not preserve the republic if we were unwilling or unprepared for general war.

It seemed to us, therefore, that the first concept differs from other aims, objectives, or policies. We thought a more useful and descriptive word to describe this concept was the word "purpose."

In one of the important National Security papers (NSC 68) prepared in the spring of 1950, we expressed it this way:

> The fundamental purpose of the United States is laid down in the Preamble to the Constitution: ". . . to form a more perfect Union, establish Justice, insure domestic Tranquillity, provide for the general Welfare, and secure the Blessings of Liberty to ourselves and our Posterity." In essence, the fundamental purpose is to assure the integrity and vitality of our free society, which is founded upon the dignity and worth of the individual.

I should like to emphasize three points about this formulation. The first is that it is tied into the United States Constitution to which, as servants of the American people, we take our oath of office. As such it is not wholly applicable as a statement of purpose applicable to the free world coalition.

The second is that it calls for more than mere survival. It calls for the creation of conditions in which our system can live and prosper.

The third is its emphasis upon our willingness to fight if necessary to defend this purpose.

Let us now take a more thorough look at the second concept we started with, the reduction of Soviet power and influence. In a certain sense this is merely another and narrower say of saying the creation of conditions in which our system can live and prosper.

At this point we are in the center of what we are usually talking about when we refer to foreign policy.

By way of introduction it may be useful to suggest a definition of foreign policy. Foreign policy can be defined as being the projection of the will of the State to matters external to its domain; in other words, the courses of action undertaken by a government to affect matters of concern to it but beyond the span of its jurisdiction. . . . Furthermore, foreign policy relates to acting—that is, matching of ends and finite limited means.

Therefore, when we discuss as an aim the creation of conditions in which our system can live and prosper, we are talking only about one aspect of the foreign policy problem. We are talking about aims without having as yet related them to the means which we propose to use in achieving them. And we are a long way from the concrete actions which alone can be expected to achieve them.

It is when we get to the third concept, the avoidance of war, that we begin to get into the field of the means which we propose to use in achieving our ends.

One of the principles the United States has stood for is that war should not be used as an instrument of foreign policy. Obviously a disagreement about trade policy, fishing rights, adequate compensation for the taking of property, unfriendly statements, or failure to ratify a treaty are not matters where the ultimate sanction of war is appropriate.

If the fundamental purpose of the United States is threatened, if we are faced with defeat or the real prospect of eventual defeat if we cannot preserve or achieve certain vital aims, this question takes on a different meaning.

The United States has considered that an attack on any of the American states, that an attack on the European states who are members of NATO, including Greece and Turkey, that an attack on Western Germany, Berlin, or Japan, that an attack on the Philippines, Australia, New Zealand or on Formosa would constitute such a threat, and has registered this either by treaty or presidential declaration. We have gone further to give solemn warnings with respect to other areas, such as Yugoslavia and Indochina. We have gone into a limited war over an attack on the Republic of Korea.

The question remains, however, as to whether we should resort to general war against the U.S.S.R. in order to bring about a recession of Soviet power from the satellites and from China. It is this question which underlies much of the argument as to liberation versus containment.

In the same NSC paper to which I referred earlier, the policy of containment was described as follows:

As for the policy of "containment," it is one which seeks by all means short of war to (1) block further expansion of Soviet power, (2) expose the falsities of Soviet pretensions, (3) induce a retraction of the Kremlin's control and influence and (4) in general, so foster the seeds of destruction within the Soviet system that the Kremlin is brought at least to the point of modifying its behavior to conform to generally accepted international standards.

It was and continues to be cardinal in this policy that we possess superior overall power in ourselves or in dependable combination with other like-minded nations. One of the most important ingredients of power is military strength. In the concept of "containment," the maintenance of a strong military posture is deemed to be essential for two reasons: (1) as an ultimate guarantee of our national security and (2) as an indispensable backdrop to the conduct of the policy of "containment." Without superior aggregate military strength in being and readily mobilizable, a policy of "containment"—which is in effect a policy of calculated and gradual coercion—is no more than a policy of bluff.

At the same time, it is essential to the successful conduct of a policy of "containment" that we always leave open the possibility of negotiation with the U.S.S.R. A diplomatic freeze—and we are in one now—tends to defeat the very purposes of "containment" because it raises tensions at the same time that it make Soviet retractions and adjustments in the direction of moderated behavior more difficult. It also tends to inhibit our initiative and deprives us of opportunities for maintaining a moral ascendancy in our struggle with the Soviet system.

In "containment" it is desirable to exert pressure in a fashion which will avoid so far as possibly directly challenging Soviet prestige, to keep open the possibility for the U.S.S.R. to retreat before pressure with a minimum loss of face and to secure political advantage from the failure of the Kremlin to yield or take advantage of the openings we leave it.

The continuing requirements of a program of gradual coercion without resort to general war are very great indeed. These requirements are in part economic. It is a very expensive business both for us and for our allies to build and to maintain for as long as may be necessary military power superior to that which the Soviets and its [sic] satellites have and are building. The political requirements in the form of fortitude and continued willingness to make real sacrifices for a slow-moving policy are also very great.

There is therefore continued pressure to find some quicker and easier road to the attainment of our objectives. This pressure finds its expression in a number of suggestions as to the conduct of our foreign policy.

These suggestions group themselves into distinct categories. It was once suggested that we might call them the seven pillars of unwisdom.

The first pillar is victory through reorganization. The advocates of world government, Atlantic Union, sole reliance on the United Nations fall into this category.

The second pillar is victory through lung power. Those who believe that through threats, promises, hortatory speeches, or merely through the simple clear exposition of our aims the walls of Jericho will collapse, fall into this category.

The third pillar is victory through change of personalities. In this group fall those who believe that the United States is inherently omnipotent and that insofar as there are problems in the world they must spring from the incompetence or treasonableness of individuals. If we were to remove them, our problems would fall away.

The fourth pillar is victory through eliminating our allies. This group believes that the sins of the British or the French, or some other foreigners on our side, are so corrupting our position that if we could eliminate them and pursue a pure United States foreign policy victory would be easy.

The fifth pillar is victory through retreat. It being apparent that our commitments exceed our capabilities, assuming that we are not to increase our present efforts, it therefore follows that we should withdraw our commitments even if this means going back to the Western Hemisphere.

The sixth pillar is victory through personal diplomacy. If we only had people competent to talk turkey to our allies or to the enemy, or if those who are competent were permitted to conduct our diplomacy as their experience indicated, our problems would fall away.

The seventh pillar is victory through technology—or concentration on new weapons, particularly atomic weapons. This group tends to move over to the "drop the bomb now," and "we should have dropped the bomb earlier" school.

Now each of these points has in it an element of wisdom. It is only when the proposition is made that one can rely solely on a partial element and that it is not necessary to devote energy to other essential elements that one is led into unwisdom. . . .

To go back then to the three concepts that we started with, the preservation of the republic, the reduction of Soviet power and influence, and the avoidance of war, their interrelationship and hierarchy stand out clearly. The first one, the preservation of the republic, is at the heart of our fundamental purpose as a nation; the second one is an aim which is part of a wider aim, the creation of conditions in which the republic can live and prosper; the third one is a limitation upon the means which we propose to employ in achieving this aim. To put these three concepts in a hierarchy of relative importance the order would be preservation of the republic first; the avoidance of general war, second; and the reduction of Soviet power and influence, third.

A New International System

From "The Recovery of Ethics," 1960

International politics presents even more difficulties, as a field in which to sort out the role of ethics, than does the field of domestic politics.

In the international arena, no one has a monopoly of the legitimate use of force and the most basic values may be in conflict—even the values associated with the survival of entire nations or civilizations. There is no executive controlled by a constitution, balanced by a judicial and a legislative branch and subject to the restraints of *habeas corpus* and due process. But even the international arena need not be wholly without order.

From 1815 to 1914, a certain degree of international order was maintained. The balance of power system among the European states preserved a certain degree of stability. England, with control of the seas, could act as a balance wheel. Economic institutions based on the gold standard and centering on the London capital market provided an economic framework within which large portions of the world, including the United States, were able to make tremendous forward strides in developing their economies. Above all, wars were kept limited as to objective and limited in extent.

The two world wars shattered the system which existed prior to 1914. Today the fundamental issue in the international arena is that of who will construct a new international order, appropriate to today's world, to take the place of the one that was shattered in those two world wars.

Until the spring of 1947, we in the United States did not face up to the fact that that was the issue and that we had to do something about it, because no one else had the will or resources to do it. Few of us remember the intense activity of the six months beginning in March 1947 with the Truman Doctrine, announcing our determination to help those willing to fight for their independence. This was followed by the Greek–Turkish Aid Program, the merger of the Western zones of Western Germany leading to restoration of German sovereignty, the Marshall Plan, the Rio Treaty, and the National Security Act of 1947, creating the Defense Department, the Central Intelligence Agency, the National Security Council, and the National Security Resources Board. That intense activity in 1947 was subsequently followed up with the filling out of our treaty arrangements, including NATO and the ANZUS Pact, the Mutual Defense Assistance Act, Point Four, the restoration of sovereignty to

Japan, and, finally, the decision to intervene in support of the Republic of Korea against overt aggression.

As one looks back on the overall pattern of the actions undertaken in those years, one can ask what is it that we were trying to do? I think one can summarize it by saying that we were trying to lay the foundations for an international system which would substitute, in the circumstances existing in the modern world, for the system which the balance of power in Europe, supported and managed by the British—relying on their control of the seas—had maintained during the century following the Congress of Vienna. This new structure had to have its political, its economic, and its military aspects. It had to provide for certain overall world-wide functions within which closer regional institutions could be developed. A unique role in this system had continuously to be borne by the United States because we alone had the resources and the will to tackle the job. And while this system was being developed it had to be continuously protected against the hostile and destructive efforts of the Soviet–Chinese Communist bloc which was dedicated to the construction of another and antithetical system. . . .

The object was to create a structure sufficiently flexible to house the diverse interests and requirements of the entire non-Communist world. Even with respect to the Communist world it was hoped that the structure would have something to offer and would, by its attractive power, either draw off portions of the Communist world, as it did in the case of Yugoslavia, or result in a weakening of the bonds within the Communist world, as it did in the case of Poland but failed to do in the case of Communist China.

In 1952 and 1953 only a portion of the United States population was persuaded that an effort as enormous as that entailed in the contruction and maintenance, with the United States bearing the principal responsibility, of a new international system was really necessary. Could we not look more to our own interests as a nation and leave to others the worries about an international system? Others thought that so burdensome an external policy would inevitably prove inconsistent with the preservation of our domestic political traditions. Still others thought that, though the aims of our foreign policy might be all right, there must be some easier and cheaper way of going about the business. And there were those who were disappointed in the prospect of an effort extending indefinitely into the future. If we not only had to get such a system going, but then had to keep it going, in spite of the apathy of a large portion of the world and the bitter hostility of another large portion, would we not be at the job forever? . . .

If the nation, or nations, principally responsible for a given international system appear to lose faith in that system and appear to be following their narrow national interests, the other nations of lesser power are bound to become uncertain in their policy. These lesser powers know that they, without the co-operation and leadership of the great powers, cannot hope to make the system work. They must then decide whether the faltering by the great powers is temporary or whether they must prepare to adjust themselves to some quite different system.

After the Cold War

For much of the era between 1914 and 1989, Hamiltonian realists and Wilsonian globalists, agreeing, for different reasons, that U.S. intervention in the world wars of Eurasia was necessary, have been allied against isolationists—pro-German isolationists in the first two World Wars, and pro-communist isolationists on the left during the Cold War. During the three world wars (the Cold War was World War III) the boundaries between globally minded Hamiltonian realism and muscular Wilsonian idealism became very blurred, with both groups tending to support anti-Soviet alliances like NATO and free trade (which Hamiltonians favored as an expedient to unite the anti-Soviet coalition, and which Wilsonians treated as a good in itself). Even after the end of the Cold War, the need to defend a grand strategy of forward defense in Europe, Asia, and the Middle East continued to unite Hamiltonian realists and Wilsonian globalists in the American foreign policy elite against their neo-Jeffersonian isolationist critics. In the decades to come, however, events might produce a parting of the ways between Hamiltonian proponents of an active but limited and nationalist foreign policy and Wilsonian believers in collective security and world federation.

FAREED ZAKARIA

Fareed Zakaria, managing editor of *Foreign Affairs* and a contributing editor of *Newsweek,* is the author of *From Wealth to Power: The Unusual Origins of America's World Role* (1997/8). Zakaria reflects on the distinctions between American and continental European realism in "The Ultimate Resume" (review of Godfrey Hodgson, *The Colonel: The Life and Wars of Henry Stimson, 1867–1950*) in *The National Interest,* Summer 1991.

American Realism

American Realism proceeds from the assumption that the Pax Britannica of the nineteenth century was a blessing, preserving peace, trade, and travel around the globe. The United States has taken Britain's place as the balancer of the world, ensuring that expansionists are thwarted in their efforts to unsettle the world. By implication, of course, American hegemony is not feared because it is benign. While eagerly accepting national power and the need for force, proponents of this ideology tame the Rooseveltian imperial faith in war as a "moral adventure." They take from Europe's great power game the need for calculation, wariness, and an understanding of the limits of power, but they cannot play the game as unselfconsciously as the Europeans did. Admittedly, these lessons in skepticism have been difficult to master, and—as realists like George Kennan have often pointed out—many of America's foreign policy failures can be attributed to its inability to temper idealism with prudence.

Part of the problem is that advocates of American Realism . . . have never been sure which aspects of liberalism they accept and which they reject.

International liberalism can be divided into three components: *commercial,* *republican,* and *regulatory liberalism.*[2] In the past, American realists, even when they have forcefully promoted free trade, have considered commercial liberalism's faith in the pacific effects of commerce to be naïve. Though they have often supported nasty regimes, American statesmen have frequently and increasingly accepted republican liberalism—believing that a nation's domestic system has an effect on its external behavior and that democracies are more peace-loving than dictatorships. And while European *realpolitik*'s principal criticism of liberalism is its misguided emphasis on collective security, American statesmen have never been able entirely to reject regulatory liberalism and its advocacy of international organizations, laws, and regimes. In practice, they have placed their faith in the pacific effects of free trade, democracy, and international organizations, believing that these measures enhance peace and stability, at least in the "civilized" world.

For all this intellectual confusion, many American foreign policy successes contain a wise blend of idealism and *realpolitik.* Consider the greatest triumph . . . the postwar rehabilitation of Europe and Japan. This rested on a belief that the greatest threat that Europe faced was not one involving military security—the focus of *realpolitik*—but rather a political threat. The solution was even bolder: domestic reconstruction. Europe had to be made socially, politically, and economically confident enough not to succumb to pro-Soviet communism.

The motives for American aid were, of course, part self-interest and part generosity, but more striking is the American faith that Germany and Japan could be rebuilt into peace-loving, prosperous democracies. No European great power, it must be said, was ever so generous with its vanquished enemies, and few had the arrogance to believe that ancient civilizations could be remade. . . . That the United States succeeded in its task, achieving liberal ends through often illiberal means, suggests that American Realism may have appreciated aspects of the modern world—the universal appeal of democracy and the promise of the free market, for example—which make it more *realistic* than the Old World's cynicism.

---

2. These distinctions are drawn from Robert Keohane, "International Liberalism Reconsidered," in John Dunn's *The Economic Limits to Modern Politics* (Cambridge: Cambridge University Press, 1990).

JAMES CHACE

James Chace, a former managing editor of *Foreign Affairs,* is the editor of the *World Policy Journal* and the author of a number of books on U.S. foreign policy, including *The Consequences of the Peace* (1992), from which this excerpt is taken.

The Realist Vision

The stable structure of peace that F.D.R. hoped for rested on four pillars: a significantly expanded role for the United States abroad; an accommodation with the Soviet Union; a major role for postwar China; and the end to colonialism. All of these aims have at last been achieved.

Haunted by the arms buildup and the self-defeating economic nationalism of the 1930s, Roosevelt's internationalism also encompassed a world in which free trade would lead to an ever expanding prosperity. With the war still under way, a series of conferences, mostly initiated by Washington, began to shape the world we have lived in for the past half-century—Bretton Woods (which, through the establishment of the International Monetary Fund and the World Bank, provided for currency stabilization); Dumbarton Oaks (which drew up plans for the United Nations); Hot Springs (for food and agriculture); Washington (for relief and rehabilitation); and Chicago (for civil aviation). In calling for free markets, full employment, and human rights, the Rooseveltian vision became the postwar vision for the Western world.

It was also the failure of the postwar victors to implement the peace that brought about the breakdown of the postwar order F.D.R. had hoped for. In the Declaration on Liberated Europe, which Stalin, Churchill, and Roosevelt signed at Yalta, the Big Three promised that "the liberated peoples" of Eastern Europe would be permitted "to choose the form of government under which they will live," "to create democratic institutions of their own choice," and to establish "through free elections . . . governments responsive to the will of the people." The Yalta accords, in short, called for the democratic Eastern Europe that may be coming into being—after nearly a half-century when Europe was split into hostile ideological camps, precisely because Stalin broke the pledges he had given in the Crimea in 1945. . . .

The collapse of the Soviet empire, the end of the struggle for ideological supremacy between Moscow and Washington, the absolute necessity to rethink our military commitments and force structures, all this presents a signal occasion for embracing a new American internationalism. It would rest on the proposition that a global balance of powers is coming into being. It would require the United States to abandon any pretense to being the only superpower, yet it would preclude a withdrawal into ourselves. It would require us to use all our efforts to sustain the global balance, taking nothing for granted in our ability to remain economically and militarily vigorous. Roosevelt's vision was of a world of democratic nations, united "in a permanent system of general security" and in a freely trading international economy—a vision, if we recognize it, that we can now hope to achieve as a consequence of the peace.

SAMUEL P. HUNTINGTON

Samuel P. Huntington is Albert J. Weatherhead III University Professor at Harvard, where he is also director of the John M. Olin Institute for Strategic Studies and chairman of the Harvard Academy for International and Area Studies. Huntington has served in government both during the Vietnam War and during the Carter administration, when he was coordinator of security planning of the National Security Council, 1977–78. His classic and often controversial books on U.S. foreign policy and domestic politics include *The Soldier and the State* (1957); *Political Order in Changing Societies* (1968); *American Politics: The Promise of Disharmony* (1981); and *The Clash of Civilizations* (1996). The following selection is from "Why International Primacy Matters," in *International Security,* Spring 1993.

International Primacy

PRIMACY IN WHAT?

First, what do we mean by primacy? Primacy in what? Politics is concerned with primacy in power. In international politics power is the ability of one actor, usually but not always a government, to influence the behavior of others, who may or may not be governments. International primacy means that a government is able to exercise more influence on the behavior of more actors with respect to more issues than any other government can. . . .

To ask whether primacy matters is to ask whether power matters. And the answer can only be: of course, it matters in most human relationships, even in families, and it obviously matters in national and international affairs. It does make a difference whether one party, politician, branch of government, interest group, public official, or national government has more or less power than another. . . . It matters to hundreds of millions of people throughout the world whether the United States, Japan, Germany, Europe, Russia, China, or some other entity has primacy in shaping decisions affecting the world. Political science is, indeed, the study of why, how, and with what consequences people get and exercise power in major collective entities. If power and primacy did not matter, political scientists would have to look for other work. . . .

With respect to wealth, in some circumstances actors may prefer absolute gains and in others relative gains. . . . With respect to power, however, absolute gains are meaningless. An actor gains or loses power compared to other people. Since it concerns the ability of people to influence each other, power is only relative. Lord Acton and others may have talked about "absolute power," but they do not mean absolute in the meaning it has in the term absolute gains. Absolute power itself is relative. . . . International primacy means a state has more power than other actors and hence primacy is inherently relative.

Even if power is relative, the question remains: Why do people want power? A variety of motives are possible. The contest for power itself may be satisfying and enjoyable. So also may be the exercise of power once it is acquired. To be powerful and to be viewed by others as such surely enhances the self-esteem of individuals and nations. Power enables an actor to shape his environment so as to reflect his interests. In particular it enables a state to protect its security and prevent, deflect, or defeat threats to that security. It also enables a state to promote its values among other peoples and to shape the international environment so as to reflect its values. States and other actors who are powrful can, and do, do evil. But power is also the prerequisite to doing good and promoting collective goals. Almost nothing beneficial in the world happens except by the exercise of power.

IS HISTORY ENDING?

It is a fact well-known since Thucydides that it matters which state exercises the most power in the international system. At no time in history has this been more true than in the twentieth century: one has only to consider what the world would have looked like if Nazi Germany had won World War II, or the Soviet Union won the Cold War. No reason exists to assume that what has been true for millennia will cease to be true in the next hundred years.

Does it matter to the United States or the world that American primacy is maintained? Obviously that depends on what the alternative distribution of power might be. Logically there are two other possibilities. Some other state could displace the United States as the only superpower in the world, or there could be a condition in which no state was in a position of international primacy and there was a rough equilibrium of power among the major states. Would either of these situations be more desirable for the United States or for the world than the maintenance of U.S. primacy?

It is quite erroneous to think that the principal reason states pursue international primacy is to be able to win wars, and that hence if war is unlikely primacy is unimportant. States pursue primacy in order to be able to insure their security, promote their interests, and shape the international environment in ways that will reflect their interests and values. Primacy is desirable not primarily to achieve victory in war but to achieve the state's goals without recourse to war. Primacy is thus an alternative to war. A state such as the United States that has achieved international primacy has every reason to maintain that primacy through peaceful means so as to preclude the need of having to fight a war to maintain it.

Some argue that the end of the Cold War means the end of history as we have known it. Unfortunately every day's newspaper contains dramatic and tragic evidence that the end of the Cold War means the return to history as we used to know it. Conflicts among nations and ethnic groups are escalating. Controversies are intensifying between the United States and other major powers. This is to be expected. The end of a significant war or conflict, whether among individuals, groups, or states, creates the basis for the generation of new conflicts. The end of war leads to the breakup of the coalition of powers fighting the war. There is no reason why the end of the Cold War should have any different consequences. The alliances of the United States with Japan and with the Western European countries in NATO rested on three fundamentals: shared political and economic values; common economic interests; and the Soviet security threat. Without the last of these three, the alliances would never have come into existence. Now, however, the Soviet threat is gone, and common economic interests are giving way to competing economic interests. Shared political and economic values remain the principal glue holding together the grand alliances of the Cold War. Those common values are real, and they mean that wars are most unlikely between these countries. They do not mean that these countries will have shared or even congruent interests. Instead the disappearance of the common enemy means that conflicting interests that were subordinated to the common need to unite against the Soviet security threat during the Cold War will now emerge with a vengeance. This is not likely to lead to the physical mayhem that occurred in Bosnia, but it will lead to intense conflicts over political and economic interests. Competition—the struggle for primacy—we all recognize as natural among individuals, corporations, political parties, athletes, and universities. It is no less natural among countries.

DOES ECONOMIC PRIMACY MATTER?

In the coming years, the principal conflicts involving the United States and the major powers are likely to be over economic issues. U.S. economic primacy is now being challenged by Japan and is likely to be challenged in the future by Europe. Obviously the United States, Japan, and Europe have common interests in promoting economic development and international trade. They also, however, have deeply conflicting interests over the distribution of the benefits and costs of economic growth and the distribution of the costs of economic stagnation or decline. The idea that economics is primarily a non-zero-sum game is a favorite conceit of tenured academics. It has little connection to reality. In the course of the economic competition that may produce economic growth, companies go bankrupt; bankers forfeit their investments; factories are closed; managers and workers lose their jobs; money, wealth, well-being, and power are shifted from one industry, region, or country to another.

Economists argue that in economic competition what counts are absolute not relative gains; to economists this is a self-evident truth. It is, however, self-evident to almost no one but economists. The American public as a whole, various groups in American society, and the leaders and publics in other societies do not buy it for a moment. Why are the economists out in left field? They are there because they are blind to the fact that economic activity is a source of power as well as well-being. It is, indeed, probably the most important source of power, and in a world in which military conflict between major states is unlikely, economic power will be increasingly important in determining the primacy or subordination of states. Precisely for this reason Americans have every reason to be concerned by the current challenge to American economic primacy posed by Japan and the possible future challenge that could come from Europe. . . .

WHAT'S THE WORLD'S INTEREST?

The maintenance of U.S. primacy matters for the world as well as for the United States.

First, no other country can make comparable contributions to international order and stability. The security consequences of a multipolar world have been dramatically evident in the dismal failure of the major European powers to deal with the Yugoslav catastrophe on their doorstep. Leaders and publics throughout the world recognize the need for an American presence and American leadership in maintaining stability in their region. These are, as the prime ministers of Japan and Korea said, "indispensable" to Asian security. Crowds chanting "Americans go home!" are not much in evidence these days. The fear is, instead, that Americans may well turn isolationist again and do exactly that. The ability of the United States to provide international order is obviously limited and, despite the constant demands, the United States cannot settle every dispute in every part of the world. Yet the fact remains that, as General Colin Powell, Chairman of the Joint Chiefs of Staff, put it, "One of the fondest expressions around here is that we can't be the world's policeman. But guess who gets called when suddenly someone needs a cop?" As Bosnia, Somalia, and many other places evidence, the answer to that question is obvious. And, given the nature of the world as it is, is there any remotely plausible alternative or better answer? If the United States is unable to maintain security in the world's trouble spots, no other single country or combination of countries is likely to provide a substitute.

Second, the collapse of the Soviet Union leaves the United States as the only major power whose national identity is defined by a set of universal political and economic values. For the United States these are liberty, democracy, equality, private property, and markets. In varying degrees other major countries may from time to time support these values. Their identity, however, is not defined by these values, and hence they have far less commitment to them and less interest in promoting them than does the United States. This is not, obviously, to argue that these values are always at the forefront of American foreign policy; other concerns and needs have to be taken into consideration. It is, rather, to argue that the promotion of democracy, human rights, and markets are far more central to American policy than to the policy of any other country. . . . To argue that primacy does not matter is to argue that political and economic values do not matter and that democracy does not or should not matter.

A world without U.S. primacy will be a world with more violence and disorder and less democracy and economic growth than a world where the United States continues to have more influence than any other country in shaping global affairs. The sustained international primacy of the United States is central to the welfare and security of Americans and to the future of freedom, democracy, open economies, and international order in the world.

PART FIVE

THE GENERAL WELFARE

The historical differences between the Hamiltonian and Jeffersonian traditions in American politics have been greatest in the areas of domestic economic and social policy. For generations Hamiltonians have favored a national and international industrial-capitalist economy, promoted by federal support for industry, national banking, and "internal improvements" (infrastructure). Jeffersonians, for most of American history, fought for an alternate vision of the United States as a largely agrarian, decentralized republic in which the states rather than the federal government assumed responsibility for public goods like transportation and education.

By the early twentieth century, the Hamiltonian vision had prevailed—but only after many delays and disasters, of which the Civil War was the most devastating. From the election of Thomas Jefferson in 1800 to the election of Abraham Lincoln in 1860, the Hamiltonian party—known successively as the Federalists, the National Republicans, the Whigs, and the Republicans—was usually out of power. In the antebellum period Congress, the Presidency and the Supreme Court were usually controlled by Southerners imbued with the Jeffersonian hostility to the federal government, banks, and industry. The First and Second Banks of the United States were created and then abolished, ambitious projects for federal infrastructure development were rejected, and the tariff-based industrialization policy that Hamilton's successor Henry Clay dubbed "the American System" was realized only in part.

217

SAMUEL H. BEER

In the following excerpt from his book *To Make a Nation: The Rediscovery of American Federalism* (1993), the contemporary American political scientist Samuel H. Beer attempts to define the essential differences between the Hamiltonian and Jeffersonian conceptions of the goals and means of domestic government.

Hamilton and Activist Government

Hamilton's nationalism was expressed not only in his belief that Americans were "one people" rather than thirteen separate peoples but even more emphatically in his commitment to governmental activism. This concern that the American people must make vigorous use of their central government for the tasks of nation-building separated him sharply from Thomas Jefferson, Washington's Secretary of State, who leaned toward the compact theory [of states' rights]. The classic expression of this difference of opinion between the two members of the cabinet—the champion of federal power and the champion of states' rights—was their conflict over the proposed Bank of the United States. Jefferson feared that the bank would corrupt his cherished agrarian order and discovered no authority for it in the Constitution. Hamilton, believing that a central bank was necessary to sustain public credit, to promote economic development, and—in his graphic phrase—"to cement more closely the union of the states," found in a broad construction of the "necessary and proper" clause ample constitutional authorization.

Should the words "necessary and proper" be construed narrowly, as Jefferson said, or broadly, as Hamilton advised? A generation later the question came before the Supreme Court in *McCulloch* v. *Maryland* (1819). Speaking for the Jeffersonian reply, appellants advanced the theory that the

Constitution was a compact of sovereign states and therefore should be strictly construed, in order to safeguard state power against the federal government. In the Court's decision, however, John Marshall argued from the national theory that the Constitution was "ordained and established" directly by the people of the United States and concluded in almost the same words used by Hamilton that the crucial phrase "necessary and proper" should be broadly construed to mean not "indispensable" but "appropriate." Looking back today and recognizing that the words of the disputed clause could bear either construction, but that American government could never have adapted to the needs of a complex modern society in the absence of the doctrine of implied powers, the reader must feel relieved that at this critical moment in the development of our juristic federalism the national idea prevailed.

Hamilton was not only a nationalist and centralizer, he was also an elitist. Along with the bank, his first steps to revive and sustain the public credit were the full funding of the federal debt and the federal assumption of debts incurred by the states during the war of independence. These measures had their fiscal and economic purposes. Their social impact, moreover, favored the fortunes of those members of the propertied classes who had come to hold the federal and state obligations. This result, while fully understood, was incidental to Hamilton's ultimate purpose, which was political. As with the bank, that purpose was to strengthen the newly empowered central government by attaching to it the interests of these influential members of society. Hamilton promoted capitalism, not because he was a lackey to the capitalist class—indeed, as he once wrote to a close friend, "I hate moneying men"—but just the opposite: his elitism was subservient to his nationalism.

In the same cause he was not only an elitist but also an integrationist. I use that term expressly because of its current overtones, wishing to suggest Hamilton's perception of how diversity need not be divisive but may lead to mutual dependence and union. Here again he broke from Jefferson, who valued homogeneity. Hamilton, on the other hand, planned for active federal intervention to diversify the economy by the development of commerce and industry. His great report on manufactures is at once visionary and far-seeing—"the embryo of modern America," a recent writer termed it.

The economy he foresaw would be free, individualist, and competitive. The federal government, however, would take action to make it more likely that entrepreneurs invested their money in ways more advantageous to the national welfare. Bounties, premiums, and other aids, in addition to a moderately protective tariff, would be employed to develop industry, along with a federal commission to allocate funds. There would be federal inspection of manufactured goods to protect the consumer and to enhance the reputation of American goods in foreign markets. The purpose was to make the country rich and powerful. At the same time, the interdependence of agriculture and industry and especially of South and North would enhance the union. The outcome, writes a biographer, would be to make the United States "one nation indivisible, bound together by common wants, common interests and common prosperity."

Hamilton is renowned for his statecraft—for his methods of using the powers of government for economic, political, and social ends. But that emphasis obscures his originality, which consisted in his conceptualization of those ends. His methods were derivative, being taken from the theory and practice of state-builders of the seventeenth and eighteenth centuries from Colbert to Pitt. Hamilton used this familiar technology, however, to forward the unprecedented attempt to establish republican government on a continental scale. In his scheme, the unities of nationhood would sustain the authority of such a regime. By contrast, those earlier craftsmen of the modern state in Bourbon France or Hohenzollern Prussia or Whig Britain could take for granted the established authority of a monarchic and aristocratic regime. They too had their technique for enhancing the attachment of the people to the prince. But in America the people *were* the prince. To enhance their attachment to the ultimate governing power, therefore, meant fortifying the bonds that united them as a people. If the authority of this first nation-state was to suffice for its governance, the purpose of the state would have to become the development of the nation. This was the essential Hamiltonian end, to make the nation more of a nation.

HERBERT CROLY

In this selection from *The Promise of American Life* (1909), the leader of
the twentieth-century Progressive intellectual movement contrasts the
different approaches to government of Hamiltonians and Jeffersonians.

Hamiltonianism Versus Jeffersonianism

Underlying the several aspects of Hamilton's policy can be discerned a definite
theory of governmental functions. The central government is to be used, not
merely to maintain the Constitution, but to promote the national interest and
to consolidate the national organization. Hamilton saw clearly that the
American Union was far from being achieved when the Constitution was accepted by the states and the machinery of the Federal government set in motion. A good start had been made, but the way in which to keep what had
been gained was to seek for more. Unionism must be converted into a positive policy which labored to strengthen the national interest and organization,
discredit possible or actual disunionist ideas and forces, and increase the national spirit. All this implied an active interference with the natural course of
American economic and political business and its regulation and guidance in
the national direction. It implied a conscious and indefatigable attempt on
the part of the national leaders to promote the national welfare. It implied the
predominance in American political life of the men who had the energy and
the insight to discriminate between those ideas and tendencies which promoted the national welfare, and those ideas and tendencies whereby it was
imperiled. It implied, in fine, the perpetuation of the same kind of leadership
which had guided the country safely through the dangers of the critical period, and the perpetuation of the purposes which inspired that leadership. . .

221

[Hamilton] succeeded in imbuing both men of property and the mass of the "plain people" with the idea that the well-to-do were the peculiar beneficiaries of the American Federal organization, the result being that the rising democracy came more than ever to distrust the national government. Instead of seeking to base the perpetuation of the Union upon the interested motives of a minority of well-to-do citizens, he would have been far wiser to have frankly intrusted its welfare to the good-will of the whole people. . . .

It did not take Hamilton's opponents long to discover that his ideas and plans were in some respects inimical to democracy, and the consequence was that Hamilton was soon confronted by one of the most implacable and unscrupulous oppositions which ever absued a faithful and useful public servant. This opposition was led by Jefferson, and while it most unfortunately lacked Hamilton's statesmanship and sound constructive ideas, it possessed the one saving quality which Hamilton himself lacked. Jefferson was filled with a sincere, indiscriminate, and unlimited faith in the American people. He was according to his own lights a radical and unqualified democrat, and as a democrat he fought most bitterly what he considered to be the aristocratic or even monarchic tendency of Hamilton's policy. Much of the denunciation which he and his followers lavished upon Hamilton was unjust, and much of the fight which they put up against his measures was contrary to the public welfare. They absolutely failed to give him credit for the patriotism of his intentions or for the merit of his achievements, and their unscrupulous and unfair tactics established a baleful tradition in American party warfare. But Jefferson was wholly right in believing that his country was nothing, if not a democracy, and that any tendency to impair the integrity of the democratic idea could be productive only of disorder.

Unfortunately Jefferson's conception of democracy was meager, narrow, and self-contradictory; and just because his ideas prevailed, while Hamilton toward the end of his life lost his influence, the consequences of Jefferson's imperfect conception of democracy have been much more serious than the consequences of Hamilton's inadequate conception of American nationality. In Jefferson's mind democracy was tantamount to extreme individualism. He conceived a democratic society to be composed of a collection of individuals, fundamentally alike in their abilities and deserts; and in organizing such a society, politically, the prime object was to provide for the greatest satisfaction of its individual members. The good things of life which had formerly been monopolized by the privileged few, were now to be distributed among all the people. It was unnecessary, moreover, to make any very artful arrangements, in order to effect an equitable distribution. Such distribution would take care of itself, provided nobody enjoyed any special privileges and everybody had equal opportunities. Once these conditions were secured, the motto of a democratic government should simply be "Hands Off." There should be as little government as possible, because persistent governmental interference implied distrust in popular efficiency and good-will; and what government there was, should be so far as possible confided to local authorities. The vitality of a democracy resided in its extremities, and it would be diminished rather than increased by specialized or centralized guidance. Its individual members needed merely to be protected against privileges and to be let alone, whereafter the native goodness of human nature would accomplish the perfect consummation. . . .

On this, as on so many other points, Hamilton's political philosophy was much more clearly thought out than that of Jefferson. He has been accused by his opponents of being the enemy of liberty; whereas in point of fact, he wished, like the Englishman he was, to protect and encourage liberty, just as far as such encouragement was compatible with good order, because he realized that genuine liberty would inevitably issue in fruitful social and economic inequalities. But he also realized that genuine liberty was not merely a matter of a constitutional declaration of rights. It could be protected only by an energetic and clear-sighted central government, and it could be fertilized only by the efficient national organization of American activities.

JOHN QUINCY ADAMS

Though he was not the most effective President of the United States, John Quincy Adams (1767–1848) may have been the most intelligent and erudite. In addition to serving as President, member of Congress, and a diplomat, Adams learned to read and translate from numerous languages, taught Rhetoric and Belles Lettres at Harvard, and compiled a lifelong diary that is one of the masterpieces of American literature.

The son of the second president, John Adams, John Quincy Adams was elected in 1824 by the House of Representatives even though Andrew Jackson had received the most electoral votes in a race that had produced no electoral college majority (the other two candidates were Treasury Secretary William H. Crawford and Henry Clay). Jackson supporters denounced the appointment by Adams of Clay as Secretary of State (after Clay's supporters in the House had voted for Adams) as a "corrupt bargain." The controversy hastened the split of the Democratic-Republican party, which had been the only national party since the demise of the Federalist party after the War of 1812, into Hamiltonian "National Republicans" and Jeffersonian "Democratic Republicans." In time the National Republicans became the Whigs and the Democratic Republicans the Federalists.

Lacking a strong constituency, Adams accomplished little in his four years as President and was swept out of power in 1828, when Jackson was elected in a landslide. Adams returned to politics and served in the congressional delegation from Massachusetts until his death in 1848. In his later years "the old man eloquent" became one of the nation's most determined and articulate opponents of slavery. Here is an excerpt from his First Annual Message, December 6, 1825.

The Spirit of Improvement

The great object of the institution of civil government is the improvement of the condition of those who are parties to the social compact, and no government, in whatever form constituted, can accomplish the lawful ends of its institution but in proportion as it improves the condition of those over whom it is established. Roads and canals, by multiplying and facilitating the communications and intercourse between distant regions and multitudes of men, are among the most important means of improvement. But moral, political, intellectual improvement are duties assigned by the Author of our existence to social no less than to individual man. For the fulfillment of those duties governments are invested with power, and to the attainment of the end—the exercise of delegated powers is a duty as sacred and indispensable as the usurpation of powers not granted is criminal and odious. Among the first, perhaps the very first, instrument for the improvement of the condition of men is knowledge, and to the acquisition of much of the knowledge adapted to the wants, the comforts, and enjoyments of human life public institutions and seminaries of learning are essential. So convinced of this was the first of my predecessors in this office, now first in the memory, as, living, he was first in the hearts of our countrymen, that once and again in his addresses to the Congresses with whom he cooperated in the public service he earnestly recommended the establishment of seminaries of learning, to prepare for all the emergencies of peace and war—a national university and a military academy. With respect to the latter, had he lived to the present day, in turning his eyes to the institution at West Point he would have enjoyed the gratification of his most earnest wishes; but in surveying the city which has been honored with his name he would have seen the spot of earth which he had destined and bequeathed to the use and benefit of his country as the site for an university still bare and barren.

In assuming her station among the civilized nations of the earth, it would seem that our country had contracted the engagement to contribute her share of mind, of labor, and of expense to the improvement of those parts of knowledge which lie beyond the reach of individual acquisition, and particularly to geographical and astronomical science. Looking back to the history only of the half century since the declaration of our independence, and observing the generous emulation with which the Governments of France, Great Britain, and Russia have devoted the genius, the intelligence, the treasures of their respective nations to the common improvement of the species in these three branches of science, is it not incumbent upon us to inquire whether we are not bound by obligations of a high and honorable character to contribute our portion of energy and exertion to the common stock? The voyages of discovery prosecuted in the course of that time at the expense of those nations have not only redounded to their glory, but to the improvement of human knowledge. We have been partakers of that improvement and owe for it a sacred debt, not only of gratitude, but of equal or proportional exertion in the same common cause. Of the cost of these undertakings, if the mere expenditures of outfit, equipment, and completion of the expeditions were to be considered the only charges, it would be unworthy of a great and generous nation to take a second thought. One hundred expeditions of circumnavigation like those of Cook and La Perouse would not burden the exchequer of the nation fitting them out so much as the ways and means of defraying a single campaign in war. But if we take into account the lives of those benefactors of mankind of which their services in the cause of their species were the purchase, how shall the cost of those heroic enterprises be estimated, and what compensation can be made to them or to their countries for them? Is it not by bearing them in affectionate remembrance? Is it not still more by imitating their example—by enabling countrymen of our own to pursue the same career and hazard their lives in the same cause?

In inviting the attention of Congress to the subject of internal improvements upon a view thus enlarged it is not my design to recommend the equipment of an expedition for circumnavigating the globe for purposes of scientific research and inquiry. We have objects of useful investigation nearer home, and to which our cares may be more beneficially applied. The interior of our own territories has yet been very imperfectly explored. Our coasts along many degrees of latitude upon the shores of the Pacific Ocean, though much frequented by our spirited commercial navigators, have been barely visited by our public ships. . . . With the establishment of a military post there or at some other point of that coast, recommended by my predecessor and already matured in the deliberations of the last Congress, I would suggest the expediency of connecting the equipment of a public ship for the exploration of the whole northwest coast of this continent. . . .

Connected with the establishment of an university, or separate from it, might be undertaken the erection of an astronomical observatory, with provision for the support of an astronomer, to be in constant attendance of observation upon the phenomena of the heavens, and for the periodical publication of his observations. It is with no feeling of pride as an American that the remark may be made that on the comparatively small territorial surface of Europe there are existing upward of 130 of these light-houses of the skies, while throughout the whole American hemisphere there is not one. If we reflect a moment upon the discoveries which in the last four centuries have been made in the physical constitution of the universe by means of these buildings and of observers stationed in them, shall we doubt of their usefulness to every nation? And while scarcely a year passes over our heads without bringing some new astronomical discovery to light, which we must fain receive at second hand from Europe, are we not cutting ourselves off from the means of returning light for light while we have neither observatory nor observer upon our half of the globe and the earth revolves in perpetual darkness to our unsearching eyes? . . .

The Constitution under which you are assembled is a charter of limited powers. After full and solemn deliberation upon all or any of the objects which, urged by an irresistible sense of my own duty, I have recommended to your attention should you come to the conclusion that, however desirable in themselves, the enactment of laws for effecting them would transcend the powers committed to you by that venerable instrument which we are all bound to support, let no consideration induce you to assume the exercise of powers not granted to you by the people. But if [the powers of the federal government] enumerated in the Constitution may be effectually brought into action by laws promoting the improvement of agriculture, commerce, and manufactures, the cultivation and encouragement of the mechanic and of the elegant arts, the advancement of literature, and the progress of the sciences, ornamental and profound, to refrain from exercising them for the benefit of the people themselves would be to hide in the earth the talent committed to our charge—would be treachery to the most sacred of trusts.

The spirit of improvement is abroad upon the earth. It stimulates the hearts and sharpens the faculties not of our fellow-citizens alone, but of the nations of Europe and of their rulers. While dwelling with pleasing satisfaction upon the superior excellence of our political institutions, let us not be unmindful that liberty is power; that the nation blessed with the largest portion of liberty must in proportion to its numbers be the most powerful nation upon earth, and that the tenure of power by man is, in the moral purposes of his Creator, upon condition that it shall be exercised to ends of beneficence, to improve the condition of himself and his fellow-men. While foreign nations less blessed with that freedom which is power than ourselves are advancing with gigantic strides in the career of public improvement, were we to slumber in indolence or fold up our arms and proclaim to the world that we are palsied by the will of our constituents, would it not be to cast away the bounties of Providence and doom ourselves to perpetual inferiority? In the course of the year now drawing to its close we have beheld, under the auspices and at the expense of one State of this Union, a new university unfolding its portals to the sons of science and holding up the torch of human improvement to eyes that seek the light. We have seen under the persevering and enlightened enterprise of another State the waters of our own Western lakes mingle with those of the oceans. If undertakings like these have been accomplished in the compass of a few years by the authority of single members of our Confederation, can we, the representative authorities of the whole Union, fall behind our fellow-servants in the exercise of the trust committed to us for the benefit of our common sovereignty by the accomplishment of works important to the whole and to which neither the authority nor the resources of any one State can be adequate?

The American School of National Economy

During the nineteenth century the dominant school of American political economy was the "American School" of developmental economic nationalism. (It might just as accurately be called the American–German–Japanese School, given its influence on the modernization of all three of today's leading capitalist states.) The patron saint of the American School was Alexander Hamilton, whose *Report on Manufactures* (1791) had called for federal government activism in sponsoring infrastructure development and industrialization behind tariff walls that would keep out British manufactured goods, though not British investor's money. The American School, elaborated in the nineteenth century by economists like Henry Carey (who advised President Lincoln), inspired the "American System" of Henry Clay and the protectionist import-substitution policies of Lincoln and his successors in the Republican party well into the twentieth century.

The national economists believed that the classical or laissez-faire economists like Adam Smith and David Ricardo (whose school was sometimes called the English School) defined national wealth too narrowly, overlooking what would nowadays be called "human capital" and "technological productivity." They also accused the English School of mistakenly adopting a static rather than a dynamic vision of economic policy. According to theorists of the American School, the economic policy that a country should pursue ought to depend on its circumstances and on its level of economic development. Like their precursor Hamilton, the national economists believed in the "infant-industry" theory of industrialization through (temporary, not permanent) protection of the domestic market of a developing country. Enormously influential in the nineteenth century (Lincoln among others studied their

229

writings), the national economists fell out of favor in their own country in this century, when the United States had become the world's leading financial and exporting power and sought to open foreign markets through free trade. Such a shift, from infant-industry protection to free trade at a later stage once competitive industries had matured, had been called for by the national economists themselves, although it is doubtful that they would have approved of the unilateral free trade policy which the United States adopted during the Cold War in order to bribe Japan and Europe into remaining in the American-led anti-Soviet alliance.

Through Friedrich List, a liberal German émigré who lived for a time in the United States, the ideas of the American Hamiltonians inspired Bismarck's pro-industrial policies and found a home in the Wilhelmine German academy in the form of the "Historical School" of economics, which included Wilhelm Roscher, Bruno Hildebrand, Karl Knies, and Gustav Schmoller. After the Meiji Restoration in 1868, Japanese who had been sent abroad to learn how to modernize their country's economy rejected English laissez-faire doctrine and introduced the ideas of the American and German economic nationalists.

Predictably, the very U.S. industrialists who had attacked laissez-faire theory when they had wanted protection for their infant industries became converts to free-market ideology once they began seeking foreign markets and were faced with growing popular concern about unchecked capital. Laissez-faire theory underwent a revival in turn-of-the-century American universities, as the academic profession adopted both classical Smithian economics and the variant of laissez-faire liberalism promoted by the so-called Austrian School. In reaction, the maverick American economist Thorstein Veblen wrote *The Theory of the Leisure Class* (1899) and founded what became known as institutional economics. As developed by pre–World War II economists like Wesley Clair Mitchell (a student of Veblen's) and John Rogers Commons, institutional economics focused on real-world questions about the institutional framework in which business activity takes place. Commons, along with Rexford Guy Tugwell, a member of FDR's Brain Trust, promoted liberal reforms like social security. The influence of institutionalism can be seen in the concept of the separation of ownership and control in the modern corporation explored by Adolf Berle and Gardiner Means in *The Modern Corporation and Private Property* (1932).

The institutional school had begun to gain in prestige and influence during the New Deal years. European émigrés fleeing Hitler in the academy, particularly members of the Austrian School like Ludwig van Mises and Fritz Machlup, however, helped to persuade most of the American economics profession that abstruse mathematical modeling provides the test of whether a theory is truly "scientific." Ironically, many of the Austrian economists who became famous and influential in the postwar United States had not been able to find teaching positions in prewar Austria and Germany, where the leading economists of the non-mathematical, pragmatic German Historical School were the intellectual heirs, by way of Friedrich List, of Alexander Hamilton. For the Austrian economists, FDR's New Deal was no different in kind from Hitler's mercantilism or Soviet planning; it was all "socialism." This kind of economic fundamentalism—alien to the older American and British conservative traditions—became interwar Vienna's legacy to Reaganism and Thatcherism. Liberal and leftist economists of the neo-Hamiltonian German Historical School, adapting Disraeli's mocking phrase "Manchester Liberalism," called the Austrian School *Manchestertum*.

DANIEL RAYMOND

Daniel Raymond was a Baltimore lawyer and influential American political economist. The following excerpts from Daniel Raymond's 1823 treatise *The Elements of Political Economy* illustrate the major themes of the American School of national economy. According to the editor of Friedrich List's collected works, Raymond was a "positive influence" on the thinking of List, and thus on policymaking in Germany and Japan in the later nineteenth and twentieth centuries.

National Wealth

Political economy is a science which teaches the nature of public or national wealth, the sources from which it is derived, and the causes by which it is produced. It professes to teach the most effectual means of promoting a nation's wealth and happiness, and it embraces every subject which has a tendency to promote them. . . .

The great source of error on this subject has been the confounding of national with individual wealth, than which no two things can be more different and distinct. . . . It is most unfortunate for the science of political economy that the word *wealth* has been applied indiscriminately to nations and to individuals. . . .

A nation, it is true, is an artificial being, or a legal entity, composed of millions of natural beings; still, it possesses all the properties and attributes of a being, which are as distinct and strongly marked as the properties and attributes of any natural being. . . .

The interests of a nation, and the interests of individuals who are constituent parts of that nation, may be, it is true, and often are, in unison. They

232

may be identical, but they are not necessarily so—so far is this from being the case, that they are often directly opposed. . . .

What is the true definition of national wealth?

I shall define, *a capacity for acquiring the necessaries and comforts of life.* . . .

This capacity never can exist independent of labor. Its extent, however, will depend upon a great variety of other circumstances. It will be materially influenced by the nature of the government. The energies of a nation can be more fully developed under a free than under an arbitrary or tyrannical government. . . .

A nation may possess the most extensive and fertile country, susceptible of being made to yield in the greatest abundance all the most valuable products of the earth; still, if the people have not industry, it will profit them nothing; they will be poor and wretched. On the contrary, let a country be ever so sterile by nature, yielding most sparingly the fruits of the earth, still, with industry, the people may possess a much greater capacity for acquiring the necessaries and comforts of life, than their idle neighbors who are blessed with all the advantages of climate and soil. . . .

Industrious habits, therefore, constitute a very important item in the stock of national wealth. . . .

When we speak of national wealth, we speak, or at least should speak, of the condition of the whole nation, and not of any constituent part of it. If the whole territory and all the property of nation is engrossed by a few, while a much greater number are sunk into a state of hopeless poverty and wretchedness, it matters not how great the sum total of individual wealth may be provided the nation is to be considered as a UNITY composed of all its citizens, it can never be said to enjoy a high degree of national wealth. . . .

There is a much greater degree of national wealth in England and in Holland than in Spain, Portugal or Russia, not merely because the amount of property is greater in proportion to the number of inhabitants, but for the reasons above stated. National wealth prevails to a much greater degree in New England than in Virginia, not beacuse the territory is more extensive or the land more fertile, for in these respects Virginia has the advantage, but because property in New England is more equally divided; because the people are more industrious and have made greater progress in the arts; and because they are not cursed with slavery.

It may possibly be objected to this definition of national wealth that it has no relation to the power of a nation, or to its ability to raise taxes and carry on war; that, according to this definition, a small nation may be more wealthy than a large one. But national wealth is a thing totally distinct from military power, and a small nation may enjoy a greater portion of wealth, in comparison to the number of its people, than a large one. . . .

It has usually been supposed that "the totality of the private property of its individuals" was the most accurate definition or description of a nation's wealth. . . . If that property should happen to be so unequally divided, as we know it may, as to enable a few to riot in the most extravagant luxury, while a great majority of the people are reduced to the most hopeless poverty and want, the nation would not enjoy a high degree of prosperity and happiness, although it might possess a very great amount of property in proportion to its inhabitants. . . .

It is essential to national prosperity and happiness that wages should be high, or in other words, receive a due portion of the product, and it is very certain that labor will be low in proportion as property is unequally divided. . . .

It is the duty of every man in society to do something towards promoting the general prosperity and happiness; no man has a right, whatever his condition in life, to be a drone or an idler, or to pursue an occupation which is either useless or injurious to the community. . . .

It is the imperious duty of government to suppress all occupations which are positively injurious to society, and to discourage, so far as practicable, all that are useless. . . .

The true policy for every wise legislator is to consider the nation immortal, and to legislate for it as though it was to exist forever; but, unfortunately, most legislators . . . instead of adopting a policy which looks prospectively to future generations and centuries . . . adopt one which looks only to themselves and the present . . . and, too frequently, one which looks only to the interests of some particular individuals, or classes in the community, instead of the interests of the nation. . . .

The fundamental error, as I apprehend, into which Adam Smith and most other writers have fallen, and which has caused the greatest portion of the ambiguity and uncertainty charged upon the science [of political economy], is their not having distinguished between public and private wealth. . . .

[Adam Smith] takes great pains . . . to prove that national affairs are best administered when let entirely alone, and every man suffered to pursue his own affairs in his own way. . . .

[T]he absurdity of this doctrine of not legislating at all, and permitting every man to pursue his own interest in his own way, is manifest from its utter impracticability. It can never be adopted, until all government shall be abolished and man return to a state of nature. The question, therefore, is not, and never will be, between law and no law, regulation and no regulation, but it must always be between the wisdom of different laws and different regulations. . . .

So far as the writings of Adam Smith have tended to restrain rash and in-experienced legislation, their influence has been highly salutary, but when he undertakes to maintain that there is any great public interest which cannot be promoted by judicious legislation he asserts a doctrine altogether untenable. . . . That restrictions may be too numerous and extensive is no proof that there should be none at all. . . .

Adam Smith was the champion of the agricultural, in opposition to the mercantile system. He was the champion of free trade, in opposition to navi-gation laws, colonial monopolies, and protective duties. In short, he adopted the theory of the French economists, so far as he went, and he only differs from them by not pushing the governing principle of their theory to the same extent that they do. They say that agricultural labor is alone productive; Smith, that it is the most productive. He almost invariably reprobates the pol-icy of the English government, in which the principle of the mercantile has predominated over that of the agricultural system.

It is no doubt true that the mercantile system adopted by England has been pushed to an extreme prejudicial to her interests, and she is now reaping the evil consequences of it; but there can be little doubt but what that system has contributed most essentially to her unexampled wealth and power. . . .

The maritime superiority of England, which enabled her, in a great mea-sure, to engross the commerce of the world whenever she was at war with the other maritime nations of Europe; her great colonial possessions, a monopoly of whose trade she has taken for herself, so far as she has found it for her in-terest to do so; her navigation laws; the liberality and freedom of her political institutions in comparision with those of other European nations, comprise all the advantages which England has enjoyed over the other nations of Europe; and to these must be attributed her great ascendancy over them in wealth and power.

FRIEDRICH LIST

Friedrich List (1789–1846) had the unusual distinction of being one of the most influential political economists in the nineteenth century in two of the three countries that would be the major capitalist powers at the end of the twentieth: the United States and Germany. Persecuted in Germany for his liberal and nationalist views, List emigrated to the United States, where he absorbed Hamiltonian economic doctrines, proselytized for internal improvements like railroads in the United States, and helped to found what became the National Association of Manufacturers. In 1827 he published *The Outlines of American Political Economy*, defending tariff-based industrialization. A critic in the U.S. Congress complained, "We appear to have imported a professor of Germany, in absolute violation of the doctrines of the American system, to lecture upon its lessons." List later served as a diplomatic envoy of the Jackson administration in Germany. In his later years he resided in France and Germany, and worked to bring about a democratic and liberal United States of Germany. Bismarck's German Empire, established in 1870, fulfilled only part of List's vision—it was a federal state that adopted economic nationalist modernization policies, but it was neither liberal nor democratic. Far closer to List's ideal was the post-1945 Federal Republic of Germany. Another of List's dreams, a common market among industrialized European democracies, has been achieved with the growth of the European Union. List's dream of a common global market uniting all of the advanced and democratic nations has yet to be realized.

In his time and later, List was criticized both by Karl Marx, who considered him a "bourgeois nationalist," and by adherents of the English school of laissez-faire and free trade. Joseph Finkelstein and Alfred L. Thimm write that List believed "in the dynamic growth of progressive capitalism. It is easy to think of List as being very much at home among the supporters of the early New Deal or, with any stretch of the imagination, in the coterie of followers of President Johnson's Great Society."[1] The following selection is from *The Natural System of Political Economy* (1837). (For more about List and his influence, see the excerpt from James Fallows below.)

Economic Nationalism

If the inhabitants of a town, a group of towns, or a number of provinces are able to exchange goods freely among themselves, their standard of living will improve in a way that would not be possible if the movement of goods were restricted by imports or prohibitions. Similarly the wealth of the various nations in the world would reach a maximum if universal freedom of trade were established. . . .

Particular countries may achieve an overwhelming industrial ascendancy owing to the special aptitudes of the inhabitants, the introduction of improvements in the manufacturing processes, or to natural advantages. In brief the advantages bestowed by nature or by history may enable a country to become—and to remain—a great industrial power. Such a country will be able to supply the world with the best goods at the lowest prices. And in this way the manufacturing power of the whole world will quickly reach hitherto unimagined heights to the advantage of all humanity.

At the same time the economic progress of the agrarian countries will expand in the most natural and sensible manner. Their prosperity will grow as they sell their raw materials and agricultural products to industrial countries while they can buy the manufactured products, the tools, and the most efficient machines that they require. Their increased wealth and their contacts with industrial countries will enable them to improve their political and social institutions. The time will come when these agrarian states will themselves become manufacturing countries. Moreover the surplus capital and workers in the industrial states will inevitably move to agrarian countries when they are ripe for industrial development.

As each country prospers and becomes more civilised it acquires an aptitude for the manufacturing arts and in due course it will become an industrial state.

For this prosperity to be procured by every nation and by the whole human race it is necessary to have universal peace. Conflicts between nations—

---

1. Joseph Finkelstein and Alfred L. Thimm, *Economists and Society: The Development of Economic Thought from Aquinas to Keynes*, 2d ed. (Schenectady, NY: Union College Press, 1981), pp. 118–19.

whether settled by force of arms or by other means—must be replaced by an alliance of all peoples governed by laws of universal application. A world republic, as envisaged by J. B. Say, is necessary to secure the fulfilment of the dreams of the free traders.

. . . In the previous chapter we summarised the main features of the most widely accepted economic doctrine of our time. This doctrine is clearly concerned only with individuals and with a universal republic embracing all members of the human race. But this doctrine omits a vital intermediate stage between the individual and the whole world. This is the nation, to which its members are united by ties of patriotism.

At present the world is divided into a number of different states, each with its particular national characteristics. Each individual—be he a manufacturer, farmer, merchant, professional man, or pensioner—is a member of the country in which he lives. The state protects him and helps him to achieve the aims that he pursues as an individual.

Individuals owe to a nation their culture, their language, their opportunity to work, and the safety of their property. Above all they depend upon the state in their relations with people in other countries. They share in the nation's glory and in its misfortunes; they share in its memories of the past and its hopes for the future; they share its wealth and its poverty. From the nation they draw all the benefits of civilisation, enlightenment, progress, and social and political institutions, as well as advances in the arts and sciences. If a nation declines, the individual shares in the disastrous consequences of its fall.

So it is right and proper that the individual should be prepared to sacrifice his own interests for the benefit of the nation to which he belongs.

As yet no universal republic exists. What is called "international law" is, for the time being, only the embryo of a future world state. Common sense and—as we saw in our first chapter—mutual interests should induce nations to abate their natural envy and their distrust of each other. Common sense tells us that war between nations is as stupid and savage as duels between individuals. Mutual interests would suggest the establishment of perpetual peace as well as free trade between nations which would bring the greatest prosperity to us all. Nevertheless it is not yet safe for the lamb to lie down with the lion.

So far there are only a few people, even in the most enlightened countries, who have grasped the fact that perpetual peace and universal free trade are both desirable and necessary. Nations have not yet attained a state of political and social development which would make such a reform possible. Moreover the civilised and enlightened countries in the world cannot be expected to disarm and to renounce warfare so long as there are in existence powers which reject the ideas of peaceful prosperity for the whole human race and are bent upon conquering and enslaving other nations.

Just as the discovery of gunpowder enabled states to establish law and order in their towns and in isolated regions so it now seems that only some new (and so far unknown) invention will persuade people of the possibility—indeed the necessity—of establishing a system of law which will enable them to live together in peace throughout the world.

At present a nation may be regarded from two distinct points of view with regard to its relations with other countries:

(i)   First, a nation is a sovereign political body. Its destiny is to safeguard and to maintain its independence by its own efforts. Its duty is to preserve and to develop its prosperity, culture, nationality, language, and freedom—in short, its entire social and political position in the world.

(ii)   Secondly, a nation is a branch of human society. It is the duty of a nation—as far as its own special interests permit—to join with other countries in the task of promoting the welfare and prosperity of the whole world.

Regarded from the first point of view a nation should adopt an independent "national economy." Regarded from the second point of view it should adopt a "cosmopolitan economy." An analogy between the "national" and "cosmopolitan" economics would be the two kinds of legal system which exist in the world. There are "national" systems of law which are in force in particular countries and there is a "cosmopolitan"—or international—system of law which is in force all over the world.

Cosmopolitan economics—or universal free trade between all the countries in the world—is only in the very earliest stage of development. Nations can only move slowly, step by step, towards the attainment of world free trade. They can do so only insofar as it is advantageous and not disadvantageous for them to adopt such a policy.

A nation which dismantled its fortresses and demobilised its armed forces would not enjoy the benefits of eternal peace, despite the fact that our religion teaches us to love and to help one another. Similarly a nation which abolished its import duties while other countries retained their tariffs, would not enjoy the benefits of world free trade.

The doctrine of national economics teaches us that a country which hopes to attain the highest degree of independence, culture and material prosperity should adopt every measure within its power to defend its economic security from any foreign attack, whether such an attack takes the form of hostile legislation or military action. To enable a country to protect itself it is essential that it should establish industries and foster their development—insofar as this is possible with available physical and human resources.

The foundations upon which national independence can be built are quite inadequate without the development of industries. A country of farmers and peasants can never maintain the military power—or the human and physical means to defend itself—that can be maintained by an industrialised country. The position of an agrarian country is worsened by the fact that just when it needs to defend itself it may be unable to find markets for its agricultural products and it may thus be deprived of the capital with which to create new industries. Moreover those of its merchants who live abroad—men who are half foreigners already—will in wartime never be such sound patriots as manufacturers and farmers whose entire livelihood depends upon the maintenance of their country's independence.

In time of war every country is forced to establish factories to make those goods which were formerly imported from abroad in exchange for products made at home. The result is the same as that achieved by a prohibitive fiscal policy in peace time. The nation is forced to demand great sacrifices from consumers in order to create new industries. And this happens just when the means available for the establishment of manufactures have been reduced to a minimum. If free trade is introduced when hostilities cease the newly established industries will be thrown to the tender mercies of foreign competitors. In these circumstances a country will lose all the capital, all the experience, and all the work of the war years and will return to its former position of weakness and dependence upon foreigners.

In the event of war or of the threat of war it is essential for a Great Power to establish industries. And in peacetime a government should foster the establishment of new branches of manufacture to safeguard the prosperity and the culture of the nation.

We saw in the previous chapter how the division of labour and the co-operation of productive powers follow automatically from the adoption of the policy of free trade. But if the natural growth of the economy is hindered by the hostile political actions of other states it would be foolish to expect that the same growth will take place that would have occurred if universal free trade existed. In such circumstances a nation can expect the industrial sector of the economy to grow only if defensive measures are taken through political action. . . .

From this point of view the imposition of a protective tariff in no way hampers the natural growth of the economy. The object of a tariff is to frustrate any hostile action by foreigners to harm a country's economy by political action or by acts of war. While achieving its immediate objective a protective

FRIEDRICH LIST · 241

tariff will also foster the natural and normal expansion of home industries. A protective tariff establishes free trade within the frontiers of a single state, as an alternative to the establishment of universal free trade. In the world in which we live it is impossible to introduce universal free trade just now because the various nations into which it is divided are intent upon pursuing their own selfish economic interests.

In these circumstances one would fail to appreciate the nature of the relations between a state and the individuals who compose it if one were to argue that a national commercial policy designed to control trade with foreign countries could in any way prejudice the rights and interests of the individuals who form the nation. We have already observed that the fortunes or misfortunes of individuals are dependent upon the maintenance of the independence and progress of the whole nation. We have seen that each country can secure economic growth by means of a specially designed tariff. It is obvious therefore that the freedom of the individual must be restricted to secure the freedom of all the individuals who make up a nation. In doing this a state acts in the same way as it does when it demands part of an individual's wealth to pay for the administration of the country or when it calls upon its citizens to serve in the armed forces, at risk of life and limb, to defend its independence. . . .

In his *Traité d'economie politique* (1824), *discours preliminaire,* Say writes: "Political science, which ought properly to be regarded as the study of the organisation of society, has long been confused with economics, which examines how the wealth which satisfies our needs is created, distributed, and consumed. The wealth of a country is really independent of its political organization. A state will become rich if it is well administered, whatever its constitution may be. Nations ruled by absolute monarchs have prospered, while those governed by popular assemblies have seen their economies ruined. It is only indirectly that political liberty may be more favorable (than a dictatorship) to economic prosperity—or for that matter to the progress of cultural activities." All history refutes this notion. The truth is the very opposite. No nation has ever achieved success as an industrial power without also enjoying a high degree of political freedom. No country ruled by a despot has ever been able to establish manufactures on a large scale or to achieve economic prosperity. Free peoples have declined and have become poor and weak, but this has occurred only after they have lost their liberty. A despot has sometimes secured a certain degree of prosperity for his subjects but this has happened only if he had the good fortune to employ a number of exceptionally able ministers and officials. But, as the Emperor Alexander once remarked, that is only a fortunate chance. As soon as the services of able officials are no longer available the economy of the country declines. Liberty and industry are synonymous and cannot be separated. Only a strong democratic element in society can bring opulence to a monarchical or an aristocratic state. The nobles of Venice committed suicide as soon as they effectively weakened the democratic element in the city state. Industry demands a democratic government which pursues the same economic policy for many hundreds of years.

The validity of this proposition is supported not only by historical evidence but also by no less an authority than Montesquieu who writes in his *Esprit des lois* (Part II, p. 192): "In a servile state people work to preserve what they have got rather than to increase their wealth. In a free society people work to acquire riches rather than to preserve wealth."

HENRY C. CAREY

Henry C. Carey (1793–1879) inherited his economic nationalist views along with his fortune from his father Matthew Carey (1760–1839), an Irish-American immigrant. Imprisoned in 1784 for libel after he had criticized the London parliament, Carey emigrated to Philadelphia, where he set up a publishing company and wrote pamphlets on political economy advocating the Hamiltonian program of a protective system. His son Henry, inheriting the firm, turned it into the largest publisher in the United States at the time. The wealth this generated permitted Henry to withdraw from business in 1835 and devote himself to writing on political economy. Like his father, the younger Carey advocated government support for internal improvements and a protective tariff to promote infant industries (although Henry, who began as a free-trader, always emphasized that the ultimate goal of policy was free trade among industrial nations, once each had developed its own industries by means of protection).

The Irish connection made the Careys particularly aware of how Britain's advocacy of global free trade during the nineteenth century served British interests by making it difficult for late-developing nations like the United States, or subordinate nations like Ireland and India, to compete in industries in which Britain already held the lead (in 1865 Henry Carey wrote a book entitled *The Way to Outdo England Without Fighting Her*). Instead of a world dominated by a single advanced economy, Carey, like the other national economists, envisioned a polycentric world economy that would result from the voluntary merger of national markets that had developed first behind protectionist barriers.

Carey became one of the most famous economists in the world. His writings were criticized by J. S. Mill (who disapproved of anti-British protectionism) and by Karl Marx (who scoffed at the idea of government intervention in the economy encouraging harmony between the classes—an idea that American School economists shared with European National Liberals like Friedrich List). Carey's major works, including *The Principle of Political Economy* (3 volumes, 1837–40) and *Principles of Social Science* (3 volumes, 1858–59), were translated into German, Italian, Russian, and Spanish. Lincoln read and admired Carey, and corresponded with the economist during his presidency. Here is a selection from *The Past, the Present, and the Future* (1859).

Against British Economic Hegemony

According to several eminent writers, there exist various races of men; and some of the most eminent of the writers of our time have been disposed to attribute to the antipathy of those races many of the phenomena to which we have referred. A more careful study of history might, however, as we think, satisfy them that although men are of various colors, white, red, brown and black, there have existed from the creation to the present time but two races, to wit, the great race and the small one; the race of the few and that of the many; the races that lives by the labor of others, and that which lives by their own; the race of the plunderers and that of the plundered. . . .

By all the advocates of the Ricardo doctrine, the prosperous condition of the people of the United States is attributed to the abundance of fertile land, yet, in all other countries men have been most poor where land was most abundant, and where the inhabitants had, apparently, the most choice of soils. Fertile land, uncultivated, abounded in the days of the Edwards, yet a supply of food was then obtained with far more difficulty than now. It is more abundant, by far, in Mexico than in the United States, yet inferior food is obtained at the cost of far more labor. The whole agricultural product of Mexico, with a population of eight millions, is far less than that of a single American state. It is more abundant in Russia, South America, India, Ceylon and Brazil, yet in all food is far more scarce. The reason why labor is in demand and largely paid is, that peace having been maintained, the whole people have been engaged in the work of production instead of that of carrying muskets and sabres, and therefore wealth has rapidly increased. . . .

Nearly a century has now rolled round, since, by the battle of Plessy, the ascendency of England in that great country [India] was secured; and such is the result. The Hindoo raises cotton, but he consumes only so much as will give him a strip to cover his loins. He raises rice; but he eats little, for he may not even clean it; and all this is done that England may be the workshop of the world, and that great manufacturers may accumulate millions by aid of the labor of over-worked and under-fed operatives. . . . Canada stagnates; and governors and forms of government are changed, but Canada remains still motionless. Ireland starves, and Irishmen shoot agents; and curfew laws, and bills prohibiting the carrying of arms, are passed; but Ireland still starves and borrows, and *will not* pay, because she *cannot.* Jamaica tries hill-coolies and free negroes; and coolies and negroes fail; and Jamaica still is poor. . . . Australia raises, on the poorest soils, a small supply of wool for which she must be paid; while paying nothing for six millions of dollars annually charged to her account. . . . India will grow rich, and rapidly grow, when India shall be independent, and shall protect herself against the radical error of the English system; but until she shall do so, until she shall acquire power to place the consumer by the side of the producer, she must remain poor. In few countries of the world would population and wealth grow so rapidly, were she left alone; but so long as she must remit twenty millions to pay interest, and raise so many other millions to pay armies and officers, while compelled to cultivate the poorest soils with the worst machinery, neither can increase. England may change, and change again, abroad; but, before she can effect any improvement, she must learn to look at home, and not abroad. . . . She must increase her producers, and she must permit others to increase their consumers; and when she shall do that, India and Canada, Jamaica and Australia, will grow rich, while she will grow richer; but she will then cease to want colonies, or armies, or great men. . . .

Let but the people of the United States set the example of a determined resistance to the system [of English economic hegemony], and it will be followed by all Europe. . . .

The people of the United States owe this to themselves, and to the world. They enjoy a higher degree of happiness than has fallen to the lot of any other nation, and they should desire to aid their fellow men in England, in Ireland, in Germany and in India, and by helping themselves they will help them. As colonies, India and Ireland will remain poor. As independent nations, they will become rich, for they too will insist on the right of placing the consumer by the side of the producer. . . .

Thus far, resistance to the great error of English policy has been in the form of tariffs having for their object the raising of revenue, and thereby affording incidental protection to the consumer of food, and cotton, and wool, who wishes to place himself by the side of the producer. The system is vicious and unsound. . . .

To the unsoundness of the [English] system it is due that throughout the world protective tariffs exist, having for their object the exclusion of British manufactures. Nothing less could have introduced the system of protection into the United States. Everywhere, however, it has been attempted to correct error resulting from the effort by England at indirect taxation, by other error in desiring to use tariffs as a means of similar taxation at home. It has been the substitution of plunder by a pickpocket for that of a highwayman. . . .

Tariffs for revenue should have no existence. Interferences with trade are to be tolerated only as measures of self-protection. Every man who enjoys security should contribute directly for its maintenance, and then he would have cheap government, and good government. . . .

With its correction, every obstacle to the establishment of perfect freedom will disappear, and the tariff will pass out of existence. Its enactment would be a declaration of war for the establishment of peace and free trade, and when the object of the war should be attained a continuance of hostilities would be found unnecessary.

HENRY CLAY

Henry Clay (1777–1852) was one of the leading American Senators of the nineteenth century and a central figure in the American Hamiltonian tradition of democratic nationalism. Born, raised, and admitted to the bar in Virginia, he moved to Kentucky to practice law. In 1803 he was elected to the Kentucky legislature, and he was appointed to fulfill unexpired terms in the U.S. Senate in 1806 and 1809. His long career in the U.S. Congress continued when he was elected to the House in 1810. A leader of the mostly Southern "war hawks," Clay helped pressure President Madison into submitting a declaration of war against Britain to punish the former mother country for its harassment of American shipping during the Napoleonic wars and to provide the United States with an excuse to seize Florida and Canada. After the American bid for expansion had failed, Clay was one of the commissioners who took part in negotiating the Treaty of Ghent between Britain and the United States.

Clay, who hoped to become President, used his influence in the House in 1824 to elect John Quincy Adams instead of Clay's rival, Andrew Jackson. Clay's machinations backfired, though. His appointment by Adams as Secretary of State permitted Jackson's followers to claim that their hero had been the victim of a "corrupt bargain," a claim that hurt Clay's attempt to win the presidency in 1832 and again in 1840, when he was the Whig nominee.

From 1831 until his death in 1852, Clay served in the U.S. Senate. There he devoted himself to the attempt to balance preservation of the Union with the phased abolition of slavery. His economic program served his larger unionist goals. Unlike other nineteenth-century American statesmen in the Hamiltonian tradition like Lincoln and Webster, whose economic views have been ignored by later generations of Americans, Clay is remembered today for his advocacy of "the American

247

System," a term introduced in the speech excerpted below. Although he was a Southerner, Clay was a fervent Unionist. The American System was an updated version of Hamilton's plan for modernizing the United States by means of internal improvements and tariff-based industrialization. During the War of 1812, Clay had learned how important an adequate industrial base is for national defense. Note Clay's admiration for Napoleon, whose failed "Continental System," designed to protect the French empire in Europe from British economic warfare, may have influenced Clay's own conception of the American System.

On American Industry

From a speech in the House of Representatives, March 30–31, 1824

Two classes of politicians divide the people of the United States. According to the system of one, the produce of foreign industry should be subjected to no other impost than such as may be necessary to provide a public revenue; and the produce of American industry should be left to sustain itself, if it can, with no other than that incidental protection, in its competition, at home as well as abroad, with rival foreign articles. According to the system of the other class, while they agree that the imposts should be mainly, and may under any modification be safely, relied on as a fit and convenient source of public revenue, they would so adjust and arrange the duties on foreign fabrics as to afford a gradual but adequate protection to American industry, and lessen our dependence on foreign nations, by securing a certain and ultimately a cheaper and better supply of our own wants from our own abundant resources. Both classes are equally sincere in their respective opinions, equally honest, equally patriotic, and desirous of advancing the prosperity of the country. In the discussion and consideration of these opposite opinions, for the purpose of ascertaining which has the support of truth and reason, we should, therefore, exercise every indulgence, and the greatest spirit of mutual moderation and forebearance. And, in our deliberations on this great question, we should look fearlessly and truly at the actual condition of the country, retrace the causes which have brought us into it, and snatch, if possible, a view of the future. We should, above all, consult experience—the experience of other nations, as well as our own—as our truest and most unerring guide. . . .

The great desideratum in political economy is the same as in private pursuits; that is, what is the best application of the aggregate industry of a nation, that can be made honestly to produce the largest sum of national wealth?

Labor is the source of all wealth; but it is not natural labor only. And the fundamental error of the gentleman from Virginia, and of the school to which he belongs, consists in their not sufficiently weighing the importance of the power of machinery. In former times, when but little comparative use was made of machinery, manual labor and the price of wages were circumstances of the greatest consideration. But it is far otherwise in these latter times. Such are the improvements and the perfection of machinery that, in analyzing the compound value of many fabrics, the element of natural labor is so inconsiderable as almost to escape detection. This truth is demonstrated by many facts. Formerly, Asia, in consequence of the density of the population, and the consequent lowness of wages, laid Europe under tribute for many of her fabrics. Now Europe reacts upon Asia, and Great Britain, in particular, throws back upon her countless millions of people the rich treasures produced by artificial labor, to a vast amount, infinitely cheaper than they can be manufactured by the natural exertions of that portion of the globe. But Britain is herself the most striking illustration of the immense power of machinery. Upon what other principle can you account for the enormous wealth which she has accumulated, and which she annually produces? A statistical writer of that country, several years ago, estimated the total amount of the artificial or machine labor of the nation to be equal to that of one hundred millions of able-bodied laborers. . . . If we suppose the machine labor of the United States to be equal to that of ten millions of able-bodied men, the United States will operate, in the creation of wealth, by a power (including all their population) of twenty millions. In the creation of wealth, therefore, the power of Great Britain, compared to that of the United States, is as eleven to one.

That these views are not imaginary will be, I think, evinced by contrasting the wealth, the revenue, the power of the two countries. Upon what other hypothesis can we explain those almost incredible exertions which Britain made during the late wars of Europe? Look at her immense subsidies! Behold her standing, unaided and alone, and breasting the storm of Napoleon's colossal power, when all continental Europe owned and yielded to its inflexible sway; and finally, contemplate her vigorous prosecution of the war, with and without allies, to its splendid termination on the ever-memorable field of Waterloo! . . .

From this exhibit we must remark that the wealth of Great Britain, and consequently her power, is greater than that of any of the other nations with which it is compared. The amount of the contributions which she draws from the pockets of her subjects is not referred to for imitation, but as indicative of their wealth. The burden of taxation is always relative to the ability of the subjects of it. A poor nation can pay but little. And the heavier taxes of British subjects, for example, in consequence of their greater wealth, may be more easily borne than the much lighter taxes of Spanish subjects, in consequence of their extreme poverty.

The object of wise governments should be, by sound legislation, so to protect the industry of their own citizens against the policy of foreign powers, as to give it the most expansive force in the production of wealth. . . .

Is there no remedy within the reach of government? Are we doomed to behold our industry languish and decay yet more and more? But there is a remedy, and that remedy consists in modifying our foreign policy, and in adopting a genuine AMERICAN SYSTEM. We must naturalize the arts in our country; and we must naturalize them by the only means which the wisdom of nations has yet discovered to be effectual; by adequate protections against the otherwise overwhelming influence of foreigners. This is only to be accomplished by the establishment of a tariff. . . .

But it is said that, wherever there is a concurrence of favorable circumstances, manufactures will arise of themselves, without protection; and that we should not disturb the national progress of industry, but leave things to themselves. If all nations would modify their policy on this axiom, perhaps it would be better for the common good of the whole. Even then, in consequence of natural advantages and a greater advance in civilization and in the arts, some nations would enjoy a state of much higher prosperity than others. But there is no universal legislation. The globe is divided into different communities, each seeking to appropriate to itself all the advantages it can, without reference to the prosperity of others. Whether this is right or not, it has always been, and ever will be the case. Perhaps the care of the interests of one people is sufficient for all the wisdom of one legislature; and that it is among nations as among individuals, that the happiness of the whole is best secured by each attending to its own peculiar interests. . . .

The next objection . . . which I shall briefly notice is, that the manufacturing system is adverse to the genius of our government, in its tendency to the accumulation of large capitals in a few hands; in the corruption of the public morals, which is alleged to be incident to it; and in the consequent danger to the public liberty. The first part of the objection would apply to every lucrative business, to commerce, to planting, and to the learned professions. Would the gentleman introduce the system of Lycurgus? If his principle be correct, it should be extended to any and every vocation which had a similar tendency. The enormous fortunes in our country—the nabobs of land—have been chiefly made by the profitable pursuit of that foreign commerce, in more propitious times, which the honorable gentleman would so carefully cherish. Immense estates have also been made in the South. The dependents are, perhaps, not more numerous upon that wealth which is accumulated in manufactures than they are upon that which is acquired by commerce and by agriculture. . . .

The principle of the system under consideration has the sanction of some of the best and wisest men, in all ages, in foreign countries as well as in our own—of the Edwards, of Henry the Great, of Elizabeth, of the Colberts, abroad; of our Franklin, Jefferson, Madison, Hamilton, at home. But it comes recommended to us by a higher authority than any of these, illustrious as they unquestionably are—by the master-spirit of the age—that extraordinary man, who has thrown the Alexanders and the Caesars infinitely further behind him than they stood in advance of the most eminent of their predecessors—that singular man who, whether he was seated on his imperial throne, deciding the fate of nations and allotting kingdoms to the members of his family, with the same composure, if not with the same affection, as that with which a Virginia father divides his plantations among his children, or on the miserable rock of St. Helena, to which he was condemned by the cruelty and the injustice of his unworthy victors, is equally an object of the most intense admiration. He appears to have comprehended, with the rapidity of intuition, the true interests of a State, and to have been able, by the turn of a single expression, to develop the secret springs of the policy of cabinets. We find that Las Casas reports him to have said:

"He opposed the principles of economists, which he said were correct in theory, though erroneous in their application. The political constitution of different States, continued he, must render these principles defective; local circumstances continually call for deviations from their uniformity. Duties, he said, which were so severely condemned by political economists, should not, it is true, be an object to the treasury; they should be the guaranty and protection of a nation, and should correspond with the nature and objects of its trade. . . .

" 'I have not fallen into the error of modern systematizers,' said the emperor, 'who imagine that all the wisdom of nations is centred in themselves. Experience is the true wisdom of nations. And what does all the reasoning of economists amount to? They incessantly extol the prosperity of England, and hold her up as our model; but the custom-house system is more burdensome and arbitrary in England than in any other country. They also condemn prohibitions; yet it was England set the example of prohibitions; and they are in fact necessary with regard to certain objects. . . .

" 'Industry or manufactures, and internal trade, made immense advances during my reign. The application of chemistry to the manufactures caused them to advance with giant strides. I gave an impulse, the effects of which extended throughout Europe. . . .

"'Thus I naturalized in France the manufacture of cotton. . . .

"'I at first confined myself merely to prohibiting the web; then I extended the prohibition to spun cotton; and we now possess, within ourselves, the three branches of the cotton manufacture, to the great benefit of our population, and the injury and regret of the English; which proves that, in civil government, as well as in war, decision of character is often indispensable to success. . . .'"

Mr. Chairman, our confederacy comprehends, within its vast limits, great diversity of interests: agricultural, planting, farming, commercial, navigating, fishing, manufacturing. No one of these interests is felt in the same degree, and cherished with the same solicitude, throughout all parts of the Union. Some of them are peculiar to particular sections of our common country. But all these great interests are confided to the protection of one government—to the fate of one ship—and a most gallant ship it is, with a noble crew. If we prosper, and are happy, protection must be extended to all; it is due to all. It is the great principle on which obedience is demanded from all. If our essential interests cannot find protection from our own government against the policy of foreign powers, where are they to get it? We did not unite for sacrifice, but for preservation. . . .

Even if the benefit of the policy were limited to certain sections of our country, would it not be satisfactory to behold American industry, wherever situated, active, animated, and thrifty, rather than persevere in a course which renders us subservient to foreign industry? But these benefits are twofold, direct, and collateral, and, in the one shape or the other, they will diffuse themselves throughout the Union. All parts of the Union will participate, more or less, in both. As to the direct benefit, it is probable that the North and the East will enjoy the largest share. But the West and the South will also paricipate in them. . . .

[T]he bill may be postponed, thwarted, defeated. But the cause is the cause of the country, and it must and will prevail. It is founded in the interests and affections of the people. It is as native as the granite deeply imbosomed in our mountains. And, in conclusion, I would pray God, in his infinite mercy, to avert from our country the evils which are impending over it, and, by enlightening our councils, to conduct us into that path which leads to riches, to greatness, to glory.

ABRAHAM LINCOLN

Saints and godlike martyrs do not concern themselves with mundane things like banks and railroads. Lincoln's posthumous deification explains the complete neglect by historians of the economic views of this prosperous railroad lawyer who studied the works of Henry Carey and other national economists and devoted himself as a politician, in both Springfield and Washington, D.C., to promoting Whig and Republican economic-nationalist measures like national banking, federally subsidized internal improvements, and a high tariff to protect American manufacturing (Lincoln's notes for an argument in favor of protection survive as "Fragments of a Tariff Discussion," December 1, 1847). Most Americans, even most scholars, are not aware that Lincoln devoted more of his political career to these Hamiltonian issues than he did to the debates over slavery and national union for which he is remembered. To this date there has been only one major study of the central concerns of Lincoln's political life, *Lincoln and the Economics of the American Dream* by Gabor S. Borritt (1978, 1994). Borritt points out that "during his thirty-three years of public life Lincoln probably spoke more about broad topics of economics than any other issue" and calculates that "Lincoln's speeches on national banking, in a single year alone, had they been recorded, could have taken up a volume in his" collected works.[2]

---

2. Gabor S. Borritt, *Lincoln and the Economics of the American Dream* (Chicago: University of Illinois Press, 1994), p. 324, footnote 8.

On National Banking

In this Illinois address of December 26, 1839, Lincoln made the Whig case for a national bank against the independent treasury or subtreasury favored by the Jeffersonian Democrats. Lincoln repeated the argument made by his Hamiltonian predecessors for a broad construction of the constitutional powers of the federal government.

As a sweeping objection to a National Bank, and consequently an argument in favor of the Sub-Treasury as a substitute for it, it often has been urged, and doubtless will be again, that such a bank is unconstitutional. We have often heretofore shown, and therefore need not in detail do so again, that a majority of the Revolutionary patriarchs, whoever acted officially upon the question, commencing with Gen. Washington and embracing Gen. Jackson, the larger number of the signers of the Declaration, and of the framers of the Constitution, who were in the Congress of 1791, have decided upon their oaths that such a bank is constitutional. We have also shown that the votes of Congress have more often been in favor of than against its constitutionality. In addition to all this we have shown that the Supreme Court—that tribunal which the Constitution has itself established to decide Constitutional questions—has solemnly decided that such a bank is constitutional. Protesting that these authorities ought to settle the question, ought to be conclusive, I will not urge them further now. I now propose to take a view of the question which I have not known to be taken by anyone before. It is, that whatever objection ever has or ever can be made to the constitutionality of a bank, will apply with equal force in its whole length, breadth and proportions to the Sub-Treasury. Our opponents say, there is no express authority in the Constitution to establish a bank, and therefore a Bank is unconstitutional; but we, with equal truth, may say there is no *express* authority in the Constitution to establish a Sub-Treasury, and therefore a Sub-Treasury is unconstitutional. Who, then, has the advantage of this "express authority" argument? Does it not cut equally both ways? Does it not wound them as deeply and as deadly as it does us?

Our position is that both are constitutional. The Constitution enumerates expressly several powers which Congress may exercise, superadded to which is a general authority "to make all laws necessary and proper" for carrying into effect all the powers vested by the Constitution of the Government of the United States. One of the express powers given Congress is "To lay and collect taxes; duties, imposts, and excises; to pay the debts, and provide for the common defence and general welfare of the United States." Now Congress is expressly authorized to make all laws necessary and proper for carrying this power into execution. To carry it into execution, it is indispensably necessary to collect, safely keep, transfer, and disburse revenue. To do this, a Bank is "necessary and proper." But, say our opponents, to authorize the making of a Bank, the necessity must be so great, that the power just recited, would be nugatory without it; and that that necessity is expressly negatived by the fact that they have got along ten whole years without such a Bank. Immediately we turn on them, and say that that sort of necessity for a Sub-Treasury does not exist, because we have got along forty whole years without one. And this time, it may be observed, that we are not merely equal with them in the argument, but we beat them forty to ten, or which is the same thing, four to one. On examination, it will be found that the absurd rule which prescribes that, before we can constitutionally adopt a National Bank as a fiscal agent, we must show an indispensable necessity for it, will exclude every sort of fiscal agent that the mind of man can conceive. A Bank is not indispensable, because we can take the Sub-Treasury; the Sub-Treasury is not indispensable because we can take the Bank. The rule is too absurd to need further comment. Upon the phrase "necessary and proper" in the Constitution, it seems to me more reasonable to say, that some fiscal agent is indispensably necessary; but, inasmuch as no particular sort of agent is thus indispensable, because some other sort might be adopted, we are left to choose that sort of agent, which may be most "proper" on grounds of expediency.

On Internal Improvements

Lincoln returned to the theme of a broad construction of federal power in a speech in the U.S. House of Representatives (June 20, 1848) on another subject dear to Hamiltonian democratic nationalists—federally sponsored internal improvements or infrastructure projects. Lincoln treats Hamilton's admirer and successor Chancellor Joseph Kent of New York, one of the country's leading proponents of the nationalist interpretation of the constitution, as the ultimate authority on questions of federal power.

Mr. Chairman, on the third position of the [Democratic argument against federal internal improvements], the constitutional question, I have not much to say. Being the man I am, and speaking when I do, I feel that in any attempt at an original constitutional argument I should not be, and ought not to be, listened to patiently. The ablest and the best of men have gone over the whole ground long ago. I shall attempt but little more than a brief notice of what some of them have said. In relation to Mr. Jefferson's views, I read from Mr. Polk's veto message:

> President Jefferson, in his message to Congress in 1806, recommended an amendment to the constitution, with a view to apply an anticipated surplus in the Treasury "to the great purposes of the public education, roads, rivers, canals, and such other objects of public improvements as it may be thought proper to add to the constitutional enumeration of the federal powers;" and he adds: "I suppose an amendment to the constitution, by consent of the States, necessary, because the objects now recommended are not among those enumerated in the constitution, and to which it permits the public moneys to be applied." In 1825, he repeated, in his published letters, the opinion that no such power has been conferred upon Congress.

I introduce this, not to controvert, just now, the constitutional opinion, but to show that on the question of expediency Mr. Jefferson's opinion was against the present president; that this opinion of Mr. Jefferson, in one branch at least, is, in the hands of Mr. Polk, like McFingal's gun: "Bears wide, and kicks the owner over."

But to the constitutional question: In 1836, Chancellor Kent first published his Commentaries on American Law. He devoted a portion of one of the lectures to the question of the authority of Congress to appropriate public monies for internal improvements. He mentions that the question had never been brought under judicial consideration, and proceeds to give a brief summary of the discussions it had undergone between the legislative and executive branches of the government. He shows that the legislative branch had usually been for, and the executive against the power, till the period of Mr. J. Q. Adams' administration, at which point he considers the executive influence as withdrawn from opposition and added to the support of the power. In 1844 the chancellor published a new edition of his commentaries, in which he adds some notes of what had transpired on the question since 1826. . . .

It is not to be denied that many great and good men have been against the power [of the federal government to undertake internal improvements]; but it is insisted that quite as many, as great and as good, have been for it; and it is shown that, on a full survey of the whole, Chancellor Kent was of opinion that the arguments of the latter were vastly superior. This is but the opinion of a man, but who was that man? He was one of the ablest and most learned lawyers of his age, or of any age. It is no disparagement to Mr. Polk, nor, indeed, to anyone who devotes much time to politics, to be placed far behind Chancellor Kent as a lawyer. His attitude was most favorable to correct conclusions. He wrote coolly, and in retirement. He was struggling to rear a durable monument of fame; and he well knew that truth and thoroughly sound reasoning were the only sure foundations. Can the party opinion of a party president, on a law question, as this purely is, be at all compared, or set in opposition to that of such a man, in such an attitude, as Chancellor Kent?

This constitutional question will probably never be better settled than it is, until it shall pass under judicial consideration; but I do think no man who is clear on the questions of expediency need feel his conscience much pricked upon this. . . .

[L]et the nation take hold of the larger works, and the states the smaller one; and thus, working in a meeting direction, discreetly, but steadily and firmly, what is made unequal in one place may be equalized in another, extravagance avoided, and the whole country put on that career of prosperity which shall correspond with its extent of territory, its natural resources, and the intelligence and enterprise of its people.

From the Civil War to the Progressive Era

The Hamiltonians at last came to power once more in the federal government with Abraham Lincoln and the Republican party in 1861. During and after the Civil War, the Republicans—most of them former Whigs—enacted many of the Hamiltonian measures that had been stymied when Southern Democrats had controlled the government. The railroads were subsidized by federal land grants, a national banking system was established (culminating with the Federal Reserve act of 1913), and U.S. industries flourished behind high tariff walls. The United States was at its most "Hamiltonian" during the period of Republican Party dominance, between the Civil War and the Depression.

By the early twentieth century, the success of the Hamiltonian program for government-sponsored industrial modernization posed new problems for government, including widening class divisions and the unchecked political power of the new national and multinational corporations. What might be called the "Old Hamiltonians" of the Republican Party, based in Lincoln's Midwest, favored a continuation of the policies that had proved so successful, like protection for industry and government–business collaboration at the expense of labor. Those complacent "conservatives" (who had been the liberals and radicals of the Civil War era) were opposed by the mostly Republican Progressives like Theodore Roosevelt and Herbert Croly, who believed that creative measures were necessary to deal with the problems of an integrated nation-state with an industrial economy. Both TR and Croly saw Progressive reforms as logical developments of the democratic nationalist tradition of Hamilton, Clay, Webster, and Lincoln.

HENRY CABOT LODGE

Although he has been caricatured as a reactionary because of his opposition to the League of Nations and European immigration, Lodge was quite progressive in many of his views, from the time that he gave his first speeches in Congress in favor of federal voting-rights enforcement. In his Senate speech defending the tariff, excerpted below, he brilliantly and amusingly demolishes the laissez-faire or, as he calls it, the "let-alone" doctrine that has become the orthodoxy once again in the United States at the end of the twentieth century. Even more relevant today are Lodge's warnings about what today is called the global "race to the bottom"—the pressure on advanced industrial countries to lower the wages of their workers as an alternative to transferring production to low-wage countries like China. Lodge's warning about low-wage competition from Asian countries proved to be premature, because of the disruption of the world economy by the two world wars and the Cold War. The end of the Cold War, however, has been followed by a massive transfer of industrial production to take advantage of cheap labor in poor countries, at the expense of workers and unions in North America, Europe, and Japan. Lodge's solution—a "social tariff" eliminating the advantage of low-wage countries—is today advocated only by the far left and maverick populists like Patrick J. Buchanan. The problem that Lodge diagnosed in a speech in the Senate on April 10, 1894, which is excerpted here is nevertheless real, if an article in *International Business* (April 1995) is to be believed: "U.S. multinationals are under relentless competitive pressures to produce at the lowest cost possible. . . . Cheaper and better educated workers are more available than ever before as developing countries seek to grow and modernize their economies. . . . And U.S. firms can easily move to these workers. With worldwide unemployment now close to 900 million, it will be a buyer's market for labor for a long time."

The Let-alone Theory

Two questions are involved in this bill. One is the effect upon our business prosperity, the wages of our working-men, and the welfare of our people of a given set of tariff schedules and duties on imports. The other is a much wider and deeper question, and involves nothing less than a conflict between two hostile theories of government, upon the outcome of which is staked the so-cial and political fabric which embodies our modern civilization. The first question is domestic and of the gravest and most immediate importance. But it neither belittles nor underrates it to say that it falls far short of the second in its scope and in its influence upon the fortunes of civilized man.

In what I shall say I propose to discuss the second and larger question first, for on that I think the cause in which I believe must surely rest. Protection and free trade are merely expressions in one direction of the differing theories of society and government which have been struggling for recognition and ac-ceptance during this century, with the control of the affairs of the civilized world as the great prize set between them. They serve, however, to illustrate and exhibit the conflict of the contending forces of which they are only the outward sign and manifestation. In examining the history of these two op-posed tariff policies, we are able as readily as in any other way to reach the great principles which underlie them, and of which, as I have said, they are merely one expression.

At the outset in treating of protection and free trade, it is well to clear our minds of cant. A tariff policy in its largest sense, as a part of a general theory and system of government, and in its farthest results, may affect a nation so-cially, morally, and politically; it may so modify the distribution of wealth as to give it a wider and better scope, and by defending wages and standards of living may influence the whole arrangement and growth of society. On the other hand, a tariff policy in the usual and narrow sense, and especially from the standpoint of the free trader, is purely an economic matter, a question of the pocket, of dollars and cents, and of the national method of doing business. In this latter aspect certainly there is nothing either sacred or moral about a tariff system.

I have had the pleasure in recent years of hearing a number of persons dis-course about free trade as a great moral issue. This attitude of mind has all the imperishable charm of springtime, and these same people have been very fond of likening themselves to the early Abolitionists and Free Soilers, as the fore-runners, and, if need be, the noble but not suffering martyrs, of a great moral movement for the redemption of mankind. No one likes to lay an irreverent hand upon such beatitude as this, but it seems unavoidable to do so. There is nothing moral about the tariff question, in the narrow sense just described, nor is the morality of free trade greater than that of protection. It seems hardly necessary to quote authority on this point, but if authority is needed, we have that of the great hero of the free traders, Adam Smith. That eminent man wrote the "Wealth of Nations," a very remarkable book, containing much of great value, and pointing out the pathway to be pursued by enlightened self-ishness in its search for national prosperity. That book has been widely read and greatly admired. Its author, however, looked upon it as covering only half of the scheme of human society and human action, for seventeen years before the publication of the "Wealth of Nations" he had written another book, which was complementary to the "Wealth of Nations," and which covered what that omitted. This earlier book he entitled "Moral Sentiments." It is quite forgotten now. I have never met a free trader who had read it, and very few who had heard of it. The "Moral Sentiments" have not proved as attractive as the methods of enlightened selfishness for getting rich, but the book demonstrates that Adam Smith knew that moral sentiments were not necessarily involved in a mere system of money-making, and established the distinction so broadly and clearly that he was justified, perhaps, in hoping that his followers and worshippers would understand it.

Let us rest, then, if we need to do so, on the authority of Adam Smith, that "moral sentiments" are a thing apart from the "wealth of nations," or from tariff policies merely as such. To suppose otherwise, indeed, is as great an error as another theory which I have seen advanced, to the effect that the American manufacturer is a "robber baron," who ought to be as destitute of rights as a black man under the Dred Scott decision, while the New York importer, generally of foreign birth and often with "no fatherland but the till," is a disinterested being so pure and good that if it were not for the imperfection of our earthly state we might expect to see angel wings springing from his shoulders. The truth is that both are men with the usual supply of human nature and of enlightened selfishness about them, although I greatly prefer the American manufacturer, because his enlightened selfishness is more profitable to his own countrymen than that of the importer.

It is always well to look at things as they are, even if the thing be free trade, to which some pesons in beautiful language have consecrated themselves. It is best, if we would treat it intelligently, to know that by itself and of itself the tariff is a business question, and that protection and free trade only take on a different and far deeper meaning when they are considered as parts of a question between far-reaching principles, which I believe involves the future of our race and the existence and progress of the highest civilization. It is in the latter and far graver aspect, as I have already said, that I prefer first to treat them.

To the practical man of affairs the theoretical and convinced free trader is generally extremely exasperating. But to the student of history and to the disinterested observer, to men of philosophic minds and blessed with a sense of humor, he is one of the most interesting and entertaining of human phenomena. These convinced free traders generally have some education, and invariably think that they have a great deal. They are provided with a set of little sayings and aphorisms, which can be carried without intellectual strain in a very small compass, and which to their thinking are complete solutions of all social and economic questions. These they draw forth on all occasions and present them to the world with entire confidence in the finality of their little sentences and a profound contempt for all persons who venture to differ from them, and who do not think that the difficulties of humanity can be so easily dealt with. . . .

It is very interesting to know that there are men who really think that the complex affairs of humanity can be disposed of by a collection of epigrammatic half truths and watch-pocket memoranda, and who firmly believe that they can regulate the vast mechanism of modern society with a latch-key because that simple instrument suffices to open their own front doors. They are interesting, also, in another way, for, to use the expressive slang of the day, "They know it all." The curious thing about it is that they really do know it all, if by "it" you mean free trade. It is possible for anyone to know everything about free trade, because its doctrines reached maturity fifty years ago and have stood still ever since, untaught by history and unchanged by facts.

The only condition necessary to this complete knowledge, besides being able to read, is that you should know nothing else except free trade. You must close your eyes and shut your ears to everything that has happened since the time of the Manchester School; you must take English opinion as the ultimate expression of human wisdom, and then you know all about free trade, and that is all you will know. Thus the free trader and his doctrine stand stationary and immovable. You cannot affix to them Galileo's sentence, which an American wit declared to be the proper motto for Italian locomotives, "And yet it moves." There is no motion about the free trader or his doctrine. To him human wisdom culminated and found its complete expression in the free-trade measures of the Manchester school—doctrines which Thomas Carlyle irreverently christened "The Dismal Science" and the "Calico Millennium."' . . .

Much has happened since then; many facts have appeared which contradict all their theories; many of their prophecies have failed of fulfillment. They neither know nor care. The world has been moving steadily forward, with many struggles and much suffering, along the dusty highroad of human progress ever since 1840; but the free trader, perched like a wee bird on the

fence rail by the roadside, chirps and twitters his little song in bland uncon-
sciousness of the great procession which has been marching steadily onward
for fifty years in a direction quite different from that upon which the
Manchester school decided that it must move. . . .

The physical revolt against [the monarchies of the *ancien régime* in Europe]
carried with it an intellectual revolt against state interference of any kind, and
paternalism came to be regarded as the equivalent of the hideous despotisms
which the French Revolution destroyed.

This confusion of these two ideas was natural, and perhaps at the same
time wholesome. In any event, it had an immense effect upon the philosophy
and theory of government, for out of this period came the doctrine that the
least government is the best, and the economic theory known as *laissez faire*
and *laissez aller*. The pendulum under the influence of this great movement
against personal government, as was to have been expected, swung with corresponding violence to the opposite extreme. Men swiftly concluded that, because the interference of the state under the monarchies of the eighteenth
century was evil, the true secret of freedom, happiness, and success was to be
found in going as far as possible in the opposite direction, in reducing government to its lowest terms, and in getting as near as possible to no government at all. In other words, the world in its political and economic theories
rushed from the system of tyrannous interference by a personal government,
under which it had sorely suffered, to extreme individualism and unrestrained
competition as a sure haven where all would be peace, gentleness, and prosperity. All this was very natural, but, like all extremes, very dangerous, and,
like all Utopias, was in practice very uncertain and disappointing. The theory
that state interference is always and necessarily a wholly bad thing, of which
we must have as little as possible, was in reality a too hasty generalization. It
depended on the proposition that state interference and paternalism as shown
in the case of a personal monarchy were wholly bad. On this precise state of
facts the let-alone theory in politics rested, and from it the same theory in eco-
nomical questions took its widest extension. The foundation was insecure,
and the glittering formula soon began to break down. It could not do otherwise, for it depended on a half truth. Men began to perceive, as time went on
and the steady progress of the democratic movement was assured, that there
was more than one kind of state, and that it did not at all follow because the
meddling tyranny of a personal monarchy was bad that the limited and intelligent interference of every other kind government must be bad too. The wide
difference between the action of a state composed of Louis XIV and a state
composed of the people themselves began to be apparent. In proportion as
this truth has grown visible to men, so has the reaction against state interfer-

ence, which began at the close of the last century and culminated in the adoption of free trade by England, declined.

Except to the English free trader and his imitators in this country, for whom history ended fifty years ago, and to whom the observation of historic and economic facts which do not fit their theory appears a mere impertinence, this change of opinion and advance of knowledge are very obvious. Men and nations have alike discovered that unrestrained individualism and unrestricted competition are capable of producing a social system quite as cruel and oppressive as the darkest forms of feudalism, to which some free-trade orators are fond of likening protection, apparently with the notion that feudalism was an economic policy. Having made this discovery, men have revolted against the doctrine which denied that any relief could be obtained by invoking the strength of the whole community united in government to remedy the glaring evils and miseries which unrestricted individualism and unrestrained competition were helpless to modify or cure. This revolt has been successful at various points, yet its importance rests not on its success, but on the fact that the let-alone theory has in this way been proved to be unsound in many directions. This fact is fatal, for if the general let-alone doctrine is not sound and correct at all points, it cannot be assumed to be correct at any. It is no longer sufficient to say that any given social or economic policy rests on the let-alone theory, for that theory has broken down completely as a general truth, and therefore no part of it, and no expression of it, is necessarily correct. Free trade rests entirely on the let-alone doctrine—that is, upon the doctrine that the least interference of the state is best; or, in other words, that the state ought not to interfere at all in the affairs of its individual members, except to maintain order at home or abroad, or in defense of public morals and public health; and even these are logically infractions of the doctrine of absolute individualism. Free trade, comparatively speaking, is not a very large question. It is merely the expression in one limited direction of a much broader principle. If the let-alone theory is correct as a general economic principle, and if the experience and practice of mankind show that it is correct, then free trade is of course correct as one of its parts. But if, on the other hand, the let-alone doctrine can be proved in many directions to be incorrect, if it has been abandoned again and again in practice by the most civilized nations, then the presumption is against free trade or any other single expression of the central principle. . . .

The public-school system and the post office are absolute violations of the let-alone theory. Yet who disputes their value, or who proposes to give them up? In almost every State of the Union there are statutes regulating the hours of labor, employers' liability, the management of railroads, and a thousand other acts great and small which interfere more or less directly with all the force of the government in the affairs of individuals. It is the same with the nation as with the states. Our statute book is filled with provisions which utterly disregard the let-alone theory of government, and every time we dredge a harbor or deepen a river or open a canal we set it at naught.

There is no need to go on and pile up examples. They occur every day, and stare at us from every page of our constitutions and statutes. If the let-alone doctrine on which free trade rests is correct, then these laws, from those providing for public education down, are all wrong. They should be swept from the statute books. In the jargon of the Democratic orator, they are fetters upon freedom. They set at defiance the darling epigrams that the free trader carries in his pocket and produces year in and year out, with the comfortable belief that they are both new and true, instead of being the damaged utterances of half a century ago. Let us look for a moment at two of these precious aphorisms, these beautiful expressions of the let-alone doctrine to the effect that you must "buy in the cheapest and sell in the dearest market," and that everything must be settled by the unrestrained and unqualified economic law of supply and demand. Let us see how these profound antitheses bear the test of actual legislation in the United States. We have upon our statute books at this moment a law to prevent the importation of contract labor, a law very imperfectly enforced, I am sorry to say. What put that law upon the statute book? The demand of the laboring men of the United States that they should be protected against that form of competition. The workingmen of the United States called for and secured this legislation in order to prevent the lowering of their rates of wages by the introduction of large masses of labor, which brought with them by contract the rate of wages of other countries where wages were lower than in the United States. On what portion of the let-alone system do you rest the economic correctness of these laws, supported by both political parties and questioned in their soundness by no one? If the free-trade doctrine be sound, by what principle do you step in and say to the employers of the United States, "You shall not buy your labor in the cheapest market?" . . .

In China, as the cheapest labor market and the greatest reservoir of low-priced labor in the world, on the theory of free trade we should have the right to buy our labor; and yet everybody is agreed that it is well to put a stop to [Chinese immigration] by law. What becomes of the precious theory of free trade in the face of a fact like that? We are right to exclude the Chinaman, who brings his cheap labor with him and lowers our standard of living and degrades our working people. If it is right to do so, then by what theory do you admit free of duty the product of this same [Chinese worker] made in his own country to compete with our product here? The product brings its rate of wages with it just as much as the man, and ocean freight no longer gives protection. If it is right to exclude the [Chinese worker], it is right to exclude the chair cane which he makes, and which brings his rate of wages and standard of life to compete with our workingmen just as surely as if the [Chinese worker] came over himself and made his chair cane in New York or Philadelphia. The underlying proposition of the free trader is that it is idle to attempt to modify by legislation the working of immutable economic laws. He forgets, or has never learned, that scarcely anything is immutable into which enter the heart and mind and emotions of humanity. The personal equation plays a large part in all things which human beings affect by their own actions. "Raise wages by law, make yourselves richer by taxation," says the free trader, bringing out again his little collection of epigrams. "It is like lifting yourself by your boot-straps." And then he fancies that he has answered the whole case. And while he thinks he has settled the universe in this simple fashion, the plain sense of the American working-men has shut out Chinese labor and contract labor, and will in no long time shut out the imported products of that same labor. . . .

The principle embodied in the contract-labor law should be enlarged, because the protection we now give by the duty on the bale of goods should be extended. There is no greater need at this time than stringent laws to sift and restrict the immigration to this country for the protection of our rates of wages and of the quality of our citizenship. This protection against excessive European immigration will come, as the exclusion of the Chinese and contract labor came, from the good sense and unerring instinct of the people, which will lead them to measures to guard their homes, their future, their race, and their civilization against forms of competition which they cannot meet if it is left unrestricted.

What, then, becomes of a doctrine which all the legislatures of the world continually disregard? What becomes of a doctrine with a hundred violations staring it in the face from every statute book, violations which even its devotees support or accept? What becomes of a doctrine that the instinct of mankind in his efforts for improvement sets at naught? All history proves that the let-alone doctrine cannot stand the shock of facts or the ordeal of practice. The truth is that in these modern times the civilized world is now entering upon a new period. The temperate zone . . . is very nearly absorbed. . . . Over against us are the crowded masses of the tropics. Relieved in many instances by the rule of [colonial powers] from the effect of the wars, famines, and floods which formerly decimated them, they are multiplying with enormous rapidity. . . . They have standards far below ours. They live under conditions of climate and habits impossible to us. Millions of men in India subsist on from fourteen to twenty dollars a year, and those men in India as well as in Japan are beginning to manufacture, thus closing to us their own markets and threatening our markets with an industrial competition which is deadly if you do not shut it out. You may lower wages and reduce costs beyond the wildest dreams of the free-trade orator, and in this temperate zone, where we and those like us dwell, you never can meet that tropical standard of living. Are we to sit down with our great civilization and bring about free trade, in order to be gradually overwhelmed by the labor of the tropics after a desperate strug- gle with the overcrowded people of our own race in Europe? Are we to be told that the laws of supply and demand, of buying in the cheapest and selling in the dearest markets, are eternal truths, and that everything would be right if we only adhered to them? Are we to accept these shattered dogmas of fifty years ago, and yield without a struggle to the ruin of our labor and the degra- dation of our standard of living? . . .

[The inhabitants of the advanced countries] will not submit; they have al- ready begun to resist. . . . They will exclude every sort of low labor brought by the [immigrant] himself, and they will in process of time equalize that same labor with their own by proper duties, when it is brought down the ship's gangway, not in the form of a human being, but in the form of a bale of goods, and carrying the same low rate of wages. The law of self-preservation is a higher law than any that political economy has ever invented, and, although it is the outcome of human nature, it is immutable. That law will in the lapses of the years, if not now, give us the protection which the free trader playing with his wrinkled little puppets would deny.

The fundamental error of the supporters of the let-alone theory, as I have al- ready said, is that they believe that what they call economic laws are fixed and certain, like those which govern the motions of the stars. But, although men, like stars, may differ from one another in glory, they are unlike stars in most other respects. Laws which are grounded upon the action of humanity are not fixed, but empirical. With rare exceptions, the most that we can hope for in this field is an approximation, some general rule with many exceptions. Human policies of society or government are subject to infinite variations. That which is most wise at one time may be most unwise at another. That which is excellent for one people would be ruin to another. Soil, climate, situ- ation, the size of the country, the race and character of the people, the condi- tions of the moment, and the possibilities of the future must all be considered in the adoption of any policy. The states and the people who have recognized this great controlling truth, and have put *a priori* theories behind them, have been the successful and governing races of the world. The Abbé Sieyes drew one ideal constitution after another for France. They were all perfect in theory, and they all perished from the face of the earth. Washington and his associates made but one constitution. It embodied few theories and much practice. It had inconsistencies and compromises, but it met the wants of the time and of the people, and it has stood strong and flourishing for a hundred years. The free trader is like the French Abbé; he would bind human development in the tight bandages of a theory, without regard to the infinite complexity of all things pertaining to humanity. He may by so doing attain symmetry, but it will be the symmetry of the Egyptian mummy, and the result will be quite as lifeless. That which applies to constitutions and government applies also to economic policies. We must look for guidance not to closet theories, but to the great book of history and experience, and see what has been done and attempted and what results have been achieved. Men are learning the lessons of history. They have long since put those lessons into practice. They are now beginning to formulate them as a theory, and to understand the philosophy which underlies them. It is apparent to all whose eyes are not hermetically sealed by the traditions of a fading past that, because a personal monarchy or state socialism is bad and oppressive, it does not therefore follow that unrestrained individualism and unrestricted competition are always and everywhere the only good things. Because some state interference is hurtful, all forms of it are not necessarily so. It is a question of degree, not of kind. Somewhere between the extremes of unlimited individualism on the one hand and personal monarchy or state socialism on the other can be found the golden mean, in which it is possible to use the united power of the community expressed in the state for the benefit of mankind and the protection of civilization.

Just how far we can go profitably in the use or in the refusal to use the powers of the state can be determined only by patient and cautious experiment, through which all the slow steps of civilization have been thus far painfully won. It is no doubt true that it is a grievous mistake to suppose that we can cure by law every evil which afflicts humanity, and that it is a weakness to look helplessly to legislation for everything we desire. But it is equally true, and has been proved in practice, that legislation and government can in many cases be employed with advantage to help the affairs of men. In other words, the aggregate power of the community can sometimes bring beneficial results which individuals by their divided efforts can never reach. If it be said, as it always is said, that this is a futile attempt to overhear natural laws by artificial devices, the answer is that the so-called economic laws are neither natural nor final; that statute law can often modify or call into action economic laws, and is constantly doing so, and that the whole fabric of human civilization to which those supposed laws are thought to apply is artificial. If we put away from us everything that is artificial, everything which man has established by means of law and custom, we should sink back to the condition of the men of the caves and the river drift. . . .

The let-alone theory, as a complete guide, when tried by the broad history of man, fails utterly. It has no support. Tried even by the standards of the limited application of it attempted in this century in new directions it fails, and can have no other fate, for it gives the lie to all that men have done and suffered in order to reach the point they have now attained, and sets at naught all the teachings of history. If, then, as I have said, the general doctrine breaks down, no single expression of it can stand except on its own merits. The general doctrine of let-alone in government has been invaded, abandoned, and disproved in hundreds of cases ever since it reached its highest point fifty years ago. Free trade is one expression of the let-alone doctrine. The general theory cannot sustain it. It must, therefore, stand on its own merits alone as one expression of a principle broken at a hundred points, and must prove, by the benefits it confers, its right to exist as an exception to the great law of human development through which all civilization has been reached.

The next point, therefore, is to determine whether free trade, contrary as it is to the general principles on which human society has been built up, can justify its existence. . . . England did not take up free trade because she was suddenly convinced of its scientific truth and believed that it ought therefore to prevail, even if the heavens fell. She adopted it, as nations generally adopt an economic policy, because she was satisfied, after much discussion, that it would pay. . . .

After the adoption of free trade those who brought it about immediately proclaimed, in the fashion of the English when they have entered upon some scheme which they think profitable, that the new system was a great and eternal truth; that every other nation ought to adopt it; that everyone who did not agree with them was either vicious or ignorant, and probably both. This outcry had but little effect upon other nations, but in the United States there is a class of persons who are still intellectually in the colonial stage of development, and who are sadly distressed by any disagreement with the views of England. Hence has arisen among us a free-trade propaganda. It was sustained at first by the existence of slave labor, which condemned a large section of our country to the production of a single great staple, and which, where it flourished, checked all industrial development. With the fall of slavery the gospel of free trade passed out of sight, and only in late years has it regained some of its lost ground. But now that, sustained by a desire for sectional reconciliation, it again has a political standing, we have a right to demand, when it asks us to imitate the British policy, an exhibition of British results. . . .

England has many more doubters of the truth of free trade now. . . . If Thomas Carlyle were to come back to life, instead of crying in the wilderness against the "calico millennium," he would find many allies even in his native land. Among others, no less a person than a late prime minister of England, Lord Salisbury, who has not hesitated to sneer in public at the dogmas of free trade. And if Carlyle were to look across the North Sea to the land of one of his heroes, he would find another German, Prince Bismarck, worthy to stand by the side of the great Frederick, declaring that the prosperity of the United States was largely due to the policy of protection, and himself embodying that policy in the legislation of the mighty empire which he has created. According to the Manchester school, free trade was to become straightway universal, and was to bring in the place of war peace on earth and good will among men. Free trade has not become universal, for no nation but England has adopted it, and England herself has had a war on her hands on an average of about once a year ever since. As prophets of peace and universal free trade, the Manchester school has been a failure. . . .

The true and lasting source of wealth is production, while trade, even though it enhances the value of the product, is at the same time a tax upon production, on account of the cost of transportation. A nation without trade may be permanently rich and prosperous, but a nation without production and dependent solely on trade holds riches and prosperity by a frail tenure. . . .

Trade is very brisk at Monte Carlo, and large sums of money are made and lost there by the exchange of what represents real values. Yet the prosperity of Monte Carlo is not desirable. Trade is most active in the Paris Bourse, the London Stock Exchange, and on Wall Street. In all those places that which represents real values passes rapidly from hand to hand, and vast fortunes are lost and won. In no place is barter, so beloved of the free trader, carried to such an ideal height; yet the stock exchanges of the world add nothing to the real wealth of the community. They are conveniences, but they create nothing. They deal in the symbols of wealth, but the wealth itself is made elsewhere—on the farm and in the factory, in the mine and the workshop. . . .

The free trade . . . is always prompt to exclaim that a manufacturer who can export ought not to have any protection. They forget that such manufacturers have reached this exporting point because the home market was secure. If you throw down the barriers which protect them at home you force them to struggle for the home market as for the foreign market, weakening their hold on the former and thereby losing the latter. More important still than the general proposition is the fact, which by itself is conclusive, that this increase of the export of manufactures is chiefly to countries with which we have lately formed reciprocity treaties, impossible without a protective tariff, for without protection you will have nothing to give for the advantages you ask and receive.

As reciprocity of this sort cannot exist without protection, the Democratic party proposes to destroy it, as they do not seem to care for any extension of trade where the foreign country is obliged to make concessions to us. Under their scheme nothing is to be exacted from foreigners, but we are to give everything. The price which we are to pay is not a limited mission to our market, but our market itself. They promise us an opportunity to compete, not for the markets of the world, but for a limited number of foreign markets, with nations having lower labor costs than ours. In return they ask us to abandon reciprocity, which is increasing our exports of manufactured products, and to throw our own market open to those same [low-wage] nations as well as to all others. . . .

[W]e can prevent increased importations by making them unprofitable. Unfortunately the only way we can make them unprofitable is by making our own costs lower than those of the foreigners, and there is no way to lower costs except by lowering wages. Thus we come back at every turn of the free-trade policy to a reduction of wages, and every free trader who knows anything of his subject, and is not talking for political effect, will admit this to be true. . . .

With a duty equal to the difference in labor costs, our rates of wages can be maintained against outside competition. With the removal of such duties we must bring our labor costs down to theirs, or we must cease to manufacture and compete. To maintain these [high] rates of wages is the whole purpose of protection, after we have got beyond the stage of establishing our industrial independence.

To maintain high rates of wages and to give, if possible, the fullest scope for their increases, I believe to be essential, because I believe good wages absolutely vital to the stability of our institutions and of our society. Protection and free trade present a social far more than an economic question, for on high wages and high standards of living depends the stability of society, and especially in a republic where every man has a vote, and where no privileged classes exist. Protection in its widest aspect is something far more than a mere question of schedules or of national bookkeeping. It is an effort to defend by legislation our standards of living. . . . I feel sure that in the end we shall not cast aside the policies which are to protect us from the lowering and deadly competition of races with lower standards of living than our own. . . .

I turn . . . to the broad principle . . . which I have already discussed. . . . That is the principle of let-alone in the government, the refusal to use the power of the state to benefit the community. Protection rests on the broad doctrine that the power of the community can be widely used in certain cases for the benefit of the whole body politic. There is no magic in it. We leave to the free trader the privilege of claiming that he has a panacea for all human ills in a patent tariff policy. We uphold a system of tariff protection because we believe it is one important method of defending the standards of living in the United States from a fatal and degrading competition [with low-wage foreign labor]. We believe in maintaining, defending, and uplifting the standards of living of the American people, because upon those standards rest our civilization and the onward march of our race. Men have struggled up from the darkness which shrouds their beginnings by slow and strenuous endeavor. They have fought their way to the light through many defeats and with much labor. They have not done it by any doctrine of *laissez faire* or "let-alone," but by united and unresting effort. The same force which has created good nations has created civilization, and great nations are the denial of the let-alone theory.

THEODORE ROOSEVELT

By the beginning of the twentieth century, the Hamiltonian program of tariff-based industrialization and government-promoted infrastructure development, in the form of railroad construction, had succeeded in transforming the United States into the world's leading industrial state. That success had brought with it new problems, such as growing class conflict and the formation of urban working classes subject to the vicissitudes of the national and global economies. The most successful American corporations had grown from fledgling enterprises dependent on public support into monopolies whose owners and directors dominated the state and national legislatures.

Americans disagreed about how those evils should be addressed. The answer of the Populist Democrats, who found a champion in William Jennings Bryan, was to use government in order to protect and preserve a small-town, rural America. Populism was the last stand of the old Jeffersonianism, a reactionary, backward-looking movement that sought to defend rural America against the industrial and urban America that Hamilton had planned and that Lincoln and his successors had created.

Another prescription for curing the ills of the industrial age was provided by socialists. American socialists came from varied backgrounds— some emerged from Jeffersonian rural radicalism, others from the reformist tradition of New England and the Northern tier states. In the twentieth century, American socialism and communism were dominated by European immigrants, particularly Jewish immigrants from Russia and Eastern Europe. Unlike the Jeffersonian Populists, socialists were reconciled to the industrial age; they simply wanted industrialism without capitalists.

The attempt to reconcile social reform with industrial capitalism fell to Republicans in the tradition of Hamilton and Lincoln. The defeat of

Bryan, the Democratic presidential candidate, by the Republican William McKinley, in the critical election of 1896, rescued the country from the possibility of a disastrous Jeffersonian revival. At the same time, McKinley's victory led to growing tension between the conservative wing of the Republican party, which was satisifed with the status quo, and the Progressives, mostly Republican. The rift would grow when McKinley's assassination in 1901 led to the succession of his Vice President, Theodore Roosevelt. In 1912 Roosevelt would bolt the Republican party and run for president as the nominee of the short-lived Progressive or "Bull Moose" party.

At the dedication in 1910 of the John Brown Cemetery at Osawotomie, Kansas, Theodore Roosevelt, in a speech that Herbert Croly helped to draft, called for a "New Nationalism" capable of addressing the problems that had arisen from the success of the Hamiltonian nationalist program.

The New Nationalism

We come here today to commemorate one of the epoch-making events of the long struggle for the rights of man—the long struggle for the uplift of humanity. Our country—this great Republic—means nothing unless it means the triumph of a real democracy, the triumph of popular government, and, in the long run, of an economic system under which each man shall be guaranteed the opportunity to show the best that there is in him. That is why the history of America is now the central feature of the history of the world; for the world has set its face hopefully toward our democracy; and, O my fellow citizens, each one of you carries on your shoulders not only the burden of doing well for the sake of your own country, but the burden of doing well and of seeing that this nation does well for the sake of mankind.

There have been two great crises in our country's history: first, when it was formed, and then, again, when it was perpetuated; and, in the second of these great crises—in the time of stress and strain which culminated in the Civil War, on the outcome of which depended the justification of what had been done earlier, you men of the Grand Army, you men who fought through the Civil War, not only did you justify your generation, but you justified the wisdom of Washington and Washington's colleagues. If this Republic had been founded by them only to be split asunder into fragments when the strain came, then the judgment of the world would have been that Washington's work was not worth doing. It was you who crowned Washington's work, as you carried to achievement the high purpose of Abraham Lincoln.

Now, with this second period of our history the name of John Brown will be forever associated; and Kansas was the theater upon which the first act of the second of our great national life dramas was played. It was the result of the struggle in Kansas which determined that our country should be in deed as well as in name devoted to both union and freedom; that the great experiment of democratic goverment on a national scale should succeed and not fail. In name we had the Declaration of Independence in 1776; but we gave the lie by our acts to the words of the Declaration of Independence until 1865; and words count for nothing except insofar as they represent acts. This is true everywhere; but, O my friends, it should be truest of all in political life. A broken promise is bad enough in private life. It is worse in the field of politics. No man is worth his salt in public life who makes on the stump a pledge which he does not keep after election; and, if he makes such a pledge and does not keep it, hunt him out of public life. I care for the great deeds of the past chiefly as spurs to drive us onward in the present. I speak of the men of the past partly that they may be honored by our praise of them, but more that they may serve as examples for the future.

It was a heroic struggle; and, as is inevitable with all such struggles, it had also a dark and terrible side. Very much was done of good, and much also of evil; and, as was inevitable in such a period of revolution, often the same man did both good and evil. For our great good fortune as a nation, we, the people of the United States as a whole, can now afford to forget the evil, or, at least, remember it without bitterness, and to fix our eyes with pride only on the good that was accomplished. Even in ordinary times there are very few of us who do not see the problems of life as through a glass, darkly; and when the glass is clouded by the murk of furious popular passion, the vision of the best and the bravest is dimmed. Looking back, we are all of us now able to do justice to the valor and the disinterestedness and the love of the right, as to each it was given to see the right, shown both by the men of the North and the men of the South in that contest which was finally decided by the attitude of the West. We can admire the heroic valor, the sincerity, the self-devotion shown alike by the men who wore the blue and the men who wore the gray; and our sadness that such men should have had to fight one another is tempered by the glad knowledge that ever hereafter their descendants shall be found fighting side by side, struggling in peace as well as in war for the uplift of their common country, all alike resolute to raise to the highest pitch of honor and usefulness the nation to which they all belong. As for the veterans of the Grand Army of the Republic, they deserve honor and recognition such as is paid to no other citizens of the Republic; for to them the Republic owes its all; for to them it owes its very existence. It is because of what you and your comrades did in the dark years that we of today walk, each of us, head erect, and proud that we belong, not to one of a dozen little squabbling contemptible commonwealths, but to the mightiest nation upon which the sun shines.

I do not speak of this struggle of the past merely from the historic standpoint. Our interest is primarily in the application today of the lessons taught by the contest of half a century ago. It is of little use for us to pay lip-loyalty to the mighty men of the past unless we sincerely endeavor to apply to the problems of the present precisely the qualities which in other crises enabled the men of that day to meet those crises. It is half melancholy and half amusing to see the way in which well-meaning people gather to do honor to the men who, in company with John Brown, and under the lead of Abraham Lincoln, faced and solved the great problems of the nineteenth century, while, at the same time, these same good people nervously shrink from, or frantically denounce, those who are trying to meet the problems of the twentieth century in the spirit which was accountable for the successful solution of the problems of Lincoln's time.

Of that generation of men to whom we owe so much, the man to whom we owe most is, of course, Lincoln. Part of our debt to him is because he forecast our present struggle and saw the way out. He said: "I hold that while man exists it is his duty to improve not only his own condition, but to assist in ameliorating mankind."

And again: "Labor is prior to, and independent of, capital. Capital is only the fruit of labor, and could never have existed if labor had not first existed. Labor is the superior of capital, and deserves much the higher consideration."

If that remark was original with me, I should be even more strongly denounced as a communist agitator than I shall be anyhow. It is Lincoln's. I am only quoting it; and that is one side; that is the side the capitalist should hear. Now, let the working man hear his side.

"Capital has its rights, which are as worthy of protection as any other rights. . . . Nor should this lead to a war upon the owners of property. Property is the fruit of labor; . . . property is desirable; is a positive good in the world."

And then comes a thoroughly Lincolnlike sentence: "Let not him who is houseless pull down the house of another, but let him work diligently and build one for himself, thus by example assuring that his own shall be safe from violence when built."

It seems to me that, in these words, Lincoln took substantially the attitude that we ought to take; he showed the proper sense of proportion in his relative estimates of capital and labor, of human rights and property rights. Above all, in this speech, as in many others, he taught a lesson in wise kindliness and charity; an indispensable lesson to us of today. But this wise kindliness and charity never weakened his arm or numbed his heart. We cannot afford weakly to blind ourselves to the actual conflict which faces us today. The issue is joined, and we must fight or fail.

In every wise struggle for human betterment one of the main objects, and often the only object, has been to achieve in large measure equality of opportunity. In the struggle for this great end, nations rise from barbarism to civilization, and through it people press forward from one stage of enlightenment to the next. One of the chief factors in progress is the destruction of special privilege. The essence of any struggle for healthy liberty has always been, and must always be, to take from some one man or class of men the right to enjoy power, or wealth, or position, or immunity, which has not been earned by service to his or their fellows. That is what you fought for in the Civil War, and that is what we strive for now.

At many stages in the advance of humanity, this conflict between the men who possess more than they have earned and the men who have earned more than they possess is the central condition of progress. In our day it appears as the struggle of freemen to gain and hold the right of self-government as against the special interests, who twist the methods of free government into machinery for defeating the popular will. At every stage, and under all circumstances, the essence of the struggle is to equalize opportunity, destroy privilege, and give to the life and citizenship of every individual the highest possible value both to himself and to the commonwealth. That is nothing new. All I ask in civil life is what you fought for in the Civil War. I ask that civil life be carried on according to the spirit in which the army was carried on. You never get perfect justice, but the effort in handling the army was to bring to the front the men who could do the job. Nobody grudged promotion to Grant, or Sherman, or Thomas, or Sheridan, because they earned it. The only complaint was when a man got promotion which he did not earn.

Practical equality of opportunity for all citizens, when we achieve it, will have two great results. First, every man will have a fair chance to make of himself all that in him lies; to reach the highest point to which his capacities, unassisted by special privileges of his own and unhampered by the special privilege of others, can carry him, and to get for himself and his family substantially what he has earned. Second, equality of opportunity means that the commonwealth will get from every citizen the highest service of which he is capable. No man who carries the burden of the special privileges of another can give to the commonwealth that service to which it is fairly entitled.

I stand for the square deal. But when I say that I am for the square deal, I mean not merely that I stand for fair play under the present rules of the game, but that I stand for having those rules changed so as to work for a more substantial equality of opportunity and of reward for equally good service. One word of warning, which, I think, is hardly necessary in Kansas. When I say I want a square deal for the poor man, I do not mean that I want a square deal for the man who remains poor because he has not got the energy to work for himself. If a man who has had a chance will not make good, then he has got to quit. And you men of the Grand Army, you want justice for the brave man who fought, and punishment for the coward who shirked his work. Is not that so?

Now, this means that our government, national and state, must be freed from the sinister influence or control of special interests. Exactly as the special interests of cotton and slaver threatened our political integrity before the Civil War, so now the great special business interests too often control and corrupt the men and methods of government for their own profit. We must drive the special interests out of politics. That is one of our tasks today. Every special interest is entitled to justice—full, fair, and complete—and, now, mind you, if there were any attempt by mob violence to plunder and work harm to the special interest, whatever it may be, that I most dislike, and the wealthy man, whomsoever he may be, for whom I have the greatest contempt, I would fight for him, and you would if you were worth your salt. He should have justice. For every special interest is entitled to justice, but not one is entitled to a vote in Congress, to a voice on the bench, or to representation in any public office. The Constitution guarantees protection to property, and we must make that promise good. But it does not give the right of suffrage to any corporation.

The true friend of property, the true conservative, is he who insists that property shall be the servant and not the master of the commonwealth; who insists that the creature of man's making shall be the servant and not the master of the man who made it. The citizens of the United States must effectively control the mighty commercial forces which they have themselves called into being.

There can be no effective control of corporations while their political activity remains. To put an end to it will be neither a short nor an easy task, but it can be done.

We must have complete and effective publicity of corporate affairs, so that the people may know beyond peradventure whether the corporations obey the law and whether their management entitles them to the confidence of the public. It is necessary that laws should be passed to prohibit the use of corporate funds directly or indirectly for political purposes; it is still more necessary that such laws should be thoroughly enforced. Corporate expenditures for political purposes, and especially such expenditures by public-service corporations, have supplied one of the most principal sources of corruption in our political affairs. . . .

I believe that officers, and, especially, the directors, of corporations should be held personally responsible when any corporation breaks the law.

Combinations in industry are the result of an imperative economic law which cannot be repealed by political legislation. The effort at prohibiting all combination has substantially failed. The way out lies not in attempting to prevent such combinations but in completely controlling them in the interest of the public welfare. . . .

The absence of effective state and, especially, national restraint upon unfair money-getting has tended to create a small class of enormously wealthy and economically powerful men, whose chief object is to hold and increase their power. The prime need is to change the conditions which enable these men to accumulate power which it is not for the general welfare that they should hold or exercise. We grudge no man a fortune which represents his own power and sagacity, when exercised with entire regard to the welfare of his fellows. Again, comrades over there, take the lesson from your own experience. Not only did you not grudge, but you gloried in the promotion of the great generals who gained their promotion by leading the army to victory. So it is with us. We grudge no man a fortune in civil life if it is honorably obtained and well used. It is not even enough that it should have been gained without doing damage to the community. We should permit it to be gained only so long as the gaining represents benefit to the community. This, I know, implies a policy of a far more active governmental interference with social and economic conditions in this country than we have yet had, but I think we have got to face the fact that such an increase in governmental control is now necessary.

No man should receive a dollar unless that dollar has been fairly earned. Every dollar received should represent a dollar's worth of services rendered— not gambling in stocks, but service rendered. The really big fortune, the swollen fortune, by the mere fact of its size acquires qualities which differentiate it in kind as well as in degree from what is possessed by men of relatively small means. Therefore, I believe in a graduated income tax on big fortunes, and in another tax which is far more easily collected and far more effective— a graduated inheritance tax on big fortunes, properly safeguarded against evasion and increasing rapidly in amount with the size of the estate. . . .

Of conservation I shall speak more at length elswhere. Conservation means development as much as it does protection. I recognize the right and duty of this generation to develop and use the natural resources of our land; but I do not recognize the right to waste them, or to rob, by wasteful use, the generations that come after us. I ask nothing of the nation except that it so behave as each farmer here behaves with reference to his own children. That farmer is a poor creature who skins the land and leaves it worthless to his children. The farmer is a good farmer who, having enabled the land to support himself and to provide for the education of his children, leaves it to them a little better than he found it himself. I believe the same thing of a nation.

Moreover, I believe that the natural resources must be used for the benefit of all our people, and not monopolized for the benefit of the few. . . . That is one of the fundamental reasons why the special interests should be driven out of politics. Of all the questions which can come before this nation, short of the actual preservation of its existence in a great war, there is none which compares in importance with the great central task of leaving this land even a better land for our descendants than it is for us, and training them into a better race to inhabit the land and pass it on. Conservation is a great moral issue, for it involves the patriotic duty of insuring the safety and continuance of the nation. Let me add that the health and vitality of our people are at least as well worth conserving as their forests, waters, lands, and minerals, and in the great work the national government must bear a most important part. . . .

Nothing is more true than that excess of every kind is followed by reaction; a fact which should be pondered by reformer and revolutionary alike. We are face to face with new conceptions of the relations of property to human welfare, chiefly because certain advocates of the rights of property as against the rights of men have been pushing their claims too far. The man who wrongly holds that every human right is secondary to his profit must now give way to the advocate of human welfare, who rightly maintains that every man holds his property subject to the general right of the community to regulate its use to whatever degree the public welfare may require it.

But I think we may go still further. The right to regulate the use of wealth in the public interest is universally admitted. Let us admit also the right to regulate the terms and conditions of labor, which is the chief element of wealth, directly in the interest of the common good. The fundamental thing to do for every man is to give him a chance to reach a place in which he will make the greatest possible contribution to the public welfare. Understand what I say there. Give him a chance, not push him up if he will not be pushed. Help any man who stumbles; if he lies down, it is a poor job to carry him; but if he is a worthy man, try your best to see that he gets a chance to show the worth that is in him. No man can be a good citizen unless he has a wage more than sufficient to cover the bare cost of living, and hours of labor short enough so that after his day's work is done he will have time and energy to bear his share in the management of the community, to help in carrying the general load. We keep countless men from being good citizens by the conditions of life with which we surround them. We need comprehensive workmen's-compensation acts, both state and national laws to regulate child labor and work for women, and, especially, we need in our common schools not merely education in book-learning, but also practical training for daily life and work. We need to enforce better sanitary conditions for our workers and to extend the use of safety appliance for our workers in industry and commerce, both within and between the states. Also, friends, in the interest of the working man himself we need to set our faces like flint against mob violence just as against corporate greed; against violence and injustice and lawlessness by wage-workers just as much as against lawless cunning and greed and selfish arrogance of employers. If I could ask but one thing of my fellow countrymen, my request would be that, whenever they go in for reform, they remember the two sides, and that they always exact justice from one side as much as from the other. I have small use for the public servant who can always see and denounce the corruption of the capitalist, but who cannot persuade himself, especially before election, to say a word about lawless mob violence. And I have equally small use for the man, be he a judge on the bench, or editor of a great paper, or wealthy and influential private citizen, who can see clearly enough and denounce the lawlessness of mob violence, but whose eyes are closed so that he is blind when the question is one of corruption in business on a gigantic scale. Also remember what I said about excess in reformer and reactionary alike. If the reactionary man, who thinks of nothing but the rights of property, could have his way, he would bring about a revolution; and one of my chief fears in connection with progress comes because I do not want to see our people, for lack of proper leadership, compelled to follow men whose intentions are excellent, but whose eyes are a little too wild to make it really safe to trust them. Here in Kansas there is one paper which habitually denounces me as the tool of Wall Street, and at the same time frantically repudiates the statement that I am a socialist on the ground that that is an unwarranted slander of the socialists.

National efficiency has many factors. It is a necessary result of the principle of conservation widely applied. In the end it will determine our failure or success as a nation. National efficiency has to do not only with natural resources and with men but it is equally concerned with institutions. The state must be made efficient for the work which concerns only the people of the state; and the nation for that which concerns all the people. There must remain no neutral ground to serve as a refuge for lawbreakers, and especially for lawbreakers of great wealth, who can hire the vulpine legal cunning which will teach them how to avoid both jurisdictions. It is a misfortune when the national legislature fails to do its duty in providing a national remedy, so that the only national activity is the purely negative activity of the judiciary in forbidding the state to exercise power on the premises.

I do not ask for overcentralization; but I do ask that we work in a spirit of broad and far-reaching nationalism when we work for what concerns our people as a whole. We are all Americans. Our common interests are as broad as the continent. I speak to you here in Kansas exactly as I would speak in New York or Georgia, for the most vital problems are those which affect us all. The national government belongs to the whole American people, and where the whole American people are interested, that interest can be guarded effectively only by the national government. The betterment which we seek must be accomplished, I believe, mainly through the national government.

HERBERT CROLY

In this excerpt from his Progressive manifesto *The Promise of American Life* (1909), the founding editor of *The New Republic* calls for a "democratic Hamiltonianism" suitable for the conditions of the twentieth century.

Democratic Hamiltonianism

Reform is both meaningless and powerless unless the Jeffersonian principle of non-interference is abandoned. The experience of the last generation plainly shows that the American economic and social system cannot be allowed to take care of itself, and that the automatic harmony of the individual and the public interest, which is the essence of the Jeffersonian democratic creed, has proved to be an illusion. Interference with the natural course of individual and popular action there must be in the public interest; and such interference must at least be sufficient to accomplish its purposes. The house of the American democracy is again by way of being divided against itself, because the national interest has not been consistently asserted as against special and local interests; and again, also, it can be reunited only by being partly reconstructed on better foundations. If reform does not and cannot mean restoration, it is bound to mean reconstruction.

The reformers have come partly to realize that the Jeffersonian policy of drift must be abandoned. They no longer expect the American ship of state by virtue of its own righteous framework to sail away to a safe harbor in the Promised Land. They understand that there must be a vigorous and conscious assertion of the public as opposed to private and special interests, and that the American people must to a greater extent than they have in the past subordinate the latter to the former. They behave as if the American ship of state will hereafter require careful steering; and a turn or two at the wheel has given them some idea of the course they must set. On the other hand, even the best of them have not learned the name of its ultimate destination, the full difficulties of the navigation, or the stern discipline which may eventually be imposed upon the ship's crew. They do not realize, that is, how thoroughly Jeffersonian individualism must be abandoned for the benefit of a genuinely individual and social consummation; and they do not realize how dangerous and fallacious a chart their cherished principle of equal rights may well become. In reviving the practice of vigorous national action for the achievement of a national purpose, the better reformers have, if only they knew it, been looking in the direction of a much more trustworthy and serviceable political principle. The assumption of such a responsibility implies the rejection of a large part of the Jeffersonian creed, and a renewed attempt to establish in its place the popularity of its Hamiltonian rival. On the other hand, it involves no less surely the transformation of Hamiltonianism into a thoroughly democratic political principle. . . .

If the integrity of a democracy is injured by the perpetuation of unearned economic distinctions, it is also injured by extreme poverty, whether deserved or not. . . . It stands to reason that in the long run the people who possess the political power will want a substantial share of the economic fruits. A prudent democracy should anticipate this demand. Not only does any considerable amount of grinding poverty constitute a grave social danger in a democratic state, but so, in general, does a widespread condition of partial economic deprivation. The individuals constituting a democracy lack the first essential of individual freedom when they cannot escape from a condition of economic dependence.

The American democracy has confidently believed in the fatal [inevitable—M.L.] prosperity enjoyed by the people under the American system. In the confidence of that belief it has promised to Americans a substantial satisfaction of their economic needs; and it has made that promise an essential part of the American national idea. The promise has been measurably fulfilled hitherto, because the prodigious natural resources of a new continent were thrown open to anybody with the energy to appropriate them. But those natural resources have now in large measure passed into the possession of individuals, and American statesmen can no longer count upon them to satisfy the popular hunger for economic independence. An ever larger proportion of the total population of the country is taking to industrial occupations, and an industrial system brings with it much more definite social and economic classes, and a diminution of the earlier social homogeneity. The contemporary wage-earner is no longer satisfied with the economic results of being merely an American citizen. . . . What the wage-earner needs, and what it is to the interest of a democratic state that he should obtain, is a constantly higher standard of living. The state can help him to conquer a higher standard of living without doing any necessary injury to his employers and with a positive benefit to general economic and social efficiency. If it is to earn the loyalty of the wage-earners, it must recognize the legitimacy of his demand, and make the satisfaction of it an essential part of its public policy. . . .

It is entirely possible, of course, that the promise can never be kept, —that its redemption will prove to be beyond the patience, the power, and the wisdom of the American people and their leaders; but if it is not kept, the American commonwealth will no longer continue to be a democracy.

The New Deal

The triumph of the conservatives over the Progressives in the Republican party after World War I drove many Hamiltonians into the Democratic party during the New Deal era. Unlike the Progressives, the New Dealers were not clearly in the Federalist-National Republican-Whig-Republican tradition. The New Deal Democratic party owed as much to Southern and Western Jefferson–Jackson populism and to the Marxist-influenced socialism and social democracy of immigrant labor in the Northeast as it owed to the "democratic Hamiltonianism" advocated by Herbert Croly and other Progressives. Even so, in an era when pro-business conservatives in the mid-century Republican party attacked federal government activism in the name, not of the American Hamiltonian tradition, but of the English laissez-faire school of Adam Smith and Herbert Spencer, Franklin D. Roosevelt and his great successors Harry Truman and Lyndon Johnson were the closest equivalents to Hamiltonian statesmen on the scene. The "Modern Republican" school associated with Dwight Eisenhower, Richard Nixon, and Nelson Rockefeller is best viewed as an attempt by Republicans to co-opt elements of the New Deal, not as a survival of the older Hamilton-to-TR tradition.

FRANKLIN DELANO ROOSEVELT

Franklin Delano Roosevelt (1882–1945) was the greatest President of the twentieth century, and with Washington and Lincoln one of the three greatest American Presidents to date. A member of the patrician New York family to which Theodore Roosevelt belonged, Roosevelt graduated from Columbia Law School and was elected to the New York senate in 1910. In 1913 he became Assistant Secretary of the Navy in the Wilson administration. He was nominated for Vice President in 1920. In 1921 FDR was stricken by polio, which left him handicapped. He emerged from that ordeal to serve for two terms as Governor of New York, beginning in 1928.

Succeeding Herbert Hoover as the Depression deepened in 1932, FDR restored the morale of Americans with his ebullience and his willingness to experiment with new forms of economic and political organization. Although his New Deal programs did not end the Depression, FDR achieved many of the goals of Progressive reformers, establishing Social Security and federal utility agencies such as the Tennessee Valley Authority (TVA) and the Lower Colorado River Authority (LCRA) that FDR's protégé Lyndon Baines Johnson helped to create in Texas. Stymied by conservative resistance in the late 1930s, FDR moved the United States toward intervention against the Axis in World War II, despite the bitter resistance of isolationists, many of them Progressives or New Dealers. The United States was already engaged in an undeclared naval war with Germany as an ally of Britain when the Japanese attack on Pearl Harbor sank American isolationism along with much of the U.S. Pacific fleet. After being elected to an unprecedented fourth term as President, FDR died in 1945, as Hitler's empire and Japan were on the verge of defeat.

FDR transformed American conceptions of the presidency in ways that ranged from the trivial (the use of initials by JFK and LBJ) to the profound—the idea of the president as chief legislator as well as chief executive. Woodrow Wilson had sought to turn the traditionally weak American president into the leader of his party and a tribune of the people; FDR succeeded in doing so. In addition, FDR left a darker legacy: the abuse of the vastly expanded powers of the presidency. The abuses of power by President John F. Kennedy and his brother, Attorney General Robert Kennedy, and by President Richard Nixon, who treated the executive branch as their personal fiefdom and believed they were above the law, showed the danger inherent in "the imperial presidency" when it was led by individuals lacking FDR's character and common sense.

Roosevelt's New Deal coalition was an incoherent collection of Southern and Western farmers, Northern union members, immigrant Marxists, and Northern and West Coast Progressives. Accused by other Democrats of betraying the small-government, states'-rights Jeffersonian tradition of the party, FDR responded by claiming that he and his allies were the "true" Jeffersonians. As Lincoln had earlier redefined Jeffersonianism to mean legal and political equality promoted by the federal government, FDR attempted to redefine Jeffersonianism to mean economic equality and security brought about by an activist federal government. FDR never referred to Hamilton, who had been the hero of the Republicans, except with scorn, although he did seek to adopt Lincoln as a predecessor. If we ignore FDR's sly propaganda and concentrate on what he did, it is clear that he was in the Northern Hamiltonian tradition, and that the New Dealers were the descendants, if only collateral descendants, of the neo-Hamiltonian Progressives. As a wartime President, FDR combined rhetorical Wilsonianism with practical Hamiltonian realism.

FDR's campaign speech at the San Francisco Commonwealth Club on September 23, 1932, shows the "Progressive" side of America's greatest twentieth-century President. No genuine Jeffersonian could have uttered the Hamiltonian sentiment: "The day of enlightened administration has come."

A Greater Social Contract

I want to speak not of politics but of Government. I want to speak not of parties, but of universal principles. They are not political, except in that larger sense in which a great American once expressed a definition of politics, that nothing in all of human life is foreign to the science of politics. . . .

The issue of Government has always been whether individual men and women will have to serve some system of Government or economics, or whether a system of Government and economics exists to serve individual men and women. This question has persistently dominated the discussion of Government for many generations. On questions relating to these things men have differed, and for time immemorial it is probable that honest men will continue to differ.

The final word belongs to no man; yet we can still believe in change and progress. Democracy, as a dear old friend of mine in Indiana, Meredith Nicholson, has called it, is a quest, a never-ending seeking for better things, and in the seeking for these things and the striving for them, there are many roads to follow. But, if we map the course of those roads, we find that there are only two general directions.

When we look about us, we are likely to forget how hard people have worked to win the privilege of Government. The growth of the national Governments of Europe was a struggle for the development of a centralized force in the Nation, strong enough to impose peace upon ruling barons. In many instances the victory of the central Government, the creation of a strong central Government, was a haven of refuge to the individual. The people preferred the master far away to the exploitation and cruelty of the smaller master near at hand.

But the creators of national Government were perforce ruthless men. They were often cruel in their methods, but they did strive steadily toward something that society needed and very much wanted, a strong central State able to keep the peace, to stamp out civil war, to put the unruly nobleman in his place, and to permit the bulk of individuals to live safely. The man of ruthless force had his place in developing a pioneer country, just as he did in fixing the power of the central Government in the development of Nations. When the development among the Nations of Europe, however, had been completed, ambition and ruthlessness, having served their term, tended to overstep their mark.

There came a growing feeling that Government was conducted for the benefit of a few who thrived unduly at the expense of all. The people sought a balancing—a limiting force. There came gradually, through town councils, trade guilds, national parliaments, by constitution and by popular participation and control, limitations on arbitrary power.

Another factor that tended to limit the power of those who ruled, was the rise of the ethical conception that a ruler bore a responsibility for the welfare of his subjects.

The American colonies were born in this struggle. The American Revolution was a turning point in it. After the Revolution the struggle continued and shaped itself in the public of the country. There were those who because they had seen the confusion which attended the years of war for American independence surrendered to the belief that popular government was essentially dangerous and essentially unworkable. They were honest people, my friends, and we cannot deny that their experience had warranted some measure of fear. The most brilliant, honest and able exponent of this point of view was Hamilton. He was too impatient of slow-moving methods. Fundamentally he believed that the safety of the republic lay in the autocratic strength of its government, that the destiny of individuals was to serve that government, and that fundamentally a great and strong group of central institutions, guided by a small group of able and public spirited citizens, could best direct all government.

But Mr. Jefferson, in the summer of 1776, after drafting the Declaration of Independence turned his mind to the same problem and took a different view. He did not deceive himself with outward forms. Government to him was a means to an end, not an end in itself; it might be either a refuge and a help or a threat and a danger, depending on the circumstances. We find him carefully analyzing the society for which he was to organize a government. "We have no paupers. The great mass of our population is of laborers, our rich who cannot live without labor, either manual or professional, being few and of moderate wealth. Most of the laboring class possess property, cultivate their own lands, have families and from the demand for their labor, are enabled to extract from the rich and the competent such prices as enable them to feed abundantly, clothe above mere decency, to labor moderately and raise their families."

These people, he considered, had two sets of rights, those of "personal competency" and those involved in acquiring and possessing property. By "personal competency" he meant the right of free thinking, freedom of forming and expressing opinions, and freedom of personal living, each man according to his own lights. To insure the first set of rights, a government must so order its functions as not to interfere with the individual. But even Jefferson realized that the exercise of the property rights might so interfere with the rights of the individual that the government, without whose assistance the property rights could not exist, must intervene, not to destroy individualism, but to protect it.

You are familiar with the great political duel which followed, and how Hamilton, and his friends, building toward a dominant centralized power, were at length defeated in the great election of 1800, by Mr. Jefferson's party.

Out of that duel came the two parties, Republican and Democratic, as we know them today.

So began, in American political life, the new day, the day of the individual against the system, the day in which individualism was made the great watchword of American life. The happiest of economic conditions made that day long and splendid. On the Western frontier, land was substantially free. No one, who did not shirk the task of earning a living, was entirely without opportunity to do so. Depressions could, and did, come and go; but they could not alter the fundamental fact that most of the people lived partly by selling their labor and partly by extracting their livelihood from the soil, so that starvation and dislocation were practically impossible. At the very worst there was always the possibility of climbing into a covered wagon and moving west where the untilled prairies afforded a haven for men to whom the East did not provide a place. So great were our natural resources that we could offer this relief not only to our own people, but to the distressed of all the world; we could invite immigration from Europe, and welcome it with open arms. Traditionally, when a depression came a new section of land was opened in the West; and even our temporary misfortune served our manifest destiny.

It was in the middle of the nineteenth century that a new force was released and a new dream created. The force was what is called the industrial revolution, the advance of steam and machinery and the rise of the forerunners of the modern industrial plant. The dream was the dream of an economic machine, able to raise the standard of living for everyone; to bring luxury within the reach of the humblest; to annihilate distance by steam power and later by electricity, and to release everyone from the drudgery of the heaviest manual toil. It was to be expected that this would necessarily affect government. Heretofore, government had merely been called upon to produce conditions within which people could live happily, labor peacefully, and rest secure. Now it was called upon to aid in the consummation of this new dream. There was, however, a shadow over the dream. To be made real, it required use of the talents of men of tremendous will and tremendous ambition, since by no other force could the problems of financing and engineering new developments be brought to a consummation.

So manifest were the advantages of the machine age, however, that the United States fearlessly, cheerfully, and, I think, rightly, accepted the bitter with the sweet. It was thought that no price was too high to pay for the advantages which we could draw from a finished industrial system. The history of the last half century is accordingly in large measure a history of a group of financial Titans, whose methods were not scrutinized with too much care, and who were honored in proportion as they produced the results, irrespective of the means they used. The financiers who pushed the railroads to the Pacific were always ruthless, often wasteful, and frequently corrupt; but they did build railroads, and we have them today. It has been estimated that the American investor paid for the American railway system more than three times over in the process; but despite this fact the net advantage was to the United States. As long as we had free land; as long as population was growing by leaps and bounds; as long as our industrial plants were insufficient to supply our own needs, society chose to give the ambitious man free play and unlimited reward provided only that he produced the economic plant so much desired.

During this period of expansion, there was equal opportunity for all and the business of government was not to interfere but to assist in the development of industry. This was done at the request of business men themselves. The tariff was originally imposed for the purpose of "fostering our infant industry," a phrase I think the older among you will remember as a political issue not so long ago. The railroads were subsidized, sometimes by grants of money, oftener by grants of land; some of the msot valuable oil lands in the United States were granted to assist the financing of the railroad which pushed through the Southwest. A nascent merchant marine was assisted by grants of money, or by mail subsidies, so that our steam shipping might ply the seven seas. Some of my friends tell me that they do not want the government in business. With this I agree; but I wonder whether they realize the implications of the past. For while it has been American doctrine that the government must not go into business in competition with private enterprises, still it has been traditional, particularly in Republican administrations, for business urgently to ask the government to put at private disposal all kinds of government assistance. The same man who tells you that he does not want to see the government interfere in business—and he means it, and has plenty of good reasons for saying so—is the first to go to Washington and ask the government for a prohibitory tariff on his product. When things get just bad enough, as they did two years ago, he will go with equal speed to the United States government and ask for a loan; and the Reconstruction Finance Corporation is the outcome of it. Each group has sought protection from the government for its own special interests, without realizing that the function of government must be to favor no small group at the expense of its duty to protect the rights of personal freedom and of private property in all its citizens.

In retrospect we can now see that the turn of the tide came with the turn of the century. We were reaching our last frontier; there was no more free land and our industrial combinations had become great uncontrolled and irresponsible units of power within the State. Clear-sighted men saw with fear the danger that opportunity would no longer be equal; that the growing corporation, like the feudal baron of old, might threaten the economic freedom of individuals to earn a living. In that hour, our anti-trust laws were born. The cry was raised against the great corporations. Theodore Roosevelt, the first great Republican Progressive, fought a presidential campaign on the issue of "trust busting" and talked freely about malefactors of great wealth. If the government had a policy it was rather to turn the clock back, to destroy the large combinations and to return to the time when every man owned his individual small business.

This was impossible; Theodore Roosevelt, abandoning the idea of "trust busting," was forced to work out a difference between "good" trusts and "bad" trusts. The Supreme Court set forth the famous "rule of reason" by which it seems to have meant that a concentration of industrial power was permissible if the method by which it got its power, and the use it made of that power, were reasonable.

Woodrow Wilson, elected in 1912, saw the situation more clearly. Where Jefferson had feared the encroachment of political power on the lives of individuals, Wilson knew that the new power was financial. He saw, in the highly centralized economic system, the despot of the twentieth century, on whom great masses of individuals relied for their safety and their livelihood, and whose irresponsibility and greed (if they were not controlled) would reduce them to starvation and penury. The concentration of financial power had not proceeded so far in 1912 as it has today; but it had grown far enough for Mr. Wilson to realize fully its implication. It is interesting, now, to read his speeches. What is called "radical" today (and I have reason to know whereof I speak) is mild compared to the campaign of Mr. Wilson. "No man can deny," he said, "that the lines of endeavor have more and more narrowed and stiffened; no man who knows anything about the development of industry in this country can have failed to observe that the larger kinds of credit are more and more difficult to obtain unless you obtain them upon terms of uniting your efforts with those who already control the industry of the country, and nobody can fail to observe that every man who tries to set himself up in competition with any process of manufacture which has taken place under the control of large concentrations of capital will presently find himself either squeezed out or obliged to sell and allow himself to be absorbed." Had there been no World War—had Mr. Wilson been able to devote eight years to domestic instead of international affairs—we might have had a wholly different situation at the present time. However, the then distant roar of European cannon, growing ever louder, forced him to abandon the study of this issue. The problem he saw so clearly is left with us as a legacy; and no one of us on either side of the political controversy can deny that is a matter of grave concern to the government.

A glance at the situation today only too clearly indicates that equality of opportunity as we have known it no longer exists. Our industrial plant is built; the problem just now is whether under existing conditions it is not over-built. Our last frontier has long since been reached, and there is practically no more free land. More than half of our people do not live on the farms or on lands and cannot derive a living by cultivating their own property. There is no safety valve in the form of a Western prairie to which those thrown out of work by the Eastern economic machines can go for a new start. We are not able to invite the immigration from Europe to share our endless plenty. We are now providing a drab living for our own people.

Our system of constantly rising tariffs has at last reacted against us to the point of closing our Canadian frontier on the north, our European markets on the east, many of our Latin-American markets to the south, and a goodly proportion of our Pacific markets on the west, through the retaliatory tariffs of those countries. It has forced many of our great industrial institutions which exported their surplus production to such countries, to establish plants in such countries, within the tariff walls. This has resulted in the reduction of the operation of their American plants, and opportunity for employment.

Just as freedom to farm has ceased, so also the opportunity in business has narrowed. It still is true that men can start small enterprises, trusting to native shrewdness and ability to keep abreast of competitors; but area after area has been preempted altogether by the great corporations, and even in the fields which still have no great concerns, the small man starts under a handicap. The unfeeling statistics of the past three decades show that the independent business man is running a losing race. Perhaps he is forced to the wall; perhaps he cannot command credit; perhaps he is "squeezed out," in Mr. Wilson's words, by highly organized corporate competitors, as your corner grocery man can tell you. Recently a careful study was made of the concentration of business in the United States. It showed that our economic life was dominated by some six hundred odd corporations who controlled two-thirds of American industry. Ten million small business men divided the other third. More striking still, it appeared that if the process of concentration goes on at the same rate, at the end of another century we shall have all American industry controlled by a dozen corporations, and run by perhaps a hundred men. Put plainly, we are steering a steady course toward economic oligarchy, if we are not there already.

Clearly, all this calls for a reappraisal of values. A mere builder of industrial plants, a creator of more railroad systems, an organizer of more corporations, is as likely to be a danger as a help. The day of the great promoter or the financial Titan, to whom we granted anything if only he would build, or develop, is over. Our task now is not discovery or exploration of natural resources, or necessarily producing more goods. It is the soberer, less dramatic business of administering resources and plants already in hand, of seeking to reestablish foreign markets for our surplus production, of meeting the problem of underconsumption, of adjusting production to consumption, of distributing wealth and products more equitably, of adapting existing economic organizations to the service of the people. The day of enlightened administration has come.

Just as in older times the central government was first a haven of refuge, and then a threat, so now in a closer economic system the central and ambitious financial unit is no longer a servant of national desire, but a danger. I would draw the parallel one step farther. We did not think because national government had become a threat in the eighteenth century that therefore we should abandon the principle of national government. Nor today should we abandon the principle of strong economic units called corporations, merely because their power is susceptible of easy abuse. In other times we dealt with the problem of an unduly ambitious central government by modifying it gradually into a constitutional democratic government. So today we are modifying and controlling our economic units.

As I see it, the task of government in its relation to business is to assist the development of an economic declaration of rights, an economic constitutional order. This is the common task of statesman and business man. It is the minimum requirement of a more permanently safe order of things.

Happily, the times indicate that to create such an order not only is the proper policy of government, but it is the only line of safety for our economic structures as well. We know, now, that these economic units cannot exist unless prosperity is uniform, that is, unless purchasing power is well distributed throughout every group in the Nation. That is why even the most selfish of corporations for its own interests would be glad to see wages restored and unemployment ended and to bring the Western farmer back to his accustomed level of prosperity and to assure a permanent safety to both groups. That is why some enlightened industries themselves endeavor to limit the freedom of action of each man and business group within the industry in the common interest of all; why business men everywhere are asking a form of organization which will bring the scheme of things into balance, even though it may in some measure qualify the freedom of action of individual units within the business.

The exposition need not further be elaborated. It is brief and incomplete, but you will be able to expand it in terms of your own business or occupation without difficulty. I think everyone who has actually entered the economic struggle—which means everyone who was not born to safe wealth—knows in his own experience and his own life that we have now to apply the earlier concepts of American government to the conditions of today.

The Declaration of Independence discusses the problem of government in terms of a contract. Government is a relation of give and take, a contract, perforce, if we would follow the thinking out of which it grew. Under such a contract rulers were accorded power, and the people consented to that power on consideration that they be accorded certain rights. The task of statesmanship has always been the redefinition of these rights in terms of a changing and growing social order. New conditions impose new requirements upon government and those who conduct government. . . .

I feel that we are coming to a view through the drift of our legislation and our public thinking in the past quarter century that private economic power is, to enlarge an old phrase, a public trust as well. I hold that continued employment of that power by any individual or group must depend upon the fulfillment of that trust. The men who have reached the summit of American business life know this best; happily, many of these urge the binding quality of this greater social contract.

The terms of that contract are as old as the Republic, and as new as the new economic order.

Every man has a right to life; and this means that he has also a right to make a comfortable living. He may by sloth or crime decline to exercise that right; but it may not be denied him. We have no actual famine or dearth; our industrial and agricultural mechanism can produce enough and to spare. Our government formal and informal, political and economic, owes to everyone an avenue to possess himself of a portion of that plenty sufficient for his needs, through his work.

Every man has a right to his own property; which means a right to be assured, to the fullest extent attainable, in the safety of his savings. By no other means can men carry the burdens of those parts of life which, in the nature of things, afford no chance of labor; childhood, sickness, old age. In all thought of property, this right is paramount; all other property rights must yield to it. If, in accord with this principle, we must restrict the operations of the speculator, the manipulator, even the financier, I believe we must accept the restriction as needful, not to hamper individualism but to protect it.

These two requirements must be satisfied, in the main, by the individuals who claim and hold control of the great industrial and financial combinations which dominate so large a part of our industrial life. They have undertaken to be, not business men, but princes of property. I am not prepared to say that the system which produces them is wrong. I am very clear that they must fearlessly and competently assume the responsibility which goes with the power. So many enlightened business men know this that the statement would be little more than a platitude, were it not for an added implication.

This implication is, briefly, that the responsible heads of finance and industry instead of acting each for himself, must work together to achieve the common end. They must, where necessary, sacrifice this or that private advantage; and in reciprocal self-denial must seek a general advantage. It is here that formal government—political government, if you will—comes in. Whenever in the pursuit of this objective the lone wolf, the unethical competitor, the reckless promoter, the Ishmael or Insull whose hand is against every man's, declines to join in achieving an end recognized as being for the public welfare, and threatens to drag the industry back to a state of anarchy, the government may properly be asked to apply restraint. Likewise, should the group ever use its collective power contrary to the public welfare, the government must be swift to enter and protect the public interest.

The government should assume the function of economic regulation only as a last resort, to be tried only when private initiative, inspired by high responsibility, with such assistance and balance as government can give, has failed. As yet there has been no final failure, because there has been no attempt; and I decline to assume that this Nation is unable to meet the situation.

The final term of the high contract was for liberty and the pursuit of happiness. We have learned a great deal of both in the past century. We know that individual liberty and individual happiness mean nothing unless both are ordered in the sense that one man's meat is not another man's poison. We know that the old "rights of personal competency," the right to read, to think, to choose and live a mode of life, must be respected at all hazards. We know that liberty to do anything which deprives others of those elemental rights is outside the protection of any compact; and that government in this regard is the maintenance of a balance, within which every individual may have a place if he will take it; in which every individual may find safety if he wishes it; in which every individual may attain such power as his ability permits, consistent with his assuming the accompanying responsibility.

All this is a long, slow talk. Nothing is more striking than the simple innocence of the men who insist, whenever an objective is present, on the prompt production of a patent scheme guaranteed to produce a result. Human endeavor is not so simple as that. Government includes the art of formulating a policy, and using the political technique to attain so much of that policy as will receive general support; persuading, leading, sacrificing, teaching always, because the greatest duty of a statesman is to educate. But in the matters of which I have spoken, we are learning rapidly, in a severe school. The lessons so learned must not be forgotten, even in the moral lethargy of a speculative upturn. We must build toward the time when a major depression cannot occur again; and if this means sacrificing the easy profits of inflationist booms, then let them go; and good riddance.

Faith in America, faith in our tradition of personal responsibility, faith in our institutions, faith in ourselves demand that we recognize the new terms of the old social contract. We shall fulfill them, as we fulfilled the obligation of the apparent Utopia which Jefferson imagined for us in 1776, and which Jefferson, Roosevelt and Wilson sought to bring to realization. We must do so, lest a rising tide of misery, engendered by our common failure, engulf us all. But failure is not an American habit; and in the strength of great hope we must all shoulder our common load.

LYNDON BAINES JOHNSON

After FDR, Lyndon Baines Johnson (1908–73) was the most important of the three great New Deal Democratic Presidents (Roosevelt, Truman, Johnson), who did the most to implement a version of the "democratic Hamiltonianism" for which Croly had called and for which TR had fought. As a young New Deal volunteer in Texas, and later as a member of Congress, Johnson impressed FDR and became one of the leading protégés of the second Roosevelt. The record of legislative accomplishment that Johnson compiled after succeeding to the presidency following the assassination of his ineffectual predecessor, the playboy millionaire John F. Kennedy, is matched only by FDR's achievement.

Indeed, a case can be made that Johnson's accomplishment was even greater than FDR's. Of FDR's reforms, only Social Security remains unchallenged; President Clinton, pressured by the Republican Congress, abolished Aid for Families with Dependent Children, the New Deal–era basis of federal welfare policy until the 1990s, and New Deal farm subsidies have long been under attack by liberals as well as conservatives as wasteful and counterproductive. Far more of Johnson's Great Society programs remain popular with liberals and conservatives alike—Medicare and Medicaid, student loans, Head Start. What is more, Johnson, unlike his hero and mentor FDR, sought to complete two revolutions at the same time—the progressive-liberal revolution, and the civil rights revolution. FDR had been afraid to alienate Southern whites by promoting racial justice, and Truman had undertaken tentative reforms like integrating the military only with reluctance; Johnson, however, brought all of his formidable skill and passion to bear on the task of eradicating the centuries-old American caste system.

Johnson's reputation was harmed, if only temporarily, by the debacle of the war in Vietnam, in which he merely carried out the ultimately successful containment policy of Truman and Eisenhower—a policy which itself was part of America's twentieth-century grand strategy of denying control of the European and East Asian littoral to hostile great powers. The U.S. military fought the wrong war in Vietnam, combating an insurgency with conventional-war techniques whose destructiveness and ineffectiveness led to the erosion of public support not only for the war in Vietnam but for the Cold War, which the United States in effect unilaterally abandoned between 1968 and the Soviet invasion of Afghanistan in 1979. Even so, the determination of Johnson and his predecessors not to allow the United States to be expelled from Indochina and Southeast Asia may come to look prudent in retrospect, if the United States in the twenty-first century finds itself confronting a hostile China or some other nation determined to eliminate American influence in Asia.

Johnson's reputation has also suffered in the aftermath of the annihilation of the New Deal Democratic coalition of Southern and Western populists and Northern Catholics by the post-1968 left-liberal coalition of Northern Protestants, Jews, and blacks, who in effect created a new party under the old name of the Democrats. The acolytes of George McGovern who wrested control of the Democratic party from supporters of Johnson's successors Hubert Humphrey and Henry M. "Scoop" Jackson consisted chiefly of two groups: socialists and social democrats, influenced by Marxism, who derided the democratic Hamiltonianism of New Deal reformers as mere "corporate liberalism," and black radicals who rejected color-blind integrationism, calling instead for racial preferences ("affirmative action") and even for reparations for slavery. In only two decades, the left-liberal capture of the Democratic party reduced the once dominant party of FDR to the minority party in Congress and to minority status in the presidency as well, if the period from 1968 to 2000 is counted. If the democratic nationalist tradition ever revives in the United States, its adherents will repudiate the misguided left-liberal synthesis of isolationism, Nordic-style social democracy, and multiculturalism, and Lyndon Johnson will be restored to his proper position in the pantheon of great American leaders. No single President, not excepting Lincoln and FDR, did more to promote both economic opportunity and racial equality for all Americans, while refusing to appease those aggressive communist empires, the Soviet Union and China, and their proxies like North Vietnam.

In the excerpt which follows from Johnson's State of the Union Address in January 1965, following his election in one of the greatest landslides in American political history, the last of the major New Deal presidents sets forth his vision of "the Great Society."[3] [See footnote, p. 301]

The Great Society

We are entering the third century of the pursuit of American union. Two hundred years ago, in 1765, nine assembled colonies first joined together to demand freedom from arbitrary power. For the first century we struggled to hold together the first continental union of democracy in the history of man. One hundred years ago, in 1865, following a terrible test of blood and fire, the compact of union was finally sealed. For a second century we labored to establish a unity of purpose and interest among the many groups which make up the American community. That struggle has often brought pain and violence. It is not yet over. But we have achieved a unity of interest among our people that is unmatched in the history of freedom.

And so tonight, in 1965, we begin a new quest for union. We seek the unity of man with the world that he has built—with the knowledge that can save or destroy him—with the cities which can stimulate or stifle him—with the wealth and machines which can enrich or menace his spirit. We seek to establish a harmony between man and society which will allow each of us to enlarge the meaning of his life and all of us to elevate the quality of our civilization.

This is the search that we begin tonight.

But the unity we seek cannot realize its full potential in isolation. For today the state of the union depends, in large measure, upon the state of the world. . . .

Our first aim remains the safety and well-being of our own country. We are prepared to live as good neighbors with all, but we cannot be indifferent to acts designed to injure our interests, or our citizens, or our establishments abroad. The community of nations requires mutual respect. We shall extend it—and we shall expect it. . . .

World affairs will continue to call upon our energy and courage. But today we can turn increased attention to the character of American life. We are in the midst of the greatest upward surge of economic well-being in the history of any nation. . . .

We worked for two centuries to climb this peak of prosperity. But we are only at the beginning of the road to the Great Society. Ahead now is a summit where freedom from the wants of the body can help fulfill the needs of the spirit.

---

3. The term, originating with the English Fabian socialist Graham Wallas, passed into American political discourse via Walter Lippmann, who used it to mean a metropolitan, heterogeneous society (of the sort preferred by Hamiltonians) as opposed to a small-scale, homogeneous, parochial community (of the sort idealized by Jeffersonians). In Johnson's usage "great" connoted "excellent" and "splendid" and "ideal" more than merely "large" and "diverse."

We built this Nation to serve its people. We want to grow and build and create, but we want progress to be the servant and not the master of man. We do not intend to live in the midst of abundance, isolated from neighbors and nature, confined by blighted cities and bleak suburbs, stunted by a poverty of learning and an emptiness of leisure.

The Great Society asks not only how much, but how good; not only how to create wealth, but how to use it; not only how fast we are going, but where we are headed. It proposes as the first test for a nation: the quality of its people.

This kind of society will not flower spontaneously from swelling riches and surging power. It will not be the gift of government or the creation of Presidents. It will require of every American, for many generations, both faith in the destination and the fortitude to make the journey, and like freedom itself, it will always be challenge and not fulfillment.

Tonight we accept that challenge.

I propose that we begin a program in education to ensure every American child the fullest development of his mind and skills. I propose we begin a massive attack on crippling and killing diseases. I propose we launch a national effort to make the American city a better and more stimulating place to live. I propose we increase the beauty of America and end the poisoning of our rivers and the air that we breathe. I propose we carry out a new program to develop regions of our country that are now suffering from distress and depression. I propose we make new efforts to control and prevent crime and delinquency. I propose we eliminate every remaining obstacle to the right and the opportunity to vote. I propose we honor and support the achievements of thought and the creations of art. I propose that we make an all-out campaign against waste and inefficiency.

Our basic task is threefold: First, to keep our economy growing; to open for all Americans the opportunity that is now enjoyed by most Americans; and to improve the quality of life for all. . . .

A President's hardest task is not to do what is right, but to know what is right. Yet the Presidency brings no special gift of prophecy or foresight. You take an oath, step into an office, and you must then help guide a great democracy. The answer was waiting for me in the land where I was born.

It was once barren land. The angular hills were covered with scrub cedar and a few large live oaks. Little would grow in the harsh caliche soil of my country. And each spring the Pedernales River would flood our valley. But men came and they worked and they endured and they built. And tonight the country is abundant: abundant with fruit and cattle and goats and sheep, and there are pleasant homes and lakes and the floods are gone.

Why did men come to that once forbidding land? They were restless, of course, and they had to be moving on. But there was more than that. There was a dream—a dream of a place where a free man could build for himself, and raise his children to a better life—a dream of a continent to be conquered, a world to be won, a nation to be made.

Remembering this, I knew the answer.

A President does not shape a new and personal vision of America. He collects it from the scattered hopes of the American past. It existed when the first settlers saw the coast of a new world, and when the first pioneers moved westward. It has guided us every step of the way. It sustains every President. But it is also your inheritance and it belongs equally to all the people that we all serve. It must be interpreted anew by each generation for its own needs; as I have tried, in part, to do tonight.

It shall lead us as we enter this third century of the search for "a more perfect Union."

In addition to presiding over the greatest expansion of the American social-market state since FDR, Johnson did more to destroy institutionalized racism in the United States than any president since Lincoln, by using his skills to push the Civil Rights Act of 1964, the Voting Rights Act of 1965, and other epochal civil rights measures through Congress. Johnson and his allies realized that striking down formal barriers to black advancement would not by itself help the black poor. Like other liberal integrationists, Johnson rejected the tokenist policy of racial preferences (which only later came to be camouflaged by the innocuous name "affirmative action"). "We are not going to solve the problem by promoting minorities," Johnson told Mexican-Americans in Los Angeles. "That philosophy is merely another way of freezing the minority group status system in perpetuity."

With the help of a White House aide (and later New York's U.S. Senator), Daniel Patrick Moynihan, a social scientist who had written a controversial report on the crisis of the black American family, Johnson proposed a program of race-neutral federal action to help the black poor in the inner cities. The eruption of black riots and the rise of black radicalism, combined with the white backlash against the Civil Rights Revolution, which began affecting politics as early as the 1966 congressional elections, ensured that the Johnson-Moynihan approach would never be tried (their approach has often been confused with the War on Poverty, an ill-conceived left-liberal initiative to circumvent white Democratic urban leaders about which Johnson had misgivings). In the quarter-century since, the same Congresses that routinely renew welfare programs for corporations and affluent white retirees have claimed that there is no money to improve schools and housing and police in the inner cities. In 1996 the Republican Congress, with the consent of Democratic President Clinton, abolished the major federal welfare policies, which white voters had come to identify with the urban black poor.

Affirmative action, a leftist proposal which the Johnson administration had quashed, was adopted by the Nixon administration as a divide-and-rule ploy that would pit white workers against black activists. The Nixon aide John Ehrlichman wrote: "Nixon thought that Secretary of Labor George Schultz had shown great style in constructing a political dilemma for the labor union leaders and civil rights groups."[4] Ironically, Johnson's commencement speech at Howard University on June 4, 1965 (excerpted here), calling for color-blind programs in education, housing, health, and welfare in order to improve the "ability" of black Americans to compete on the basis of merit, has been misread by both the Left and the Right as a manifesto for a policy of racial preferences in hiring, school admissions, and political redistricting, which Johnson and other liberal integrationists opposed.

To Fulfill These Rights

Our earth is the home of revolution. In every corner of every continent men charged with hope contend with ancient ways in the pursuit of justice. They reach for the newest of weapons to realize the oldest of dreams, that each may walk in freedom and pride, stretching his talents, enjoying the fruits of change.

Our enemies may occasionally seize the day of change, but it is the banner of our revolution that they take. And our own future is linked to this process of swift and turbulent change in many lands in the world. But nothing in any country touches us more profoundly, and nothing is more freighted with meaning for our own destiny than the revolution of the Negro American.

In far too many ways American Negroes have been another nation: deprived of freedom, crippled by hatred, the doors of opportunity closed to hope.

In our time change has come to this Nation, too. The American Negro, acting with impressive restraint, has peacefully protested and marched, en-

---

4. John D. Ehrlichman, *Witness to Power* (New York: Simon & Schuster, 1982), pp. 228–29.

tered the courtrooms and seats of government, demanding a justice that has long been denied. The voice of the Negro was the call to action. But it is a tribute to America that, once aroused, the courts and the Congress, the President and most of the people, have been the allies of progress.

LEGAL PROTECTION FOR HUMAN RIGHTS

Thus we have seen the high court of the country declare that discrimination based on race was repugnant to the Constitution, and therefore void. We have seen in 1957, and 1960, and again in 1964, the first civil rights legislation in this Nation in almost an entire century.

As majority leader of the United States Senate, I helped to guide two of those bills through the Senate. And, as your President, I was proud to sign the third. And now very soon we will have the fourth—a new law guaranteeing every American the right to vote.

No act of my entire administration will give me greater satisfaction than the day when my signature makes this bill, too, the law of this land.

The voting rights bill will be the latest, and among the most important, in a long series of victories. But this victory—as Winston Churchill said of another triumph for freedom—"is not the end. It is not even the beginning of the end. But it is, perhaps, the end of the beginning."

That beginning is freedom; and the barriers to that freedom are tumbling down. Freedom is the right to share, share fully and equally, in American society—to vote, to hold a job, to enter a public place, to go to school. It is the right to be treated in every part of our national life as a person equal in dignity and promise to all others.

FREEDOM IS NOT ENOUGH

But freedom is not enough. You do not wipe away the scars of centuries by saying: Now you are free to go where you want, and do as you desire, and choose the leaders you please.

You do not take a person who, for years, has been hobbled by chains and liberate him, bring him up to the starting line of a race and then say, "you are free to compete with all the others," and still justly believe that you have been completely fair.

Thus it is not enough just to open the gates of opportunity. All our citizens must have the ability to walk through those gates.

This is the next and the more profound stage of the battle for civil rights. We seek not just freedom but opportunity. We seek not just legal equity but human ability, not just equality as a right and a theory but equality as a fact and equality as a result.

For the task is to give . . . Negroes the same chance as every other American to learn and grow, to work and share in society, to develop their abilities—physical, mental and spiritual, and to pursue their individual happiness.

To this end equal opportunity is essential, but not enough, not enough. Men and women of all races are born with the same range of abilities. But ability is not just the product of birth. Ability is stretched or stunted by the family that you live with, and the neighborhood you live in—by the school you go to and the poverty or the richness of your surroundings. It is the product of a hundred unseen forces playing upon the little infant, the child, and finally the man. . . .

TO FULFILL THESE RIGHTS

There is no single easy answer to all these problems.

Jobs are one part of the answer. They bring the income which permits a man to provide for his family.

Decent homes in decent surroundings and a chance to learn—an equal chance to learn—are part of the answer.

Welfare and social programs better designed to hold families together are part of the answer.

Care for the sick is part of the answer.

An understanding heart by all Americans is another big part of the answer.

And to all of these fronts—and a dozen more—I will dedicate the expanding efforts of the Johnson administration. . . .

WHAT IS JUSTICE?

For what is justice?

It is to fulfill the fair expectations of man.

Thus, American justice is a very special thing. For, from the first, this has been a land of towering expectations. It was to be a nation where each man could be ruled by the common consent of all—enshrined in law, given life by institutions, guided by men themselves subject to its rule. And all—all of every station and origin—would be touched equally in obligation and in liberty.

Beyond the law lay the land. It was a rich land, glowing with more abundant promise than man had ever seen. Here, unlike any place yet known, all were to share the harvest.

And beyond this was the dignity of man. Each could become whatever his qualities of mind and spirit would permit—to strive, to seek, and, if he could, to find his happiness.

This is American justice. We have pursued it faithfully to the edge of our imperfections, and we have failed to find it for the American Negro.

So, it is the glorious opportunity of this generation to end the one huge wrong of the American Nation and, in so doing, to find America for ourselves, with the same immense thrill of discovery which gripped those who first began to realize that here, at last, was a home to freedom.

The Jeffersonian Backlash

Lyndon Johnson was the last Hamiltonian President of the twentieth century. Although Richard Nixon was a realist in foreign policy and a moderate Rockefeller Republican in domestic policy, his "Southern strategy" of taking advantage of white Southern hostility to blacks resulted in the capture of the Republican party by conservative Jeffersonians in the South and West. (Today conservative Republicans denounce Nixon, not for Watergate but for his "big-government liberalism.") The radical expansion of the American state and American foreign policy commitments along with disorienting revolutions in race relations and society between 1932 and 1968 produced a Jeffersonian backlash which still has not run its course.

The Jeffersonian backlash has not been limited to the Republicans. The only two Democrats to be elected President after Johnson have been two conservative Southerners, Jimmy Carter and Bill Clinton, each of them far to the right of the New Deal Presidents, on economics if not on social issues. Carter, with his ineffectual, moralistic foreign policy and his economic conservatism, had more in common with Woodrow Wilson than with FDR, Truman, or Johnson. Carter was the first President since FDR not to propose any major federal initiative. Clinton (whose middle name, appropriately enough, is Jefferson) has been even more conservative. After a failed attempt to pass what would have been the most business-friendly national health care program in the industrial world, he presided over both the destruction of FDR's national welfare policy and the collapse of the Democrats as the congressional majority party.

The slowdown of economic growth in all of the Western industrial countries, which began in 1973, has effectively prevented major new government initiatives, because the costs of providing social security and medical care for aging populations take up more and more of the budgets of every First World democracy. Because affluent old people vote and poor young people do not, the United States is generous in its welfare policies toward the white and elderly and stingy toward the nonwhite and young.

Thwarted on the home front, Hamiltonians sought to reform American trade policies in the 1980s and 1990s. Stimulated by Japan's growing merchandise trade surplus with the United States, Hamilton-List–style economic nationalism underwent a revival among dissidents in both parties. Attempts by a few maverick Republicans to replace laissez-faire conservatism with Hamiltonian economic nationalism as the doctrine of the Republican party failed, while for Democrats economic nationalism came to be identified with protecting old industries rather than nurturing new ones.

JAMES FALLOWS

In the following excerpt from his book *Looking at the Sun: The Rise of the New East Asian Political and Economic System* (1994), James Fallows, one of America's leading journalists, the editor of *U.S. News & World Report,* and a former speechwriter for President Jimmy Carter, describes how during a stay in Japan he discovered that the economic tradition of Friedrich List is still alive in East Asia, even if it has been forgotten in the United States and Britain. What Fallows calls the "Germanic" school might with equal justice be called the American-German-Japanese school of economic nationalism, as distinct from the English or Anglo-American tradition of Adam Smith and David Ricardo.

The Fallacy of Anglo-American Economics

Why Friedrich List? The more I had heard about List in the preceding five years, from economists in Seoul or Osaka or Tokyo, the more I wondered why I had virtually never heard of him when studying economics in England and the United States. By the time I saw his books in the shop beneath the cherry trees, I had come to think of him as a symbol of the strange self-selectivity of Anglo-American thinking about economics.

I emphasize "Anglo-American" because, in this area, the United States and the United Kingdom really are like each other and different from most of the rest of the world. Just how isolated they are is usually not evident to people in these Anglophone countries. Together they have dominated world politics for decades, and the dominance of the English language lets them ignore what people are saying in the vernacular overseas. The difference shows up in this way: The Anglo-American system of politics and economics, like any system, rests on certain principles and beliefs. But rather than acting as if these are the "best" principles, or the ones that their societies "prefer," Britons and Americans often act as if these were the *only possible* principles and that no one else, except in error, could choose any others. That is, political economics becomes an essentially religious question—leading to the standard drawback of any religion, the failure to understand why people outside the faith might act as they do.

To make this more specific: Today's Anglo-American worldview stands on the shoulders of three men. One is Isaac Newton, father of modern physical science. A second is Jean-Jacques Rousseau, father of liberal political theory. (If we want to keep this purely Anglo-American, John Locke can serve in his place.) And the third is Adam Smith, father of laissez-faire economics. From each of these founding titans come the principles on which advanced society, in the Anglo-American view, is supposed to work. It is supposed to understand the laws of nature, as Newton indicated. It is supposed to recognize the paramount dignity of the individual, thanks to Rousseau, Locke, and their followers. And it is supposed to recognize that the most prosperous future for the greatest number of people comes from the free workings of the market. So Adam Smith taught, with axioms that were enriched by David Ricardo, Alfred Marshall, and the other giants of neoclassical economics. . . .

Outside the United States and Britain, the matter looks quite different. About science, there is no dispute. The physics of Newton and Einstein are the physics of the world. About politics, there is more debate. . . .

But the difference is largest when it comes to economics. In the non-Anglophone world, it looks as if Adam Smith was merely one of several contending theorists with ideas about organizing economies. It is not at all self-evident—in Germany, in Korea, in Japan, in Singapore—that his theories have worn well with time.

Englishmen and Americans tend to see the last two centuries of economics as one great progression toward rationality and good sense. In 1776, Adam Smith's *Wealth of Nations* made the case against old-style mercantilism, just as the Declaration of Independence made the case against old-style feudal and royal domination. Since then, as it seems in the Anglo-American world, more and more of the world has come to the correct view. Along the way the world met such impediments as neomercantilism; guildism; radical unionism; sweeping protectionism; socialism; and, of course, communism. One by one the three worst threats have given way. Except for lamentable areas of backsliding, the world has seen the wisdom of Adam Smith's ways.

Yet during this whole time, there has been an alternate school of thought. The Enlightenment philosophers were not the only ones to think about how the world should be organized. During the eighteenth and nineteenth centuries, the Germans were also active—to say nothing of the theorists at work in Tokugawa Japan, late imperial China, czarist Russia, and elsewhere.

The Germans deserve emphasis because many of their philosophies endured. They did not take root in England or America, but they were carefully studied, adapted, and applied in parts of continental Europe and in Asia, notably in Japan. In place of Rousseau and Locke, the Germans offered Hegel. In place of Adam Smith, they had Friedrich List.

The German vision of economic life differed from the Anglo-American view in many ways, but the crucial differences were the following:

"Automatic" growth vs. deliberate development. The Anglo-American approach emphasized the unpredictability and unplannability of economics. . . .

Although List and others did not use exactly this term, the German school was more concerned about what would now be called "market failures." In the language of modern economics, these are cases in which normal market forces produce a clearly undesirable result. The standard illustration involves pollution. If the law allows factories to dump pollutants into the air or water, then every factory will have to do so. Otherwise their competitors will have lower costs and squeeze them out. This "rational" behavior would leave everyone worse off because of pollution. The answer to such a "market failure" is for all the members of the society—that is, the government—to set standards that all factories must obey.

Friedrich List, and his best-known American counterpart Alexander Hamilton, argued that there was a more sweeping sort of "market failure" when it came to industrial development. Societies did not automatically go from farming, to small crafts, to major industries just because millions of small merchants were making decisions for themselves. If every person put his money where the return was greatest, the money might not automatically go where it would do the nation the most good. Economic development could require a plan, a push, an exercise of central power. List, as we will see, drew heavily on the history of his times—in which the British government had deliberately encouraged British manufacturing, and the fledgling American government deliberately kept out foreign contributors.

List used the term "cosmopolitan theorists" to describe Adam Smith and his ilk. Their worldview, as List characterized it, rested on the belief that if individuals were left to pursue their own interests, the national economy as a whole would automatically develop in the best possible way. By the logic of this laissez-faire view, it naturally followed that government intervention could only harm an economy, by diverting it from the optimum path it would otherwise follow.

Yet any realistic look at British economic history, List said, would raise severe doubts about laissez-faire theory. Sometimes industries did flourish in certain regions, and wither in others, for essentially laissez-faire reasons. "It may be chance that leads certain individuals to a particular place to foster the expansion of an industry that was once small and insignificant," List said, "just as seeds blown by chance by the wind may sometimes grow into big trees." But often something more than chance was involved in the evolution of industries over hundreds of years:

> In England Edward II created the manufacture of woollen cloth and Elizabeth founded the mercantile marine and foreign trade. In France Colbert was responsible for all that a great power needs to develop its economy. Following these examples every responsible government should strive to remove those obstacles that hinder the progress of civilisation and should stimulate the growth of those economic forces that a nation carries in its bosom.

Consumers vs. producers. The Anglo-American approach assumed that the ultimate good of a society is measured by its level of consumption. Competition is by definition good, because it kills off the overpriced producers. Killing them off is, in its turn, good, because more efficient suppliers will give the consumers a better deal. Foreign trade is, by the same logic, best of all, because it means that the most efficient suppliers in the whole world will be able to compete. It doesn't even matter *why* competitors in other countries are willing to sell for less. They may be genuinely more efficient; they may be determined to "dump" their goods for reasons of their own. In either case, the consumer is better off. He has the ton of steel, the cask of wine, or—in today's terms—the car or computer that he might have bought from domestic manufacturers, plus the extra money he saved by buying overseas.

In the Friedrich List view, this logic led to false conclusions. In the long run, he argued, a society's well-being and its overall wealth were determined not by what it could buy but by what it could make. This is the corollary of the familiar argument about foreign aid: Give a man a fish, and you feed him for a day. Teach him how to fish, and you feed him for his life.

List's objection to consumption was not aesthetic or moral. Instead it involved both strategic and material well-being. In strategic terms, nations ended up being dependent or independent based on their ability to make things for themselves. Why were the Latin Americans, Africans, and Asians subservient to England and France in the nineteenth century? Because they could not make the machines and weapons the Europeans could.

In material terms, a society's long-run wealth was greater if it controlled more advanced activities. If you buy the ton of steel or cask of wine at bargain rates this year, you are better off, as a consumer, right away. But over ten years, or fifty, you and your children may be stronger as both consumers and producers if you learn how to make the steel and wine yourself. If you can make steel, rather than just being able to buy it, you'll be better able to make machine tools. If you're able to make machine tools, rather than just buying them, you'll be better able to make engines, robots, airplanes. If you're able to make engines and robots and airplanes, your children and grandchildren will be more likely to make advanced products and earn high incomes in the decades ahead. . . .

In the German view, then, the final measure of an economic system was what it did for producers—manufacturers, inventors—rather than its immediate effect on consumers. A society was worth as much as it could make, not as much as it could buy. . . .

Process vs. result. In economics and politics alike, the Anglo-American theory emphasized how the game was played, not who won or lost. If the rules were fair, then the best candidate would win. If you wanted better politics, or a stronger economy, you should concentrate on reforming the rules by which political and economic struggles were waged. Make sure everyone can vote; make sure everyone can bring his new products to the market. *Whatever* people choose, under those fair rules, will by definition be the best result. Abraham Lincoln or Warren Harding; *Penthouse* or Shakespeare—whatever people choose, in a fair system, will be right.

The government's role, according to this outlook, is not to tell people how they should "pursue happiness" or grow rich. Rather, its role is that of referee—making sure that no one cheats or bends the rules of "fair play," whether by voter fraud in the political realm or monopoly in the economic. . . .

The Germanic view is more paternalistic. People might not automatically choose the best society, or the best use of their money. The state, therefore, must be concerned with both the process and the result. Identifying an Asian variant of the Germanic view, the sociologist Ronald Dore has written that the Japanese—"like all good Confucianists"—believe "that you cannot get a decent, moral society, not even an efficient society, simply out of the mechanism of the market powered by the motivational fuel of self-interest." So, in different words, said Friedrich List.

Individuals vs. the nation. The Anglo-American view focuses on how individuals fare as consumers and how the whole world fares as a trading system. But it does not really care about the intermediate levels between one specific human being and all six billion—that is, about communities and nations.

This criticism may seem strange, considering that the title of Adam Smith's mighty work was *The Wealth of Nations*. It is true that Smith himself was more of a national-defense enthusiast than most people who now invoke his name. Smith said that the art of war was the "noblest" of the arts, and he approved various tariffs that would protect defense-related industries—which in those days largely meant sailcloth-making. He also said that since defense "is of much more importance than opulence, the act of navigation is, perhaps, the wisest of all the commercial regulations of England." This "act of navigation" was, of course, the blatantly protectionist provision that goods going to and from England must be carried by English ships.

Still, the assumption behind the Anglo-American model is that if you take care of the individuals, the communities and nations will take care of themselves. Some communities will suffer, as dying industries and inefficient producers go down, but other communities will rise. And as for nations as a whole, they are not assumed to have economic interests—apart from the narrow field of national defense. There is no general "American" or "British" economic interest beyond the welfare of the individual consumers who happen to live inside its borders. . . .

The German view was more concerned with the welfare—indeed, sovereignty—of people in groups, in communities, in nations. This is its most obvious link with the Asian economic strategy of today. Friedrich List fulminated against "cosmopolitan theorists" who assumed away the fact that people lived in nations and that their welfare depended to some degree on how their neighbors fared. If you make $100,000 and everyone around you makes $80,000, you feel well off. The community is prosperous, and you are a success. If you make $101,000 and everyone around you is a destitute beggar, you are worse off in any full reckoning of human well-being, even though your standing is higher in both absolute and relative terms. . . .

For the Germans, the answer to this predicament was to pay explicit attention to the welfare of the nation. If a consumer had to pay 10 percent more for a product made by his neighbors than for one bought from overseas, it would be worse for him in the short run. But in the long run, and in the broadest definitions of well-being, he might be better off. . . .

Economic policies, in the German view, would be good or bad depending on whether they promoted the strength of the nation as a whole.

Business as peace vs. business as war. By far the most uplifting part of the Anglo-American view was the idea that everyone could prosper at once. Before Adam Smith, the Spanish and Portuguese mercantilists had viewed world trade as a kind of battle. What I won, you lost. Adam Smith and David

Ricardo demonstrated that you and I could win at the same time. If I bought your wine and you bought my wool, we would both have more of what we wanted, for the same amount of work. The result would be the economist's classic "positive sum" interaction. Your well-being plus my well-being, added together, would be greater than they were before our trade.

The Germans had a more tragic, or "zero sum"–like conception of how nations dealt with each other. Some of them won; others lost. Economic power often led to political power, which in turn let one nation tell others what to do. In the post–World War II era, American politicians have often said that their trading goal is a "level playing field" for competition around the world. This very image implies a horizontal relationship among nations in which they all good-naturedly joust as equals. "These horizontal metaphors are fundamentally misleading," John Judis, an American journalist, has pointed out. . . . The same spirit and logic ran through List's arguments. Trade was not just a game. Over the long sweep of history some nations lost independence and control of their destiny if they fell behind in trade. Therefore they had to think about it strategically, not just as a matter of where they could buy the cheapest shirt this week. . . .

Morality vs. power. By the end of the twentieth century, the Anglo-American view had taken on a moral tone that was latent and embryonic when Adam Smith wrote his book. If a country disagreed with Anglo-American axioms, it wasn't simply disagreeing; it was "cheating." Japan "cheats" the world trading system by protecting its rice farmers. America "cheats" with its subsidies for sugar-beet growers and with its various other restrictions on trade. Malaysia "cheated" by requiring foreign investors to take on local partners. And on and on. If the "rules" of the trading system aren't protected from such cheating, the whole system might collapse and bring back the Great Depression. . . .

In the German view, economics is not a matter of "right" or "wrong," of "cheating" or "playing fair." It is merely a matter of strong or weak. The gods of trade will help those who helped themselves. No code of "honor" will defend the weak (as today's Latin Americans and Asians can attest). If a nation decides to help itself—by protecting its own industries, by discriminating against foreign products—then that is a *decision,* not a sin.

The Future of Hamiltonianism in America

The economic troubles of Japan in the 1990s (which resulted, in part, from the prolongation of a successful protectionist industrial policy beyond the point at which it became counterproductive) have persuaded many adherents of laissez-faire that the economic nationalist critique of Japanese mercantilism was mistaken. In fact, Japanese mercantilism has been eclipsed by a new problem: the rise in offshore manufacturing by Japanese and American multinationals in low-wage countries in Asia and Latin America. Hamilton and List never foresaw the conversion of entire poor countries into industrial sweatshops for absentee corporate owners. As noted above, Henry Cabot Lodge and other turn-of-the-century Republicans did, but their solution—a social tariff eliminating the attractiveness of poor, authoritarian states as sources of cheap labor for mobile corporations—is dismissed with horror, a century later, by academic economists and American politicians and public policy experts (many of them dependent on multinationals to finance their campaigns or to hire them as advisers).

Not content with forcing American workers to compete with hundreds of millions of poor people in Asia and Latin America, the American oligarchy has resisted all attempts to restrict labor-displacing immigration to the United States itself. At present the U.S. labor market is continually enlarged by more than a million legal immigrants every year (illegal immigration makes the number much greater). Meanwhile, in recent years there has been a net exodus of native-born white and black Americans, displaced by immigrant competition, from cities and states with high levels of immigration. Critics of immigration, when their arguments are published at all, are quickly denounced as racists. Not infrequently those who defend immigration as a moral imperative have an immigrant nanny looking after the children, an immigrant maid cleaning the house, and another immigrant caring for the yard—each of them receiving the minimum wage, if that much, with no health care benefits and often no social security. A reaction by the working and middle classes in the advanced nations against the excesses of laissez-faire globalism in trade and immigration policies—taking the form of xenophobic right-wing populism, if not of an enlightened democratic nationalism—seems inevitable in the twenty-first century.

Beginning with the Civil Rights Revolution in the 1950s and 1960s, the two parties engaged in a remarkable exchange of constituencies. The Democrats—formerly the party of white Southerners and Northern "ethnics" or Catholic European immigrants—have become a party of Northern Protestants and Jews and urban blacks, whose demographic profile resembles that of the Whigs and older Republicans. The Republicans, at the same time, have become a predominantly Southern and Western party, making inroads among ex-Democratic Catholics in the Northeast and Midwest. The antigovernment philosophy and populist style of the new Republicans show their Southern Democratic pedigree.

One might have expected this realignment to have led to a revival of Hamiltonianism in the Democratic party. This has not happened. The dominant ideas of the Democratic party since 1968 have been products not of the Progressive and New Deal traditions but of Marxist-influenced New Left radicalism. As a result of the capture of the Democratic party by McGovern's New Left followers between 1968 and 1972, and the purge of "vital-center" liberal New Dealers, the Democratic party has become focused on racial and sexual identity politics. For post-1968 Democrats, the most important goals are not protecting and extending universal economic and social programs, but defending affirmative action for women and minorities and the reproductive and sexual rights of women and homosexuals. While the Southernized Republican party has embraced a dynamic (if implausible) program of stimulating societywide prosperity through tax cuts and free trade, the Democratic party has been reduced to fighting a rear-guard action, defending New Deal and Great Society entitlements, along with the entitlement cherished by the New Left, affirmative action for white women and members of officially favored racial and ethnic minorities. Even if the Democrats regained control of the government, they no longer had an ambitious agenda of any kind, much less one rooted in Hamiltonian nationalism.

In the near future there seems little chance that the ascendant Jeffersonian Republicans of the South and West can be checked by a revival of Hamiltonian nationalism within the Democratic party. It is possible that neo-

Hamiltonians in the GOP itself will emerge (perhaps from the Northeast) to contest the resurgence of states' rights doctrines and hostility to federal activism on behalf of the nation. It is also possible that an entirely new party will replace the Democrats and promote an updated version of the Hamiltonian tradition. At the end of the twentieth century, however, none of those developments seem likely. The stage may be set for an era of neo-Jeffersonian dominance, like that of the era between 1800 and 1860. If that is the case, the results are all too easy to predict—a "race to the bottom" in social protections and living standards among states competing to win the favor of national and multinational businesses and investors; a lack of adequate investments in infrastructure and in research and development, of the kind that only governments and not profit-conscious firms can undertake; and, not least, an erosion in America's standing as a world power, inasmuch as it is impossible to combine a strong national-security state with a feeble domestic government that is starved of taxes and authority.

This last factor may ultimately put an end to today's neo-Jeffersonianism. Again and again in American history, waves of Hamiltonian reform at home have been inspired by the necessities of war and preparedness. Continental Army officers like Hamilton and Washington became supporters of the 1787 Constitution and later of the Federalist party; Henry Clay went from being a War Hawk of 1812 to sponsoring the American System; the Progressives tended to support American power-projection abroad along with reform at home; the Cold War liberals built up the American warfare state as well as the American welfare state. A global great-power conflict in the twenty-first century in which the United States found itself involved would quickly end the present period of reverence for Thomas Jefferson and Adam Smith as symbols of a domestic policy of decentralization and laissez-faire. The need to mobilize American economic resources, and to unite the population across class, racial, and regional lines, might well lead to a renaissance of Hamiltonian nationalism, in domestic as well as in foreign policy—if only at a very high price.

This section concludes with two calls from the mid-1990s for a new democratic nationalism in the United States.

JOHN JUDIS AND
MICHAEL LIND

John Judis, a senior editor of *The New Republic,* is author of *Grand Illusion: Critics and Champions of the American Century* (1992). Michael Lind, a Contributing Editor of *Harper's Magazine,* is the author of *The Next American Nation* (1995). In the following essay, which appeared in the March 27, 1995 issue of *The New Republic,* the magazine that Herbert Croly founded to promote Rooseveltian progressivism, the authors call for a "New Nationalism" in the spirit of Theodore Roosevelt and Herbert Croly.

For a New Nationalism

From "For a New Nationalism: A Manifesto for America's Future,"
The New Republic, March 27, 1995

We have found that, among Washington's policy elite, describing oneself as a populist or a nationalist invites scorn and derision. Both terms, however, describe political traditions with roots deep in the American past. Populism was the name of a movement that lasted only from about 1886 to 1896, but populist themes emanate from the country's founding and have resonated through the twentieth century. Populism has been the classic movement of America's middle class—from its small farmers of the nineteenth century to its small businessmen and industrial workers of the twentieth. Populists saw society divided between "productive" workers in the broadest sense, which included farmers, artisans, businessmen and merchants, and the "idle" and "unproductive," which included coupon-clippers, vagrants and speculators. Like all political movements, populism has had its dark side. Under the populist banner, politicians have pushed everything from arcane monetary schemes in

320

racial segregation to the expropriation of the rich. But what we would build upon is the convictions shared by populists and progressives—expressed most forcefully during this century by Theodore and Franklin Roosevelt, Harry Truman and Lyndon Johnson—that what government does must be judged by whether it benefits the great productive middle of our society.

Nationalism, too, has had its dark side, not just in Europe but also in America. Nativism was an important strain in American politics during the 1850s and the 1920s and is recurring again. But there is a constructive and inclusive current of American nationalism that runs from Alexander Hamilton through Abraham Lincoln and Theodore Roosevelt. It emphasizes not the exclusion of foreigners, but rather the unification of Americans of different regions, classes, races and ethnic groups around a common national identity. It stands opposed not only to nativism, but also to today's multiculturalism and economic or strategic globalism.

We draw our version of American nationalism from Theodore Roosevelt's "New Nationalism," which was inspired in part by Herbert Croly, author of *The Promise of American Life* (1909), and founder of this magazine. "The American people," Roosevelt declared in 1910, "are right in demanding that New Nationalism, without which we cannot hope to deal with our new problems. The New Nationalism puts the national need above sectional or personal advantage."

Roosevelt defined his "New Nationalism" on an analogy with Lincoln's nationalism of 1860. Where Lincoln was concerned with the threat of a nation half-slave and half-free and divided between North and South, Roosevelt was concerned with the conflict between capital and labor and, secondarily, with the lingering sectional divisions between North and South and East and West. In the growing class conflict of the period, he saw the prospect of a new civil war that would divide America and destroy the nation. Roosevelt was not a socialist; his solution was not to eliminate capital, but to tame and regulate it so that it could coexist harmoniously with labor. But Roosevelt also incorporated a central idea of Lincoln and of populism: that, in Lincoln's words, "labor"—defined broadly in nineteenth-century terms of productive workers—"is prior to, and independent of, capital."

America today faces a situation roughly analogous to the one Roosevelt and the progressives faced. Workers are not threatening to man the barricades against capitalism, but society is divided into mutually hostile camps: cities against suburbs, Northeast against Sunbelt, black against white. Particularly disturbing is the growing division along class lines—between a white overclass and an increasingly redundant and insecure working class in constant fear of tumbling into the underclass. It's not so much the Balkanization as the

Brazilianization of America, characterized by the increasing withdrawal of the white overclass into its own barricaded nation-within-a-nation, a world of private neighborhoods, private schools, private police and even private roads, walled off from the spreading squalor beyond. The goal of a new nationalism today is to forestall these looming divisions in American society.

Roosevelt also had a distinct idea of the American nation that differed from the right and left of his time. On the right, nativists argued that the American nation was defined by the Anglo-Saxon or Germanic race and the Protestant religion. On the left, cultural pluralists such as Horace Kallen and Randolph Bourne argued that the United States was, or should be, a federation of culturally distinct "nationalities"—Anglo-Americans, German-Americans, Italian-Americans—sharing only a common framework of institutions. Theodore Roosevelt and like-minded progressives rejected both nativism and cultural pluralism in favor of the idea of the "melting pot" (the popular play of that name was dedicated to Roosevelt).

In foreign policy, Roosevelt wanted the United States to be able to exercise military power commensurate with its economic wealth. Roosevelt's principal foes were isolationists who believed that the United States did not need to play a role in the imperial conflicts that were convulsing Europe, China and Africa. But after his death Roosevelt's allies such as Henry Cabot Lodge also opposed Woodrow Wilson's concept of collective security. Roosevelt was what we would now call a national interest realist.

Just as Roosevelt and Croly drew upon Lincoln's antebellum nationalism, we would draw upon Roosevelt's effort in the Progressive Era to define a "new nationalism." That means, first and foremost, that we must discard the illusions created by America's brief career as a military and economic hegemon. America emerged from World War II in a position of economic and military supremacy that even nineteenth-century Great Britain had never enjoyed: the United States produced half of the world's goods; our manufacturers had no peers; and our military, bolstered by the atomic bomb, had enemies but no equals. The United States formed a military alliance against its principal rival, the Soviet Union, in which it assumed the costs of deterrence, equating the security of its NATO and Asian allies with its own. Similarly, in hope of eventually creating foreign demand for its own goods, it provided economic aid and open markets to its allies without demanding similar concessions in return. Such an unquestioning commitment to free trade is the luxury of hegemonic economic powers.

Cold war globalism, in defense and economics, was also accompanied by a redefinition of American national identity. Beginning in the 1950s, American leaders, who before 1945 had tended to view the United States as an Anglo-Saxon or Euro-American society, redefined the United States as a "nation of nations," a federation of ethnic and racial groups united only by democratic idealism. The multinational United States, it was said, could serve as a model for the United Nations and a federal Europe; America was what the Soviet Union claimed to be, a multinational federation united by progressive Enlightenment ideology. Though few Americans have ever thought of their country as anything other than a nation-state, this idea of the United States as a non-national or post-national society became a staple of cold war rhetoric on the part of politicians and pundits.

Over the past two decades, but particularly in the past five years, these three pillars of cold war American globalism—strategic, economic, and cultural—have been crumbling. The cold war is over—replaced by the re-emergence of pre-World War II tensions in Asia and ethnic hatreds in Eastern Europe. Japan shows signs of its own resurgent nationalism, while a united Germany has assumed greater diplomatic independence. At the same time, the American people, with the mortal threat of Soviet communism removed, are in no mood to support American policing of the world on behalf of Europe and Japan, as public opposition to intervention in Somalia and the Balkans has shown.

The United States has also lost its unchallenged industrial supremacy. Since 1971 the United States has repeatedly run trade deficits—not only in energy products, but also in manufacturing. While the world's nations have signed a new GATT treaty, they have not prevented the re-emergence of trade conflicts among the major economic powers. Now that the contest between capitalism and socialism has been settled, a new ideological contest is emerging between national variants of capitalism—American free-market radicalism, Japanese economic nationalism, and German social-market capitalism.

The conception of the United States as a multinational democracy, epitomized by the multicultural movement, is also in retreat. Opposition to racial preferences and quotas represents a repudiation of the idea that the United States is a confederation of racial nationalities rather than a nation-state with a common culture. The backlash against escalating levels of Third World immigration reflects not just racism but genuine concerns about the displacement of the native-born working poor. Americans are sending a message: We Are Not the World.

Our challenge is to replace these outworn ideologies of cold war globalism with a politics that more accurately reflects our new situation. For that, like Theodore Roosevelt and Herbert Croly, we propose a "new nationalism."

The first pillar of this new nationalism is economic nationalism. We believe that a strategy of limited protection for developing industries was critical to America's industrialization in the nineteenth century; to the rebuilding of Western Europe and Japan after World War II and to the emergence of East

Asian capitalism today. We believe that a one-sided commitment to free trade was absolutely appropriate to mid-nineteenth-century Britain and to post–World War II America. But in the late twentieth century, the United States is in a much more ambiguous position, still possessing the world's largest market, but also highly vulnerable to foreign competition in many industries and incapable of competing in several, including areas of consumer electronics. This is not a situation in which a strategy of either rampant protection or one-sided free trade is appropriate. Instead, we advocate that the United States encourage free trade in a majority of goods and services. At the same time, it should reserve the right to protect industries such as machine tools and semiconductors that are important to the country's well-being and the right to pursue managed trade negotiations with countries such as Japan and China that have proved resistant to open trading.

We have to adopt a similar posture toward American overseas investments. In the decades after World War II, the United States clearly benefited from the export of capital overseas. It helped rebuild countries into trading partners for the United States and also, in the case of Western European nations, reinforced their commitment to democracy and the Atlantic alliance. Capital investment abroad also spurred American exports of technology. But since the early '70s, capital investment abroad has accelerated deindustrialization, which has deprived many American workers of the kind of blue-collar jobs by means of which previous generations worked their way up the economic ladder. The United States has to do something about this: America cannot export its poorer citizens as European countries have done. We should not try to impede technological change, but we must remove incentives created decades ago encouraging American firms to produce abroad.

Ultimately American economic policy must meet a single test: Does it, in the long run, tend to raise or depress the incomes of most Americans? A policy that tends to impoverish ordinary Americans is a failure, no matter what its alleged benefits are for U.S. corporations or for humanity as a whole. "I believe in shaping the ends of government to protect property as well as human welfare," Teddy Roosevelt told a Kansas audience in 1910. "Normally, and in the long run, the ends are the same; but whenever the alternative must be faced, I am for men and not for property." So are we.

The second pillar of today's new nationalism is national-interest realism in defense. We reject both indiscriminate retrenchment and indiscriminate commitment abroad. We favor a new defense policy tailored to promote concrete American security interests in the emerging multipolar world.

The isolationism of right-wingers such as Patrick Buchanan and Jesse Helms is even more of an anachronism in 1995 than it was in 1895. As

America's relative share of world military power declines, participation in countervailing coalitions against potential hegemons will become more, not less, important. In the next century, the United States may be surpassed as the world's largest economic power by an integrated Europe or by a Chinese- or Japanese-dominated pan-Asian bloc, even by a modernized India. As it did before World War II, the United States may have to help other powers prevent a hostile superpower or alliance from consolidating its control over vast resources; no wondrous weapons systems like SDI [the Strategic Defense Initiative] will ever eliminate the need for military allies.

In advocating that the United States pursue its national interests by the traditional means of a conventional great power, we reject the misleading description of the United States as "the world's only superpower." The disproportionate power of the United States relative to Western Europe and Japan was a passing phenomenon caused by World War II; notions of U.S. global hegemony were already anachronistic by 1973, as Nixon and Henry Kissinger recognized. Today those who talk about a "unipolar world" believe that, by policing the turbulent Third World regions bordering Europe and Japan, the United States can preserve its cold war dominance. But American voters will not permit the United States to act as the security guard for the Europeans and East Asians and the latter will be equally unwilling to forgo pursuing independent military strategies. That's how it should be: we fought two world wars and the cold war in order to prevent hostile powers from dominating those areas; our objective was not to achieve domination ourselves.

The third pillar of the new nationalism is a nation-uniting approach to social policy. We think the goal of social policy should be to reduce the growing disparity among economic classes. While we don't believe absolute equality is possible or desirable, we share the faith of populists and progressives that American democracy is incompatible with huge disparities in wealth and power. We also believe that the goal of social poliy should be to carry forward and complete the movement toward equal rights in our society by eliminating discrimination based on race, gender and sexual orientation. But this must be pursued with an understanding that we seek equality as citizens of the same nation.

Our concept of America as a nation is at odds with the prevailing views on the right and the left. On the right today, nativists . . . argue that the United States must preserve its European "ethnic core." Charles Murray and Richard Herrnstein warn in *The Bell Curve* about the supposed "dysgenic" effects of immigration by blacks and Latinos on the gene pool, while members of the religious right warn that the American people must preserve the United States' identity as a "Christian" or "Judeo-Christian" nation. On the left, multiculturalists view America not as a nation but as a collection of different cultures, a kind of miniature UN. The multiculturalists want to use quotas, subsidies or even reparations to achieve economic and political parity with the abstract category of white men for each of the supposed "nations" of America—blacks, Hispanics, Asians, even women of all races and homosexuals of all races and both sexes. These policies end up exacerbating the divisions among "nations" while failing to make them more equal. We reject both nativism and multiculturalism.

The new nationalism differs from multiculturalism in holding that there is an American nation; it differs from nativism by defining that nation in terms of a common vernacular culture rather than race or religion. The political corollary of Roosevelt's transracial melting-pot ideal is a revival of the color-blind integrationism of the early civil rights revolution—a revolution opposed by the racists of the right, and betrayed by the racists of the left. We believe that government-coerced tokenism should be repudiated, in favor of race-neutral programs, either means-tested or universal, that seek to integrate the disadvantaged of all races into the mainstream of American economic and social life.

In *The Promise of American Life,* the founding editor of [*The New Republic*] wrote, "There comes a time in the history of every nation, when its independence of spirit vanishes, unless it emancipates itself in some measure from its traditional illusions; and that time is fast approaching for the American people. They must either seize the chance of a better future, or else become a nation which is satisfied in spirit merely to repeat indefinitely the monotonous measures of its own past." Abraham Lincoln made the same point more succinctly in 1862: "As our case is new, so we must think anew, and act anew. We must disenthrall ourselves, and then we shall save our country."

Though the challenges we face today are different, the illusions that tempt us are the same as those that earlier nationalists warned against. It's facile to believe we can dispense with large-scale governmental and economic organization and hope that a paradise of free individuals—the family farmers of William Jennings Bryan or the Internet entrepreneurs of the Tofflers—will spring up of its own accord. It's naïve to hold that, in our international affairs, power politics is un-American, or has been rendered obsolete by commerce and spreading enlightenment. It is a delusion (shared by Andrew Carnegie and William Bennett) to hold that the problems facing American society can be addressed by individual moral reformation, rather than by the redesign of our institutions and the rethinking of our strategies.

Can we meet these challenges? In the decades between Lincoln and Theodore Roosevelt, the country floundered as badly as it has during the last few decades. Their mountebanks were no different from ours; their corruption was even more pervasive; and their sense of political paralysis even more profound. Still, they were able to think and act anew. As we prepare to enter the next century, we believe that we are on the verge of a similar era of national renewal. Those of us who believed that we had missed out on the great struggles to shape the fate of the American nation were mistaken. The end of the American century draws near; but the promise of the American nation remains to be fulfilled.

WALTER RUSSELL MEAD

Walter Russell Mead is a President's Fellow at the World Policy Institute at the New School for Social Research and the author of *Mortal Splendor* (1986). In this essay from *The New York Times Magazine* (October 15, 1995), Mead predicts that the conservative counterrevolution against liberalism will be followed by a rebirth of Hamiltonian democratic nationalism as a force in American national politics.

Progressive Hamiltonianism, Past and Future

From "Newt's Real Target: The Other Roosevelt,"
New York Times Magazine, October 15, 1995

Both of the great American political parties are in trouble, and the Democrats—the oldest continuously functioning political party in the world—may be on the verge of death. Sensing the disarray among the parties, many pundits predict the imminent demise of the two-party system.

Wrong. Underneath the surface turbulence, the political system remains extraordinarily resilient. The United States has been divided into two parties since George Washington's day. The Hamiltonian party—variously known through history as the Federalists, the Whigs and most recently the Republicans—was the party of a strong national Government in alliance with big business. The Jeffersonian party, known for most of its history as the Democrats, supported states' rights, hated the cultural elite and thought that the major banks and businesses were in unholy league with foreigners to undermine the living standards of the average American family.

That conflict is once again moving to center stage, and our political parties must and will reflect it. The names may change and the current parties may rise or fall. But when the current realignment is completed, the political landscape will most likely be familiar to each one of the guys on Mount Rushmore.

For 65 years, until [November 1994], Congress was largely a Democratic institution. Accordingly, most Democrats still think of 1994 as just a brief interruption of their long-term control, particularly in the House. Few of them seem to have noticed how the ground has shifted.

What beat the Democrats in 1994 wasn't the Contract With America. It was something much bigger: a historic shift in American politics. The white South, solidly Republican at the Presidential level since 1964, is moving monolithically into the G.O.P. column for House and Senate races.

Of the 22 men sent to the Senate in 1962 by the states of the former Confederacy, 21 were Democrat. Dixie had 106 votes in the House in 1962, 99 of them Democrats. After the 1994 elections, Southern Democrats held 10 Senate seats and 61 (out of 125 Southern seats) in the House. By the turn of the century, the Democrats will be lucky to have held onto more than four Senate seats and about 30 House seats.

Thus, to regain control of Congress, the Democrats must make substantial gains in the North and West. This doesn't look likely. They may hold their own in the North—and they may even pick up some voters disgusted by G.O.P. pandering to the white South on religion and race—but they are unlikely to offset the tidal change now under way.

So why does all this mean trouble for the G.O.P.? Easy question, for those who remember their history.

Ever since Abraham Lincoln debated Stephen Douglas, the G.O.P. has been a Hamiltonian party. Its founders were in the tradition of the Federalists, America's first governing party, which was crushed by the Jeffersonians in 1800. The Whigs replaced the Federalists and themselves broke up in a welter of third and fourth parties in the 1840's and 50's. Lincoln got the formula right and the Republicans stuck with it until the Depression.

The Republican Party fought the Civil War against Democrats who believed in states' rights. Like the Federalists and the Whigs, the classic G.O.P. was not only pro-big business and big government but also anti-populist. On racial issues especially, Republicans prided themselves on their enlightened views. Woodrow Wilson, a Democrat revered today as a symbol of American high-mindedness and idealism, imposed segregation on Washington and gave a White House screening to D. W. Griffith's racist film "Birth of a Nation." Teddy Roosevelt, by contrast, shocked Southern opinion by inviting Booker T. Washington to the White House and appointing African-Americans to Federal posts in the South.

Teddy Roosevelt was one of the most vigorous opponents of Republican Hamiltonianism. While he tried to disentangle the G.O.P. from an uncritical embrace of every big business, his faith in big government remained strong.

"There was a time," Roosevelt said, "when the limitation of governmental power meant increasing liberty for the people. In the present day, the limitation of governmental power, of governmental action, means the enslavement of the people by the great corporations."

Republican domination of the Presidency and Congress broke down in the Depression, when their traditional policies no longer worked; Herbert Hoover's refusal to use the full power of the Government gave Franklin Roosevelt the chance to look Hamiltonian, using the national government to bolster the national economy. With the success of the New Deal, Democrats broke out of their Southern ghetto to rule for two generations. On those occasions when Republicans took power, they did so only with the help of men like Eisenhower and Nixon, whose views placed them squarely in the Hamiltonian tradition.

The current upheaval in American politics has come about because neither the Democrats nor the Republicans adequately represent either the underlying Jeffersonian or Hamiltonian parties. Ron Brown's Commerce Department and Bill Clinton's trade policy are sure enough big government, big business approaches but the Democrats' ties to labor and the left make them suspect to the business establishment.

The Republicans, on the other hand, are increasingly split between their historic Hamiltonianism and the yahoo Jeffersonianism of their new Southern allies. Jesse Helms and Strom Thurmond have little in common with Abraham Lincoln, Theodore Roosevelt or Dwight Eisenhower. Pat Robertson thinks that the world's central bankers are the lackeys of Satan, while traditional Republicans revere them as the custodians of the faith. This split can only widen. Christ and Antichrist cannot run on the same ticket.

In fact, the Democrats are all that hold the Republicans together now. Big business wants to get rid of the remaining shackles and government-imposed costs of the New Deal era. With the exception of farm subsidies, that is fine with the white South. The yahoo Jeffersonians for very different reasons also want to trim back the Government.

But once this has been accomplished there will be a struggle between the Jeffersonian and Hamiltonian wings. The winners will consolidate their hold on the Republican name; the losers will ultimately form a new party. Both sides will bid for the support of the remaining Democrats. Most conservative and liberal centrists in the Democratic Party—people like Senators Sam Nunn and Bill Bradley—will move toward the Hamiltonians. So will most African-Americans. Labor will be torn between the anti-business stance of the Jeffersonians and the Hamiltonian sympathy for reasonable regulation of business in the national interest.

In the end, the United States will once again have a strong two-party system, with the Republicans of 2010 possibly the rough equivalent of the Democrats of 1896. The new G.O.P. will be strong in the white South, anti-elitist and anti–big business. It will be pro-military but isolationist. It will stand for states' rights against Federal intrusions. It will be a party of protest, for those left behind by economic and social change. It will be a stormy party, combining genuine heartfelt cries for economic justice with demagogic rhetoric on subjects like immigration, culture, religion and trade. In retrospect, the 1994 election may ultimately be seen not as the triumph of the Republicans' Southern strategy, but as the triumph of the white South's Republican strategy.

The other party will be internationalist, pro-business and moderately progressive. Looking more to Theodore Roosevelt than to his cousin Franklin, it will favor a relatively strong Federal Government and a basic social safety net, but it will not attempt to recreate the network of subsidies and social programs of the New Deal era. It will be moderately conservative on social and cultural issues, but it will also be tolerant.

The next historic movement in American politics is likely to be the emergence of such a moderately progressive Hamiltonian party—a party that might reach from Jack Kemp on the right through Colin Powell and William Weld in the center to Bill Bradley and Daniel Patrick Moynihan on the left. Jesse Jackson might not like it, but a new generation of African-American leaders would find it their least bad choice.

Thus, no matter what happens to the Republican Party, Newt [Gingrich]'s war with Teddy Roosevelt is doomed to defeat. Progressive Hamiltonianism is a permanent feature of American political life.

ADDITIONAL READING

The Hamiltonian tradition of American democratic nationalism, from the Federalists to the Progressives and beyond, has long been neglected by historians, despite the central importance of this tradition in U.S. history. Most of the leading American historians in the past half-century have been either partisan Democrats devoted to finding roots of the New Deal in the populism of Jefferson and Jackson, or leftists who have abandoned synthetic national political history in order to provide separate usable pasts for the political constituencies of the post-McGovern Democratic party—political radicals, blacks, immigrants, feminists.

The best discussion of Alexander Hamilton's life and work in print is Forrest McDonald's *Alexander Hamilton: A Biography* (New York: W. W. Norton, 1979). Readers can also profit from Harvey Flaumenhaft, *The Effective Republic: Administration & Constitution in the Thought of Alexander Hamilton* (Durham, NC: Duke University Press, 1992), and Thomas K. McGraw, "The Strategic Vision of Alexander Hamilton," in *The American Scholar* (Winter 1994).

Samuel H. Beer provides a brilliant and highly readable overview of the origins of the rival nationalist and states'-rights schools of American constitutional thought in *To Make a Nation: The Rediscovery of American Federalism* (Cambridge, MA: Harvard University Press, 1993). The best political history of the debate between Hamilton and Jefferson during the Washington administration is *The Age of Federalism: The Early American Republic, 1788–1800* (New York: Oxford University Press, 1993), by Stanley Elkins and Eric McKitrick. A spirited exposition of the nationalist interpretation of *The Federalist* is found in Edward Millican, *One United People: The Federalist Papers and the National Idea* (Lexington: The University Press of Kentucky, 1990). For an account of the origins of the rival Jeffersonian ideal of an agrarian, decentralized, isolationist society, see Drew R. McCoy, *The Elusive Republic: Political Economy in Jeffersonian America* (New York: W. W. Norton, 1980).

The liberal melting-pot conception of American identity has been opposed throughout the twentieth century not only by the racist right but by the American intellectual left, which has preferred cultural pluralism, multiculturalism, or democratic globalism (cosmopolitanism). For liberal defenses of the ideal of a syncretic national culture, see Arthur M. Schlesinger, Jr., *The Disuniting of America: Reflections on a Multicultural Society* (New York: W. W. Norton, 1992) and Michael Lind, *The Next American Nation: The New Nationalism and the Fourth American Revolution* (New York: The Free Press, 1995).

Another subject that has been insufficiently studied is the American tradition of continental expansion and great-power realism. Conventional accounts that treat American expansion in terms of two isolated episodes—"Manifest Destiny" in the 1830s and 1840s and "imperialism" at the end of the nineteenth century—are worthless. So are post-1945 academic realist studies which claim that the United States was an isolationist country with a naïvely idealist foreign policy tradition before the arrival of wise European émigré professors of *Realpolitik* during and after World War II. The summaries of American foreign policy by twentieth-century American realists, like Walter Lippmann and George Kennan (whose "realism" has been indistinguishable from conservative isolationism since the 1950s), use history selectively to bolster topical policy arguments, and should be used with caution. The Marxist Wisconsin School of the late William Appleman Williams and his disciples was justified in attempting to trace continuities in U.S. foreign policy but utterly mistaken in ignoring the context of world politics and attempting to explain American geopolitical strategies solely in terms of domestic economic pressures. The cartoon-like nature of Marxist analyses of American history is revealed when they are compared with the rich synthesis of geopolitics, economics, and ethnoregional culture theory in D. W. Meinig's *The Shaping of America: A Geographical Perspective on 500 Years of History,* a projected four-volume series of which only the first two volumes have been published: *Atlantic America, 1492–1800* (New Haven: Yale University Press, 1986), and *Continental America, 1800–1867* (New Haven: Yale University Press, 1993). Many of Meinig's conclusions about the importance of Anglo-American regional cultures in the United States are reinforced by David Hackett Fischer's magisterial *Albion's Seed: Four British Folkways in America* (New York: Oxford University Press, 1989). A comprehensive analytical history of American foreign policy would have to draw on studies like these. To the narrower subject of the history of U.S. civil-military relations, the best guide remains Samuel P. Huntington's *The Soldier and the State* (Cambridge, MA: Harvard University Press, 1985, orig. 1957).

Daniel Walker Howe's *The Political Culture of the American Whigs* (Chicago: The University of Chicago Press, 1979), is still the standard introduction to the Whig political tradition that links Hamilton's Federalists with Lincoln's Republicans. Robert A. Ferguson gives a good account of Daniel Webster's nationalist oratory in *Law and Letters in American Culture* (Cambridge, MA: Harvard University Press, 1984). No comprehensive studies of the American School of economics or the historical evolution of the Hamiltonian program for American economic development have been written; indeed, almost all the books by "national economists" like Daniel Raymond, the Careys, and Friedrich List have been out of print for a century and a half. Because the American elite after World War II rejected protectionism and adopted unilateral free trade as part of a strategy for reconstructing Western Europe and Japan, historians and academic economists have treated the long prior history of protectionism in the United States as an embarrassment, if they have acknowledged it at all. The main exception is Alfred E. Eckes, Jr., *Opening America's Market: U.S. Foreign Trade Policy Since 1776* (Chapel Hill: University of North Carolina Press, 1995). Paul Bairoch describes American economic development in its global context in *Economics and World History: Myths and Paradoxes* (Chicago: The University of Chicago Press, 1993). The only book devoted to Friedrich List and his worldwide influence is Roman Szporluk's indispensable *Communism and Nationalism: Karl Marx Versus Friedrich List* (New York: Oxford University Press, 1988). Gabor S. Borritt depicts Lincoln as a mainstream Whig-Republican economic nationalist in *Lincoln and the Economics of the American Dream* (Chicago: University of Illinois Press, 1994, orig. 1978). The subject of how the Federalist-Whig-Republican-Progressive tradition in political economy influenced the New Deal—particularly in its developmental, state-capitalist aspect—still awaits its historian.

INDEX